In Defense of Tort Law

In Defense of
Tort Law

Thomas H. Koenig and Michael L. Rustad

NEW YORK UNIVERSITY PRESS
New York and London

NEW YORK UNIVERSITY PRESS
New York and London
www.nyupress.org

First published in paperback in 2003

Library of Congress Cataloging-in-Publication Data
Koenig, Thomas H.
In defense of tort law / Thomas H. Koenig and Michael L. Rustad.
p. cm.
Includes index.
ISBN 0-8147-4757-4 (cloth : alk. paper)
ISBN 0-8147-4758-2 (pbk. : alk. paper)
1. Torts—United States.   I. Rustad, Michael. II. Title.
KF1250 .K57 2001
346.7303—dc21   2001002494

Manufactured in the United States of America
c 10 9 8 7 6 5 4 3 2 1
p 10 9 8 7 6 5 4 3 2 1

This book is dedicated to the memory of
Thomas F. Lambert Jr.

Contents

Acknowledgments

Many people contributed their time and talents to this manuscript, and we greatly appreciate their help. We would particularly like to thank Adele Barnaby, who provided us with excellent secretarial support through many drafts. Adele took an active interest in the contents of the manuscript and made many valuable suggestions. We would like to thank Don Feeney for suggesting the title. We would also like to thank Sarah Swan, who provided secretarial support during the final drafts. Our students at Northeastern University and Suffolk University Law School have been a great resource to draw upon. Many of them read and commented on earlier versions of the manuscript. Brian Flaherty, Elizabeth McKenzie, and Susan Sweetgall provided excellent research librarian support.

Many persons have contributed to the ideas in this book, most of all Tom Lambert. Elizabeth Lambert made useful suggestions for the book proposal. Edward Bander gave us important guidance on the organization of the book and prepared the index. Jim Johnson, attorney and *Legal Times* contributor, provided many useful suggestions. Russell Mohbiker, Jerry Phillips, and Joanne Doroshow also shared their insights with us.

Our research assistants at Suffolk University Law School were especially helpful: Stephen Brown, Chaz Landry, Anne-Maria Paone, Tanisha Roebuck, Punam Sharma, and Gina Takemori. Theresa Mursick-Meyer, Esq., provided valuable editorial assistance. Peter Stecher, Class of 2004, Suffolk University Law School, gave us editorial suggestions for several chapters. Ronald Kaplan helped solve computer problems.

Thomas Koenig would like to thank Maureen Norton-Hawk for her continuing support during this long project. Michael Rustad would like to thank his wife, Chryss Knowles, for her editorial work on this

In Defense of Tort Law

Preface

In Defense of Tort Law

Tort law is the chief guardian of the institutions, which are central to our civilization; it protects bodily integrity; the right to enjoy property and do business and such basic liberties as freedom of speech, reputation, and family relations . . . Tort law has been progressive and dynamic.—Thomas F. Lambert, Jr.

Introduction: Tort Rights Under Siege

William L. Prosser, in his classic treatise, observed that, "perhaps more than any other branch of the law, the law of torts is a battleground of social theory."[1] Torts is the branch of law that provides compensation for injuries to persons and property caused by the fault of another. Tort law has always been contested legal terrain because of fundamental disagreements over who should bear the financial burden for an injury and what wrongs should be compensable. Tort law inevitably involves balancing individual and social interests. Today, many tort remedies are under siege, including those for consumers injured by defective products or reckless HMO cost containment, as well as victims of sexual harassment, dangerous railroad crossings, hate crimes, drunk drivers, environmental injuries, Internet fraud, and other civil wrongs.[2] This struggle mirrors deep cultural and political divisions in contemporary American society.

Prosser describes torts as "a body of law which is directed toward the compensation of individuals rather than the public for losses which they have suffered."[3] This view is a narrower one than ours. We believe that there are both *manifest* and *latent* functions in American tort law.[4] The most important manifest function of torts is to restore plaintiffs to the position they were in prior to the injury by awarding monetary damages.

1

In the case of wrongful death, the estate receives the damages. In the absence of tort law, the injury or property loss would fall to the victim, his or her family members, or the taxpayers.

The latent function—the hidden face—of tort law is its public role of addressing corporate misconduct without requiring a rigid government bureaucracy. Private tort litigants serve the public interest by uncovering dangerous products and practices.[5] This public law purpose of torts is rarely recognized in law school classes, court decisions, or by the litigants. Professional responsibility courses emphasize the duty of the lawyer to zealously advance the interests of the client. However, the trial attorney also serves a less visible public policy function by uncovering and punishing corporate malfeasance. Thus, tort law not only performs the manifest function of alleviating "the plight of the injured," but it also fulfills the latent function of furthering "the cause of social justice."[6] "Punitive damages . . . are awarded to the injured party as a reward for his public service in bringing the wrongdoer to account."[7]

This latent function has sometimes been referred to as the role of the "private attorney general."[8] Trial lawyers, acting as private attorneys general, have uncovered numerous "smoking gun" documents unmasking corporate culpability. An industry-wide cover-up of the deadly consequences of unprotected exposure to asbestos dust, which destroyed the health of hundreds of thousands of American workers, was unmasked in asbestos products liability cases. Johns-Manville Corporation, for example, had definite knowledge as early as the 1930s of the dangers of exposure to asbestos dust but had a corporate policy of not informing employees that x-rays taken by company doctors revealed clear evidence of asbestosis.[9] Johns-Manville executives claimed that this policy was motivated by concern for employees, so that they could "live and work in peace and the company benefit by their many years of experience."[10] The asbestos industry lulled government regulators into complacency for decades with false assurances that their products posed no health hazard.[11]

Private attorneys general have been particularly effective in protecting the health and safety of women. Dangerously defective products that have been taken off the market or modified after tort litigation include the Dalkon Shield and Copper-7 intrauterine devices associated with reproductive injuries, high-absorbency tampons linked to toxic shock syndrome, oral contraceptives that caused kidney failures, and silicone-gel breast implants with a high rupture rate.

In the field of medical malpractice, torts have provided female patients with remedies for mismanaged childbirth, sexual exploitation by medical personnel, botched cosmetic surgeries, and the failure of providers to obtain informed consent.[12] All Americans are safer as the result of private attorneys general whose medical malpractice lawsuits led to liability-limiting policies such as post-surgery sponge and instrument counts, greater screening of affiliating physicians, and improved protocols for emergency room treatment. Elderly and disabled residents of nursing homes have benefited from the contingency fee system, which allows them to have the means to obtain legal representation to redress neglect and substandard treatment by profit-seeking corporations.[13]

The film *Erin Brockovich*, starring Julia Roberts, depicts the true story of a young woman who helped to launch a toxic torts lawsuit that ultimately resulted in a $333 million class action settlement against a California utility for polluting the local water supply.[14] Legal crusaders like Erin Brockovich protect the public by uncovering corporate conduct that threatens the community. In the real life case that inspired the film, Erin Brockovich discovered chromium 6 in the well water of a California town.[15] Tort law, like sunlight, acts as a disinfectant by exposing hidden threats to the public welfare.[16]

This book discusses the past, present, and future of tort law as a protector of core American values. Tort law shapes public policy by punishing the irresponsible distribution of handguns, reallocating the financial burden of caring for tobacco smokers, and increasing the accountability of health maintenance organizations.[17] In June 1997, the states reached a multibillion-dollar settlement with Big Tobacco. In 1998, Congress expanded the settlement to $516 billion over twenty-five years.[18] Tort remedies for injured consumers are opposed by what Tom Lambert called "habitual defendants."[19] This used to refer to railroads, streetcar companies, corporations, and utilities and now includes product manufacturers, managed-care organizations, tobacco companies, securities firms, and environmental polluters, as well as their insurance company allies and ideological friends, all of whom seek to nullify tort remedies.

"Whoever controls the language, the images, controls the race,"[20] noted the late poet Allen Ginsberg. This observation clearly applies to the tort reform debate. The proponents of tort retrenchment are winning by controlling the language and imagery of the political struggle.[21] On the basis of remarkably little empirical study, thirty states have enacted tort reform statutes during the last five years alone.[22] This book defends American tort law, making its case that retrenchment will only produce new injustices with systematic data, featured cases, and historical examples.

The corporate-insurance establishment uses carefully crafted language to portray corporations as the victims of a litigious society rather than focusing on the plight of the true victims: those who have suffered because of defective products, negligent medicine, or unreasonably dangerous practices. The term *tort reform* implies that caps and other limitations on injured plaintiffs' recovery improve the functioning of the American civil justice system. In reality, applying the word *reform* to these restrictions is as misleading as referring to nuclear weapons as "peacekeepers." Tort reform is a code phrase for one-sided, liability-limiting statutes that favor corporate interests.[23] Questionable lawsuits brought by corporate interests, such as the product libel suit filed by Texas ranchers against Oprah Winfrey for injuring the reputation of U.S. beef, are not targeted by these "reformers."[24]

Tort law, like any other body of law, can be improved, but the tort reformers do not take an evenhanded approach in analyzing its strengths and shortcomings. The future of tort law is in doubt because of the success of the tort reform movement in convincing legislatures to reduce the price of corporate wrongdoing. A recent study concludes that tort reform groups

> [c]laim to speak for average Americans and represent themselves as grassroots citizens groups determined to protect consumer interests. But their tax filings and funding sources indicate that they actually represent major corporations and industries seeking to escape liability for the harm they cause consumers—whether it be from defective products, medical malpractice, securities scams, insurance fraud, employment discrimination or environmental pollution.[25]

The coalition opposing plaintiffs' rights unites around the theme of federalizing tort law.[26] The Supremacy Clause of the U.S. Constitution makes it likely that federal tort reforms preempt common law remedies. The chief source of tort law is common law—the legal rules that have evolved from court decisions over many centuries. During the past twenty years, there has been a downturn in tort law's common law foundation. All fifty states have enacted at least one limitation on common law tort recovery during this period. Tort reform–inspired statutes undermine the greatest social benefit of tort law: its ability to evolve in order to constrain new forms of oppression.

As a nineteenth-century New York court noted: "It is the peculiar merit of the common law that its principles are so flexible and expansive as to comprehend any new wrong that may be developed by the inexhaustible resources of human depravity."[27] Tort law has expanded to redress new dangers and hazards from the Internet. State tort law has the flexibility to redress unfair, deceptive, and oppressive practices. The federal takeover of tort law would undermine this unique strength, namely, its latent function of evolving to protect the public interest from emergent threats.

This book dispels civil justice myths so that evolutionary tort law can continue to protect the public from the hazards that Americans will face in the twenty-first century. Courts are already applying old tort causes of action to Internet-related harms. Tort law remedies are increasingly punishing online consumer fraud, cyberstalking, defamatory e-mail messages, theft of corporate trade secrets, invasions of corporate espionage, privacy, and other wrongs committed at the click of a mouse. Misperceptions about the American civil justice system fostered by the tort reformers deflect attention from the crucial role tort law plays in improving public safety.

A Tale of Two Torts: Tire Explosions and a Hot Coffee Spill

[A] Tread Separations in Bridgestone-Firestone Tires

Private attorneys general, not government regulators, discovered that Firestone tires mounted on Ford Explorers caused hundreds of rollover accidents due to tread separation. Many deaths linked to defective Firestone tires occurred in accidents involving Ford Explorers.[28] The high center of gravity in Ford's sport utility vehicles makes them more difficult to control after tire failure.[29] Trial attorneys found that Firestone had recalled this model of tires in other countries without informing the National Highway Traffic Safety Administration (NHTSA) of the potential danger to American drivers.[30] NHTSA based its recall of 6.5 million tires on information provided by plaintiff's counsel, not by government investigators.

Firestone and Ford stand accused of causing the deaths of over one hundred Americans by failing to inform government regulators of the hazardous design defects.[31] If Ford is found liable for concealing safety information from NHTSA, the maximum fine the agency can impose is a mere $925,000,[32] obviously an inadequate amount to deter wrongful conduct by a corporation that earns $800,000 per hour.

This is the second class action suit against Firestone for defective tires.

Tread separations of Firestone 500 steel-belted radial tires caused dozens of deaths and hundreds of injuries in the 1970s.[33] The company's defense in the Firestone 500 suit closely parallels its central defense in today's mass tort disaster: Firestone claimed that tread separations were caused by "owner abuse, road damage, or under-inflation."[34] In fact, Firestone tires had a "design defect in which the steel belt did not bond to the tire carcass."[35] Most Americans welcome the nationwide recall of Firestone tires. However, when Americans think about the civil justice system, the image that comes to mind is not of deaths caused by Firestone's tread separations, but McDonald's hot coffee.

[B] The McDonald's Coffee Case: A Tort Reform "Poster Child"

Plaintiffs are often portrayed in the mass media as greedy or wacky claimants seeking a "judicial jackpot," rather than as victims obtaining redress for injuries caused by unreasonably dangerously products. Similarly, tort law is usually described by the media as corporate torture, as if jury verdicts were as unjust and arbitrary as the medieval ordeal by water.[36] In early feudalism, disputes were settled by arbitrary methods such as trial by fire or water.[37] The trial by ordeal consisted of tying the defendant to a chair and submerging him in water. Each time he was asked if he wished to tell the truth. If he did not say what was expected, he was again submerged. If he did not drown during the ordeal, he was innocent.[38]

Tort reformers have spun out a web of illusion in the form of misleading or false tort horror stories. The media's mischaracterization of the McDonald's hot coffee case has done more than any other tort horror story to create a climate of distrust about tort law and its remedies.

The tort reformers' distorted presentation of the McDonald's case was responsible in part for motivating state legislators to hastily enact comprehensive tort limitation statutes.[39] Two state supreme courts, Ohio and Illinois, overturned tort reform statutes after learning of the true facts behind the McDonald's litigation.[40] A number of other state courts have struck down tort reforms on state constitutional grounds.[41] The McDonald's case may not be as compelling as the Firestone tire mass disaster, but it was far from frivolous.

The most popular character on the television series *Seinfeld* was Cosmo Kramer, known for his herky-jerky movements and for barging into Jerry's apartment without knocking. In one famous *Seinfeld* episode, Kramer spilled a hot latte coffee in his lap while smuggling it into a movie theater. Kramer retained the services of Jackie Chiles, a parody of Johnnie Cochran, one of O. J. Simpson's defense attorneys, to sue the shop for selling him the too-hot coffee. But instead of following Jackie's advice to seek punitive damages for faulty design of the cup, Kramer negotiates his own settlement for a lifetime supply of latte.[42] This *Seinfeld* episode was inspired by the real McDonald's hot coffee litigation, which, at first glance, appears to be as outlandish as Cosmo Kramer's case.

Very few Americans know the true circumstances that led to the McDonald's verdict because the tort reform lobby won a public relations victory by framing the media coverage of this lawsuit. At least a thousand news stories reported that a clumsy elderly woman spilled coffee on her lap and then sued McDonald's because the hot coffee she ordered was too hot. The case was the subject of mocking monologues by late night talk show hosts Jay Leno and David Letterman. After this media blitz, it is hardly surprising that the popular view of the verdict is that it is exhibit number one in the case for tort reform.

News reporters and comedians had a lot of fun with the McDonald's hot coffee case, but there is no humor in the catastrophic injuries suffered by the plaintiff. In Albuquerque, New Mexico, seventy-nine-year-old Stella Liebeck purchased coffee at the drive-through window of a McDonald's restaurant. Contrary to most of the news stories, Mrs. Liebeck was not driving the car, nor was the coffee spilled while the vehicle was moving. Her grandson had pulled the car to the curb and stopped completely before Mrs. Liebeck placed the cup of coffee between her knees to remove the plastic lid. As she was removing the cover, the scalding coffee spilled onto her lap and was immediately absorbed by her sweat pants. Mrs. Liebeck sustained full-thickness burns because the super-heated coffee was held next to her skin by her clothing.[43] The beverage severely scalded her groin, inner thighs, and buttocks.

The coffee sold to Mrs. Liebeck was held at a temperature between 180 and 190 degrees Fahrenheit. As the temperature of coffee or any other hot liquid decreases to 155 degrees and below, the risk of serious burns is reduced exponentially. A beverage served at 180 to 190 degrees will cause third-degree burns in two to seven seconds. Coffee is typically brewed at 135 to 140 degrees for home use.

Mrs. Liebeck's severe burns required a week of hospitalization. She suffered through painful debridement procedures to remove layers of dead skin and several skin graft operations. She initially sought out a lawyer only to receive reimbursement for her medical bills, which totaled nearly $20,000.[44] Only after McDonald's refused to pay her medical bills did she file a products liability lawsuit. The New Mexico jury awarded the plaintiff $200,000 in compensatory damages, which was then reduced to $160,000 because the jury found Mrs. Liebeck partially at fault for the spill.[45] The jury also awarded the plaintiff $2.7 million in punitive damages, a judicial remedy intended to punish McDonald's and deter the company from needlessly endangering its customers. The purpose of punitive damages is "to further a state's legitimate interests in punishing unlawful conduct and deterring its repetition."[46]

The $2.7 million award represented only about two days' profit from the nationwide sales of McDonald's coffee—not two days' total earnings. The trial judge reduced the punitive award to $480,000. Eventually, the parties reached a confidential post-verdict settlement, presumably for a substantially reduced amount. In the end, McDonald's payment was the equivalent of a parking ticket for a multinational restaurant chain.

McDonald's Corporation had constructive, if not actual, notice that its coffee was too hot long before Mrs. Liebeck was scalded. Mrs. Liebeck's attorney learned through discovery that McDonald's files contained more than seven hundred reports of prior similar injuries caused by their super-heated coffee, yet the company had taken no steps to lower the heat.[47] After the New Mexico lawsuit, McDonald's reduced the temperature of its coffee to a safer level.

Journalists failed to inform the public about the underlying factual circumstances that led to the award. Few reporters even mentioned that hundreds of other McDonald's consumers had been injured by super-heated coffee. The media devoted more coverage to the restaurant chain's plight and the tort reformers' take on the incident than to the plight of the victims.

Many news reports make the questionable assertion that products liability law hurts American consumers by creating a litigation crisis, but few journalists document the many ways that Americans benefit from tort law. Products are now more thoroughly tested in the company's laboratory rather than in the consumer's home or workplace due to tort verdicts. The lesson of Firestone tires, McDonald's coffee, and a host of other awards is the continuing need for strong tort remedies to control corporate wrongdoing.[48]

Courts do not lay down general principles; rather they decide specific controversies. Each of the chapters in this book shows how individual cases are in effect public policy in disguise.

Chapter 1 traces the evolution of tort rights and remedies from Blackstone's day to the twenty-first century, with particular attention to how tort law has evolved to serve the public interest in each historical period. The common law of torts adapts to the exigencies of new technologies and is not a closed system of immutable rules. Tort law has widened the circle of civil justice in redressing harms for women, minorities, and consumers in recent years.

Chapter 2 illustrates the latent function served by private attorneys general through a study of featured cases. The human face of tort law is revealed through the stories of private litigants whose lawsuits have created a safer America. Successful lawsuits often prevent future accidents. "The plaintiff acts as the private attorney general to punish and deter future social misconduct, thereby encouraging adherence to safety standards that benefit consumers generally."[49] These cases show the considerable difficulties of taking legal action and winning and collecting an award from a large corporation, as well as the emotional burden shouldered by the litigants.

Chapter 3 presents an empirical and public policy analysis of the social consequences of tort reform on women. Over the past fifty years, forward-looking courts have increasingly recognized the biological and social role of women by expanding recovery for reproductive damage and gender-based emotional injuries. As the Dalkon Shield, breast implant, and Copper-7 mass tort cases illustrate, tort law fulfils a latent function in protecting women's health by taking defective products off the market.

Chapter 4 explores the latent function of medical malpractice lawsuits in protecting the rights of patients. Medical malpractice awards originated as a remedy against intentional misconduct or criminal manslaughter by individual doctors but has now expanded to meet the dangers inherent in bureaucratic health care. In response to the threat of litigation, preventive medicine has improved patient care in a host of areas. The question of patients' rights now centers on managed care. Arizona, Maine, Oklahoma, and Washington have enacted new remedies for greater HMO accountability. Congress is also considering a patients' rights bill to provide federal remedies for the reckless delay or denial of necessary medical care.

Chapter 5 is a study of corporate misbehavior that led to punitive damages in products liability. Punitive damages are not random lightning strikes; they are actually quite predictable. It is good public policy that companies that conceal dangers are assessed large punitive damage awards, while companies that enact prompt remedial measures reduce their litigation exposure. By punishing companies that do not practice preventive law, tort remedies serve the latent function of aligning the private and public good.

Chapter 6 speculates on the future path of tort law. Tort law needs to retain its flexibility in order to counter emergent forms of wrongdoing. Old tort doctrines such as "trespass to chattels," for example, are being employed to protect against the invasion of privacy caused by website marketers who track users' every keystroke using new surveillance tools. A court recently imposed a $675,000 Internet libel verdict against a defendant for posting a defamatory message on a Yahoo! website.[50] This is not to say that torts are always a perfect remedy. However, as Felix Frankfurter reminds us, "We do not discard a useful tool because it may be misused."[51]

1

The Path of Tort Law

§1.1. Introduction

The legal historian William Nelson argues that "no topic has captured the attention of private law theorists in America more than the law of tort."[1] This chapter is a study of the rise, fall, and future of tort law in American society. The word *tort* is "derived from the Latin 'tortus' or twisted."[2] The history of tort law can be summarized as the evolution of ever more effective remedies to control wrongdoing, from pre-industrial England to the age of the Internet.[3]

William Prosser begins his classic tort treatise with the statement that "[a] really satisfactory definition of a tort has yet to be found."[4] In order for a tort to exist, "two things must concur, actual or legal damages to the plaintiff and a wrongful act committed by the defendant."[5] Tort law assigns responsibility for injuries to the wrongdoer by requiring the payment of compensation. Injunctive relief and other equitable remedies may be ordered where legal remedies are inadequate. In some nuisance cases, a defendant's activities may be enjoined if they interfere with the possessor's use and enjoyment of land. In all tort cases, the actor is liable because his conduct (a) was intended to cause harm; (b) was negligent; or (c) created extra-hazardous risks to others.[6] Tort damages are broadly divided into three categories: economic, non-economic, and punitive. Economic damages compensate the plaintiff for injuries to person or property and may include medical bills, past and future earnings, and other direct economic expenses.[7] Non-economic damages, often referred to as "pain and suffering" damages, are also compensatory.[8] Pain-and-suffering awards include compensation for disfigurement, infertility, or reproductive injuries.

Tort remedies are chiefly monetary damages for personal injury though a plaintiff may receive a recovery for an injury in the form of personal or real property. Punitive damages, sometimes referred to as exemplary damages, are awarded above and beyond compensatory damages to punish the defendant for torts committed intentionally or with a spirit of reckless indifference to public safety, as well as to deter such future misbehavior. Punitive damages fulfill the latent function of sending a message to the entire community that torts do not pay. Punitive damages are especially warranted where there is deliberate concealed harm and the probability of detection by government regulators is low.[9] Punitive damages have been assessed in the United States for more than two hundred years, long before torts evolved as a separate branch of the law.

Tort law did not develop as a separate doctrinal field until the middle of the nineteenth century. In 1852, when torts were still in their infancy, Joseph Story called for law to be "forever be in a state of progress or change, to adapt itself to the exigencies and changes of society."[10] The path of tort law, from the pre-tort era of Blackstone to the new millennium, is thus a story of the progressive unfolding of new tort remedies to counter new social hazards.

Tort law's "continuous and profound effect upon the everyday life . . . makes it critical to chart its course."[11] Tort law is a "cultural mirror" that reflects changing societal conditions.[12] The touchstone of tort liability is not found in rigid rules of law but in protecting the way of life in a particular historical epoch. The tort timelines in this chapter depict the evolving nature of tort law and its relationship to changing social institutions.[13] In the pre-industrial period, tort law redressed seduction, criminal conversation, and other affronts to the individual, family, and community.

Nineteenth-century tort law "belonged to the corporate defense."[14] With the post–Civil War rise of the railroads, the doctrinal development of negligence burst onto the scene. In this "negligence era," tort law assumed that certain injuries were "unavoidable costs of industrialization."[15] Prosser stated that the "law of negligence in the late nineteenth century was to a considerable extent the law of railway accidents."[16] Negligence was a byproduct of the social, economic, political, and technological changes that accompanied large-scale industrialization.[17] During this period, courts developed a number of regressive doctrines such as contributory negligence, the assumption of risk, and the fellow servant rule to promote industrial development.[18] The public policy impact of broad employer immunities left the burden of injury entirely upon the victim.

Many such immunities and defenses were either rolled back or eliminated after World War II.[19] The law of torts expanded substantially during the progressive tort law era (1945–80), creating many new possibilities for obtaining redress and reparations for injuries. Since the early

1980s, this liberalizing trend has largely reversed course.[20] Forty-six states have enacted at least one new limitation on the tort remedies available to injured consumers and patients since 1980.[21] Today, the further expansion of torts is required for the Age of the Internet.[22]

The tort law timelines below traces the rise, fall, and uncertain future of progressive tort remedies from the dawn of common law to the dawn of the twenty-first century. The first part of the timeline traces the rise of medieval English law, whose shadow is still cast upon the present.[23] English tort law originally redressed only intentional injuries to persons and property, although defendants were held strictly liable for trespass to property.

§1.2. The Intentional Torts Era: 1200 to 1825

Intentional torts were first developed at early common law to provide plaintiffs with remedies for misconduct that threatened the public order, such as battery,[24] assault,[25] false imprisonment,[26] and trespass.[27] Intentional torts included injuries against the person as well as invasions against property interests.[28] Tort law later evolved to compensate a broader range of harms such as mental distress, prenatal injuries, and social dislocation.[29]

The "intent" in intentional torts refers to the state of mind of the defendant. Intentional torts redressed deliberate physical injuries to the person or invasions of common law property rights.[30] At early common law, torts preserved the social order of a pre-industrial age dominated by disputes in the local community.

Exemplary damages, the precursor of contemporary punitive damages, punished wrongdoers who maliciously committed torts that upset community tranquility. As Oliver Wendell Holmes, Jr., observed, "the first requirement of sound law is that it correspond with the actual feelings and demands of the community, whether right of wrong."[31] Tort law expanded to provide the ordinary citizen with more effective remedies against abuses of power.

[A] Intentional Tort Law Timeline

1066—The Norman institution of the jury is incorporated into the English legal system by William the Conqueror.[32]

1348 or 1349—*I de S et ux. v. W de S*[33] recognizes assault as a form of trespass to the person.[34]

1616—*Weaver v. Ward*[35] is first case to hold "that a defendant might not be liable, even in a trespass action, for a purely accidental injury occurring entirely without his fault."[36]

1647—Court rules that a man carried onto the plaintiff's land against his will by third parties is not liable for trespass.[37]

1669—Court holds that conditional threats unaccompanied by immanent hostile action do not constitute an assault.[38]

1697—*The Statute of 5-6 William and Mary c. 12* abolishes the criminal side of the writ of trespass, leaving it as a purely civil action.[39]

1704—Court rules that the least touching of another in anger constitutes a battery.[40]

1763—First court to use the phrase *exemplary damages* to describe a monetary penalty paid to the plaintiff above and beyond compensatory damages.[41]

1768—Sir William Blackstone publishes *Commentaries on the Law of England.*

1784—First American court to award punitive damages, in a case involving a physician spiking his rival's wine with Spanish fly, a pain-causing cantharide.[42]

1799—The defense of assumption of risk is applied for the first time.[43]

1799—The English case of *Merryweather v. Nixon*[44] is the first to recognize the doctrine of joint and several liability in ruling that wrongdoers cannot have redress or contribution against each other.

1808—English court rules that there is no recovery for wrongful death absent a specific statute.[45]

1846—The English Fatal Accidents Act of 1846, referred to as Lord Campbell's Act, provides a statutory remedy for wrongful death.[46]

1809—*Butterfield v. Forrester*[47] devises rule of contributory negligence barring actions where "a party . . . [who] contributes to his own injury . . . may not recover anything from the defendant."[48]

1814—Court upholds exemplary damages award where the actual damages are slight in *Merest v. Harvey*.[49]

1834—Court rules that a master is not liable for a servant's torts on the grounds that the servant was on an unauthorized "frolic"[50]; this becomes an exception to an employer's vicarious liability.

1837—First court to hold a seller liable for injuries caused by a defective product on the theory of deceit.[51]

1837—English court holds farmer liable for negligence even though he was ignorant of the danger to neighboring cottages posed by spontaneous combustion of uncured hay.[52] Court's ruling is key for developing an objective standard of reasonable care in negligence actions.[53]

1837—Court constructs the common employment or fellow servant rule barring recovery when a co-worker is at fault.[54]

1842—Privity of contract bars a lawsuit filed by a horse-drawn mail coach that overturned due to a defective wheel. Privity was the chief roadblock to the development of products liability.

1842—The pro-defendant doctrine of the "last clear chance" is first recognized in *Davies v. Mann*.[55]

1851—U.S. Supreme Court upholds punitive damages award in a trespass action, stating that the measure of damages is based upon the "enormity of the offense" rather than the compensation owed to the plaintiff.[56]

1852—Punitive damages are assessed against a pharmacy for the deadly consequences of careless mislabeling of poison by a druggist. This was a precursor to awarding punitive damages in products liability.[57]

1856—Justice Alderson defines negligence as conduct falling below the standard established by law that creates an unreasonable risk of harm.[58]

1859—First American treatise on tort law is published by Francis Hilliard.[59]

1860—First English treatise on tort law is published.[60]

1863—English court devises the doctrine of *res ipsa loquitur* or the "thing speaks for itself." That doctrine was later extended to medical malpractice cases where the unexpected outcome would not have occurred without negligence.[61]

1865—English court treats *res ipsa loquitur* as a species of circumstantial evidence.[62] Court rules that the circumstances of the accident created an inference that someone was careless and that it "arose from want of care."[63]

1873—The railroad turntable doctrine permits child trespasser to recover for injuries despite having no permission to be on the premises.[64]

1876—Court develops spousal immunity. Husbands and wives cannot sue each other on the grounds that lawsuits disrupt family harmony.[65]

1884—Justice Oliver Wendell Holmes, Jr., ruled in *Dietrich v. Northampton* that there was no remedy for prenatal injuries.[66]

1889—New York Court of Appeals recognizes consortium as an element of damages. Loss of consortium includes loss of love, companionship, affection, and sexual relations as well as solace.[67]

1897—In *Wilkinson v. Downton*[68] the court permits the plaintiff to recover for extreme emotional distress when a practical joker told a woman that her husband was seriously injured in an accident. This case led to the tort of outrage, first recognized in the modern period.

[B] Blackstone's *Commentaries*: The Intentional Torts Era

[1] *Blackstone's* Commentaries on Private Wrongs, *Volume III (1768)*

The Industrial Revolution swept across England about the time that Sir William Blackstone's *Commentaries on the Laws of England* (1765–68) was published. It was a period described by Irish poet Oliver Goldsmith as one "where wealth accumulates and men decay."[69] Blackstone's volumes were written during the last days of the writ system,[70] which originated in the thirteenth century.[71] The *Commentaries* provides a comprehensive view of tort-like causes of action in a revolutionary time,[72] shortly before the common law was exported to America.

Blackstone's causes of action were adapted to fit the unique conditions in the American colonies.[73] Colonial circuit-riding judges were reported to rely so heavily on Blackstone that they carried special editions in their saddlebags.[74] The First Continental Congress of 1774 declared that Americans were "entitled to the common law as well as all English statutes existing at the time of colonization."[75] Eleven of the thirteen colonies enacted statutes that adopted the English common law as a basis for their legal system.[76]

Historically, judge-made law was "called common because it was intended to be common or uniform for the entire English kingdom."[77] The English common law began with "the law common to the medieval king's courts."[78] The medieval era's actions for assault, battery, and mayhem were derived largely from Roman law.[79] By the eighteenth century, the law of torts vindicated "the personal security of individuals" for "injuries against their lives, their limbs, their bodies, their health, or their reputation."[80]

In Blackstone's day, tort law meant intentional torts and contained only a few pockets of absolute liability.[81] An English court in 1808 held that the survivors of victims of wrongful death had no cause of action.[82] Parliament overturned this harsh precedent when it enacted Lord Campbell's Act, permitting recovery for wrongful death.[83]

[2] *Torts Protecting Personal and Bodily Integrity*

[A] WRIT OF *TRESPASS VI ET ARMIS* AND ACTIONS ON THE CASE

Tort doctrines derive "from the reality that law arises out [of] or emerges from social activity."[84] At early common law, tort damages were awarded to injured plaintiffs incidentally to a criminal prosecution, and as late as 1694 the writ of trespass was still theoretically regarded as a criminal fine.[85] Blackstone distinguished between "private wrongs," which would evolve into the law of torts, and "public wrongs" or criminal law, which he examined in Book Four of the *Commentaries.*

Trespass actions were filed to redress any direct application of force to the person or to his clothing.[86] The writ of *trespass vi et armis,* for example, was for immediate, forcible, and direct injuries such as assault, battery, mayhem, or false imprisonment.[87] When the act of wrongdoing was indirect and not accompanied by force, the remedy sought was the *trespass upon the case.*[88] Deliberately cutting a man with a sword was *trespass vi et armis* whereas poisoning his livestock was the indirect action for *trespass on the case.*

Prior to the Industrial Revolution, there was little by way of what is today regarded as the law of negligence. Still, "persons like surgeons, apothecaries, solicitors, carriers, and innkeepers" were held accountable for their careless practices.[89] In an 1809 case, the court held a stagecoach company liable, ruling "that the burden lay upon the carrier to show that the coach was as good a coach as could be made, and that the driver was . . . skillful."[90] Prosser notes that "the old tort duty to serve arose as to common callings. . . . With the passage of time, the emphasis was shifted from the holding out of skill to the undertaking of a responsibility toward the public."[91]

[B] PRECURSORS TO OTHER INTENTIONAL TORTS

[1] Mayhem

Mayhem in Blackstone's time was defined as malicious injury that resulted in the loss of bodily parts such as noses, arms, fingers, or eyes.[92] The courts awarded fines, which varied according to the severity of the injury. The unlawful beating of another that resulted in the loss of a front tooth had a higher price than one that resulted in the loss of a jawtooth.[93] From the time of Henry VIII, mayhem that resulted in the loss of an ear was punished by statutory treble damages.[94]

At early common law, assault, battery, and mayhem were indictable criminal offenses as well as being torts. The indictment was a suit by the crown for the crime against the public, while the tort remedy resulted in damages awarded to the injured party.[95] Exemplary damages were levied for torts committed maliciously.[96]

[2] False Imprisonment

False imprisonment included unlawful confinement in public prisons, in private houses, "or in the stocks, or even by forcibly detaining one in the public streets."[97] Remedies for false imprisonment compensated persons confined under invalid warrants by legal officers and remedied the wrongful "impressing of mariners for the public service."[98] A false imprisonment action could be filed if a lawful warrant or process was served on a Sunday or in an unlawful place such as the King's court. *Habeas corpus*, "the most celebrated writ in the English law," was used to remove a prisoner from an inferior court.[99]

[3] Nuisances

In Blackstone's day, the law of nuisance fulfilled a role in governing competing land uses that also affected public health. A neighbor whose "noisome trade" "infect[ed] the air" or polluted the environment was liable for the offense of nuisance at common law.[100] Even a lawful activity that caused injury to another man's land could be enjoined by an injunction and compensated by monetary damages.[101] The absolute right of a man to enjoy his property later gave way to a "balancing of the equities" approach.[102] Today's toxic torts litigation as well as environmental statutes weigh economic value against the social costs.[103]

[4] Prefiguring Professional Negligence and Products Liability

[a] Negligence

Those who held themselves out as professionals, whether in "employment, trust, or duty," were required to perform their jobs with "integrity, diligence, and skill."[104] A tradesman who did not perform his job in a "workmanlike manner" could be assessed monetary damages as compensation.[105] A sheriff who permitted a debtor to escape after a judgment was liable for the consequences to the creditor.[106] Prosser argued that the English courts extended torts to many professions and trades: "A carpenter negligently building a house was held liable in tort, as was a porter unloading a hogshead, a jobmaster letting out a defective vehicle and a banker dishonoring a check."[107]

Businesses had a general duty to protect the rights of the larger public. Innkeepers, for example, were obligated to guard their guests' personal property and were liable if goods were lost or stolen.[108] "If an inn-keeper or other victualler hands out a sign and opens his house for travelers, it is an implied engagement to entertain all persons who travel that way."[109] The courts later refused to permit railroads to disclaim all liability to passengers for accidents or lost baggage. Courts consistently held carriers to the highest duty of care even at the height of the negligence era.[110] The same high duty of care for innkeepers also applied to physicians and other professionals as well as tradesmen.[111]

[b] Sales Law, Warranties, and Fraud

Eighteenth-century sales laws made sellers accountable for violating an implied covenant that "every transaction is fair and honest."[112] Even if the merchant made no express warranties about his goods, he was required to deliver goods "fit for the ordinary purpose," a doctrine that evolved into today's implied warranty of merchantability.[113] Sellers of goods were "customarily held liable for negligence and the liability may exist parallel with that for breach of warranty."[114]

An eighteenth-century merchant who sold tainted wine or other provisions was liable for "injuries affecting a man's health."[115] A horse that was "warranted to be sound" but was, in reality, blind in one eye would constitute a breach of warranty because "the discernment of such defects is frequently a matter of skill."[116] A buyer was expected to exercise reasonable care by inspecting goods for patent defects. No remedy was available for purchasing a horse that was missing a tail or an ear, unless the buyer was blind.[117] The concept of warranties was later extended to "other suppliers of chattels, such as the garage which rents out an automobile, or the shipper of goods over a carrier" and landlords who evicted tenants.[118]

[5] Torts to Vindicate Reputation

Eighteenth-century English law protected a person's reputation and good name through an action for defamation.[119] To this day, slander is oral defamation whereas libel takes a written form.[120] Compensation was awarded for "malicious, scandalous, and slanderous words causing damage or derogation," such as falsely accusing another man of a "heinous crime or having an infectious disease."[121] A tradesman could recover for lost business if he was wrongly accused of being insolvent.[122] Businessmen and professionals could obtain redress in the form of exemplary damages for the injurious consequences of defamation when falsehoods damaged their trade. Calling a "physician a quack or a lawyer a knave" was considered to be slander per se and could be punished with tort remedies.[123]

Words impugning a "peer, a judge or other great officer of the realm" were considered to be so heinous that they could be redressed by both an action on the case and the imprisonment of the slanderer.[124] Criminal penalties could also be levied for written libel.[125] The criminal indictment was for the public offense; the private injury was redressed by the action.[126]

[6] Domestic Torts

Wards, wives, children, and servants did not have an independent legal existence under early tort law. Four types of family relationships were protected: "husband and wife, parent and child, guardian and ward, and master and servant."[127] Domestic torts were designed to replace dueling and other extralegal remedies that threatened community peace.

Eighteenth-century tort law reflected the patriarchal family values of the era. Men enjoyed extensive rights over their chattels, which included wives, children, wards, and servants.[128] If a husband negligently or intentionally injured his spouse or any other member of the household, there was no recovery. Denying recovery in order to protect familial harmony reflected the patriarchal belief that the head of the household always operated in the best interests of the family members. Later, this doctrine evolved into interspousal immunity. Early twentieth-century courts refused to entertain intrafamilial lawsuits because they "threatened marital bliss or subverted parental discipline."[129]

[a] Husband–Wife Relationship

[1] ABDUCTION

Abduction was defined as taking away a man's wife by fraud, persuasion, or open violence.[130] Husbands could recover damages from another man who "persuaded or enticed his wife to live separate from him without a sufficient cause."[131] A husband whose wife was abused by another man could file a writ in the names of the husband and wife jointly.[132] If another man deprived a husband of "the company and assistance of his wife" by beating her severely, it was the husband who received monetary damages.[133] The rights of the family unit, of which the husband was the head, were being vindicated, not the individual interests of the wife.

Women had limited protection under the early common law, which reflected their diminished legal status during this period. At early common law if a wife fled an abusive husband and was given refuge by another man, that man "might carry her behind him on horseback to market to a justice of the peace for a warrant against her husband or to a spiritual court to sue for a divorce."[134] A husband could not forcefully regain custody and control of his errant spouse, although he was entitled to monetary damages if the defendant enticed her to leave home.

[2] ADULTERY AND SEDUCTION

Adultery was considered a serious crime against the public order as well as a civil injury to the family as a unit.[135] In an action for adultery, the jury could take into account the wife's "previous behavior and character."[136] The cuckold had an action of *trespass vi et armis* against the adulterer, "wherein the damages recovered were usually very large and exemplary."[137] Exemplary damages were "properly increased or diminished by circumstances [such] as the rank and fortune of the plaintiff and defendant."[138] Because of the remedy of exemplary damages, every tort had its price, which varied according to the wealth and status of the defendant.

[b] Parent–Child Relationship

The *writ of ravishment* provided compensation for the economic loss of children's services when they married without their father's consent. Family property rights—rather than the rights of the child—were the key issue, creating uncertainty as to whether a ravishment action could be filed for the "taking and carrying away of any other child besides the heir."[139] A father had a cognizable action to seek compensation for the seduction of his daughter since this high-handed misdeed dishonored the family unit. The father also received compensation for loss of services when his daughter was seduced and impregnated out of wedlock.

[c] Guardian–Ward Relationship

The father or, at his death, the mother was considered to be the "guardian for nature" until a child reached the age of fourteen.[140] A guardian could also be appointed for a child by a father's will or last testament.[141] The guardian had a cause of action if his or her ward was ravished or if the ward's property was stolen.[142] The guardian who was deprived of a ward could recover custody of the child as well as monetary damages through a writ.[143]

[d] Master–Servant Relationship

Just as wives and children had no independent action to vindicate their personal rights, servants derived all legal rights from the master.[144] The master could file a writ to obtain money damages if his servant was beaten, confined, or disabled by a third party.[145] A household head could file an action for compensation against a neighbor who hired away a family servant. At early common law, masters were strictly liable for their servants' torts under the doctrine of *respondeat superior*. The reasoning was that the master was in the best position to prevent his servants' wrongdoing by proper supervision, training, and discipline. This doctrine evolved into the corporation's vicarious liability for its employees' wrongdoing committed within the scope of duty.

[7] Injuries to Personal Property

A complicated system of writs governed personal property as opposed to real property, which consisted of "land, tenements and heritaments."[146] Personal property writs were divided into separate actions for the original taking of properties[147] and a separate action for "detaining them though the original taking might be lawful."[148] If, for example, a neighbor borrowed a horse and did not return it, there would be an action to recover money damages if the horse was harmed. A separate but distinct writ would be required if the horse was originally taken without permission. A special form of the writ was the *trespass de bonis asportatis* that applied when chattels were carried off or wrongfully taken.[149] In modern law, the tort of conversion still vindicates the wrongful dominion or control over personal property of another.[150]

[a] Loss or Destruction of Chattels

A defendant who hunted his neighbor's deer, shot his dogs, poisoned his cattle, or diminished the value of any of his chattels was liable under an action of *trespass vi et armis*. Eighteenth-century common law also recognized remedies where the act was not "in itself immediately injurious to another's property."[151] Contrary to popular folklore, vicious dogs did not get "one free bite." A chained mastiff that lunged at a neighbor's child would give its owner reason to know of the vicious propensities of the animal.[152] The action for trespass to chattels evolved for injuries to personal property, which would include animals.

[8] Injuries to Real Property

Real property was considered to be the source of "substantial and permanent rights" as compared to the "transitory rights" embodied in personal property.[153] *Trespass to land* was by far the most common real property injury.[154] Any "breaking of the close" by entry without the owner's permission was considered to be a strict liability offense. "For every man's land is in the eye of the law enclosed and set apart from his neighbors:

and that either by a visible and material fence . . . or by an ideal invisible boundary."[155] *Ouster*, as its name suggests, occurred when a wrongdoer unlawfully seized possession of land.

Hunters of beasts of prey such as badgers and foxes could enter the land of another without permission because of the public's interest in destroying these pests.[156] However, if a person used hunting as a pretext to enter another's land without permission, this was treated as a *trespass ab initio*.[157] Ignorance of real property boundaries was no defense to trespass.[158] An action for trespass could be pursued for nominal damages even when the unwarranted entry caused no actual damages.[159]

§1.2.1. Exemplary Damages to Punish and Deter Intentional Torts

Exemplary damages were awarded above and beyond compensatory damages for any intentional tort committed maliciously. Exemplary damages, like today's remedy of punitive damages, were awarded to punish and deter the defendant and others in the community.[160] This remedy punished serious violations of social norms such as "trespass cases against adulterers."[161]

[A] Precursors to Punitive Damages

Many ancient civilizations punished with multiple damages wrongdoing that threatened the social order.[162] The Babylonian Hammurabi Code[163] and the Hindu Code of Manu[164] refer to statutory penalties for punishing wrongdoing injurious to social order.[165] The Old Testament mentions the use of multiple damages to punish wrongdoing that threatens the public interest, prescribing this punishment as well as other draconian penalties as redress against fraud, deception, and misrepresentation.

In the New Testament, Luke 19:8 describes how Zacchaeus agreed to restitution of four times the actual damages to punish him for deceptive acts. The Qur'an also endorses the use of multiple damages to counter abuses in Muslim societies: "As for thieves, male or female, cut off their means of support and favors, take away their wealth and what they have hoarded, and make their hands and strength work . . . an exemplary punishment from Allah for their serious crime and Allah is mighty."[166]

The early Romans employed multiple damages to mediate social relations between unequal parties such as patricians and plebeians as well as to fine those who arbitrarily injured or killed slaves. *The Twelve Tables* (450 B.C.) contains numerous examples of multiple damages to punish conduct inimical to the public welfare.[167] Roman law levied quadruple damages as a creditor's remedy against those who did not pay their debts after a lapse of a year.[168] The dishonest Roman tutor who embezzled his ward's property was assessed double damages as a form of criminal restitution. There was a four-fold penalty exacted for violent damage to property by armed bands.[169] It was not until the last century of the Roman Republic that criminal law replaced private sanctions to punish and deter misconduct that threatened the social order.[170]

Civil punishment was also anticipated in the thirteenth-century English institution of *amercements*.[171] Amercements, unlike fixed fines, could consider the "offender's wealth or poverty, of the provocation that has been given him [or her]," and other circumstances that the rigid rules of ancient law had ignored.[172] Since amercements went directly into the royal treasury, the King had a socially dangerous incentive to assess these fines unjustly as a means of raising revenue.

In his poem *The Traveler*, Oliver Goldsmith wrote that "laws grind the poor, and rich men rule the law."[173] However, at the time Goldsmith's poem was written, the ordinary English citizen had at least one effective remedy to sting the rich when they abused their power—exemplary damages. The English courts punished aristocrats who abused their position of power much like the Roman legal system penalized Roman senators when they oppressed the weak.[174] As with the remedies of *The Twelve Tables*, the victim received money damages as a means of punishing wrongdoers.

The English doctrine of exemplary damages originated as a remedy to punish abuses of power by the Crown. The first reported exemplary damages award was assessed in 1763 to punish King George III's agents for an unlawful search and seizure of an oppositional newspaper. The companion cases of *Wilkes v. Wood*[175] and *Huckle v. Money*[176] were both filed on behalf of a newspaper editor and others who were detained by government agents in a warrantless search of a newspaper that had castigated King George III's foreign policies.

John Wilkes, the publisher of *The North Briton*, sued a Member of Parliament for trespass in *Wilkes v. Wood*.[177] In May of 1763, Wilkes's newspaper had attacked King George III for signing the pro-Prussian Treaty of Paris.[178] Wilkes's editorial intemperately accused King George of lending his name "to the most odious measures and the most unjustifiable public declarations from a throne ever renowned for truth, honor and unsullied virtue."[179] The King considered this editorial a "gross personal libel" and ordered Wilkes's immediate arrest.[180] The King's Bench, England's highest court,[181] found this action to be illegal because the trespass had been carried out without proper authority under a general warrant that called for the immediate arrest of the publishers of *The North Briton*.

The court upheld "large and exemplary damages" because actual damages would not be sufficient to punish or deter this type of governmental misconduct.[182] Despite the fact that there was no physical damage, the jury awarded the plaintiff, John Wilkes, 1,000 pounds sterling, quite a considerable sum at that time.

An employee of Wilkes sued for false imprisonment, trespass, and assault arising from the same events in the companion case of *Huckle v. Money*.[183] In *Huckle*, Lord Camden, the Chief Justice, coined the term *exemplary damages* to describe that portion of the award exceeding actual damages: "I think they have done right in giving exemplary damages. To enter a man's house by virtue of a nameless warrant, in order to procure evidence, is worse than the Spanish Inquisition; a law under which no Englishman would wish to live an hour; it was a most daring public attack made upon the liberty of the subject."[184] In the modern period, punitive damages are still assessed for police misconduct.[185]

[B] Exemplary Damages, Wealth, and Power

The doctrine of exemplary damages expanded to punish private individuals who maliciously committed intentional torts.[186] This remedy was employed to punish wanton acts such as the destruction of real property, willful battery, mayhem, willful taking of personal property, and willful trespasses of real property.[187] Exemplary damages also were assessed against the oppressive misconduct of indolent aristocrats when fixed fines were too small to teach them a lesson: "It has been a very frequent complaint in England, that the small fines imposed for drunkenness and disorderly conduct afford no checks to these indulgences by the rich. It is very obvious, therefore, that to allow mere pecuniary satisfaction for wrongs, in the present state of society, would be to put the laws under the control of the wealthier classes."[188]

The English remedy of exemplary damages can best be understood as a "manifestation of the law's concern with exercises and defaults in the use of power."[189] In eighteenth-century England, juries awarded exemplary damages to punish social affronts such as the seduction or mistreatment of servants, the debauching of daughters of the poor, and other acts committed by the upper class that were disruptive of the social fabric.[190]

Chief Justice Wilmot upheld a jury's exemplary damages award against the wealthy seducer of the plaintiff's daughter who lived in his house.[191] "Actions of this sort," he explained, "are brought for example's sake; and although the plaintiff's loss in this case may not really amount to the value of twenty shillings . . . the jury have done right in giving liberal damages."[192] The jury could examine "all the circumstances and the conduct of both parties" in determining the size of the award.[193]

As the eighteenth century came to a close, exemplary damages were firmly entrenched in the Anglo-American tradition. This remedy was employed to vindicate the rights of ordinary citizens such as the common soldier who was the victim of a brutal whipping by a militia colonel in a 1766 case.[194] The owner of an English poorhouse was punished by an exemplary damage verdict for maliciously shaving the head of a female pauper.[195] Often, such tort awards constituted the only remedy against powerful individuals whose arrogant wrongdoing upset the tranquility of the local community.[196]

Spiteful individuals who intentionally violated the property rights of others also felt the sting of the shilling. A wealthy and vindictive defendant in a nineteenth-century case purchased two old houses adjoining the plaintiff's premises and ordered laborers to tear them down in a manner calculated to damage the dwelling next door.[197] The jury found that the defendant's true purpose in acquiring the land was to harm his poorer neighbor and assessed him an exemplary damages award of seventy-five pounds.[198] A sampling of late nineteenth-century and early twentieth-century verdicts confirms that it was not unusual to award large punitive damages in cases of abuse of power, even when actual damages were slight.[199]

Exemplary damages could also be awarded to wealthy plaintiffs who had suffered abuse at the hands of even more powerful individuals. The plaintiff in *Merest* was a member of the House of Lords who was enjoying recreational hunting on his estate.[200] A local magistrate asked to join the shooting party. When rebuffed, the official used "very intemperate language and threatened to arrest the plaintiff in his capacity as a magistrate, and defied him to bring a trespass action."[201] The aristocrat's abuse of power was considered to be particularly reprehensible because he was an officer of the court.[202]

Chief Justice Gibbs upheld the jury's verdict for the plaintiff, observing that it "would not be overturned unless we were to lay it down that the jury are not justified in giving more than the absolute pecuniary damage that the plaintiff may sustain."[203] Justice Heath agreed, noting that the case was a natural outgrowth of the use of a civil justice remedy to restore societal peace: "I remember a case where a jury gave 500 pounds damages for merely knocking a man's hat off; and the Court refused a new trial. There was not one country gentleman in a hundred who would have behaved with laudable and dignified coolness which this plaintiff did. It goes to prevent the practice of dueling, if juries are permitted to punish insult by exemplary damages."[204]

[C] Punitive Damages in America

The doctrine of exemplary damages was exported to America soon after its birth in England. American exemplary damages were frequently called punitive damages because they were "awarded against such person to punish him for outrageous conduct."[205] Punitive damages were assessed for "assault and battery, libel and slander, deceit, seduction, alienation of affections, malicious prosecution and intentional interference with property."[206] Thus, punitive damages are neither unique nor original to the United States, and this remedy "is not an innovation of common law, it is the common law."[207] In 1875, the U.S. Supreme Court ruled that punitive damages were "too well settled now to be shaken, that exemplary damages may in certain cases be assessed."[208] Louisiana, Nebraska, Massachusetts, and Washington never recognized the common law remedy of punitive damages. New Hampshire abolished the remedy as a tort reform in 1986.[209]

In the first reported U.S. punitive damages case, *Genay v. Norris*,[210] the South Carolina Supreme Court in 1784 awarded what it called "vindictive damages" against a physician who used his knowledge of medicine to deliberately inflict pain. The plaintiff and defendant, both intoxicated, were prepared to settle their quarrel with dueling pistols. When the plaintiff agreed to a reconciliation toast, the physician secretly spiked the plaintiff's wine with a large dose of Spanish fly, causing the plaintiff to suffer excruciating pain. The court instructed the jury that "a very serious injury to the plaintiff . . . entitled him to very exemplary damages, especially from a professional character, who could not plead ignorance of the operation and powerful effects of this medicine."[211]

Like English exemplary damages, American punitive damage verdicts during this era were awarded as "smart money" to punish and deter bullies. In *Alcorn v. Mitchell*,[212] a bully was assessed $1,000 for the spiteful act of spitting in a neighbor's face. The courts were particularly inclined to award punitive damages when a powerful male initiated the offensive behavior against a physically weaker plaintiff such as a woman or child.[213] Juries redressed injuries to women victimized by assault and battery, by sexual harassment, and by rape through awards of punitive damages.[214] Such verdicts served to protect the social order by validating a remedy that punished intentional or malicious torts that violated property, domestic, reputation, or liberty interests.

By the middle of the nineteenth century, courts were beginning to openly acknowledge the role of punitive damages in controlling abuses of power. A Massachusetts court upheld a punitive damages award for trespass in 1872,[215] explaining that the jury was vindicating a societal norm: "the right of the poor against the aggressions of power and violence."[216] A Wisconsin court noted that the remedy "vindicates the right of the weak, and encourages recourse to, and confidence in, the courts of law by those wronged or oppressed."[217] Tort law served the aim of corrective justice by making the economically or physically powerful accountable for their misdeeds.

§1.2.2. The Enduring Legacy of the Intentional Torts Era

With rare exceptions, the intentional tort framework of Blackstone's era endures to this day. Old torts that emerged in Blackstone's time are now being extended to deal with new social problems. Intentional torts continue to fulfill the latent function of redressing grievances of less powerful groups in modern society.[218]

Modern intentional torts still protect physical security, but today they also include actions to protect rights such as mental tranquility.[219] In *Gomez v. Hug*,[220] an employee was the victim of a humiliating tirade of insults at his job as a supervisor of a fairgrounds. The company was found liable because the employee's supervisor repeatedly taunted the plaintiff as a "fucking spic" as part of a pattern of "vitriolic bullying." Wal-Mart was assessed punitive damages when one of its managers discharged an employee because of her relationship with a black man.[221]

The intentional infliction of emotional distress is one of the few examples of a completely new tort that emerged in the twentieth century.[222]

Yet, even the tort of outrage was prefigured in early common law. The functional equivalent of this then-nameless tort was the cause of action against innkeepers who abused guests. In the nineteenth century, common carriers were liable for such outrageous acts as forbidding a black woman to ride in the same railway car as white people. The tort of intentional infliction of emotional distress has since evolved into a mechanism to combat racial discrimination, violence against women, and harassment in the workplace.

In recent decades, the tort action for intentional infliction of emotional distress has evolved further to punish racism, sexism, and bullying in the workplace. A Mexican-American employee, for example, who was the object of racial taunting in the workplace received redress using this tort action.[223] The court observed that it was the position of authority of the abuser coupled with abusive conduct that gave "impetus to the claim of outrageous behavior."[224]

The history of tort law demonstrates a progressive recognition of societal as well as individual interests.[225] The tort remedies of early common law redressed private wrongs affecting the personal security of individuals "against their lives, their limbs, their bodies, their health, or their reputation."[226] With the coming of the Industrial Revolution, tort law shifted its focus to industrial accident law.

§1.3. *The Negligence Era in American Tort Law: 1825 to 1944*

The negligence paradigm developed in the latter half of the nineteenth century as a compensation system for the victims of industrial accidents. Negligence is "the failure to exercise the standard of care that a reasonably prudent person would have exercised in a similar situation."[227] The purpose of the law of negligence is to deter "culpable carelessness" that results in excessive preventable dangers.[228]

The law of torts entered the negligence era "around the turn of the nineteenth century as turnpikes and burgeoning industry were vastly accelerating the pulse of activity and confronting society with an accident problem of hitherto unprecedented dimensions."[229] Negligence was a compensation system that grew out of the rapid changes in transportation (particularly railroads) and industry. Under this new regime, "intentional injuries, whether direct or indirect, were grouped as a distinct field of intentional torts," while negligence provided remedies for the victims of accidents.[230]

American railways had a much higher rate of deaths and injuries than those in any European country. The first death in a railroad accident occurred on June 17, 1831, when a boiler exploded on a passenger locomotive, killing the fireman.[231] The first recorded train wreck with passenger fatalities occurred two years later in 1833.[232] The first major railroad accident occurred in 1853 when a New Haven Railroad train ran through an open drawbridge and plunged into the Norwalk River, killing forty-six passengers.[233] Perhaps the most shocking accident occurred on July 17, 1856, in Camp Hill, Pennsylvania, when two Northern Penn trains crashed head-on. Sixty-six church children bound for a picnic died in the flaming wreckage.[234] On January 25, 1871, a passenger in Chicago was crushed to death falling between two passenger trains while trying to catch a train.[235]

Another new form of transportation, the steamboat, also created new hazards. In August 1868, a bartender on a steamboat was severely injured when a boiler exploded on a trip between San Francisco and Petaluma, California.[236] A boiler explosion on a Mississippi River steamboat killed 1,547 near Memphis on April 27, 1865.[237] The "legal delinquency" in these cases was fatal negligence by the common carrier, not a desire to hurt anyone.

Negligence law, in no small part, was railway, streetcar, and steamboat accident law. It evolved to compensate the victims of accidents caused by common carriers and industrial corporations that failed to use reasonable care to protect the public.[238] It was negligent, for example, to fail to blow a whistle at a railway crossing or to operate a train without following safety procedures.[239] "The modern law of torts must be laid at the door of the Industrial Revolution, whose machines had a marvelous capacity for smashing the human body."[240]

The heyday of the negligence era was between 1850 and 1910, when courts recognized liability-limiting doctrines such as contributory negligence, the assumption of risk,[241] and the fellow servant rule.[242] The employer's common law duty to provide a safe workplace was undermined by court-constructed defenses that shifted the cost of accidents from the employer to the injured worker and his family. The negligence era timeline confirms that the "principal thrust of late nineteenth century doctrines was to restrict, rather than to expand, the compensation function of the law of torts."[243]

[A] Negligence Era Timeline

1842—Massachusetts Supreme Judicial Court adopts England's fellow servant rule in *Farwell v. Boston and W.R.R. Corp.*[244]

1850—Chief Justice Shaw advances the negligence theory in accidental injury cases by setting liability standard as whether the defendant exercised reasonable care under the circumstances.[245]

1880—The Massachusetts Supreme Judicial Court develops the locality rule in medical malpractice cases, defining negligence as a departure from local community practice as opposed to standards for the profession as a whole.[246]

1883—Court defines negligence as the failure to use ordinary care and skill in the circumstances.[247]

1887—Pharmacist is liable for negligently handing out the wrong drug prescription, injuring the plaintiff.[248]

1891—In *Vosburg v. Putney*[249] a twelve-year-old Wisconsin student kicks a fourteen-year-old classmate during class. What would have been a minimal injury turns out to be quite serious because the plaintiff had a preexisting condition. The court holds that the defendant is liable for all of the consequences of his intentional act.

1890—The right of privacy originates in a law review article by Samuel D. Warren and Louis D. Brandeis.[250]

1893—Proof of negligence is required in blasting cases unless the explosion is accompanied by an actual physical invasion of property.[251]

1896—In *Mitchell v. Rochester R.R. Co.*,[252] the court denies a plaintiff's recovery for a miscarriage caused by fright from the defendant's onrushing team of horses because of the absence of physical impact.

1906—Court holds that negligent blasting with dynamite resulting in twenty pound rock being thrown through plaintiff's window stated a valid claim even though there was no physical impact with the plaintiff.[253]

1911—The New York Court of Appeals strikes down the nation's first workmen's compensation act because it is based on strict liability.[254]

1913—A retail druggist is held liable for selling the plaintiff an injurious compound.[255]

1915—A seller is held absolutely liable for negligent manufacture if the article proves to be dangerously defective.[256]

1916—Judge Benjamin Cardozo authors opinion in *MacPherson v. Buick Motor Co.*,[257] which holds that if a defectively made article is reasonably certain to be a thing of danger and to place life and limb in peril, the seller is liable unless he acts with skill. Buick is held liable for injuries caused to the plaintiff when the wooden wheel of his Buick collapsed.

1917—New York's workers' compensation statute is held to be constitutional.[258]

1917—Court imposes a heightened standard of care upon common carriers to protect the traveling public.[259]

1920—Congress passes the Jones Act permitting recovery for negligent injuries or death of seamen injured on the high seas.

1928—Justice Cardozo authors opinion in *Palsgraf v. Long Island Railroad Co.*,[260] which becomes the basis for the risk theory of negligence. "The risk reasonably to be perceived defines the duty to be obeyed and risk imports relation; it is risk to another or to others within the range of apprehension."[261]

1929—The American Law Institute makes sellers liable for fraudulent misrepresentation provided they induce reliance from buyers.[262]

1932—Columbia University proposes a comprehensive compensation for automobile accidents.[263]

1935—Court holds that a nineteen-year-old unemancipated minor cannot sue his parent for negligent operation of a motor vehicle, invoking the doctrine of parental immunity.[264]

1938—Congress passes the Food, Drug and Cosmetic Drug Act to monitor the safety of food and drugs.

1939—American Law Institute membership approves Restatement (First) of the Law of Torts.

1944—Judge Roger Traynor's concurring opinion in *Escola v. Coca Cola Bottling Co.*[265] articulates the public policy rationale for the adoption of strict products liability.[266]

[B] Negligence in the Industrial Era

Negligence requires the fact finder to weigh the social utility of the activity against the gravity of the harm it causes. In the words of a nineteenth-century court, there is "no safety except in abandoning the use of machinery."[267] Some judges in early industrial America found this policy of allowing firms to perform cost–benefit analyses that balanced human lives against industrial profits to be immoral. Chief Justice Gibson of the Pennsylvania Supreme Court wrote that "the lives of human beings are not to be weighed in the same scales with the lives of a farmer's or grazier's stock."[268]

[1] Liability-Limiting Negligence Defenses

[A] CONTRIBUTORY NEGLIGENCE

"Contributory negligence, in its practical form, is the failure of the plaintiff to exercise that degree of care which is incumbent upon him by reason of his circumstances . . . and which would enable him to avoid the effect of the defendant's negligence."[269] Contributory negligence barred recovery where there was "concurring negligence of both plaintiff and defendant."[270]

An injured plaintiff was not entitled to any recovery for an injury "produced by the combined operation of his own want of 'ordinary care,' and the gross negligence of the defendant."[271] If the plaintiff's negligence "contributed as an efficient cause to the injury . . . the court could not balance the gradation of fault."[272] In Wisconsin, for example, the injured railroad employee "was faced with a solidified body of common law generally unfavorable to his interests in any court action arising out of injuries caused by industrial accidents."[273]

Contributory negligence "frequently meant that a momentary lapse of caution on the part of the workman was penalized by casting the entire burden of his injury upon him."[274] On February 11, 1895, a railroad employee who worked as a trackwalker and watchman was struck and killed by a freight train running a half-hour ahead of schedule. An Illinois court ruled that the man's estate was barred from recovery because he failed to look out for trains despite knowing that trains traveled at unscheduled times.[275]

Contributory negligence barred any recovery to the estate of an intoxicated passenger who was ejected from a railroad car at night for using profane language. The man's body was found the next day badly mangled, presumably having been killed by a passing train. The court gave short shrift to the question of the railroad's liability, observing that drunkenness was a "self-imposed disability" that did not relieve the person from the legal effects of contributory negligence.[276]

[B] ASSUMPTION OF RISK

"Assumed risk" was an absolute defense to liability if an employee voluntarily and knowingly assumed the risks that will be encountered on his job.[277] The assumption of risk doctrine cast "the entire burden of his injury upon him even if the employer was more negligent."[278] This pro-employer defense was particularly harsh because, in this historical period, injured workers had no social safety net to fall back on.

The Georgia Supreme Court reversed a $10,000 award to the widow of a railroad employee who was thrown from a train, drawn under the wheels, and instantly killed. The employee was held to have knowingly assumed all of the risks incident to employment in return for generous wages.[279] Similarly, in *Michigan Central R.R. Co. v. Smithson*[280] the Michigan Supreme Court ruled that a railroad was not liable for injuries suffered by a worker who was coupling cars, since he had voluntarily assumed the risk involved in carrying out such a dangerous activity.[281] The cars in question were "double dead woods," a type of coupling that had previously caused many lost limbs and lives.[282] One expert witness testified that the "double woods" coupling was as likely to catch a workers' limb as not.[283] The court noted that the railroad paid higher wages to compensate for the employees' higher risks.[284] The railroads sometimes hired "their watchmen, signalmen, messengers and gatemen from amongst their employees who had lost an arm or leg in the line of their employment."[285]

Railroad employees looked on while a train accident victim bled to death rather than summon medical help. In a 1903 opinion, the appeals court held that there was no negligence because the railway employees owed no duty to the bystander.[286] Courts denied recovery even in cases in which a worker continued his work while protesting its unsafe character.[287] The employer, however, could be held liable when the "master gave an assurance of safety or a promise to remedy the defect" and the worker was injured relying upon the false promise.[288]

[C] FELLOW SERVANT RULE

During this era, the employer was not liable for injuries to an employee caused solely by the negligence of a fellow employee.[289] The fellow servant rule was first recognized in 1842, in the Massachusetts case of *Farwell v. Boston and Worcester Railroad*.[290] In *Farwell*, the railroad engineer suffered the loss of a hand in an accident caused by the negligence of a switchman.

Chief Justice Lemuel Shaw observed that the "general rule is that he who is engaged in the employ of another for the performance of specified duties and services, for compensation, takes upon himself the natural and ordinary risks and perils incident to the performance of such services, and in legal contemplation, the compensation is adjusted accordingly."[291] The fellow servant rule was widely accepted by courts in both England and America. The employer's duty to provide a safe workplace "was reduced to any empty gesture by a number of ruses to balk recovery and so reduce the overhead cost of industrial operations."[292]

§1.4. Compassionate Tort Law or Subsidy to Industry?

[A] Subsidy Thesis

The liability-limiting rules during the heyday of negligence spurred the rapid industrialization of nineteenth-century America.[293] Morton Horwitz argues that these pro-defendant rules "broke with the traditional principle of just compensation for injury, in effect subsidizing industrial development at the expense of workers and consumers."[294] At early common law, the employer was required to maintain a safe workplace or be held accountable for any injuries. The doctrines of the fellow servant rule, assumption of risk, and contributory negligence abridged the absolute common law duty to protect employees.[295]

[B] The Common Law's Uncommon Compassion

Gary Schwartz takes issue with Horwitz's subsidy theory in his empirical study of nineteenth-century tort appellate decisions. Schwartz's research reveals that the liability-limiting doctrines were primarily confined to workplace cases and that judges frequently found an excuse to ignore immunities out of sympathy for the injured. Schwartz concludes that nineteenth-century courts "exhibited a keen concern for victim's welfare" and tended to "bypass harsh doctrines holding corporations accountable for their misconduct."[296] Prosser argued that juries apportioned damages in a way that could only be the result of "diminution of the damages because of the plaintiff's fault."[297]

[C] Tort Law's Dual Character

Our reading of the nineteenth-century cases finds some support for both sides of this debate. The tort law of this era was a battleground between two mutually opposed models of justice. On the one hand, negligence defenses subsidized and justified the risky activities inherent in a developing industrial economy. On the other hand, some judges did moderate the harsh consequences of rules that, "though originally sound, [had become] unsuited to new physical and social conditions."[298] Nineteenth-century tort law contained many regressive doctrines, but judges had greater sympathy for the plaintiff than acknowledged by Horwitz.[299]

Some courts applied principles of equity to side-step pro-defendant doctrines. A Wisconsin judge argued that every accident "involved a sacrifice upon industry's altar, which must inevitably, in the end, be cast upon the consumers of the products of industry. Pity's that these inevitable sacrifices fall first upon the weakest members of society . . . and do not reach the final resting place . . . without the waste and injustice of the present system."[300]

[1] Sidestepping the Fellow Servant Rule

Some courts allowed plaintiffs to recover by holding employers to the common law duty of maintaining a safe workplace. In *Shanny v. Androscoggen Mills*,[301] a worker lost two fingers when her hand came in contact with unguarded gears in a textile mill. The Maine Supreme Court held that the "fellow servant" rule did not exempt the employer from its common law duty to provide a safe workplace and "to furnish suitable machinery for carrying on his work."[302] The court rejected the employer's defense that another employee had failed to maintain the gears properly, observing that even when the gears "are fixed in the usual way, they were not free from danger."[303]

In *Railroad Co. v. Fort*,[304] the U.S. Supreme Court refused to extend the fellow servant doctrine to a case in which a sixteen-year-old boy had his arm severed by a revolving shaft. The boy was ordered by the superintendent of the machine shop to climb a ladder amidst rapidly revolving machinery, where the accident occurred. The Court reversed the lower court, holding that the fellow servant rule did not apply because it was the supervisor's careless order that placed the boy in a "position of peril."[305]

In *Fallon v. Cornell Steamboat Co.*,[306] a circuit court refused to extend the fellow servant rule to shipboard accidents in a wrongful death case. The decedent was a fireman on a tugboat who drowned as the result of a collision caused by a drunken operator.[307] The court held that the application of the doctrine would be unjust and enforcement would reflect a judicial tendency "to cite a rule and forget the justification."[308]

[2] Evading Contributory Negligence

[A] LAST CLEAR CHANCE

Negligence era judges employed the doctrine of "last clear chance" to bypass the harsh contributory negligence defense. The "last clear chance" rule held that a plaintiff could recover despite his contributory negligence, so long as the defendant had one last opportunity to avoid the accident.[309] The doctrine was first articulated in 1842, in an English case in which a farmer tied his donkey too close to the highway, where it was struck by the defendant's horse cart.[310] The court permitted the plaintiff to recover for the loss of his animal despite his negligence in leaving it on the edge of a busy roadway, because the defendant had the last clear chance to avoid the crash.[311]

[B] "HELPLESS PLAINTIFF" RULE

Some jurisdictions recognized the closely allied doctrine of the "helpless plaintiff."[312] Courts tended to apply this doctrine to situations in which the defendant's degree of fault was either "willful" or "wanton" as compared to simple negligence on the part of the plaintiff.[313] Decisions applying the helpless plaintiff rule appeared to reflect an "astonishing lack of reasoning" because the court's hidden agenda was generally to absolve the plaintiff in cases where the negligence doctrine would produce an obvious injustice.[314]

§1.5. Controlling Corporations in the Negligence Era

[A] Vicarious Liability

Vicarious liability is a form of "imputed negligence," sometimes referred to by the Latin phrase *respondeat superior*.[315] This doctrine imposes tort liability upon an employer for the misconduct of an employee. By allocating the full cost of wrongdoing to the enterprise, vicarious liability encouraged companies to make vigorous attempts to monitor their workers.[316] Judge Henry Friendly observed that under this rule, an "enterprise cannot justly disclaim responsibility for accidents which may fairly be said to be characteristic of its activities."[317] The corporation is expected to spread any unavoidable risk by increasing prices or by securing liability insurance.[318]

[1] "Frolic of His Own" Exception

A corporation was not liable for the misdeeds of an employee whose wrongdoing was considered to be a "frolic" or a personal detour from his assigned duties.[319] The "frolic" exception was first recognized in an 1834 English case in which servants took an unauthorized pleasure ride into the city. The horses, being unfamiliar with urban traffic, panicked and injured the plaintiff.[320] The master argued that the horse and cart were driven only in the country and were not authorized to go into the city where the accident took place. The court ruled that the master was "not liable, if as you suggest, these young men took the cart without leave."[321]

American jurisdictions followed the rule that a master would not be held liable if a servant was engaged in a "frolic of his own."[322] However, a master was held liable for a servant's detour if it was not extreme enough to amount to a frolic.[323] This distinction between a frolic and a detour later became important in automobile accident cases. An employer would be held liable if his employee was only on a detour while driving a company vehicle. In *Bryan v. Bryan*,[324] the plaintiff was struck by an employee who was driving the company's motor truck to his home for lunch after being instructed to return to the shop. The court concluded that the comparatively slight deviation by the employee from the direct route back to the shop was a detour and not a frolic. By the 1940s, courts had largely abandoned the narrow "frolic or detour" approach in favor of a negligence test, which asks whether the employer should have foreseen his employee's wrongdoing.

§1.6. Tort Wars in the Negligence Era

[A] Punitive Damages against Corporations

In the second half of the nineteenth century, big steel, big oil, big railroads, and the other cartels controlled by the robber barons came to dominate the smokestack-based American economy. For a time, the newly created railway monopolies and other powerful corporations seemed immune from any meaningful legal constraints. An 1852 law review article argued:

> The great increase of wealth and its gradual accumulation in a few hands . . . have necessarily introduced a corresponding change in the effect of judicial proceedings. . . . While the amount of wrong caused by an unlawful act remains very much the same, the case, at least among the richer classes, with which compensation can be made and the very trifling expense of a law suit, have deprived the latter of that vindictive character it once had, and rendered the former a mere question of profit and loss. . . . The only

question to an offender as to how often the process should be repeated, would be how far he could afford it.[325]

The actions—or dangerous inaction—of the large companies could cause injuries on a vast scale with seeming impunity.

Since "power begets wealth, and added wealth opens ever new opportunities for the acquisition of wealth and power,"[326] tort remedies were increasingly necessary to counter the new risks to the public welfare. As the Maine Supreme Court observed: "There is but one vulnerable point about these ideal existences called corporations; and that is the pocket of the moneyed power that is concealed behind them; and if that is reached, winces."[327]

Courts increasingly assessed punitive damages against defendants in commercial transactions that were characterized by malice, fraud, insult, misrepresentation, or wanton and reckless disregard of the rights of the plaintiff. The remedy corrected unethical business practices that threatened the marketplace for both buyers and sellers.[328] However, since the mental state required to prove punitive damages was equal to or greater than the standard for criminal manslaughter, only the most egregious misbehavior led to these awards.

Even during the heyday of negligence, corporations were held accountable for train wrecks, collisions, and trestle collapses. In 1839, the New Hampshire Supreme Court upheld a punitive damages award against the owner of a bridge that collapsed due to grossly negligent maintenance, on the grounds that safe bridges are a key public interest.[329] By the mid-1800s, public utilities, industrial corporations, railroads, commercial enterprises, and other corporations were habitual defendants in accident and intentional tort cases.

The use of punitive damages as a remedy for corporate misbehavior was well established in the post–Civil War period. In *Western Union Tel. Co. v. Eyser*,[330] the Colorado Supreme Court imposed punitive damages for that "class of acts extremely injurious to individuals, of which the criminal law takes no cognizance, and yet that which [affects] the public interest."[331] In 1869, the Maine Supreme Judicial Court wrote:

We think every candid-minded person must admit that it [punitive damages] is no new doctrine. . . . A corporation is an imaginary being. It has no mind but the mind of its servants; it has no voice but the voice of its servants; and it has no hands with which to act but the hands of its servants. All its schemes of mischief, as well as its schemes of public enterprise, are conceived by human minds and executed by human hands; and these minds and hands are its servants' minds and hands. . . . And yet under cover of its name and authority, there is in fact as much wickedness, and as much that are deserving of punishment, as can be found anywhere else.[332]

Railroads were frequently assessed punitive damages in their capacity as common carriers of passengers. A historical study of a few years of Mississippi verdicts found railroads to be habitual defendants. Punitive damages were awarded for a conductor's wrongful ejection of passengers; for maliciously carrying passengers past their stations; for accosting patrons in an insulting manner; for failing to stop when signaled; for not caring for a person known to be sick; for refusing to carry the blind; for allowing insults and fights; for spitefully detaining passengers; and for endangering the public by obstructing the tracks.[333]

Railway litigation was common in many other states as well. In New Hampshire, a husband recovered for injuries suffered by his wife in a train collision caused by gross carelessness.[334] Railroads were involved in innumerable tort lawsuits brought on behalf of women, invalids, children, the elderly, handicapped persons, and other vulnerable individuals who were physically attacked or humiliated by railway employees. A Texas court, for example, upheld a $1,200 punitive damages award against a malicious conductor who assaulted a female passenger.[335] A railroad was held liable when a fireman threw a shovel full of live embers from a locomotive engine on a woman standing near a crossing.[336] The court upheld a $5,000 punitive damages award against the railroad for its fireman's wanton misconduct, which caused the plaintiff to suffer disfiguring burns and blindness.[337] In *Maryville and Lexington Ry. Co. v. Herrick*,[338] a Kentucky court upheld punitive damages based on a railway's reckless disregard of its obligation to keep its tracks in good repair.

In 1870, an Illinois court upheld a $200 award in favor of a "colored woman" who was treated rudely by a conductor and excluded from riding in a "ladies only" railway car, stating that this racist act "in front of strangers and friends" was an indignity without the "shadow of excuse."[339] Tort law continues to produce a more just society by granting remedies for victims of discrimination.

[B] Limiting Punitive Damages

The railroads and other corporate interests fought back vigorously against the remedy of punitive damages. The first wave of pro-defendant "tort reforms" occurred in the nineteenth century when punitive damages against corporations became the subject of intense controversy. Justice Foster denounced the remedy of punitive damages as a "monstrous heresy . . . an unsightly and unhealthy excrescence, deforming the symmetry and body of the law."[340]

In nineteenth-century American jurisprudence, academics divided all law into two discrete spheres, the public and the private, and any legal doctrine had to fit into one of these two clearly defined categories. Influential law professors, lawyers, and some prominent jurists characterized punitive damages as an impermissible legal anomaly because they blended the civil and criminal sides of law. The critics of punitive damages contended that the goals of punishment and deterrence were, as they saw it, inconsistent with tort law's sole role of compensating individuals who were injured.

Several nineteenth-century arguments prefigured the constitutional challenges to punitive damages of today's tort reformers. Some reformers advanced the proposition that if punitive damages were to be permitted at all, the award should go directly into the state's treasury since it had been given to advance the public interest,[341] an issue that remains controversial today.[342]

Harvard Law School professor Simon Greenleaf spearheaded the movement to abolish punitive damages, arguing that the remedy had no doctrinal basis. In an 1834 lecture, Greenleaf proposed that law students adopt the methodology of the physical scientist, classifying legal doctrine into categories much as botanists created a taxonomy of plant life. This black-or-white legal taxonomy had no room for a remedy that lay on the borderland between public and private law. "Damages," opined Greenleaf, "are given as a compensation, recompense, or satisfaction to the plaintiff, for an injury actually received by him or her from the defendant."[343] For the legal formalist, punitive damages had no legitimacy; their practical utility and deterrent effects were irrelevant.

The proponents of punitive damages found their most capable spokesperson in Theodore Sedgwick, a legal editor and influential practicing attorney. Sedgwick exemplified a pragmatically oriented group of lawyers who found the logic-chopping of the legal formalists ridiculous.[344] Such tidy compartmentalizing of the law was viewed as unrealistic and impractical. Sedgwick and his allies stressed the need for a counterweight that ordinary citizens could employ against the malicious acts of powerful individuals and institutions. The nineteenth-century assault against the punitive damages remedy was successful in only a few states.

[C] Contingency Fees

The contingency fee system is an arrangement in which the plaintiff agrees to pay a fixed percentage of the recovery to his or her attorney, generally a third if they prevail and nothing if they lose.[345] This payment system is permitted in all states.[346] Jurisdictions vary as to what amount the attorney may receive and what explanation must be given to the plaintiff about the fee arrangement. Tort reformers favor an English rule in which the "loser pays" the legal fees of the opponent. The result of the English rule is to restrict access to courts by injured plaintiffs without the means of paying the legal fees of a Fortune 500 defendant.[347]

Contingency fees have long been attacked for encouraging unnecessary litigation. A lawyer who represented a hospital in Philadelphia at the start of the twentieth century claimed that "there was not an accident case brought to [the hospital he represented] that there were not at least a dozen lawyers coming in to see the injured man and trying to get to represent him on a contingent fee."[348] Plaintiffs' advocates responded that the contingent fee system made "possible the enforcement of legitimate claims which otherwise would be abandoned because of the poverty of the claimants."[349]

The Erie County Bar Association convened a committee in the fall of 1908 to examine the "evils which have grown up in connection with the contingent fee practice."[350] Some of the plaintiffs' lawyers objected to questioning the contingent fee contract, recommending that measures be taken instead against corporate abuses "in securing releases from injured persons, while they are in pain and suffering, on inadequate consideration."[351] The Erie County Bar Association adopted a majority report proposing legislation regulating "the releases obtained by corporations from injured persons immediately after accidents and before the sufferer is in a condition to judge whether he wants to settle at once or take action."[352] The American Bar Association "proposed that all contingency fees be subject to scrutiny and approval by the court."[353] As a result of this campaign, many states limit the amount that the plaintiffs' attorneys may receive in a contingency fee payment.

[D] Attacking Ambulance Chasers

The tort reformers of this era denounced "ambulance chasers,"[354] persons who were paid by an attorney to solicit negligence cases.[355] However, the representatives of the railroads, streetcar companies, and insurers were also known to chase ambulances in order to secure releases.[356] Courts often upheld one-sided settlements, which were signed while the victim lay injured in the hospital. A New Jersey court ruled that a release was valid even though it was obtained at a hospital soon after the victim's arm had been amputated.[357] The one-armed plaintiff signed a settlement agreement releasing all claims in return for $100 in cash.[358]

In *Nelson v. Chicago and Northwest Ry. Co.*,[359] the court referred to numerous cases in which railroads and other industrial employers obtained releases of claims for personal injuries using fraud, undue influence, or false representations. Corporations sometimes colluded with physicians to induce injured workers to sign releases under the false promise that they would soon recover their health. Courts could use the mutual mistake doctrine of contract law to invalidate releases when the physician purposely misinformed the patient. In *Nelson*, the court invalidated a release that was signed based on fraudulent statements made by a physician working in cooperation with the railroad.[360]

Unfair settlements by overzealous claim adjusters were also sometimes nullified. A 1910 law review editorial observed that there were "a great many cases in the reports where releases for a ridiculous consideration were secured under such circumstances that juries refused to countenance the transaction."[361] Defense counsel was frequently accused of arriving on the scene as quickly as possible after an accident, in order to purchase affidavits from witnesses to the accident.[362] The very success of corporations in leaving accident victims with no legal remedy led Congress and the states to enact compensation statutes.

[E] Replacing Torts with Statutory Remedies

[1] Federal Statutes

[A] SAFETY APPLIANCE ACT OF 1893

The high injury rate among railway workers at the end of the nineteenth century was attributable to the industry's failure to adopt safety improvements. Pro-defendant tort defenses made it cheaper to replace crippled workers than to improve equipment. An Indiana court ruled that a railroad worker who had lost his hand in a coupler accident had voluntarily assumed the risk.[363] In a similar Alabama case, a young and inexperienced brakeman was denied compensation for having lost his hand in a coupling accident.[364] The court observed that the danger of couplings "was open, plain and manifest" and that the railroad had no duty to even warn "of this obvious danger."[365]

Congress enacted the Safety Appliance Act of 1893 in order to reduce the carnage caused by the railroads. This federal statute required the railroad industry to install automatic couplers and power-driven wheels in locomotives to "protect the lives and limbs of men."[366] The U.S. Supreme Court upheld this statute in a case where a railroad worker suffered a traumatic amputation injury when the bumpers between an engine and dining car caught his wrist.[367]

[B] FEDERAL EMPLOYER'S LIABILITY ACT

Congress abolished all negligence-based defenses in order to provide compensation to workers when it passed the Federal Employer's Liability Act of 1908 (FELA).[368] Under FELA, contributory negligence of the plaintiff did not bar recovery for injuries caused in part by the defendant's negligence.[369] Justice William O. Douglas stated that FELA placed "on the railroad industry some of the cost for the legs, eyes, arms, and lives which it consumed in its operations."[370] Justice Douglas noted that FELA "lifted from employees 'the prodigious burden'" of personal injuries which the system had placed upon them.[371]

[2] Workers' Compensation Legislation

By the first decades of the twentieth century, many Americans were of the opinion that the liability-limiting doctrines for workplace accidents placed an intolerable burden upon society. One judge railed against these corporate immunities:

> All thoughtful persons agree that present conditions call for legislative, judicial or economical relief one or all. Enterprises such as railroads, streetcar lines, interurban lines, manufacturing plants of all kinds, with rapidly moving machinery, usually hazardous with the dangerous invisible electrical current of high voltage, the agency of steam, geared with cogwheels, belts, pulleys and other appliances are killing and crippling thousands and thousand every year. This is so even when the employees are sober, attentive and watchful and is materially increased when such persons or some of them are negligent. This means poverty and distress, and is followed by charity and too often, filling the poor houses and sanitariums.[372]

During the height of the negligence era, the "vast proportion of industrial accidents remained uncompensated and the burden fell upon the workman, who was least able to support it."[373]

"Between 1910 and 1920 the method of compensating employees injured on the job was fundamentally altered in the United States."[374] New York passed the first workers' compensation statute in 1910.[375] Employers contributed to an insurance fund, which gave workers a limited but certain recovery for lost wages and medical expenses. In return, the employees give up their right to sue under tort law.[376]

In the beginning, corporate defendants fought workers' compensation vigorously. The first wave of workers' compensation statutes were struck down on grounds such as liberty of contract and the denial of due process.[377] The Wyoming Supreme Court rejected a Seventh Amendment challenge to the workers' compensation act because it required corporations as well as workers to give up their right to a jury trial on damages.[378] An Iowa court observed that it was rather humorous that corporations objected to the denial of a trial by jury since "it is seldom asked or desired by the employers of laborers."[379]

[F] Insurance and Loss Spreading

Insurance policies became a critical component of American tort law in the late nineteenth century. Insurance companies have always been advocates of liability-limiting tort reforms because the companies ultimately pay the bill for most judgments against corporations. Liability insurance originated "in England in 1880, and developed first as a means of protecting employers against the increased liability resulting from employer's liability and workers compensation acts."[380] Motor vehicle insurance is the best known example of the insurer as loss spreader.[381]

In the modern age, insurers play a key role in the defense of toxic torts, products liability, and medical malpractice cases. The ability of companies to insure against potential tort liability has been controversial from the beginning. A corporation that is insured against tort liability may be less likely to vigilantly protect the public interest. Opponents of the insurability of tort risks argued that insurance was a form of "maintenance, by which professional litigants were provided to replace the true defendants."[382] Tort liability insurance is well accepted today and insurance companies even offer policies covering e-commerce and Internet-related risks.

States remain sharply divided as to whether the insurability of punitive damages violates public policy since insurance undermines the punishment function of these verdicts. Punitive damages may not be covered by insurance policies in the eighteen states that prohibit indemnification on public policy grounds, and in eleven of those states punitive damages are insurable for a principal's imputed negligence or vicarious liability.[383] Standard form insurance policies do not exclude punitive damages.[384] Courts have interpreted this fact as creating a "reasonable expectation of coverage" for the policyholder.[385]

§1.7. The Progressive Tort Law Era: 1945 to 1980

The American law of torts was a relatively sleepy outpost prior to the 1940s. Plaintiff-oriented tort expansion began shortly after the Second World War and was in high gear by the mid-1960s. Barrier after barrier to victims' tort recovery was repealed or diminished by state legislatures and common law courts. Liability-limiting rules, defenses, and immunities "retreated like a melting glacier" after the Second World War.[386] The tort timeline below reflects the progressive unfolding of tort law, which occurred from 1945 to 1980.

The principal current of American tort law following World War II was an expansion of rights and remedies. Prior to the 1960s, manufacturers were shielded from liability by the doctrine of privity and other barriers to recovery. A manufacturer was not liable for injuries caused by defective products unless it joined in the making of a contract with a consumer.[387] Absent a direct contractual link, there was no liability of a manufacturer to an injured consumer. One critic charged: "We let our victims fall where they may, redressing only the injuries of the 'privity-privileged.'"[388]

Since it was rare that a national distributor of a company directly contracted with the ultimate consumer, there was almost no products liability prior to the 1960s. Exceptions to the privity rule "first yielded in the food products cases, surrendered next in cases of drugs and cosmetics, and finally capitulated in the case of any and all products which are dangerous if defective."[389] By 1965, there were at least thirty-two cases in which courts extended "strict privity-free tort and warranty rule beyond food and drink."[390] Strict products liability assigned losses based upon the public policy decision that the manufacturer is in the best position to avoid the perils of defective products.

Medical malpractice also emerged as a means of providing patients with remedies for lethal medicine. Today, medical malpractice remedies punish negligent nursing home chains, dishonest insurance companies, and irresponsible health care entities that damage the public welfare through indifference or in order to increase corporate profits. The timeline below shows that the postwar period belonged to the plaintiff.

[A] Tort Liberalization Timeline

1945—England abolishes doctrine of contributory negligence.[391]

1946—First case to permit recovery for prenatal injuries.[392]

1947—The American Law Institute amends the Restatement of Torts to recognize the tort of intentional infliction of emotional distress.[393]

1947—Judge Learned Hand, in *United States v. Carroll Towing, Inc.*,[394] develops a negligence formula, which compares the burden of precaution to the probability and severity of the injury.

1950—The U.S. Supreme Court, in *Feres v. United States*,[395] holds that the federal government is immune from any suit filed by soldiers for injuries sustained while serving in the military.

1951—Sixteen states introduce legislation abolishing contributory negligence.[396]

1952—*State Rubbish Collectors Assoc. v. Siliznoff* is the first judicial recognition of the tort of the intentional infliction of emotional distress.[397]

1954—Court requires proof of physical injury to recover for the tort of the intentional infliction of mental distress.[398]

1959—In *Martin v. Reynolds Metal Co.*,[399] the Oregon Supreme Court extends the law of trespass to cover polluting of another's land. In this case, the corporation permitted gases and particulate to settle on the plaintiff's land, making it unfit for raising livestock.

1960—In *Henningsen v. Bloomfield Motors, Inc.*,[400] the New Jersey Supreme Court finds an automobile manufacturer liable to a customer's wife despite the seller's disclaimers and the lack of privity. This case launches the field of products liability.

1960—Ronald Coase publishes famous essay arguing that when parties compete for the same resource, it makes no different to the allocation of resources which way the court imposes liability.[401] Coase's article launches the law and economics theory of tort law.

1961—Constitutional torts remedies recognized in case in which the City of Chicago is held liable for its police officers' torts committed against a black couple.[402]

1961—Kentucky overrules doctrine of charitable immunity.[403]

1962—New York overrules long-standing rule that there can be no recovery for the negligent infliction of mental distress in the absence of physical impact.[404]

1963—*Greenman v. Yuba Power Prods., Inc.*[405] is the first appellate case to recognize the doctrine of strict products liability, in an opinion authored by Justice Roger Traynor.

1964—The U.S. Supreme Court, in *New York Times v. Sullivan*,[406] holds that the constitutional protection given to speech and the press limits defamation lawsuits brought by public officials.

1965—The American Law Institute approves the Restatement (Second) of Torts, §402A, which recognizes strict products liability.

1965—Professors Keeton and O'Connell propose a no-fault automobile accident compensation plan.[407]

1965—The American Law Institute approves §519, which recognizes strict liability for "abnormally dangerous activities."

1965—The Ohio Supreme Court rules that a defendant doctor in a medical malpractice action could be cross-examined as to accepted medical practice.[408] This ruling permitted malpractice victims to counter the "conspiracy of silence" in which doctors refused to testify against other doctors.

1965—Kentucky Supreme Court abolishes that state's doctrine of municipal immunity in a case in which negligence led to a seven-year-old child drowning in a city swimming pool.[409]

1967—African-American plaintiff is held to have a valid cause of action for assault and battery when he was approached in a buffet line by a restaurant employee who "snatched the plate from his hand and shouted that no Negro could be served in the club."[410]

1967—Court denies recovery for new tort of wrongful life.[411] Court rejects argument that mother would have undergone abortion if she had known of the risks of contracting German measles during pregnancy.

1967—First appellate case approving the awarding of punitive damages in a strict products liability action. Merrell-Richardson, the defendant, was charged with falsifying test results and marketing the unsafe anti-cholesterol drug, MER-29.[412]

1968—An automobile manufacturer was held to have a duty of care in designing a crash-worthy vehicle.[413]

1968—California Supreme Court abolishes landowner categories of trespasser, licensee, and invitee in favor of a standard of reasonable care in *Rowland v. Christian.*[414]

1969—New York Court of Appeals overrules long-established precedent that actual proof of negligence is required in blasting cases absent physical invasion. Chief Judge Fuld rules that the question is which party should bear the cost of resulting damage from dangerous activities, not whether the activity was lawful.[415]

1969—New York Court of Appeals abolishes the parent–child immunity rule.[416]

1969—Minnesota and Florida abolish interspousal immunity.[417]

1970—Arizona repudiates parent–child immunity.[418]

1970—Ralph Nader brings an invasion of privacy lawsuit against General Motors for a campaign of dirty tricks and harassment to suppress his crusade against unsafe automobiles.[419] With the proceeds of the judgment, Nader establishes public interest law group devoted to exposing corporate wrongdoing.[420]

1970—An owner of an apartment building is found liable for negligent security in a case involving a criminal attack on a tenant in a common hallway. *Kline v. 1500 Massachusetts Avenue Apartments Co.*[421] became a precedent for the development of premises liability.[422]

1970—California court recognizes tort of outrage against insurance company for bad faith refusal to settle a claim.[423] This case launches the field of bad faith insurance claims.

1971—The Supreme Court upholds a Federal Tort Claims Action against police officers in an unreasonable arrest and search action.[424]

1973—Florida replaces contributory negligence with comparative negligence.[425]

1975—In *Li v. Yellow Cab Co.,*[426] the California Supreme Court adopts a pure comparative negligence statute based upon the extent of fault of the parties.[427]

1976—In *Tarasoff v. Regents of University of California,*[428] the Supreme Court of California holds that a psychiatrist has an affirmative duty to warn of his patient's dangerous propensities.

1976—New Jersey partially abolishes parental immunity doctrine.[429]

1979—Court finds a professional football player liable for the intentional infliction of injury.[430]

1980—California Supreme Court adopts market share liability permitting DES daughters to recover for reproductive injuries occurring many decades after their mothers ingested anti-miscarriage drugs.[431]

1980—Congress enacts the federal Superfund law governing hazardous waste sites.[432]

[B] The Progressive Era in American Tort Law: 1945–1980

We think of the 1950s and 1960s as the golden days, as depicted in *Ozzie and Harriet, I Love Lucy,* and the *Andy Griffith Show,* but these decades were not happy days when it came to consumer product safety. Before the mid-1960s, there were no products liability cases for design defects or for failure to warn consumers about potential product dangers.

"The Commission on Product Safety's description of product hazards of the 1960s reads like a surrealistic nightmare. Crib slats strangled infants, easily toppled steam vaporizers scalded, and rotary power mowers clipped off fingers and toes. Thousands of television sets caught fire from poorly insulated wires. Exploding household cleaning products maimed numerous consumers. Wringer washing machines crushed the limbs of the young or unwary. Thousands of glass doors shattered, creating makeshift guillotines.[433] Nightmare, yes, but this gruesome catalogue was no dream."[434] These terrible products are no longer on the market because of preventive and remedial measures instituted by corporations in response to expanded products liability.

American automobile executives of the 1950s and 1960s believed that good looks, rather than safety, sold.[435] Seat belts were unknown and vehicle fires common. Drivers were impaled on rigid steering wheel columns, which were then standard features on American cars.[436] Steering wheels in many models would needlessly tattoo drivers with the permanent imprints of decorative emblems.[437] Unpadded dashboards and the sharp edges of ashtrays gouged out eyes and caused easily preventable head and facial injuries.[438] Prior to the rise of products liability, automobiles were not crashworthy and "crumpled like a Japanese lantern" in rollover accidents.[439]

Ralph Nader's book *Unsafe at Any Speed* documented the fact that Corvairs could unexpectedly turn on their drivers.[440] This lightweight, rear-engine automobile would veer out of control and flip over under normal driving conditions because of the Corvair's dangerously defective swing-axle suspension.[441] Nader noted that the hazardous decorative fins on the Cadillac "bore an uncanny resemblance to the tail of the stegosaurus, a dinosaur that had two sharp rearward-projecting horns."[442] Cadillac fins and sharp decorative grills gouged pedestrians due to the lack of safety engineering.[443]

Today, we have none of these deadly design features, thanks to the role of products liability in driving defective automobiles off the market. The entire industry has improved the safety of its product line. In the past ten years alone, motor vehicle deaths have dropped 11 percent.[444] From 1982 to 1996, an estimated 85,396 lives were saved by safety belts.[445]

Strict liability for products that were defectively designed or marketed with inadequate instruction became quite common by the early 1970s. Automobile manufacturers, for example, were required to design their automobiles to be crashworthy and to better protect their occupants in the foreseeable event of accidents.[446] Today, automobile design cases focus on the effectiveness of restraint systems, fuel system integrity, collapsed seatbacks, rollover defects, airbag defects, inadequate side protections, and door-liftgate latches.[447]

In the early 1970s there were 20 million injuries and 30,000 deaths caused each year by ordinary household products.[448] An annual toll of 30,000 to 60,000 people, primarily infants and the elderly, suffered serious burns from gas-fired floor furnaces in the 1960s.[449] The floor grates would reach a temperature of 400 degrees Fahrenheit, a temperature suitable for cooking roast beef.[450] Thousands of American children were branded with the distinctive "waffle patterned scars from the grills of such furnaces."[451] Expanded liability played a key role in eliminating such dangerous products.[452]

We no longer have sliding doors that guillotine children or windshields that shatter into shards. In the summer months, hospital emergency rooms are no longer filled with the victims of ultra-hazardous lawn mowers or of weed whackers marketed without safety guards. Motorcycles now incorporate side-protection to prevent serious leg injuries, after an expensive punitive damages lawsuit.[453] The Dalkon Shield and Copper-7 intrauterine contraceptive devices were removed from the market as the result of mass products liability.[454]

Lathes, augers, and farm machinery were retrofitted with guards after the manufacturers of these unnecessarily hazardous products were assessed tort damages.[455] Dangerous televisions, revolvers, and automobiles have been redesigned or taken off the market as a response to the deterrent effect of lawsuits.[456] Corporations have instituted multimillion-dollar safety campaigns as an impressive lesson learned from litigation.[457]

Much remains to be done. Products liability benefits the larger society by reducing the social and financial cost of injury.[458] The comprehensive cost of unintentional injury in the United States was an estimated $1.53 trillion in 1997.[459] Children continue to be harmed by dangerous toys and household products. Bunk beds, for example, entrap youngsters between the wall and the mattress if guardrails are not properly installed.[460] Battery-powered children's riding vehicles present fire and injury hazards.[461]

[1] Comparative Negligence

By the 1960s, pro-defendant tort defenses and immunities of all kinds were in rapid retreat. The law of comparative negligence has largely displaced the regressive doctrine of contributory negligence since the 1970s.[462] Under contributory negligence, plaintiffs had no cause of action for negligence if they had contributed in any way to the accident. The defendant could be 99 percent at fault, but the plaintiff's 1 percent fault would preclude recovery. Even if the defendant was grossly negligent or reckless, contributory negligence was an absolute bar against recovery.

Comparative negligence may also reduce verdicts on a percentage-of-fault basis rather than barring all recovery. Mississippi became the first state to adopt comparative negligence in 1919.[463] A number of states apportioned damages in state "employers' liability acts" covering railroad employees.[464] Comparative negligence was adopted for "certain specified occupations, usually hazardous, such as mining or lumbering, in Arizona, Florida, and Oregon, and to all employees of intrastate corporations in Arkansas."[465]

The California Supreme Court abolished the "all or nothing" contributory negligence doctrine in *Li v. Yellow Cab Co.*[466] The *Li* court held that the contributory negligence defense "must give way to a system of comparative negligence, which assesses liability in direct proportion to fault."[467] Forty-four states had adopted some form of comparative responsibility by 1988.[468] Six southeastern states—Alabama, Delaware, Maryland, North Carolina and Virginia—still follow the contributory negligence rule.[469]

The two major types of comparative negligence are *pure* and *modified*. Under the pure regime, a plaintiff may recover even if her negligence constitutes 90 percent or more of the fault for an accident.[470] "Recoverable damages must be reduced in the proportion which the plaintiff's fault . . . bears to the total fault of plaintiff and defendant."[471] The modified system places a limit on the degree of the plaintiff's negligence. In some states, if a plaintiff's negligence exceeds 50 percent, no recovery is permitted.[472] California's *Li* decision applied a pure form of comparative negligence that assessed liability in proportion to fault even if the plaintiff was at fault equally to or more than the defendant. The death of the contributory negligence rule was part of a larger movement in tort law to base judgments on "reason, modern policy, and the logic of the fault principle."[473]

[2] Statutes of Limitations

A statute of limitations is an absolute bar to filing a tort cause of action because too much time has passed. Many states have statutes of limitations for tort liability, which generally range from two to three years. The statute of limitations may be particularly unjust in occupational exposure cases, such as the asbestos litigation, where the injury does not manifest itself for decades. Since World War II, many states have adopted a more progressive discovery rule, which postpones the statute of limitations until a plaintiff has a reasonable opportunity to discover his or her condition. The discovery rule expanded "from doctors to dentists, accountants, architects, lawyers, manufacturers of defective products and a miscellany of negligence and other tort actions."[474]

[3] Death of Immunities

[A] WAIVER OF SOVEREIGN IMMUNITY

Governmental entities have long enjoyed sovereign immunity from lawsuits, except where this has been statutorily waived.[475] Each state has "the legal authority to limit the terms of consent to be sued and limit the total dollar amount to which it is willing to subject itself to liability on a claim."[476] The states began to waive immunity in lawsuits brought against government units beginning in the 1940s.

The federal government also has the legal authority to limit the causes of action for which it can be sued. The Federal Tort Claims Act (FTCA), for example, permits recovery for property damage and personal injury caused by the negligence of government employees acting within their scope of duty, a remedy that had previously been denied as a violation of sovereign immunity.[477] The FTCA contains many exceptions, including no recovery for punitive damages,[478] intentional torts,[479] or the failure of officials to perform discretionary functions.[480] All of the states have some form of tort claims act, which provides for recovery for negligence by state officials. As with the FTCA, the waiver of sovereign immunity does not extend to punitive damages, intentional torts, or discretionary acts.[481] The effect of the waiver is only to waive immunity from "unrecognized causes of action and not to visit the Government with novel and unprecedented liabilities."[482]

[B] CHARITABLE IMMUNITY

Charitable immunity is the common law principle "that relieves a charitable organization or trust from tort liability."[483] At least forty states recognized charitable immunity by 1938, but the tide began to turn in the 1940s and 1950s.[484] By 1985, charitable immunity had been abolished or modified in every jurisdiction.[485] Six states have a regime of partial charitable immunity, limiting claims against nonprofit institutions.[486] The abolition of charitable immunity opened the court door to expanded liability for medical malpractice.

In recent years, a number of states have reinstated charitable immunity for nonprofit organizations and volunteers as a tort reform. Congress enacted the Volunteer Protection Act in 1997, which "bars negligence lawsuits against people for volunteer for nonprofits or government agencies."[487]

[C] PRIVACY TORTS

Privacy as a tort cause of action first crystallized in the second half of the twentieth century, having originated in an 1890 article by Samuel Warren and Louis Brandeis.[488] Georgia became the first state to recognize privacy torts, which are now accepted in the vast majority of jurisdictions.[489] Many states recognize four kinds of privacy-based torts: (1) unreasonable intrusion upon the seclusion of another; (2) appropriation of the other's name or likeness; (3) unreasonable publicity given to the other's life; or (4) publicity that unreasonably places the other in a false light before the public.[490] States vary in the scope of their recognition of privacy-based torts. Virginia, for example, does not recognize intrusion upon seclusion or the disclosure of private facts. Despite these state differences, privacy torts have generally provided expanded protection since the 1940s.

[D] PRENATAL INJURIES

Prior to World War II, courts universally denied recovery for a negligently caused prenatal injury. By 1965, the overwhelming majority of courts reversed course, ruling that prenatal injuries were compensable.[491]

In a parallel development, the majority of courts permitted recovery for prenatal injuries leading to stillbirths even for a pre-viable fetus.[492] If a pregnant woman was injured, "and as a result the child subsequently born suffers a deformity or some other injury, nearly all of the decisions prior to 1946 denied recovery to the child."[493] In *Stemmer v. Kline*[494] a woman complained of suffering from severe abdominal distress. The physician gave his patient protracted x-rays, misdiagnosing a pregnancy as an abdominal tumor. The child was born profoundly retarded as a microcephalic without skeletal recovery. The court held that the physician owed no duty of care to the unborn child. Some courts reasoned that a defendant had no duty to a person not yet in existence; other courts denied recovery because of the difficulty of proving a fetal injury.[495] Today, fetal injuries are compensable in all states.

[E] OTHER EXPANSIONS OF TORT RIGHTS AND REMEDIES

[1] Redress for Negligently Inflicted Mental Injuries

The fault-based negligence paradigm frequently denied recovery for injury because of the doctrine of limited duty. A defendant was thought not to owe the plaintiff a duty "where the physical harm was not immediately the result of the plaintiff's fright or shock. A mother could have suffered a nervous breakdown from witnessing her beloved toddler dying in the street after being struck by a negligently driven vehicle and have no remedy unless she was also struck."[496]

New York was the first state to overrule the "no impact" rule.[497] Other courts adopted the "zone of danger" test to permit recovery by plaintiffs who suffered mental distress from being in the close vicinity of an accident but had not suffered any physical impact.[498] When close family members were killed or severely injured in the presence of the plaintiff, courts used this legal fiction to permit recovery. There was no recovery in the "zone of danger" for unrelated bystanders because of courts' fears of collusive lawsuits.[499] Courts imposed a requirement that the emotional distress be accompanied by verifiable medical symptoms.[500]

[2] Intentional Infliction of Emotional Distress

Recovery for the tort of outrage evolved in the 1940s and 1950s.[501] "The tort of the intentional infliction of serious mental distress requires that the defendant engage in outrageous and extreme conduct which results in intentionally or recklessly inflicted severe emotional distress."[502]

The standard for the tort of outrage is conduct that is "atrocious and utterly intolerable in a civilized community."[503] An action for the intentional infliction of emotional distress did not extend to "mere insults, indignities, threats, annoyances, petty oppressions or other trivialities."[504]

[3] The Rise of Products Liability

Judge Benjamin Cardozo's 1916 landmark opinion in *MacPherson v. Buick Motor Co.*[505] extended a manufacturer's duty of care to the ultimate purchaser, where the product, if negligently manufactured, was likely to cause injury. The court stated that the manufacturer must have "knowledge of a danger, not merely possible, but probable."[506] Products liability was soon extended to "no privity" negligence by most courts.[507]

The 1960 case of *Henningsen v. Bloomfield Motors, Inc.*[508] was by far the most influential products liability verdict decided under the law of sales. In *Henningsen*, Chrysler sold an automobile to Bloomfield Motors, a New Jersey automobile dealership. Bloomfield Motors, in turn, sold the Chrysler to Mr. Henningsen. Henningsen's wife suffered a severe injury when the car's steering gear malfunctioned and her vehicle careened into a wall.[509] Chrysler defended on the grounds of no contractual privity and no notice of rejection under the Uniform Sales Act. Justice John Francis of the New Jersey Supreme Court held the dealer and manufacturer liable without a showing of negligence, notice, or privity, ruling that "absence of agency between the manufacturer and the dealer who makes the ultimate sale is immaterial."[510]

The Uniform Commercial Code has also sharply limited privity, extending the benefit of warranties to family members or household guests in every state. Many jurisdictions have extended privity "to any person who may reasonably be expected to use, consume or be affected by the goods and who is injured by breach of the warranty."[511]

[4] The Rise of Strict Products Liability

Strict liability is imposed in the absence of intent or fault. Trespass was considered to be a strict liability offense at early common law. Absolute liability was also imposed for injuries caused by wild animals that escaped because harboring dangerous beasts was intrinsically dangerous. Strict liability did not permit defendants to argue that they took reasonable precautions in preventing the peril.[512]

By the nineteenth century, strict liability was imposed for abnormally dangerous uses of land. Strict liability was a policy decision to assign responsibility without a finding of fault where the activity was particularly hazardous. Products liability, which developed in the mid-1960s, is the most controversial expansion of strict liability.[513]

The Supreme Court of California was the first to recognize the doctrine of strict products liability in *Greenman v. Yuba Power Products, Inc.*,[514] In *Greenman*, the plaintiff was injured when a malfunctioning Shopsmith lathe turned a piece of wood into a missile that struck him in the forehead.[515] The plaintiff did not give the manufacturer notice of the claimed breach of warranty until he filed suit ten months later. The manufacturer defended on the grounds that the implied warranty action was barred for failure of timely notice. Justice Roger Traynor held that strict liability rather than warranty applied in this case: "Under these circumstances, it should not be controlling whether plaintiff selected the machine because of the statements in the brochure, or because of the machine's own appearance. . . . To establish the manufacturer's liability it was sufficient that plaintiff proved that he was injured while using the Shopsmith in a way it was intended to be used as a result of a defect in design and manufacture of which plaintiff was not aware."[516]

[1] Restatement (Second) of Torts, §402A

Justice Traynor's opinion in *Greenman v. Yuba Power Products, Inc.*,[517] had an immediate influence in shaping Section 402A of the Restatement (Second) of Torts, which was approved by the American Law Institute in 1965. This section, which was entitled "Special Liability of Seller of Product for Physical Harm to User or Consumer," was adopted by all but a few jurisdictions by the 1980s.[518] Section 402A abolished privity as well as fault from a plaintiff's burden of proof. The "consumer expectation test" of Section 402A, focusing on whether the defect was unreasonably dangerous to the consumer or ultimate user and caused his injury, was cited in more than nine thousand court decisions.[519] The underlying policy rationale is that the manufacturer is in the best position to protect the user and therefore should shoulder the burden of precaution.[520]

Products liability may be subdivided into three categories: (1) manufacturing flaws; (2) design defects; and (3) failure to warn or instruct.[521] Under any of these theories, the plaintiff must prove three elements: "(1) the injury resulted from a condition of the product; (2) the condition was an unreasonably dangerous one; and (3) the condition existed at the time the product left the defendant's control."[522]

[A] MANUFACTURING DEFECTS

In a manufacturing flaw case, the seller is liable for injuries caused by foreign objects, a bad batch, or a mismanufactured good "even though all possible care was exercised in the preparation and marketing of the product."[523] Manufacturing defect cases are the oldest branch of products liability. "As early as 1266, criminal statutes imposed liability upon victualers, vintners, brewers, butchers, cooks and other persons who supplied contaminated food and drink."[524]

The doctrine of *res ipsa loquitur* found the manufacturer liable for exploding bottles or when "the foreign object in the can is a set of false teeth."[525] Manufacturing defect cases were more common before companies instituted product safety and testing divisions.[526] The first successful tobacco products liability actions were based upon foreign objects found in chewing tobacco. In *Pillars v. R. J. Reynolds Tobacco Co.*,[527] a plaintiff suffered from ptomaine poisoning as the result of unknowingly eating the remains of a human toe embedded in a plug of tobacco. The plaintiff's mouth began to foam after chewing tobacco containing the crumbled toe. R. J. Reynolds was the defendant in a similar case in which the plaintiff was injured by a fishhook in his chewing tobacco.[528] Defendants also paid judgments to plaintiffs who ingested tobacco containing rat or squirrel claws and wooly worms.[529] Other manufacturing defect cases include a consumer injured by a sewing needle in a loaf of bread[530] and one made ill by a decomposed mouse in a soft drink.[531]

[B] DESIGN DEFECT

The more controversial cases in products liability occur in design defect cases. In the manufacturing flaw cases, it is a single item that is mismanufactured, while in design cases the litigant must show that the entire product line is unreasonably dangerous. In the Firestone litigation, the design defect was inadequate bonding between the steel radial and the tire carcass, which led to deadly tread separations.[532]

The traditional consumer expectation test requires expert testimony proving that the product was more dangerous than an ordinary consumer would expect.[533] The Firestone case should easily pass the "consumer expectation" test because it is unlikely that drivers would expect their tires to explode. Courts are increasingly retreating from the strict liability standard in favor of a negligence-based risk-utility test. The risk-utility analysis balances utilities against dangers or risks in a product.[534]

[C] FAILURE TO WARN

The defect in a failure-to-warn case is the lack of instruction on how to use a product safely.[535] In medical products cases, the manufacturer has a duty to warn prescribing or treating physicians of the risks of a drug or device. Women filed products liability actions for the failure of the manufacturer to warn their physicians of the increased risk of having a stroke created by taking high-estrogen oral contraceptives.[536] In another design defect case, a thirteen-year-old boy lost his arm when his uncle's weed whacker swung violently after hitting a rock. The court upheld a products liability judgment on the grounds that "the warnings given were inadequate to apprise consumers of the [weed whacker's] violent kickback potential."[537]

The most recent expansion of product liability is in the negligent marketing and distribution of dangerous instrumentalities such as handguns.[538] A number of municipalities have filed negligent marketing claims against gun manufacturers, with only limited success.

[D] OTHER PROGRESSIVE DEVELOPMENTS

Premises liability is a cause of action against the owners of buildings with unsafe conditions.[539] The development of premises liability permitted the victims of crimes to file lawsuits for unsafe conditions in shopping malls, apartment buildings, and residential property. Hotels and motels across the country have improved security after premises liability lawsuits were filed by guests (or their estates) who were robbed, raped, or murdered by intruders.[540]

The MGM Grand Hotel fire of 1980 killed eighty-five and injured another five hundred guests. Three thousand claims were filed against the hotel for its inadequate sprinkler and alarm system. After these lawsuits, the MGM Grand was rebuilt with improved state-of-the-art ventilation, a new sprinkler system, and carefully monitored alarms.[541]

§1.8. Tort Law Retraction: 1981 to the Present

American tort law has been in retraction during the past two decades as Congress and the state legislatures have enacted a wave of pro-defendant statutes. Many states have capped punitive and non-economic damages,[542] restricted comparative negligence, and eliminated joint and several liability.[543]

These "reform" statutes undermine the greatest social benefit of tort law: its ability to evolve in order to constrain new forms of oppression. As a nineteenth-century New York court noted: "It is the peculiar merit of the common law that its principles are so flexible and expansive as to comprehend any new wrong that may be developed by the inexhaustible resources of human depravity."[544] The federal takeover of tort law would undermine its latent function of evolving to protect the public interest from emergent threats. The timeline below reflects the predominant trend toward retreat and retrenchment.

[A] Tort Retrenchment Timeline

1981—California appellate court remits punitive damages award in famous Ford Pinto products liability case from $125 million to $3.5 million.[545]

1981—In *Vietnamese Fishermen's Association v. Knights of the Ku Klux Klan,*[546] the court concludes that the Klan is guilty of statutory violations for intimidating Vietnamese fishermen and also liable in tort for the wrongful interference with contractual relations.

1983—California Supreme Court recognizes a negligent cause of action for the mispositioning of a telephone booth close to a major roadway.[547] This case became a favorite tort horror story of President Ronald Reagan.

1986—New Hampshire abolishes the remedy of punitive damages.[548]

1986—The American Tort Reform Association (ATRA) is organized to form legislative coalitions and mobilize corporate citizens for tort reform. Tort limitations enacted in the states are spearheaded by ATRA.[549]

1987—New Jersey, Ohio, and Oregon adopt a Food and Drug Administration (FDA) defense to punitive damages. Drug and medical device manufacturers are immunized from punitive damages if they can prove that they complied with pre-approval processes and did not withhold from or misrepresent to the agency any information that was "required, material, and relevant."

1987—The court in *Ayers v. Jackson Township*[550] finds that the plaintiff's ingestion of water contaminated with toxic chemicals was an "immediate and direct physical impact and injury" permitting recovery for emotional distress.

1987—Georgia enacts a tort reform statute requiring tort claimants to remit 75 percent of all punitive damages to the state treasury. Georgia, Iowa, Kansas, Montana, New Jersey, North Dakota, Ohio, and Oregon enact tort reform statutes increasing the burden of proof for recovering punitive damages to "clear and convincing evidence."

1989—Minnesota federal district court upholds a $7 million punitive damages award in a products liability case involving the Copper-7 intrauterine device,[551] leading to the settlement of thousands of similar cases.[552]

1989—Hawaii court raises standard of proof in punitive damages from preponderance of evidence to clear and convincing evidence.

1993—Fifth Circuit U.S. Court of Appeals holds that FDA approval preempts state tort liability in medical device case.[553] First Circuit holds that pre-market FDA approval of collagen preempts all tort liability.[554]

1993—California Supreme Court reverses action for intentional infliction of emotional distress where there was no showing that the defendant knew that depositing toxic materials in a landfill close to the plaintiffs' home would cause extreme distress.[555]

1993—U.S. Supreme Court affirms $10 million punitive damages award in business torts cases. Court rejects claim that punitive damages award is excessive and violates defendant's due process rights.[556]

1993—In *Daubert v. Merrell Dow Pharm., Inc.*,[557] the Court places new limits on expert testimony, making the trial judge responsible for determining whether a theory has a valid scientific basis.

1994—In *Honda Motor Co. v. Oberg*,[558] the U.S. Supreme Court holds that an Oregon statute that prohibits judicial review of the size of punitive damages is unconstitutional.

1994—The General Aviation Revitalization Act of 1994 becomes the first federal tort reform statute enacted. The measure imposes an eighteen-year statute of repose[559] for small aircraft.[560]

1995—Restatement (Third) of the Law of Torts: Product Liability is approved by the American Law Institute.

1995—Caps on punitive damages are instituted as a tort reform in Illinois, Indiana, New Jersey, North Carolina, and Oklahoma. Indiana enacts an FDA defense to punitive damages. Texas enacts a far-reaching statute raising the standard for obtaining punitive damages, capping damages, and limiting choice of venue.

1996—U.S. Supreme Court finds a punitive damages award grossly excessive, violating the due process clause of the Fourteenth Amendment.[561] This is the first time in American history that the U.S. Supreme Court has found a punitive damages award to violate a defendant's due process rights.

1997—Texas becomes the first state to permit lawsuits against HMOs for denying medical treatment.[562]

1997—President Clinton signs the Amtrak Reform and Accountability Act of 1997, which imposes a $200 million cap on damages for Amtrak accidents.[563]

1997—U.S. Supreme Court rules that a class action by diverse asbestos claimants violates Rule 23 of the Federal Rules of Civil Procedure.[564]

1998—The Biomaterials Access and Assurance Act of 1998 immunizes the suppliers of raw materials incorporated into medical products from products liability lawsuits.

1999—A California jury awards the victim of a products liability case $107 million in compensatory damages and $4.8 billion in punitive damages. The trial judge remits the punitive damages award to $1 billion in a case where the plaintiff is severely burned by an exploding gas tank in a General Motors vehicle.[565]

1999—Federal government sues the cigarette industry to recoup medical expenses of smokers.[566]

1999—Florida governor Jeb Bush signs a comprehensive bill limiting joint and several liability, capping damages, instituting a twelve-year statute of repose, and limiting the liability of rental companies.

2000—A six-person Miami, Florida, jury awards $145 billion in punitive damages against five tobacco companies. In the first phase of the trial, the jury finds cigarettes to be dangerously defective and the companies' conduct in marketing cigarettes as warranting punitive damages.

2000—In *Pegram v. Herdrich*,[567] the U.S. Supreme Court holds that treatment decisions by HMOs through their physician employees are preempted by the Employee Retirement Income Security Act of 1974 (ERISA).[568]

[B] Tort Retrenchment Movement

[1] State Tort Reforms

The tort retrenchment timeline above reveals a pattern of reversing progressive rights and remedies. States have created new immunities and defenses benefiting corporate defendants over the past thirty years. The first wave of tort reforms occurred in the early 1970s as a response to an increase in insurance premiums that was blamed on the growing number of lawsuits. In the late 1950s, only 1 in 100 doctors were sued for medical malpractice.[569] By the 1990s, the number of malpractice claims had increased ten-fold.[570] State legislatures enacted caps on non-economic damages, limitations on punitive damages, restrictions on filing medical malpractice cases, limitations on attorney's fees, and the collateral source rule in order to reduce costs.

Medical malpractice reforms did not fulfill their promise of reducing medical or insurance costs. A leading medical liability researcher argues that "the idea that containing medical liability costs will make any appreciable dent in health care costs is absurd."[571] Even if medical liability could be eliminated altogether, the savings would only amount to "two month's growth" in the nation's overall health care budget.[572]

[2] The Abolition of Strict Products Liability

In 1997, the American Law Institute (ALI) replaced Section 402A with the Restatement (Third) of Torts: Products Liability.[573] As the California Supreme Court observed, the negligence-based reasonableness standard of the Restatement (Third) "entirely abandons strict liability."[574] The ALI Reporters who drafted the Restatement (Third) argued that was necessary to keep up with the fast and furious "pace of American products liability litigation."[575] The drafters of the Restatement (Third) describe their efforts as only restating a broad consensus in products liability case law.[576] The Georgia Supreme Court finds it doubtful that this consensus exists.[577] The Nebraska Supreme Court rejected Section 6(c) of the Restatement (Third), which bans liability against prescription drugs or medical devices even if an alternative safer design is available.[578]

The Restatement (Third) applies to those who (1) are engaged in the business of selling; (2) have marketed a defective product; and (3) have caused harm to persons or property. Section 402A of the Restatement (Second) adopted a "consumers expectation test," which has been displaced by a risk-utility test in the Restatement (Third).[579] Plaintiffs are required under the new restatement to prove that "foreseeable risks of harm posed by the product could have been reduced or avoided by the adoption of a reasonable alternative design."[580] The Reporters argue that "the rule developed for manufacturing defects is inappropriate for the resolution of claims of defective design and defects based on inadequate instructions or warnings."[581] Section 2(c) of the Restatement (Third)

replaces strict liability with a negligence approach in warning cases. It remains to be seen whether courts will follow the Restatement (Third) in
substituting old fault-based principles for strict products liability.

Since 1986, thirty-five states have restricted the plaintiff-oriented doctrine of joint and several liability, and another thirty-two have placed one
or more restrictions on the recovery of punitive damages.[582] Since 1986,
twenty-two states have abolished or restricted the collateral source rule
and another thirteen states limited the recovery of non-economic damages.[583] The collateral source rule does not reduce the plaintiff's recovery
for benefits received such as free care at a Veteran's hospital or insurance
benefits. The purpose of the collateral source rule is to ensure that the defendant pays the entire price of wrongdoing. Fifteen states have enacted
restrictions on products liability.[584] Tort reform is not confined to legislative retrenchment in the states. Nationalizing the law of products liability
is a top priority for the tort retrenchment movement.

[3] Federalization of Products Liability

Tort reformers often justify the federal preemption of state tort law by
arguing that the present variations among the states create unpredictabil-
ity and confusion for manufacturers who market across state lines. Federal tort reform, however, is not designed to solve this problem. Federal
product liability reform would preempt none of the state law provisions
that presently limit tort rights and remedies. The reformers' goal is to further restrict the tort rights of injured Americans.

The proposals do not attempt to create uniformity by introducing
punitive damages into states that do not presently recognize the remedy.
Colorado, for example, requires plaintiffs to prove punitive damages by
the criminal law standard of "beyond a reasonable doubt." If the supporters of federal products liability were truly interested in uniformity, Colorado's standard of proof would be rolled back to the standard of "clear
and convincing evidence" proposed in the federal tort reform bills. This
one-way preemption requires all states with a preponderance-of-the-evi-
dence standard raise their standard of proof, making it more difficult for
plaintiffs to recover punitive damages.

The first comprehensive federal products liability bill was proposed in
1979.[585] Since then, there has been at least one federal tort reform bill
filed in each session of Congress. "In 1986 alone, approximately 1400 tort
reform bills were introduced in state legislatures."[586] Thirty-eight states

enacted at least one tort reform statute affecting products liability rights and remedies during the 1970s and 1980s.[587]

President Clinton vetoed the Common Sense Legal Standards Reform Act of 1995, stating that the bill "interfered unduly with state prerogatives and unfairly tilts the legal playing field to the disadvantage of consumers."[588] This federal statute would have capped punitive damages in products liability at the greater of $250,000 or two times the compensatory damages awarded by a jury. The traditional basis for awarding punitive damages is the defendant's wealth and aggravating circumstances rather than some arbitrary ratio of the value of the plaintiff's loss or injury. The statute would have abolished joint liability for persons suffering non-economic damages such as the permanent loss of health, disfigurement, blindness, or sterility. Federal tort reform bills are the culmination of a twenty-year campaign to narrow and restrict the tort remedies of injured victims.

[4] Industry-Specific Federal Tort Reforms

A number of industry-specific federal tort reforms were enacted during the 1990s. The General Aviation Revitalization Act of 1994 is a special-purpose federal tort reform benefiting the small aircraft industry. This federal tort reform imposed an eighteen-year statute of repose for small aircraft. Congress passed the Small Business Job Protection Act of 1996, which contained a provision for the tax deductibility of punitive damages and non-economic damages. The Amtrak Reform and Accountability Act of 1997 granted tort relief by imposing a $200 million cap on damages for Amtrak accidents.[589] The suppliers of raw materials or components for medical implants have been given immunity from products liability lawsuits by the Biomaterial Access Assurance Act of 1998.

[5] State Punitive Damages Restrictions

Forty states have enacted at least one limitation on the recovery of punitive damages in the past two decades.[590] Colorado, for example, caps punitive damages to the amount of compensatory damages. Connecticut caps punitive damages at twice compensatory damages in products liability actions. In Delaware, punitive damages are limited to the greater of three times the compensatory damages or $250,000. Maryland caps punitive damages at four times compensatory damages.

Florida and Indiana impose a punitive damages limit of three times compensatory damages.

Georgia caps punitive damages in products liability cases at $250,000 and places limits on multiple punitive damages for the same course of conduct. Kansas limits punitive damages to the lesser of $5 million or the defendant's annual gross income. Nevada has a complicated formula that caps punitive damages at three times compensatory damages if the award is $100,000 or greater. New Jersey, North Dakota, Oklahoma, Texas, and Virginia also cap punitive damages.[591] Thirteen states require a prevailing plaintiff to remit a portion of punitive damages to a state fund.[592] Twelve jurisdictions require that the amount of punitive damages be determined in a bifurcated proceeding.[593] Since 1970, the majority of states require plaintiffs in punitive damages cases to prove liability by "clear and convincing evidence," which is a heightened standard of proof.[594]

[6] Medical Malpractice Retrenchment

The tort reformers have targeted medical malpractice rights and remedies, which had expanded rapidly in the 1970s. To prevail in a medical malpractice case, the plaintiff must prove that the health care provider violated a professional standard of care.[595] Medical malpractice plaintiffs fare even worse than products liability claimants do, winning only 30 percent of their cases.[596] Every state enacted at least one new restriction on patients' rights to compensation for medical negligence in the 1970s and 1980s.

Tort reforms have been passed without systematic empirical investigation about their possible consequences. Before state tort law is nationalized, tort reformers should meet some minimal burden of persuasion that there is a nationwide litigation crisis. States that have weakened tort remedies are experiencing unanticipated negative consequences. For example, when the owner of a day care center sexually abused an infant girl who was under his care, caps on the size of verdicts required the trial judge to reduce the non-economic damages award to the legally permitted maximum of $500,000. The victim will require extensive therapy, yet she will not obtain all of her non-economic damages because of California's tort reform statute.[597]

In 1988, racist thugs in Portland, Oregon, beat an Ethiopian man to death with their fists, a baseball bat, and steel-toed boots. The victim was inadvertently dropped off in front of his home just as a skinhead meeting was breaking up.[598] Morris Dees of Klanwatch filed a tort lawsuit on behalf of the decedent's estate against the White Aryan Resistance, an organization that actively "encouraged the skinheads to take actions to kill the defendant."[599]

White Aryan Resistance and three of its leaders were jointly and severally assessed $10 million in punitive damages, $479,000 for the loss of future wages, and $2 million for pain and suffering and other damages. The trial judge, however, was forced to reduce the award of $2 million in non-economic damages to $500,000 under Oregon's damages cap statute.[600] It is doubtful whether the Oregon legislators intended to benefit a racist hate group when they enacted tort reform.

§1.9. Conclusion: The Future of Tort Law

The power of the law of torts lies in its ability to adapt to changing social conditions. In the eighteenth century, torts compensated individuals injured by their neighbors. In contrast, in the 1970s and 1980s, mass tort law litigation evolved to compensate the victims of occupational exposure to toxic substances. The greater the outrage and the more prominent the defendant, the greater the punishment. "Power alone can limit power."[601]

The inherent flexibility of tort law allows it to mediate social inequities as they arise. Just as tort law protected less powerful individuals against King George III's agents or from the excesses of abusive employees of the railroads, torts continue to evolve to meet the challenges of the new millennium. There is a logical continuity from the early cases against powerful aristocrats to the modern products liability cases against powerful corporate interests. The information age and advances in biotechnology create the opportunity for new forms of oppression, which must be controlled by tort law. Torts have consistently evolved to provide protection for the average citizen against entities too powerful to be constrained by lesser remedies.

Today, the tort system is under unremitting attack. Corporate America is calling for "reforms" that actually constitute a radical revision of the American civil justice system. It is difficult to think of one sub-field of tort law that has not been retrenched or reversed during the past two decades. The demand for further evisceration continues unabated, with one tort revisionist recently asserting: "By all reasonable measures, the American tort system is a disaster. It resembles a wealth-distribution lottery more than an efficient system designed to compensate those injured by the wrongful actions of others."[602]

The key assertion of the tort reformers is that punitive damages awards in products liability and medical malpractice are spiraling out of control. Chapter 2 will begin our empirical investigation of these assertions by revealing the human face of tort litigation. Awards are extremely hard to win, even when the plaintiff has been seriously injured by clear-cut corporate misbehavior. By reviewing four typical products liability cases in depth, we will acquaint the reader with the ways that dangerously substandard products harm consumers and the role of tort law in establishing a safer America.

2

The Human Face of Tort Law

§2.1. A Civil Action: *David vs. Goliath*

The 1997 movie *A Civil Action* relates the ordeal of several families who sue two Fortune 500 corporations because their predecessor companies dumped industrial solvents into the Woburn, Massachusetts, water supply. The movie, based on a 1996 book by the same name, depicts the tragedy of families needlessly losing children to leukemia due to environmental polluters, and the further suffering inflicted by the legal process upon those who sought redress.[1]

A Civil Action is based on a real case of toxic torts, *Anderson v. W. R. Grace*,[2] in which eight Massachusetts families sued W. R. Grace and Beatrice Foods for alleged contamination of the Woburn ground water with chemicals, including trichloroethylene and tetrachloroethylene. W. R. Grace operated the Cryovac Plant, which was suspected to be the source of chemicals that leached into the public water supply.[3] Beatrice Foods was the successor in interest to a neighboring property formerly occupied by a tannery. The Woburn plaintiffs sought to hold both successor corporations liable for the environmental pollution that occurred over many decades.

The plaintiffs' theory was that two of Woburn's water wells, Wells G and H, drew upon the contaminated water until they were closed in 1979, and that the contaminated water caused local children to die of leukemia.[4] Sixteen of the twenty-eight living plaintiffs were relatives of the children who died of cancer. Three of the claimants were suffering from leukemia and were being treated for the disease; the other plaintiffs alleged that the contaminated water caused a variety of illnesses and damages.[5] The plaintiffs also sought recovery of damages for the emotional trauma of witnessing the slow death of their children from leukemia and for the risk of developing future illness and emotional injuries.[6]

Although Massachusetts is one of five states in which punitive damages are not recoverable under the common law, this remedy may be sought under the Massachusetts Wrongful Death Act.[7] Identifying a statute under which one can sue is just the first step in what is often a long, frustrating struggle. Despite a determined search, the Woburn families could not find a law firm willing to take on their case. Finally, one very small firm simply could not refuse the families' pleas, a decision that would lead to its bankruptcy. The human and financial expenses of litigating a toxic torts case defended by armies of legal talent hired by Fortune 500 companies are crushing.

The Woburn defendants were represented by two of Boston's leading law firms: Hale and Dorr, and Foley, Hoag and Eliot. The defendants argued that several of the wrongful death actions were barred by the statute of limitations. One of the children who consumed Woburn water had died more than eight years before the lawsuits were filed. The plaintiffs responded that the action was timely because Massachusetts follows a discovery rule that delays the statute of limitations until a plaintiff knows or reasonably should know that he or she has been harmed by the defendant's action.[8] However, the causal connection between the contamination that contributed to the plaintiffs' illnesses was difficult to establish even with the help of geologists and other experts.

The film accurately portrays the David versus Goliath nature of a toxic tort lawsuit: the powerful corporate defense firms against understaffed and poorly financed plaintiffs' attorneys. Even where the alleged harm done is so grave, the American legal system places a cruel and almost insurmountable burden on the small, individual plaintiff. The grieving Woburn families had to endure mountains of motions and years of acrimonious litigation because of the difficulties of proving a causal connection and the nature of the scientific evidence. The expert testimony from hydrologists, geologists, and ground water supply scientists was complex and expensive. Walter Skinner, the U.S. federal district judge who tried the case, separated or bifurcated the proceedings into two phases: one for causation and one for damages. Only if a defendant was found liable for causing the pollution would it then be tried in the damages phase.[9]

The jury found W. R. Grace liable for environmental pollution and Beatrice Foods not liable for tainting the water supply. On appeal, the trial verdict was reversed and remanded. In 1986, the Woburn litigants agreed to settle the case against W. R. Grace for approximately $8 million rather than face a retrial on all the issues. This settlement agreement satisfied none of the parties; it certainly did not satisfy the concept of justice held by the plaintiffs. While $8 million seems like a great deal of money, the litigation expenses were so high that the eight families received only a small fraction of the settlement. The plaintiffs' law firm collected too little to remain solvent.

A Civil Action is emblematic of a tort litigation system that is too often unable to deliver justice. As Justice Harlan Stone once stated: "The most elementary conceptions of justice and public policy require that the wrongdoer shall bear the risk of the uncertainty which his own wrong has created."[10] In *Woburn*, those who dumped chemicals into the water supply decades earlier were no longer in business to stand trial for their misdeeds. Yet, this case did increase corporate accountability. W. R. Grace acknowledges that it "made mistakes in addressing the concerns of the community and government agencies regarding the impact of waste disposal practices at our Woburn plant in the 1960s and 1970s."[11] The manufacturer notes that it had spent more than a decade learning from the events in Woburn, Massachusetts.

W. R. Grace has completely revamped its environmental policies in the wake of this litigation and has been commended for its social responsibility by the community of Woburn and the Environmental Protection Agency (EPA).[12] The lesson from *A Civil Action* is that ordinary Americans can force powerful companies to address the concerns of the community. Toxic tort cases such as this have resulted in a safer environment for all citizens. The EPA and W. R. Grace worked cooperatively in cleaning up contaminated ground water. The purpose of the tort system is, quite simply, to make the wrongdoer accountable for damages inflicted or injuries caused, whether by malfeasance, misfeasance, or nonfeasance. W. R. Grace's latest legal crisis is from a rapidly growing number of asbestos product liability claims.[13]

§2.2. The War against Tort Victims

The general public has an unfavorable impression of injured plaintiffs that stems from a carefully orchestrated campaign to portray civil litigants as greedy, stupid, or fringe lunatics. Courts are depicted as being bogged down with frivolous lawsuits to which the media have attached such pejorative headlines as "Burned in the Act," "Junk Food, Junk Lawsuit," "Man Sues Lifesavers," "Cold Cuts," "Sue Thy Neighbor," "Obey the Law, Get Sued," "Fear of Not Flying," "Bad Hair Day," "Spook Suit," and "Bombed Man Bombs Self and Then Sues Everyone."[14] A particularly outstanding "wacky lawsuit" was the bank robber "with a hearing problem who was arrested because he did not realize a teller had tripped the alarm. He sued the bank for exploiting his disability!"[15] Journalists do not mention that the truly loony lawsuits are dismissed at an early stage of the legal process and have minimal significance in our civil litigation system.

[A] Tort Horror Stories That Blame the Victim

Tort horror stories are disseminated by a corporate-funded "outrage industry" whose long-term goal is to reallocate the cost of injuries from corporate wrongdoers to the victims.[16] The American Tort Reform Association (ATRA)[17] celebrates National Lawsuit Awareness Week each year and sponsors a five-mile "Tort Trot" to benefit the hydrocephalic infants whose access to medical products is supposedly threatened by frivolous products liability lawsuits.[18]

ATRA tells the story of customer who sued a nightclub claiming that its topless dancer gave him whiplash by bumping him with her huge silicone implant–augmented breasts. The tort reformers mock product warnings used on bathing suits: "This is an article of clothing and in no way is intended to be used as a flotation device or serve as protection from harmful rays of the sun." Tort reformers suggest the next generation of warnings will be even more bizarre: "Batman costumes: Cape does not enable user to fly."[19]

[B] The Insurance Industry's Advocacy Advertisements

The contemporary campaign against tort law arose as a response to the expansion of tort rights in the post–World War II era. Prior to the 1940s, defendants had few worries about product liability because privity of contract stymied most cases against national manufacturers.[20] Doctors were seldom sued for malpractice because of charitable immunities and the difficulty of getting physicians to testify against other doctors. The abolition of many immunities and defenses, the adoption of "strict liability," and an "emerging concern about toxic exposures and a broader-based rise in claims consciousness on the part of the public" led to an increase in awards.[21]

Corporate America has been fighting since the 1950s to return to the "good old days" when consumers had very limited remedies.[22] The insurance industry placed full-page advocacy advertisements in popular magazines such as the *Saturday Evening Post* and *Life Magazine*[23] that were calculated to turn the public against injured plaintiffs.[24] A 1953 advertisement appearing in several national magazines asserted:

> This could be any courtroom in the country. Behind the locked door, twelve men and women are reaching a verdict involving a defendant protected by a casualty insurance company. What they decide affects your pocketbook. All claims against insurance companies have to be paid out of funds created by premiums from policyholders. When these funds are insufficient, insurance rates must be increased.
>
> Casualty insurance companies have been losing an average of $11 on every $100 of earned automobile liability premiums. More accidents are partly responsible. So are excessive jury awards, rendered by jurors who feel they can afford to be generous with the 'rich' insurance company's money. Actually, jurors who are responsible for awards in excess of what is just and reasonable are soaked by rising insurance rates.[25]

The natural tendency of most Americans is to be sympathetic to the plight of a crippled plaintiff and to the grief of the surviving dependents. The insurance industry's concerted effort is to push the jury away from its natural moorings by portraying the corporation as the true victim in tort liability cases—that is, the corporations as victim of a tort system run amuck. An insurance industry advertisement from the 1950s depicted jurors taking their oath, with the following printed message underneath the picture:

> A True Verdict Rendered According to the Law and the Evidence
>
> Jury service is often a difficult responsibility because, when making decisions, we always are tempted to listen to our hearts as well as our heads.
>
> But the Juror's Oath demands that jurors decide 'according to . . . the evidence.' Jurors sometimes forget this. Ruled by emotion rather than facts, they arrive at unfounded or excessive awards . . . verdicts occasionally even higher than requested!
>
> These men and women may be scrupulously honest. But, as jurors, they feel in their hearts that the injured person—although he may have caused the accident—is entitled to an award.
>
> Because insurance rates depend on claim costs, these honest jurors cost millions of policyholders, including themselves, countless extra dollars in premiums every year. When you, as a juror, sit in judgment on a suit involving personal injuries, be fair with the public's—and your—money. Reach a decision according to the evidence.[26]

The public—the pool of potential jurors—is told that the American jury decide cases because of sympathy for the injured victim, and then is importuned to consider the victimized insurance company and its policyholders, rather than the plight of widows and orphans.

In the 1970s, St. Paul Property and Liability Insurance purchased print advertisements that trumpeted, "You really think it's the insurance company that's paying for all those large jury awards?"[27] Crum and Forster Insurance Companies placed full-page advertisements that were captioned: "The jury smiled when they made the award. They didn't know it was coming out of their own pockets."[28] Aetna, too, has sponsored an extensive and sophisticated advertising campaign against the American civil jury. The insurance industry's campaign implied that jurors decide cases on raw emotion rather than on the evidence. These advertisements not only appeared in national magazines, they were distributed by civil groups, PTAs, insurance agents, and brokers.

In contrast, a recent survey of trial judges reported that 98 percent of respondents agreed the juries do at least "moderately well" in rendering fair verdicts.[29] Insurance industry advertisements strongly suggest that the tort system is little more than a thinly veiled method by which populist juries redistribute wealth from corporations to the plaintiff. While these public relations ploys make the argument that excessive jury awards have caused the jurors' own insurance premiums to increase, they never report the profits of the insurance companies or the salaries of insurance executives. The courts have rejected claims that this propaganda campaign is improper or illegal.[30] However, a justice of the Montana Supreme Court sounds an alarm: "When insurance companies inject the issue of insurance into the consciousness of every potential juror through a high-priced advertising campaign, as has been illustrated in this case, they threaten every plaintiff's rights to an impartial jury."[31]

This public relations campaign to abridge the rights of plaintiffs continues to this day. The U.S. Chamber of Commerce promotes tort reform through television advertisements that portray plaintiffs as a "very small group of people who are trying to suck the vitality out of American industry and put it in their pockets."[32] Recently, a federal court castigated the U.S. Chamber of Commerce for running a political campaign supporting pro–tort reform judicial candidates under the guise of informing citizens about the tort reform "issue."[33] The court held that the Mississippi ads "in effect endorse candidates and must comply with election-reporting laws."[34]

A health insurance industry advertisement contends that a patients' rights bill will provide more opportunities for frivolous lawsuits.[35] Another tort reform–sponsored advertisement depicts three firefighters that appear to have rescued someone from a fire.[36] One fireman tells another: "I didn't take this job to sit around and worry about being sued." "If we don't stop lawsuit abuse, I might not be able to do my job," says another. "And my job might be to save your life."[37] The General Secretary of the International Association of Firefighters stated that the advertisement was "absolutely false" and that firefighters were not afraid of saving lives because of liability concerns.[38] The tort reformers recently purchased "a print advertisement . . . challenging Members of Congress to choose between working Americans or trial lawyers."[39]

[C] Tort Law and Personal Responsibility

Defense lawyers charge plaintiffs with refusing to take personal responsibility for their actions as the central defense in tobacco products liability lawsuits.[40] Tobacco's principal defense is to blame smokers for their poor judgment in deciding to smoke, deflecting blame from the industry.[41] The jury is told that no one forced the plaintiff to smoke. Plaintiffs' attorneys counter this "freedom of choice defense [with a] head-on rebuttal based on the addictive character of tobacco."[42] Tobacco company executives testified "shoulder to shoulder before Congress and declared with a single voice that cigarettes were not addictive."[43]

The insurance industry's advocacy advertisements also focus on personal responsibility, deflecting attention away from unsafe products and practices. Tort reformers urge Republican incumbents and challengers to make arguments about civil liability reform that will resonate with voters:

> Spill hot coffee on your lap? Sue the company that made the coffee! Your kid misses a pop fly and bruises his face? Sue the volunteer Little League coach! Have an accident going 100 mph in a 35-mph zone? Sue the engineering firm that designed the road! Since America's tort system now divorces action from responsibility, it encourages outrageous lawsuits.[44]

A cloud is cast over even worthy claims by this victim-blaming strategy.

Plaintiffs' attorneys are attacked for enriching themselves through frivolous suits. An advertisement entitled "Smoke" charges that trial lawyers are behind new legislation that would give HMO patients a right to sue their medical insurer. The announcer states: "Laws that make trial lawyers rich by drowning the courts with new lawsuits, but could cost almost two million Americans their health insurance . . . they call that patient protection. But you know who they're really protecting."[45] An HMO advocacy group broadcast a television commercial that portrayed trial lawyers as sharks: "America's richest trial lawyers are circling—and your health plan is the bait: call Congress today."[46]

Because of this deliberate campaign to belittle tort plaintiffs and their lawsuits, stories about supposed lawsuit abuse have become "urban legends": "true-sounding but utterly false stories that pass from person to person even in this modern day."[47] Public relations experts concoct many of these tort tales by selective distortion of the facts of real cases. Their objective is to persuade ordinary Americans that the injury problem is not the responsibility of corporate defendants, but rather the product of crazy or greedy individuals.

In real life, the consequences of the tort reform movement fall upon those Americans who have suffered catastrophic injury or death at the hands of corporations. Considering the number of people injured or killed by dangerously defective products every year in the United States, it is surprising how few Americans ever obtain any redress for their injuries. Like the plaintiffs in *A Civil Action*, most injury victims face great difficulties even in the initial task of finding a lawyer willing to cover the upfront costs of pursuing a complex case.[48] "At best, litigation, even successful litigation, is an inconvenience, at worst an ordeal."[49]

The actual toxic tort case portrayed in the film cost millions of dollars to pursue, leading to financial as well as emotional ruin for the plaintiffs' attorneys. Tort reform has increased the already difficult hurdles that must be overcome before undertaking a lawsuit, often closing the courtroom door to ordinary citizens injured by corporate America.

The tort reform campaign against the civil jury is paying big dividends for the business community. Employment and economic security are top priorities for many Americans, and tort reformers argue that the tort system costs jobs.[50] According to a 1991 survey nearly 90 percent of Americans agree that there are too many lawsuits.[51] A 1992 survey showed that more than four out of ten Americans believe that "only about half of the plaintiffs in [civil lawsuits] have just cause to file suit."[52] As a result of tort reform campaigns, state after state has enacted statutes limiting the ability of plaintiffs to recover for their injuries.

A number of state courts have overturned tort reforms on state constitutional grounds.[53] In 1995, the Alabama Supreme Court overturned a tort reform that imposed a $1 million cap on wrongful death recoveries. The plaintiff in that case died after a physician misplaced an endotracheal tube connected to a mechanical respirator. The court reduced a $4.5 million punitive damages award to $1,276,873 to comply with the state's cap. The Alabama Supreme Court struck down the statute, ruling that it violated state constitutional guarantees to equal protection and a jury trial.[54]

Four years earlier, the Alabama Supreme Court struck down a $400,000 cap on economic damages on similar grounds.[55] A trial judge had been given no choice but to reduce the award of a plaintiff who suffered amputation of her finger and endured permanent pain in her right arm from a negligently administered injection. The Alabama Supreme Court struck down the state cap on the grounds that it violated Alabama's jury trial provision and equal protection guarantee.[56]

In 1995, Illinois passed a comprehensive tort reform statute capping non-economic damages, punitive damages, and restricting doctrines such as joint and several liability. The Illinois Supreme Court ruled that the $500,000 non-economic damages cap was unconstitutional because it constituted special legislation, violated Illinois's single subject rule, and was also invalid on separation of powers grounds.[57]

The Ohio Supreme Court struck down a 1995 tort reform statute in *Ohio Academy of Trial Lawyers v. Sheward*.[58] The Ohio tort reform statute capped non-economic damages, limited punitive damages, limited joint and several liability, and abolished the collateral source rule. The court found that the statute violated the right of the citizens of Ohio to a trial by jury, due process, and equal protection, as well as violating that state's separation of powers clause.[59] Caps on plaintiff's recovery have been held to violate the open courts doctrine found in a number of state constitutions. The Texas Constitution, for example, guarantees that "all courts shall be open, and every person for an injury done him, in his lands, goods, person, or reputation, shall have a remedy by due course of law."[60]

[D] Restricting Individual Rights, Not Corporate Rights

The tort reform movement does not seek to restrict in any way the rights of businesses to sue each other, nor does it advocate capping the amounts to be awarded in business contract damages. Businesses are not pressing for legal reforms to stem the rising tide of business tort or contract lawsuits. Tort reform is a code phrase for one-sided, liability-limiting statutes that favor corporate interests. Questionable lawsuits such as the product libel suit filed by Texas ranchers against Oprah Winfrey for injuring the reputation of U.S. beef, are not targeted by the "reformers."

Corporations are free to sue other businesses for failing to perform services in a diligent and reasonably skillful manner.[61] Nearly half of the federal court cases that were filed between 1985 and 1991 involved business-versus-business litigation.[62] Punitive damages are used as leverage to generate bad publicity and to pressure competitors to withdraw advertisements. *USA Today* called this tactic "Corporate America's way of screaming: 'Liar, Liar, Pants on Fire!'"[63] There is an epidemic of punitive damage awards, but it is in business contract and competition cases, not personal injury cases. Here are some examples of recent business lawsuits that could be characterized as frivolous:

> The American Express Company settled a punitive damages case against Chase Manhattan Corporation over Chase's print and mail advertisements, which praised its award earned from J. D. Power and Associates for its credit cards.[64]
>
> Federal Express filed a lawsuit seeking treble damages over the U.S. Post Office's "What's Your Priority?" advertising campaign.[65]
>
> The drug company Merck's 1995 television campaign for Tagamet became the basis of a lawsuit by SmithKline, which marketed a rival remedy for sour stomach and heartburn.[66] SmithKline sued Merck, seeking to "stop the defendant from deceiving the public and undermining the launch of Tagamet HB."[67]
>
> The two leading suppliers of personal computers, Compaq and Packard Bell, were involved in a bitter legal battle wherein Packard sought punitive damages for what it alleged was an unfair advertising claim.[68]
>
> The maker of Scott paper towels sued Procter and Gamble over its claim that Bounty paper towels were the "quicker-picker-upper."[69]
>
> Simmons was sued by its business rival, Sealy, for its advertisements "showing a set of bowling pins standing undisturbed after a bowling ball was dropped on a Beautyrest mattress to show its sturdiness."[70]
>
> GTE Long Distance filed a punitive damages claim against AT&T Corporation over AT&T's claims that its long-distance service is superior to GTE's service.[71]

Business-versus-business torts have resulted in a number of the largest punitive damages awards. Texaco was assessed $3 billion in punitive damages and seven and a half billion in compensatory damages for interfering with Pennzoil's contract to purchase Getty Oil.[72] A California jury awarded $173 million against a developer in a real estate fraud case involving the sale of contaminated property.[73]

Large damage awards are skyrocketing in the field of intellectual property, which has become a hotbed of litigation. The owners of famous trademarks do not hesitate to use the civil justice system to vindicate their rights. Each website has a domain address "which is an identifier somewhat analogous to a telephone number or street address."[74] Thousands of lawsuits have been filed over disputes about Internet domain name registrations.[75] Mattel Corporation, which holds a trademark on the Barbie doll, sued an Internet host who registered the domain names "barbiesplace.com" and "badbarbies.com."[76] Porsche Cars of North America sued someone for registering the domain name "Porsch.com."[77] The Hearst Corporation, which owns *Esquire* magazine, brought suit against the registered owner of the domain name "esqwire.com."[78] Such litigation is as easy to denounce as frivolous as any of the examples publicized by the insurance companies.

Businesses are also not reluctant to litigate to protect their Internet-related rights.[79] Litigation over e-commerce patents has increased spectacularly since the late 1990s.[80] Business methods had previously been regarded as unpatentable,[81] but now patent litigation is frequently employed to quash competition in the Internet economy.[82] Internet-related companies frequently find it more profitable to file patent infringement lawsuits than to produce better software or other products.

Trademark infringement lawsuits sometimes seem to epitomize frivolous litigation. In *Muppets v. Hormel Foods*, Hormel filed a trademark infringement and dilution lawsuit because in the movie *Muppet Treasure Island*, one of the new Muppets was named "Spuh-am."[83] In that case, the Minnesota-based marketer of Spam luncheon meats argued that the Spuh-am Muppet would cause the public to lose its appetite for Spam and Spam-related merchandise.[84] Pepsi Cola's Frito-Lay Division and Proctor and Gamble litigated over the disputed advertising claim that Pringles' Right Crisp potato chips were more nutritious and delicious than Frito-Lay's chips.[85] The "aggressive holders of intellectual property may act on the belief that simply filing a lawsuit and maintaining its pendency, in and of itself, accomplishes strategic goals."[86] Plaintiffs' representatives characterize these cases as the real frivolous lawsuits—businesses clogging the courts by suing other businesses.[87]

The "new angle" of tort damages is the growing use of punitive damages by companies in business torts and contracts litigation. Tort reformers show no interest in clamping down on this expanding arena of litigation, even though some cases would be easy to paint as far more frivolous than the McDonald's hot coffee case.

[E] Targeting Medical Malpractice Recovery

Tort "reform" has resulted in additional barriers in bringing medical malpractice lawsuits and obtaining a jury award or settlement. The empirical reality is that there are too few medical malpractice cases. A study of hospital negligence in New York conducted by Harvard University researchers concluded that only a small fraction of malpractice is actually reported.[88] The report concluded that "there is a substantial amount of injury to patients from medical management, and many injuries are the result of substandard care."[89] Adverse events[90] occurred in 4 percent of the hospitalizations, and one-fourth of these adverse events were the result of medical negligence.[91] The Harvard researchers found that only 8 out of the 306 victims of medical malpractice ultimately filed negligence lawsuits.[92]

The researchers attributed the low incidence of medical malpractice lawsuits "to the fact that the cost of bringing a suit is high, that less than forty percent of malpractice plaintiffs actually win their cases, and that New York State has a $250,000 limit on the amount that can be paid in a lump sum."[93] They find that "[c]ontrary to doctors' impressions, injured patients do not sue at the drop of a hat, encouraged by juries who bend over backwards to dip into the deep pockets of malpractice insurers in order to do something for needy victims."[94]

The National Academy of Sciences recently called for a new federal agency to protect patients because the number of persons killed each year by medical error and malpractice is "44,000 to 98,000, numbers that exceed those who die from highway accidents and breast cancer."[95] These findings suggest that there should be more fault-based medical malpractice lawsuits. New defenses and limitations will have a chilling effect on victims' rights to be compensated for their injuries and will lessen the financial incentives for medical providers to institute injury prevention procedures.

[F] The Injury Problem

America suffers from an epidemic of injuries, deaths, and property damage from accidents. Accidents are the leading cause of death for Americans under the age of thirty-six and the fifth cause of death overall. Consumer-product injuries alone "account for one out of every six hospital days in this country."[96] No advocacy advertisements by the insurance industry explain the financial and social costs of unsafe consumer products or the role of careless medicine in producing suffering and raising prices.

Despite progress in removing defective products from the marketplace, "there are still an average of 22,000 deaths and 29.5 million injuries annually" from consumer-product injuries, at a cost of $400 billion a year.[97] Each year there are 1,400 deaths and 310,070 injuries from "electrical, mechanical, and children's products" alone.[98] Incorrect diagnoses and administering the wrong drugs "cost the nation $8.8 billion a year."[99] The economic impact of injuries amounted to $478.3 billion in 1997.[100] Some of these accidents are due to bad luck, but many are avoidable and "result from hazardous conditions, which can be corrected, and unsafe behaviors, which can be changed."[101] The social and economic costs of preventable injury play a far more significant role than litigation expenses in raising the prices of medical treatment, insurance, and consumer products.

Products liability lawsuits comprise only .002 percent of the civil cases filed in state trial courts. Fewer than one in ten people injured by a dangerously defective product ever file a lawsuit against the responsible party. In many instances, particularly where there is a latent injury, plaintiffs may not realize that a product defect caused the harm. Further, potential plaintiffs are often deterred from initiating litigation by the impression that they are partly at fault for their own injuries.[102]

The typical products liability action costs tens of thousands of dollars for retaining experts, pursuing discovery, interviewing witnesses, and other expenses.[103] An injured consumer who is not in a position to pay these costs in advance depends upon the contingency fee system. Contingency fees provide trial lawyers with "an incentive to screen out cases with little legal merit—an incentive that is lacking with an hourly fee."[104] Contingency-fee lawyers will rarely accept products liability cases because the success rate is so low and the costs are so great.[105] Beyond the financial burdens of protracted litigation, plaintiffs incur human costs in stress, family dislocation, employment disruption, and lost time.

Americans are rarely informed that lawsuits result in safer products and practices that, in turn, prevent costly injuries and deaths. This is the latent function of tort law. In recent years, punitive damages awards have persuaded manufacturers to fortify product warnings, to redesign products to eliminate excessive preventable danger, and to scrap products in the research laboratory rather than risk the health of consumers.

§2.3. Ordinary Citizens Who Sued for Safety

In each of the cases featured below, an injured individual had the fortitude to pursue a medical malpractice or products liability lawsuit despite the long odds against winning. Each account profiles an ordinary citizen who was forced to endure extraordinary suffering and hardship, after having already suffered a substantial injury or loss due to a defective product. In several of these cases, plaintiffs rejected secret settlement offers that would have required concealing the facts of the case in order to sue for the safety of the general public. Settlements containing confidentiality clauses may obtain compensation for an individual claimant, but do not prevent future injuries or deaths by informing the public.

In the next section, we describe how the plaintiff, serving as a private attorney general, exposed dangerous products or practices undetected by federal, state, or local regulators. Even where the plaintiff received no financial benefit personally, each of these lawsuits ultimately benefited all Americans. These private attorneys general and others like them play an important social policy role in encouraging companies to recall dangerous products or, better yet, to employ risk-management procedures to keep needlessly hazardous products from being marketed in the first place. The purpose of tort law is not only to indemnify for injuries, but also to prevent future harm.

CASE STUDY #1: Products Liability Forces Withdrawal of Tractors from American Market

[A] Tractor Rollover Death

Sixty-four-year-old Athel Hunt was crushed to death on May 11, 1989, when his 2,500-pound Kubota B8200 tractor flipped over and landed on his chest, suffocating him.[106] Hunt's tractor lacked a rollover protection system (ROPS), which would have saved his life. The Kubota dealer who sold Hunt the tractor had installed a brush hog and front loader bucket on the Kubota tractor in September 1987. The front loader decreases the lateral stability of a tractor that lacks rollover protection. The Japanese manufacturer made rollover protection an option in its American sales, whereas it was a standard feature in Japan.

Hunt's tragic and preventable death led his family to file a products liability lawsuit against Kubota Tractor Corporation. The tractor that flipped over on Hunt was a 1982 model purchased in 1987. Kubota Tractor Corporation of California (KTC) was fully aware that it was risking products liability lawsuits by marketing its tractors without ROPS as standard equipment. The National Safety Council had passed a resolution requiring ROPS as standard equipment in 1967. In June 1967, the National Institute for Farm Safety (NIFS) had issued a statement noting that a great reduction in the number of injuries and fatalities could be achieved through the use of ROPS and safety belts. In 1985, years before the death of Hunt, the American Society of Agricultural Engineers reinstated a standard stating that ROPS "shall be provided" on wheeled agricultural tractors.

Alec and Susan McNaughton, the lawyers for Hunt's estate, filed a strict products liability lawsuit against the Japanese manufacturer, the exporter, the importer, and the American seller of Kubota tractors on the grounds that the vehicles were dangerously defective because they were sold without a rollover protection system. In addition, the plaintiff claimed that Kubota's tractor design did not allow adequate space between the frame and the front axle stop, which allegedly made the tractor unstable. The combination of a tractor prone to tipping over and the lack of protection had deadly consequences for Hunt.

Punitive damages were claimed on the grounds that Kubota's conduct exhibited a willful and wanton disregard for the public's safety. In Oklahoma, a product manufacturer is not liable for punitive damages unless there is proof that the company intentionally or recklessly marketed the product knowing of a deadly defect. The focus of the punitive damages issue in the rollover tractor case was what Kubota knew, when the company knew it, and what safety steps it took to protect American farmers.

Kubota Japan and KTC are interlocking corporations. Managers and consultants circulated between the Japanese parent corporation and its California subsidiary, which were in daily contact with each other. KTC's engineers reviewed prototypes formulated by Kubota Japan's technical experts. The goal of this joint consultation was to achieve a smooth introduction of Kubota Japan's tractors into the United States market.

Trading Safety for Profits

The plaintiffs' attorneys argued that Kubota was engaging in a cost–benefit analysis, balancing lives against profits. Evidence was presented at the trial that Kubota and its California subsidiary held joint meetings to discuss the relative benefits and costs associated with equipping the imported farm equipment with ROPS versus the costs of paying verdicts for foreseeable injuries and deaths. If Kubota had instituted rollover protection for its American farm equipment it would have added only $200 to the price of the tractor. However, Kubota was marketing its tractor as a low-cost alternative to American tractors, and the cost of adding rollover protection might have depressed sales. The plaintiffs' attorneys provided sales data showing that Kubota was eclipsing its American rivals in the small tractor market by keeping its prices low.

The plaintiffs introduced a large number of documents to prove Kubota's corporate culpability. An officer working for KTC drafted a memo acknowledging that tractors without rollover protection were hazardous. KTC's memorandum stated: "Approximately 237 rollover deaths in 1978 would probably have been averted had ROPS been installed on the tractors." Kubota formulated a chart weighing the risk of incurring punitive damages for failure to install ROPS as standard equipment against the "sales hazard." The "sales hazard" to Kubota's marketing goals became more critical than the "safety hazard" to American farmers.

Kubota did consider adding rollover protection to unsold tractors while Hunt's tractor sat in inventory without ROPS, and KTC did recommend to Kubota that it should consider ROPS as an integral part of the design of future models. However, KTC left ROPS as optional equipment. A 1985 KTC document noted: "Due to the uncertainty in predicting demand, it was decided that the [dealer's inventory of tractors] retrofit program will be delayed, although dealers will be encouraged to put ROPS on the tractors they have in stock." The effect of this decision was to sell tractors that lacked the safety measure that would have saved Athel Hunt's life.

The Garfield County jury imposed a $3.3 million punitive damages award jointly against Kubota and its subsidiary for marketing a product with known dangers. As expected, Kubota and its subsidiary took the jury verdict to the Oklahoma Court of Appeals. Kubota argued that it had no legal obligation to install roll bars on tractors made before 1985. The case settled prior to final disposition after a costly appellate briefing of the issues.

Athel Hunt was neither the first nor the last farmer to die from a Kubota tractor rollover. In 1987, a twenty-one-year-old heavy equipment mechanic suffered a crushing injury to his chest and 50 percent permanent disability when a Kubota tractor flipped over backwards and landed on him while he was trying to pull-start it in August 1982.[107] The plaintiff in that case sued Kubota, arguing that the tractor was dangerously defective because it was not equipped with rollover protection. The rollover victim also contended that Kubota tractors' center of gravity was located too far to the rear, with the result that the tractors had a tendency to flip over backwards. Kubota denied that there was negligent design, blaming the accident on driver error and product misuse.[108]

The Kubota rollover tractor cases illustrate how private lawsuits fulfill the latent function of suing for public safety. American farm families are safer as the result of Athel Hunt's family pursuing a products liability lawsuit against Kubota. After trial, but prior to the verdict, Kubota decided to withdraw tractors without rollover protection from the U.S. marketplace. Kubota acknowledged that the "tractors were originally built to operate mainly in Japanese rice paddies and not in the U.S. farmland environment"[109] and that "tractors have been found to roll over when driving up hills and pin drivers underneath."[110]

Kubota even placed advertisements in American newspapers warning users of the rollover hazard posed by its tractors,[111] an important step toward protecting U.S. farmers.[112] Punitive damages in this product liability case sent Kubota a clear signal that its products must comply with American standards of quality and safety.

Tort reformers argue that our law of products liability places American business at a competitive disadvantage against corporations in countries that do not permit a full recovery for defective products. But the competitive disadvantage argument is disingenuous because it implies that state tort law only restrains U.S. manufacturers, while foreign producers enjoy immunity. On the contrary, American punitive damages laws equally affect all product manufacturers that export products into the U.S. market. Foreign manufacturers such as Kubota have frequently been the subjects of American products liability lawsuits. Tort awards are a disincentive for domestic as well as foreign corporations that are tempted to sacrifice the public interest for profits.

Before any corporation falsifies test data, markets a product with a known risk, or fails to warn the public of known dangers, it has to consider the possibility that it might be subject to tort remedies. The Kubota tractor case illustrates clearly how a product manufacturer or distributor can be prevented from gaining "an unfair advantage over its more socially responsible competitors" through the imposition of punitive damages awards.[113] Contrary to the dire warnings of the tort revisionists, ethical businesses benefit from the awarding of tort damages against irresponsible or unscrupulous competitors, foreign or domestic.

CASE STUDY #2: *Carrollton Church Litigation Results in Stronger Bus Standards*

Carrollton, Kentucky, is located where the waters of the Ohio and Kentucky Rivers meet, halfway between Cincinnati and Louisville. On May 14, 1988, a church group from the town's First Assembly of God Church went on a bus trip to King's Island Amusement Park in Cincinnati. The church group, ironically called "Life Is for Everyone," carried fifty-nine children, aged ten to seventeen, and four adult chaperones on its own Ford school bus. At about 10:55 P.M., a pickup truck traveling the wrong way on the southbound lanes of Interstate 71 struck the bus. As the Toyota pickup rotated upon impact, it struck a passenger car traveling southbound in the right-hand lane near the bus. The fuel tank of the bus was punctured during the collision, and the resulting fireball engulfed the bus. The driver and twenty-six passengers died in the fire; another thirty-four bus passengers suffered burns, some of them critical. The driver of the pickup was also seriously injured by the impact of the collision.[114]

None of the twenty-seven fatalities were caused by the initial collision between the pickup and the bus.[115] Rather, they were killed when gasoline from the ruptured fuel tank geysered into the bus and ignited, sending a fireball roaring through the passenger compartment.[116] The children struggled in vain to get to the rear door. Later, when the medical examiner entered the bus, he witnessed a gruesome scene of fifteen or seventeen people "draped over the backs of seats." He recalled the nightmarish tableau of bodies "in the aisles stacked on each other." The medical examiner was completely overwhelmed by the horrendous tragedy: "I kept closing my eyes hoping that what I had seen would go away."[117]

[A] The Battle over Admissibility

Six weeks after the accident, most of the families settled claims in the range of \$500,000 to \$1 million without filing suit.[118] The two families who filed the lawsuit in the Carrollton bus disaster rejected a confidential settlement offer. Instead, they opted for litigation, which sometimes resembles war. Discovery in products liability litigation can descend into scorched earth battles over which documents must be made available and what may be admitted into evidence at trial. Shortly before the Kentucky school bus case went to trial, Ford's attorneys filed a blockbuster *in limine* motion to exclude many of the "smoking gun" documents that were the basis of the plaintiffs' punitive damages case on relevancy grounds. The disputed "smoking guns" included:

   i) Admissions of its corporate fuel system safety policy (actually a non-safety policy) from 1967 through 1977;

   ii) Documents associated with the high percentage of Pinto crash test fuel system failures;

   iii) Evidence that the company considered but rejected feasible alternative designs; evidence of in-cab truck fuel system crash test failures;[119]

   iv) Evidence that it had attempted to persuade the federal government to rescind or delay safety standards in their 301 fuel system standard. Ford moved to exclude evidence that Ford's Chief Executive Officer Lee Iacocca secretly met with President Nixon to urge him to stop or delay proposed federal safety standards including the fuel system 301 standard;[120]

   v) The Grush-Saunby memo, which was the smoking gun memorandum that led to punitive damages in the famous Ford Pinto case of *Grimshaw v. Ford Motor Co.*[121]

   vi) Evidence that it was aware of a fuel system fire in another vehicle in Reston and that the National Traffic Safety Board (NTSB) was considering safety improvements for the fuel systems of school buses.[122] Ford attempted to exclude a report that recommended that a guard be placed on their school buses' fuel system two years before the school bus involved in the Carrollton tragedy was manufactured.[123]

The exploding school bus case was prefigured by the famous Ford Pinto litigation in which a 1972 Ford Pinto hatchback automobile stalled on a freeway and was rear-ended by another car. The impact of the crash drove the Pinto's gas tank forward and caused it to be punctured by a bolt on the differential housing. The Pinto's fuel tank ruptured, engulfing the car in a fireball that incinerated the driver. Richard Grimshaw, a young passenger, was the sole survivor of the crash. He suffered disfiguring burns requiring hundreds of surgeries and skin grafts.

Design changes would have enhanced the safety of the fuel system at little cost: a "flak suit" to protect the tank would have cost five dollars per car; placement of the tank over the axle would have cost less than six dollars; and improvement and reinforcement of the bumper would have cost less than three dollars. The jury found Ford's cost–benefit analysis, which balanced lives against corporate profits, to be evidence of a conscious disregard of the probability of injury to members of the consuming public. Ford's knowledge of the dangers of fuel-fed fires from its defectively designed fuel system led to an award of punitive damages in the case.[124]

The *Grimshaw* court found that the evidence was sufficient to support a finding of Ford's malicious conduct. Through the results of its crash tests, Ford knew that the Pinto's fuel tank and rear structure would expose consumers to serious injury or death in a twenty- to thirty-mile-per-hour collision. There was substantial evidence that Ford's conduct constituted "conscious disregard" of the probability of injury to members of the consuming public.[125]

The problem of fuel tank integrity had long concerned regulators, but they were slow to adopt mandatory safety standards. In August 1973, the National Highway Traffic Safety Administration (NHTSA) gave the industry notice of a new safety standard that would prevent fuel leakage in a typical crash situation. Ford Motor Company produced an internal evaluation of the proposed standard, referred to as the Grush-Saunby Report. The report indicated that Ford's corporate officers were deferring remedial measures that would prevent fuel tank fires in order to save about ten dollars per car on the 12.5 million Pintos then on the road.

The court in the Ford Pinto case found that "[t]he conduct of Ford's management was reprehensible in the extreme. It exhibited a conscious and callous disregard of public safety in order to maximize corporate profits. . . . Unlike malicious conduct directed toward a single specific individual, Ford's tortious conduct endangered the lives of thousands of Pinto purchasers."[126] Ford Motor Company had previously been acquitted in the first and only criminal prosecution of an American manufacturer for marketing products with known defects.[127]

Information about the Ford Pinto litigation would be useful in convincing the jury that the Carrollton bus fire was part of Ford's pattern and practice of neglecting consumer safety. Counsel for the plaintiffs argued that all of the evidence Ford sought to have excluded was relevant to proving that the company had prior knowledge of the fuel system integrity problems in its school buses. The plaintiffs' position was that Ford's systematic corporate policy was to delay and obstruct safety improvements in its vehicles. They wanted to prove that the Carrollton bus tragedy was a product of the same kind of cost–benefit equation of trading safety for profits that was found in the Pinto litigation.

Ford's central defense in the case was that the school bus was not defectively designed. Federal safety standards had not been raised until one month after the vehicle was manufactured. However, Ford's own crash tests on its buses showed that, at minimum, a metal guard should have been placed around the fuel tank.

Mark Robinson, the plaintiffs' counsel in the Kentucky school bus case, had also served as attorney in the products liability action against the Ford Pinto.[128] Robinson argued (1) that Ford was making last-minute motions to exclude key evidence showing that it was guilty of willful and wanton misconduct in the preventable deaths of twenty-seven victims and serious injuries to thirty-four other passengers; (2) that Ford was seeking to excise its own corporate safety policy from the Carrollton bus crash case because it was the company's practice in the 1970s to sell vehicles with easily correctable rupture problems;[129] and (3) that Ford had a simple means of correcting the fuel-integrity problems, but continuously declined to incorporate the modifications until federal regulators absolutely required the safety improvements.

The plaintiffs acquired documents showing that Ford had long resisted federal initiatives to raise automobile safety standards. Improved safety standards proposed by NHTSA were scuttled in January 1972, eight months after a secret meeting between President Richard M. Nixon and Ford's chief executive, Lee Iacocca, in which the two men discussed derailing new federally mandated fuel system safety standards. Ford sought to exclude this evidence on the grounds that the conversation did not specifically mention the buses that were the subject of the litigation.

[B] The Case for Punitive Damages

The Kentucky school bus plaintiffs argued that the primary issue in the products liability case was whether Ford acted negligently and with a wanton or reckless disregard for safety in failing to place a fuel tank guard on the school bus. The plaintiffs asserted that Ford should be held to the standard of a reasonably prudent vehicle manufacturer under "the same or similar circumstances."[130] Counsel asserted that the evidence the defense sought to exclude provided an essential "backdrop" explaining Ford's actions, and that Ford's corporate decision-making process on the improved fuel system was part of a concerted corporate policy of trading safety for profits:

> Ford Motor Company's motions *in limine* seek to tear the heart out of the plaintiffs' case by removing the most damaging, yet most probative evidence available on the issues relating to negligence, product defect, and punitive damages. Ford concedes in its introductory brief that these motions are "inter-related." That is precisely the reason the motions should be denied, for the evidence itself is also inter-related. Despite Ford's attempts to compartmentalize, pigeonhole and segregate evidence which demonstrates its knowledge and awareness of a defect common throughout its product lines, as well as a pervasive corporate policy of profit over fuel system safety, the available evidence is all highly probative and must be viewed as a whole. Further, presentation of this evidence comes primarily from several short Ford in-house documents. The Court will be able to read these documents in less than one day. Therefore, there will not be an undue consumption of time on the punitive damages issue.[131]

Ford's corporate safety policy, the crash tests on Ford Pintos and trucks, Iacocca's secret meeting with Nixon, Ford's cost–benefit equation, and a corporate strategy to delay the implementation of federal safety standards were all key to supporting the plaintiffs' punitive damages claim.

The documents Ford sought to exclude had previously been introduced in a Georgia trial court in *Ford Motor Company v. Stubblefield*.[132] In *Stubblefield*, a fifteen-year-old girl was burnt to death when the gas tank of her Ford Mustang II was punctured in a crash with another vehicle. The *Stubblefield* court admitted the transcript of a taped conversation between President Nixon and Iacocca into evidence, observing that:

> [w]hile there was no specific discussion among the participants as to fuel system integrity, the meeting took place just one day after the decision of Ford's management to defer the adoption of protective devices for the fuel tanks until required by law, and the gist of the taped conversation concerned the necessity for the Department of Transportation to 'cool it' as to safety requirements and how the government might make those

standards more responsive to the auto maker's cost effectiveness. . . . Also, since punitive damages were sought, one of the material facts at issue in this case was whether Ford acted with conscious disregard for the consequences when making policy decisions as to fuel tank safety on the Mustang II, and this conversation clearly served to 'elucidate or throw light upon' that question.[133]

The *Stubblefield* court upheld the jury's punitive damages verdict, stating:

> The evidence here was sufficient to authorize the jury to find the sum of $8 million was an amount necessary to deter Ford from repeating its conduct; that is, its conscious decisions to defer implementation of safety devices in order to protect its profits. One internal memo estimated that the total financial effect of the Fuel System Integrity program [would] reduce Company profits over the 1973–1976 cycle by $109 million, and recommended that Ford "defer adoption of [safety measures] on all affected cars built in 1976 to realize a design cost savings of $20.9 million compared to 1974."[134]

The plaintiffs in the Kentucky school bus crash hoped to make a similar argument. Ford responded that documents dealing with passenger cars had no relevance to the design of school buses and should therefore be excluded.

Ford denied that it delayed bus safety standards, disavowing all responsibility for the design defects of the bus. Ford's strategy was to place the entire blame for the fatal crash on the drunk driver who crashed into the bus.[135] Ford portrayed itself as a model corporate citizen who had responsibly complied with all government safety standards.[136] Attorneys for the plaintiff responded by arguing that Ford had elevated profits over safety by delaying the placing of metal guards around the fuel tanks for more than a decade.[137] The end of the trial was not a Hollywood-type "climactic judgment."[138] Ford settled the case with plaintiffs for $10 million without a finding of liability for the defective design of the bus.[139]

NHTSA conducted a systematic investigation of the Kentucky school bus crash and soon after adopted a stronger set of safety standards for these vehicles. This profound tragedy has led to a nationwide movement to improve school bus safety in which the plaintiff families played a prominent part.[140] All children riding school buses are now safer because these two Kentucky families refused the offer of a confidential settlement in favor of prosecuting the manufacturer.

CASE STUDY #3: *Defense Prevails against Victim with Ruptured Implants*

[A] Violation of Informed Consent

Silicone breast implants have been marketed in the United States since the 1960s. Twenty-four-year-old Ellen Mohney underwent a subcutaneous mastectomy with reconstruction using silicone breast implants as a remedy for a recurrent fibrocystic condition in her breasts.[141] Dr. Alfred Speirs performed the surgery, using silicone gel implants that had been manufactured by Heyer-Schulte Corporation.[142] Dr. Speirs was more than a simple cosmetic surgeon; he was also a pioneering Dow Corning researcher who published studies on local tissue reaction to "silicone elastomers." Thus, Dr. Speirs was uniquely positioned to know about the dangers of liquid silicone injections. He understood that hardness and contracture were the big problems with breast implants, and he knew of the complications associated with implants, such as asymmetry, scar tissue formation, infection, bleeding, and the possibility of rupture.

Dr. Speirs testified that he warned each and every patient of the risks of silicone breast implants. But the surgeon's all-purpose consent form did not even inform Mohney that he was using a silicone gel–filled implant, much less communicate to her the known risks of these implants. Nor did Dr. Speirs inform her of the alternative of saline implants because, even though they were safer, he considered them to be aesthetically inferior.[143]

In July 1977, Dr. Speirs performed a bilateral subcutaneous mastectomy on Mohney, using Heyer-Schulte gel implants to reconstruct her breasts. Mohney's first memory after awakening from her surgery was the sensation of burning, like battery acid, on her left side. Swelling and pain occurred in her left arm. Dr. Speirs examined her and observed "a little more fluid in . . . the left breast" but reassured his patient that the healing was normal.

Mohney soon began to suffer serious health problems that grew progressively worse over the next decade. She left her job because of her deteriorating health. In 1979, Mohney sought help from her sister in caring for her children because of growing weakness and loss of stamina. In 1981, she was diagnosed with multiple radiculopathy, possible phlebitis, and asthma. By 1982, Mohney was permanently disabled, periodically needing the assistance of a walker or cane.

Naturally upset and depressed over her increasing inability to lead a normal life, Mohney consulted with a number of doctors to learn the cause of her difficulties. Dr. Thomas Reichert biopsied one of her lymph nodes and discovered the presence of silicone gel. The pathology report stated that her left axillary lymph node was "largely filled with innumerable refractile lipid like droplets surrounded by a prominent reactive infiltrate of lymphocytes, histiocyte and multinucleated giant cells." Mohney further consulted with Dr. Richard Lawrence, who performed surgery to remove the implants in February 1985. Soon after her implants were taken out, Mohney felt better; but subsequently her health again deteriorated. She had a feeling of malaise and lacked the energy necessary to perform everyday tasks. A treating neurologist diagnosed her as suffering from a "probable brain stem" infarct or stroke caused by the gravitating silicone.

Mohney was soon back to using her walker and experiencing vision problems. Another treating physician, Dr. Linda Huang, detected at least 10 cc's of free-floating silicone in her body, though it "could have been as much as an ounce." Dr. Huang performed surgery to remove the infected breast tissue, "ectopic bone formations," and bone spurs in the region of the implants. The doctor observed silicone-related scarring, lumps, muscle thinning, and nerve damage as well as a swollen lymph node, which was removed for biopsy.

[B] Products Liability Action

Once Mohney discovered that ruptured breast implants were causing her health problems, she filed lawsuits against Baxter Health care Corporation (Baxter), the successor corporation to Heyer-Schulte, and against her surgeon, Dr. Alfred Speirs. The action was filed in Colorado Springs, Colorado, a community with a large military presence and juries with a conservative predisposition.

Heyer-Schulte, not Baxter, designed and marketed the breast implants that injured the plaintiff. However, under the doctrine of successor liability, Baxter was responsible for injuries due to the defective implants designed by Heyer-Schulte. Mohney sued Baxter, arguing that the implants were defectively designed and that the company's predecessor had failed to warn her of the dangers then known about silicone-gel breast implants. Mohney's lawsuit also contended that Dr. Speirs had not given her the information necessary for an informed consent prior to her surgery.

The Colorado Springs trial was of such interest that it was televised.

Each side placed a large number of experts on the stand. Mohney's experts testified that silicone from her ruptured implants caused a variety of serious neurological and autoimmune problems. Baxter's expert, Dr. Michael Phillips, acknowledged that the plaintiff "clearly . . . had local foreign body reactivity against the silicone, and she also had some complications of that, including this fistula formation and, at least on one occasion, a low-grade infection of that area."[144] Dr. Phillips explained that silicone gel from the ruptured implants could travel in the blood stream to the brain and organs of the human body; it can cause immune system reactivity. His conclusion was "[t]here can be no doubt that Mohney suffered from a number of tragic local problems related to the breast implants, the leaking of silicone by these breast implants."[145] There was indisputable evidence that she suffered:

> thick scar tissue; pain in her breasts; thin eggshell like, fibrous growths in the area of implants, calcification of scar tissue, tissue growing towards bone; scar formation along her rib cage; ectopic bone formation due to breast implant capsule; resurgery to remove free silicone found in plaintiff's breasts; bony spurs from implant materials; company nodules in her breast tissue; area of neuroma; erosion of muscle from implant; post-surgical abscesses from operation to remove free silicone; post-surgical infection which required treatment by an internal catheter and surgical debridement in early 1993; and capsular contracture.[146]

The Food and Drug Administration (FDA) had documented many of these problems as the known risks of implants.[147] On April 10, 1991, the FDA made several findings that silicone-gel breast implants were associated with the local and regional injuries that Ellen Mohney clearly manifested, including fibrous capsular contracture, infection, silicone gel leakage and migration, and calcification of the fibrous capsule.[148]

[C] Blaming the Victim, Distracting the Jury

In July 1993, the Colorado Springs jury handed down a verdict in favor of Baxter Health Care Corp. The jury found that Ellen Mohney had suffered no injury. The jury also concluded that Dr. Alfred Speirs, the plaintiff's plastic surgeon, had not committed medical malpractice. Mohney filed a notice of appeal in October 1993, but the Colorado Court of Appeals upheld the defense verdict, leaving her without a further remedy.

The jury's verdict that the plaintiff had suffered no injury from breast implants was arguably against the manifest weight of the evidence. At a minimum, Mohney suffered local and regional injuries that were acknowledged by Dr. Phillips, Baxter's medical expert. One explanation for the defendants' victory was that the jury actually came to believe that the plaintiff had not suffered any injury. The jury might have seen her as a hypochondriac; a whiner, or worse—a fraud. A more likely explanation for the "no injury" verdict was that the jury was distracted from considering that, at minimum, the plaintiff was disfigured and had suffered local and regional injuries.

The central defense in this case was calculated to draw the attention of the jury to the character and personality of the plaintiff and away from the dangerously defective nature of the silicone-gel breast implants. Dr. Speirs's counsel told the jury: "We hear the language 'victim' all over the place. Everybody's a victim who can't stand to the line and perform and take care of themselves." This ethic of personal responsibility echoes the rhetoric used by tort revisionists in their campaign to convince the American public that most personal injury lawsuits are frivolous.

The defense argued that Mohney's injuries were all in her head. Dr. Speirs's counsel questioned "why this case came here in the first place without [plaintiff] having a full-blown psychiatric evaluation and trial of psychotherapy." The attorney developed the theme that products liability plaintiffs were driving good products off the market. He told the jury that the true silicone problem was "the movement afoot in this country . . . a traveling show that comes in to support a silicone problem."

Ellen Mohney was portrayed as a person who would make silicone products prohibitively expensive, or even illegal, thus dooming hydrocephalic babies and heart patients to certain death, and arthritis sufferers to lives of crippling disability. One of Baxter's experts, Dr. Garry Brody, testified that products liability torts were threatening "the availability of biomaterial for reconstruction joints or breasts or anything else in our society." Dr. Pierre Blais, an internationally renowned specialist and former Canadian government regulator, countered that the rubberized silicone compounds used to save hydrocephalic babies are entirely different in design than the "jello mixture of liquid . . . and elastomers or semisolids of silicone gel used in breast implants." The argument that greedy plaintiffs are driving good medical products off the market is a theme frequently used in tort reform advocacy advertisements.

All of the silicone injuries that deformed Ellen Mohney's body were dismissed as being psychosomatic. Dr. Speirs's counsel told the jury that the plaintiff suffered asthma, had "a lot of dental cavities," and wore glasses when she was young. He noted that she was "observed to be a nervous child" who suffered bouts of fainting. Mohney suffered headaches, fevers, gastrointestinal pains, adjustment problems, and had been hospitalized in the Colorado Asthma Center. All of these arguments portrayed her as a person with emotional problems, not problems with ruptured silicone-gel breast implants.

Mohney was depicted as an irresponsible and immoral complainer. Dr. Speirs's counsel informed the jury about her pre-marital sex life and the fact that she was pregnant at the time of her teenage marriage. After that marriage failed, "[s]he was married again after a very brief courtship of about two and a half months and with a second child." Dr. Speirs's counsel questioned Mohney extensively about collateral matters having no possible relevance to silicone-related injury, including her problems with marriage, her children, and the IRS. He cross-examined the plaintiff about her mother-in-law's rudeness, her ex-husband's drinking problems, her ingestion of Maalox for stomach pain, and even the quality and quantity of her urinary flow. The defense attorney noted that the plaintiff had held only "two or three jobs" over her lifetime and that she earned very little. None of this character and personality evidence was even remotely related to any legal issue in this case. Yet, the jury weighed this evidence along with the testimony of medical experts.

The plaintiffs responded that the defense's attack on Mohney's character was designed to distract the jury from fairly considering the clear evidence that she was suffering from systemic silicone-related illnesses. Whatever her psychological portrait, even the defense experts acknowledged the very serious injuries she had received from the ruptured breast implants. Defense expert Dr. Michael Phillips noted that the plaintiff had good reason to be depressed after a series of surgeries stemming from the rupture. However, the jury was left with the impression that she suffered from mental illness and had feigned her physical symptoms.

Baxter filed a motion for physical and mental evaluation of the plaintiff shortly before the trial began. The trial court initially denied the psychiatric portion of the request, but later reconsidered, ordering a mental examination.[149] The plaintiff appealed the trial court's decision to order Mohney to undergo a psychiatric examination in the middle of the trial. This was a case about products liability and whether informed consent was given, and yet the defense was making her mental state the central issue.

The common law has always held that you "take your victims as you find them." Legally, it makes no difference whether a saint or a prostitute was injured by dangerously defective breast implants, or any other medical product, but the defense will commonly engage in the tactic of "blaming the victim." The jury was apparently swept away by prejudice against Ellen Mohney and returned a "no injury" verdict against the clear weight of the evidence.[150]

[D] Discovery Wars

A number of other defense tactics at trial tended to undermine the plaintiff's case. Baxter claimed that it had no knowledge of the history of the implants that were the subject of Mohney's lawsuit. As a successor corporation, Baxter maintained that its predecessor had retained all of the records of her implants. The predecessor, in contrast, claimed to have turned all records over to Baxter. Baxter waited until the plaintiff rested her case to inform the jury that its defense attorneys had just discovered that the company was the wrong defendant because Mohney actually had 1972 thick-shell implants containing Dow Corning gel. The plaintiff's counsel vigorously objected to this last-minute introduction of an entirely new theory of the origins of the implants that burst in Mohney's body:

> We have tried this case based on the theory made—the theory that was founded on representations made to us by Baxter during this lawsuit, most recently on supplemental responses, interrogatories a week ago or so—two weeks before trial that there were no lot histories that existed for the implants in question; that the gel was General Electric at Heyer-Schulte in the '70's. . . . So far, I've only put in three Dow Corning documents. In my office, I have thousands of pages of Dow Corning documents concerning their test data on their gel from the '60's and '70's, and I would have to recall witnesses, bring in new witnesses and talk about the problems known to Dow Corning about their gel.

The trial court properly excluded Baxter from introducing its new theory through a former Heyer-Schulte employee who was located only after the plaintiff had presented much of her case.

The court found Baxter's explanation for the last- minute discovery to be "incredible":

> And I have to say . . . I simply don't understand your position that it was only on June 1st that you found out that they were going to be able to say it was produced at a certain time. I mean the only way to do that is from

information gleaned through discovery from your record and your people, so somehow that just [doesn't] make sense to me, to be honest, that this is something that you couldn't have discovered at some time in the past, and so I deny the request to endorse the witness.

Finding the front door blocked, Baxter brought substantially similar testimony in through the back door. At the conclusion of its expert Dr. Paul Ducheyne's testimony, Baxter's counsel asked him about the product identification of the implants. Dr. Ducheyne testified that the implant did not contain General Electric gel, but was filled with Dow Corning gel.

The net result of the attack on Ellen Mohney's character and the confusion about who manufactured the breast implants was a defense victory upheld on appeal. Astoundingly, the Colorado Court of Appeals found no reversible error in Baxter's withholding of information about the manufacturing history of the breast implants until the last day of the trial. Baxter had successfully made the plaintiff's personality the focus of the trial. In the end, the jury found no liability, no damages, and no medical malpractice. In today's products liability legal battles, there are no automatic victories even when a person has clearly identifiable medical problems resulting from ruptured implants.

It takes courage for an individual with severe medical problems to take on a multimillion-dollar corporation. For Ellen Mohney to endure a trial that focused on her personality and character, rather than on her ruptured implants, required great fortitude. She persevered through years of discovery, a lengthy trial, an appeal, and still lost her case. Plaintiffs' victories in other breast implant cases led to a $4.5 billion settlement entered into by Dow Corning compensating 300,000 women injured by breast implants.[151] Mohney was barred from obtaining compensation through the settlement since she had already lost her case.

CASE STUDY #4: *Justice Is Blind; or, Punishing Blinding Injustices*

[A] Products Liability for Intraocular Lenses

In a 1990 verdict, a jury in Taos, New Mexico, assessed punitive damages against Surgidev, a manufacturer of intraocular lenses that are implanted to replace the natural lens after it is removed during cataract surgeries.[152] Two plaintiffs, Enrique Gonzales and Ricardo Garduno, were each blinded in the eye in which a Surgidev Style 10 intraocular lens was implanted. In May 1985, Gonzales, a forty-nine-year-old welder, went in for surgery to remove cataracts. As part of the treatment, the surgeon removed the natural lens and replaced it with an intraocular lens manufactured by Surgidev in a procedure known as an intracapsular cataract extraction (ICCE). He began to experience excruciating pain shortly after the surgery.

Gonzales developed severe glaucoma and a corneal decompensation in his left eye as the result of the lens implants. He underwent extensive medical treatments to save his vision and to control the chronic pain in his eye, as well as a corneal transplant (to remove the intraocular lens) and two cryotherapies. The result was that Gonzales was left permanently disabled and could no longer work as a welder. By November 1990, he was totally blind in the eye containing the implant.

Garduno, an eighty-one-year-old fruit stand operator, had a similar experience. He developed chronic irritation in the eye in which the Surgidev lens was implanted. Within months after his surgery, Garduno also suffered severe pain and sun sensitivity. He was unable to continue his business of selling fruit from a roadside stand. Garduno joined Gonzales in filing a medical products liability lawsuit against the manufacturer of the intraocular lens. The plaintiffs claimed that the Surgidev lens was defectively designed and that the company failed to warn the medical community about dangers associated with implanting the lenses by the ICCE procedure.

[B] A Dangerous Procedure with a Dangerous Product

The plaintiffs argued that the intraocular lens was particularly dangerous when used with an ICCE procedure. In the ICCE procedure, the natural lenses of the eye and the capsule encasing the lens are removed along with surrounding tissue. The intraocular lens is then implanted to replace the natural lens, which has clouded over due to cataracts. The portion of the lens designed for fixation in the eye (the haptic) forms a closed loop. The plaintiffs' theory was that the haptic placed in the eye had a loop that caused a "cheese-cutter effect" on the eye. As the loop interacted with the delicate tissue of the eye, it caused chronic inflammation and scarring. This inflammation led to severe glaucoma and blindness due to corneal decompensation.

The punitive damages claim was based upon the plaintiffs' evidence that Surgidev knew of the danger of the intraocular lens when used with the ICCE procedure, but did not warn either the physicians or the patients. The manufacturer also was alleged to have failed to do adequate testing of the product and to have failed to follow FDA regulations for the testing and sale of the intraocular lenses. The Style 10 lens was sold while still classified as an investigational device by the FDA. The plaintiffs further argued that Surgidev had not complied with a 1981 FDA request to monitor sight-threatening complications in patients who received the Style 10 lens.

Surgidev's own data showed a high rate of sight-threatening complications with the lens. Patients who underwent the intracapsular cataract procedure had a complication rate three to five times higher than that of those who underwent an extracapsular cataract procedure. The FDA never gave the Style 10 lens pre-market approval, but Surgidev continued to sell the investigational device without warning of the known risks. On the basis of this information, the jury awarded Gonzales $434,990.18 in compensatory damages and $350,000 in punitive damages. Guardino was awarded $45,000 in compensatory damages and $350,000 in punitive damages.

Surgidev mounted a scorched-earth defense of the intraocular lens in its attempts to conceal key documents. A Surgidev official "testified that he stored approximately 300 boxes of material" containing internal memoranda, sales materials, and tapes.[153] These materials were hidden from the plaintiff, and only retrieved two weeks after the end of the trial. A Surgidev employee testified that the defense attorneys stated that they intended to "deep-six" the documents even though they were aware that this was in contempt of court. Particularly damaging to Surgidev's case were "internal memoranda to the sales force [which] suggested strategies that could be used in countering the criticism of the Style 10 IOL and encouraged the sales force to push sales despite the known dangers."[154]

During the trial, Surgidev concealed the existence of transcripts documenting pressure the FDA had brought to bear on the defendant to remove the intraocular lenses from the market. Surgidev was evasive "about the reason the intraocular lenses were taken off the market, the criticism of the lens, and the existence of internal and sales memoranda about the lens."[155] The trial court ordered sanctions in the amount of $151,000, finding that the defendant "willfully and intentionally failed to comply with [Appellees'] discovery requests repeatedly throughout this litigation"; "misrepresented material facts to this court"; was not credible; "willfully and intentionally violated discovery rules"; "willfully and intentionally violated court orders in regard to discovery"; "willfully and intentionally [gave] false answers to interrogatories and in testimony" "willfully, intentionally, and systematically withheld damaging evidence"; and demonstrated "a pattern of abuse of the judicial system and interference with the administration of justice."[156]

The New Mexico Supreme Court found that it would take a "stretch of the imagination to believe Surgidev 'suddenly discovered' 300 boxes only upon the conclusion of the trial!"[157] The court believed that the company would have retrieved the "information immediately had it consisted of beneficial rather than damaging material."[158]

Abuse of the discovery process is an aggravating factor that may be considered in imposing punitive damages. It is extremely important that the discovery process work properly in cases where the defendant has a virtual monopoly of information on key aspects of the subject in dispute.[159] Firestone, for example, was in a better position than individual consumers to understand the phenomenon of tread separation in its tires. The asbestos manufacturers, not the workers, were in the best position to understand the deadly consequences of unprotected exposure to asbestos dust.

Products liability cases "must rest basically on the records of the manufacturer and what was known to him."[160] Litigants are generally entitled to expect that the opposing side will comply with the rules of civil procedure.[161] Pre-trial disclosure is designed to help the parties define issues and eliminate secrets and surprises.[162]

§2.4. Conclusion

Each case in this chapter involved protracted discovery disputes, lengthy depositions, expensive expert testimony, and complex adjudication of the products liability issues. The plaintiffs and their attorneys had to undertake years of expensive litigation with no guarantee of any recovery. The entry barriers in pursuing tort litigation screen out not only frivolous cases, but far too many cases that are clearly meritorious. Further restricting rights to recovery for individual victims will reduce the effectiveness of tort law as social control.

Tort damages not only punish and deter, they create an even playing field by depriving unethical corporations of the opportunity to maximize profits by minimizing safety. The latent function underlying the remedy is to prevent a race to the bottom, as manufacturers are pressured to forgo the public's safety in order to compete in the marketplace. The cases discussed above demonstrate the effectiveness of torts in products liability situations. Chapter 3 focuses on the most important role played by tort law in both products liability and medical malpractice litigation to further gender justice.

3

Gender Justice and Tort Law

§3.1. Introduction

Tort law impacts men and women in different ways, reflecting the different roles men and women play in American society. The two sexes are typically injured in different ways. No reader of the previous chapter was surprised that the farmer crushed by a tractor rollover was male or that the plaintiff whose breast implants leaked silicone was female. Our analysis of products liability cases from 1965 to 1990 reveals that household consumer products, medical products, or drugs harmed nearly 70 percent of all women who received punitive damages.[1] Gender-related injuries reflect a variety of social and cultural factors, including discrimination against women, gender segregation, social stratification, and differential socialization.

The tort rights and remedies of women have increasingly taken into account women's caretaking roles. The common law's abolition of interspousal immunity has given women tort remedies as a counter-weapon against family violence. The right to obtain redress against bad medicine—particularly in nursing home, botched cosmetic surgery, and sexual abuse cases—also particularly benefits women. Tort retrenchment in these areas leads to a disguised form of gender injustice.[2] Lucinda Finley, for example, argues that caps on non-economic damages have the unanticipated consequence of discriminating against women's caretaking and household roles.[3]

Many scholars maintain that by not taking full account of the sociological and biological differences between males and females, the law as well as the courts are deeply biased against women.[4] Robin West argues that the law is so permeated by patriarchal assumptions that women's life experiences and values are not "reflected at any level whatsoever in contracts, torts, constitutional law, or any other field of legal doctrine."[5] The manifest function of tort law is to provide redress for injuries in a gender-neutral judicial forum, but tort remedies have inherent and unrecognized gender-specific impacts.

Our statistical examination of the national patterns of tort verdicts shows that awards may be readily subdivided into "his" and "her" tort remedies. These separate tort remedy worlds parallel Jesse Bernard's sociological finding that husbands and wives experience their marriages in dissimilar ways: "his" and "her" marriages.[6] "Her" marriage is marked by an earlier recognition of marital problems and less overall satisfaction, which is a reflection of gender differences in resources, power, and life experiences. "Her" torts are disproportionately based on reproductive injuries, sexual exploitation, nursing home neglect, cosmetic surgery, and harms produced by defective household products. "His" torts revolve around workplace injuries and recreational products.

Formal equality, without consideration of social roles, can produce gender injustice in disguise. Most jurisdictions have already weakened "his" tort remedies during the past quarter century through legislative restrictions on products liability and toxic tort remedies, causes of action for injuries disproportionately suffered by men in their occupational and recreational roles. Now, tort reformers are turning their attention to "her" tort remedies by proposing restrictions on recovery for defective, ineffective, or dangerous medicine and medical products.

As this chapter demonstrates, women are disproportionately injured by bad medicine as a result of both biological factors and the male domination of the medical profession. Examining systematic data on the gendered patterns of tort recovery against medical product manufacturers and doctors is a first step toward linking women's "personal" troubles with managed care to women's public health care issues.

Relatively excluded from the governing elite, women's voices are rarely heard in the tort reform debate. No policy discussion should ignore an affected group, much less women, who make up more than half the American population. In the words of Elizabeth Janeway:

> To understand the workings of power as a relationship one must also consider the situation of the weak, the other, second, member of the process by which society at once exists and changes. And women are the oldest, largest and most central group of human creatures in the wide category of the weak and the ruled. The adjustments that women have made to life over centuries spent as subordinate partners in a power relationship illuminates the whole range of power situations.[7]

Women have a right to know that the tort revision legislation currently being debated in Congress and state legislatures will disproportionately endanger their health and safety. As Oliver Wendell Holmes observed, "The passion for equality sometimes leads to hollow formulas."[8]

[A] The Illusion of Gender Neutrality in Tort Law

Reworkings of law may have unanticipated negative impacts on women unless gender bias is considered.[9] California's 1970 no-fault divorce reform had the unexpected result of radically increasing the feminization of poverty because its authors ignored the economic advantages of male wage-earners.[10] Medical malpractice reform in Indiana also inadvertently hurt the interests of women because damages were capped on the basis of lost earnings. Indiana researchers found patterns suggesting that, although this tort reform was neutral on its face, women received smaller awards than men because under the revision "male work and lives are valued higher than female work and lives" by the physicians who staff the arbitration boards.[11] The failure of the Indiana legislators to consider the disparate gender impact of their legislation is an example of how "the law fails to take seriously events, which affect women's lives."[12]

[B] Tort Law and the Patriarchal Society

A brief historical examination unveils the gendered nature of tort law. Traditional tort law was openly patriarchal.[13] Eighteenth-century English tort verdicts for injuries to wives were generally awarded to their husbands because "at early common law, the wife's legal identity merged with that of her husband."[14] Torts committed against females were classified as affronts to the family as a social institution, and therefore awards were given to the male as head of the household.

Females were considered personal chattels of a sort, and males filed lawsuits when other men trespassed upon their conjugal or parental property rights through improper sexual behavior. Alienation of affection, for example, was a cause of action filed by married men to punish another male for willfully and maliciously damaging the marital relationship through the theft of the husband's conjugal rights. Husbands brought a tort action for adultery against other males who engaged in sexual intercourse with their wives. "Criminal conversation" was the name given for the "[d]efilement of the marriage bed, sexual intercourse of an outsider with husband or wife, or a breaking down of the covenant of fidelity."[15]

Seduction was "the offense that occurs when a man entices a woman of previously chaste character to have unlawful intercourse with him by means of persuasion, solicitation, promises or bribes, but not force."[16] Males were awarded exemplary damages for the mortification they suffered when defendants seduced their female servants, debauched their daughters, or formed illicit sexual attachments with their wives. Often, the defendants in these tort cases were wealthy males who had committed adultery with the wives of poor men. In sharp contrast, a woman was not generally afforded compensation when she lost her philandering husband to another woman.[17] In some American jurisdictions, a wife was given the same right to pursue an action for alienation of affection that a husband had under English law.

In nineteenth-century America, punitive damages punished wrongdoers who threatened the family as a social institution. Fathers received damages to compensate them for the loss of services when seducers impregnated their daughters.[18] In *Berghammer v. Mayer*,[19] the seducer of a fifteen-year-old girl was assessed a $3,000 punitive damages award. The court observed that the girl's neighbor had not only ravished the girl but also made her pregnant, and thereby denied the father the services of his daughter. In *Reutkemeier v. Nolte*,[20] a $6,000 punitive damages verdict was awarded to the father of a fourteen-year-old girl when she was seduced and impregnated.

§3.2. Tort Remedies for Gender Injustice

In America, female plaintiffs received tort awards directly as redress for the humiliation of being seduced by the false promises of a sexual predator.[21] Wealthy males who deceived "virtuous" women of modest means by promising marriage were punished through torts. The first recorded awarding of punitive damages to a woman in the United States was the 1791 case of *Coryell v. Colobough*,[22] in which the plaintiff was wronged by her suitor's breach of his promise to marry her. In the 1918 case of *Owens v. Fanning*, a defendant was assessed $1,416 in punitive damages for leading a seventeen-year-old girl off the "path of virtue."[23] The court specifically stated that the award was warranted because of the defendant's considerable wealth and social standing in the community. In this case, the previously chaste character of the plaintiff was also an aggravating factor leading to punitive damages.[24]

The female plaintiff in *Drobnich v. Bach*[25] received a $9,000 award for a rich man's breach of his promise to marry her. The defendant's promise was deemed a deception, designed to permit the defendant to have sexual intercourse without having to "pay the price of marriage." In *Goodal v. Thurman*[26] a wealthy male was punished through tort damages for inducing a young woman to submit to his sexual advances with false promises of marriage. In these cases, the actual damages would have been too slight to punish the defendant.

During the late nineteenth and early twentieth century, U.S. juries awarded punitive damages directly to females who were victimized by intentional torts such as assault and battery. A father was punished for a brutal attack on his infant daughter in a 1904 Minnesota case;[27] an abusive father who threw his teenage daughter down a flight of stairs was assessed punitive damages in 1908;[28] tort damages were awarded to a seven-year-old girl who was viciously attacked, tied up, and severely beaten in a 1913 verdict.[29]

A $1,000 punitive damages award was imposed against a violent man whose assault on the plaintiff caused her to suffer a nervous breakdown.[30] Punitive damages were awarded to punish a defendant who brutally attacked a woman in her home.[31] Another male was assessed $385.25 in joint compensatory and punitive damages to punish him for severely injuring a woman by kicking her.[32] A defendant paid punitive damages to a woman who suffered a miscarriage as a result of an aggravated assault.[33] Another pregnant woman was awarded punitive damages from a brute who assaulted her by violently pulling her through a door.[34] A Kentucky court upheld a $700 punitive damages award in favor of the wife of a farm tenant who suffered a miscarriage as a result of being struck repeatedly by a wealthy landowner in an argument over personal property.[35]

In 1925, a black woman and her eleven-year-old daughter were evicted from a parish house in mid-winter by a mob in Colorado.[36] The masked bullies broke into a private dwelling and severely beat the woman and her daughter. The daughter was bedridden for three and a half weeks with bruises all over her body, injuries to her spine, and nervous shock caused by the mob attack. The plaintiffs were awarded $5,000 in actual damages and $10,000 in exemplary damages against the perpetrators of this vicious act.[37] The essence of these cases was the invasion of bodily integrity and emotional harm done to women in vulnerable social roles.

§3.3. *Tort Damages, Gender, and Corporations*

[A] Tort Law, Gender, and Industrialization

As the economic and societal structure of nineteenth-century America changed, old tort remedies were adapted to new realities. In an industrializing America, men and women were exposed to dangers created by the emergent forces of production and distribution, such as assembly-line factories, public utilities, and railroad systems. When mishandled, these new technologies caused disasters of gargantuan dimensions.

By the late nineteenth century, railroads were being held vicariously responsible for their employees' assaults on female passengers.[38] In *Missouri Pacific Ry. Company v. Martino*,[39] a $2,020 punitive damages award was handed down against a railway conductor who struck and threatened a female passenger. In a similar case in which a brakeman deliberately shot a female passenger, damages of $2,000 were awarded to punish the railroad.[40] The court observed sarcastically that it was the brakeman's duty to look after the comfort and safety of the passengers, rather than to shoot them, and that the public trust had therefore been breached.

Railway employees could also be found liable as individuals. A $1,250 punitive damages award was imposed against a conductor for using unnecessary force in ejecting a female passenger.[41] Punitive damages also served to punish railway employees who sexually assaulted female passengers. In one such case, a court upheld a $1,500 award against a conductor for making improper sexual advances to a female passenger and fondling her breasts.[42]

[B] Gender Justice in Modern Tort Law

Tort law has expanded to benefit women in ways that would have been almost unimaginable a hundred years ago. In nineteenth-century America, mental suffering was not compensated, nor were there any cognizable remedies for the pain and suffering of witnessing the death of a loved one—unless the plaintiff also suffered a perceivable physical impact. As torts have evolved over subsequent decades, women have gained an ever-expanding array of rights, as well as remedies to redress their injuries.

Tort law now redresses new categories of emotional injury, including a woman's suffering for the miscarriage or death of her child even if she suffers no "physical impact."[43] Courts allow bystanders outside the zone of danger or impact to recover emotional damages for consequences of "witnessing injury to a third person, usually a child, spouse or near relative."[44] Torts have evolved to protect battered women and other victims of family violence.[45] Civil actions for battery, assault, and the intentional infliction of emotional distress have been extended to the victims of domestic abuse.[46] Tort law provides remedies for passengers sexually assaulted by crew members on offshore cruise lines who are beyond the jurisdiction of American criminal law. Tort remedies are now used to police inappropriate sexual advances in the workplace.[47]

Between 1945 and 1980—what we have called the Progressive Age of Tort Law—many traditional barriers to tort recovery were eliminated. By the end of that period, a dozen courts had recognized prenatal remedies, largely because of the appointment of more progressive judges. By 1972, twenty-one states had abolished spousal immunity; by 1978, an additional six states had repealed this regressive rule.[48] Women's rights have been advanced through tort law's recognition of remedies for gender discrimination[49] and sexual exploitation.[50]

Increasingly, women have been awarded tort remedies as compensation for injuries due to pornography,[51] sexual abuse,[52] and hostile workplaces.[53] During the past quarter century, tort damages have been awarded to female victims of familial sexual exploitation[54] and acquaintance rape.[55] In *Claus v. Lee*, a court found sufficient evidence to pursue an adult daughter's claim that she was sexually abused by her father, a medical doctor.[56] The court permitted the woman to seek punitive damages to punish sexual abuse despite the fact that it occurred within the family. Before the 1950s, such a suit would almost certainly have been barred by family immunity.

Traditionally, statutory charitable immunity precluded lawsuits against hospitals, no matter how grievous the harm done. The doctrine of *respondeat superior* was not extended to hospitals, nor were hospitals liable for the torts of affiliated doctors. As this immunity retreated in the 1960s, medical malpractice cases expanded. When corporate medical liability was extended to include the torts of a hospital's affiliated physicians, hospitals were assessed damages for failing to screen out incompetent or unqualified medical personnel.

Tort remedies have evolved to punish doctors who intentionally harm patients, perform unnecessary surgeries, or sexually exploit their patients. This expanded medical malpractice liability has principally benefited women because many malpractice cases are gender-linked, especially those involving the failure of informed consent, grossly substandard cosmetic surgeries, and sexual abuse of patients by health care providers.

In corporate workplaces, women have increasingly found redress against abusive misconduct. For example, a San Francisco jury awarded $225,000 in punitive damages against Martin Greenstein, a partner in the elite law firm of Baker and McKenzie, and $6.9 million in vicarious punitive damages against the company.[57] Greenstein dropped "M and M" candies into his secretary's shirt pocket while groping her breast.[58] He put his knee in her lower back, held her arms behind her and said, "Let's see which breast is bigger."[59] The senior law partner was verbally abusive toward his secretary for spurning his advances.

Baker and McKenzie was found to be vicariously liable for ratifying its partner's wrongdoing by failing to investigate his misconduct or take disciplinary action.[60] Jurors calculated punitive damages by awarding 10 percent of the law firm's net worth. One juror explained that "any time anybody complained, they were retaliated against in some fashion, so we thought we should give [the law firm] a good wake-up call."[61] The punitive damages award was reduced in the post-verdict period to $3.5 million.

§3.4. Gender and Medical Products Liability

Women rely primarily upon tort remedies rather than government regulators to ensure the safety of medical products and procedures. Lucinda Finley found "[r]eproductive or sexual harm caused by drugs and medical devices [to have] a disproportionate impact on women because far more drugs and devices have been devised to control women's fertility or bodily functions associated with sex and childbearing than have been devised for men."[62] Over the past few decades, punitive damages have expanded from punishing intentional torts committed maliciously to controlling reckless product manufacturers and health care providers.

Many mass torts have arisen out of products developed specifically for women, including the drug diethylstilbestrol (DES), the Dalkon Shield and Copper-7 intrauterine devices (IUDs), high-absorbency tampons linked to toxic shock syndrome, oral contraceptives causing kidney failure, and ruptured silicone-gel breast implants. As a result of tort litigation, dangerously defective products have been taken off the market, recalled, and redesigned. Drug and medical device manufacturers have been held accountable for marketing products that have injured millions of women.

The market share doctrine was first developed in a case permitting recovery for daughters of women who ingested the synthetic hormone DES to prevent miscarriages. Many of the daughters of mothers who took DES developed cancer when they reached sexual maturity. Approximately two hundred different manufacturers produced this drug. The daughters were rarely able to identify the specific manufacturer of the tablets taken decades earlier by their mother. Traditional tort principles will not impose products liability unless the defendant can be identified with certainty.

The court in *Sindell v. Abbott Laboratories*[63] permitted the plaintiffs to make an industry-wide joinder, holding each manufacturer liable for the proportion of the judgment represented by its share of the market. A New York court adopting this novel market share theory observed that druggists usually filled "prescriptions from whatever was on hand. Approximately 300 manufacturers produced the drug, with companies entering and leaving the market continuously during the 24 years that DES was sold for pregnancy use. The long latency period of a DES injury compounds the identification problem."[64] The court-fashioned rule of market share liability was the high water mark for progressive tort law in sidestepping traditional principles of causation.[65]

Infertility, miscarriage, and stillbirth are some of the grievous, non-economic losses caused by defective medical products and devices. In many of these cases, as illustrated in Chapter 2, the manufacturers mount a "scorched earth" defense. The manufacturers' counsel seeks to embarrass, harass, and intimidate women into abandoning their just claims. A favorite defense tactic is to blame the victim, deflecting attention away from the defective product. Reputations and marriages are destroyed by lengthy depositions that probe the injured woman's premarital or extra-marital sexual histories.

Tort law is increasingly articulating a feminine voice that provides fair compensation for the social and economic costs of caring for others.[66] Since women are generally the primary caretakers of severely injured family members, they have a particularly strong interest in obtaining sufficient recovery to provide care for the permanently disabled. Moreover, women are often the primary plaintiffs in cases seeking compensation for birth injuries, reproductive damage, and improper management of childbirth. Caps on damages for birth injuries fall disproportionately on women who face a lifetime of caring for their severely brain-damaged infants. Tort reformers have convinced state legislatures to limit or cap non-economic damages that compensate women for the pain and suffering resulting from loss of fertility or reproductive function.[67]

$3.5. *Tort Reformers' War against Women*

[A] Claiming to Protect Women

Chapters 1 and 2 describe the emergence of a strategic political alliance among leaders of the business community, which was designed to counter the expanded corporate liability imposed in the 1960s and 1970s.[68] Such revision of tort law is not true reform, but regression to an earlier time in history when the law permitted little, if any, redress by an injured plaintiff against a corporate wrongdoer. Tort reforms that limit the total recovery of the victims of unsafe medical products will have a substantial adverse impact on women.

This push to "reform" tort law is part of a much larger effort to roll back any legislation that benefits women but conflicts with corporate self-interest:

> Contrast the largely unopposed commitment of more than $500 billion for the bailout of savings and loan associations with the sharp debate, close votes, and defeats for the rights of men and women to take unpaid parental leave. Although the classic phrase for something non-controversial that everyone must support is to call it a "motherhood" issue, and it would cost little to guarantee every woman the right to an unpaid parental leave, nonetheless this measure generated intense scrutiny and controversy.[69]

Tort reformers argue that they are advancing women's interests by freeing the medical establishment from excessive tort liability. For example, they distributed a poster to thousands of obstetricians and gynecologists, which showed a pregnant woman at the closed door of a doctor who no longer accepts obstetric patients because of the fear of lawsuits.[70] These revisionists maintain that drugs women need, such as Bendectin, have been unnecessarily withdrawn from the market because of litigation costs.

Tort law defenders, in contrast, argue that sexist biases, rather than any so-called litigation crisis, account for the failure of the medical system to adequately protect the interests of women.[71] The American Medical Association's Council on Ethical and Judicial Affairs reviewed forty-eight studies on gender discrimination in dealing with patients and concluded:

> These studies have documented gender disparities in treatment in a number of areas, including kidney transplantation, cardiac catheterization and the diagnosis of lung cancer. While biological factors account for some differences between the sexes in the delivery of medical care, the studies indicate that there may be non-biological and non-clinical factors that affect

clinical decision-making. . . . [M]ore research in women's health issues and women's health problems should be pursued. Finally, awareness of and responsiveness to socio-cultural factors which could lead to gender disparities may be enhanced by increasing the number of female physicians in leadership roles and other positions of authority in teaching, research, and the practice of medicine.[72]

Improving training for male physicians and earmarking research money for female health and reproductive issues would be far more beneficial to women than reducing their tort recoveries.

Tort reformers have had considerable success in their campaign to limit tort remedies.[73] Jury verdict research credits tort reformers for the fact that during the 1990s "juries nationwide have become markedly tougher on people who sue doctors, insurance companies,[74] and other deep-pocket defendants."[75] Even grievously injured victims may have difficulty finding a lawyer willing to underwrite the cost of medical experts and other charges, which may add up to hundreds of thousands of dollars.[76] Tort reform makes it more difficult to redress injustice in general and gender injustice in particular.

[B] Women, Pain, and Suffering

Non-economic compensatory damages are sometimes referred to as pain and suffering, or non-pecuniary, damages. "It is irreducibly difficult to translate pain and suffering, disfigurement, loss of enjoyment of life, loss of conjugal fellowship, loss of marriage prospects, inability to taste and smell, inability to lift your children into your arms and other miseries into dollars and cents."[77] A "pain and suffering" award is designed to compensate the injured plaintiff for past and future bodily suffering and for the lost or reduced quality of life. Women have greater pain and suffering awards not because they are more emotional than men are, but because of the gendered nature of their injuries.

Males are far more likely than females to be crushed, asphyxiated, and shattered by workplace injuries, accidents largely redressed with economic damages. Tort reforms have already been enacted that make it more difficult to recover for "male injuries" such as accidents caused by defective power shovels, log skidders, punch presses, or chemical drums. In contrast, women are more likely to suffer reproductive injury, sterility, or miscarriage from products that are placed inside their bodies by medical professionals. Those who suffer sexual abuse at the hands of a physician, parent, or supervisor are far more likely to be female than male. Non-economic and punitive damages make up a large percentage of the compensation for these types of injury.

If punitive and other non-economic damages are capped at some small multiple of the verdict's economic damages, as commonly advocated by tort reformers, women as a class will be adversely impacted. Women are usually awarded smaller economic verdicts for equivalent injuries because of their lower overall wages. The tracking of women into low-wage "pink collar" work has led to the "comparable worth" doctrine, which would require equal pay for women's work that requires skill and training equivalent to that of better-paid jobs in male-dominated fields.[78]

The information age economy has not ended sexism in employment. An apparently biologically based tendency for females to have superior spatial perception and fine motor control may lead women into employment in poorly paid assembly work rather than engineering, dentistry, or architecture.[79] "Even in the much storied meritocracy of high tech . . . women still make only 83¢ for every dollar men earn."[80] Tort litigants rarely perceive the role of gender in their lawsuits because the legal system requires that they focus on the facts of their individual injuries, rather than the societal roots of their problems. But personal troubles are socially constructed and situated. What appear on the surface to be merely individual misfortunes are often reflective of deeply embedded inequalities in American culture.

In general, women spend fewer years in the labor force than men and will have lower earnings over their lifetime. Limiting their potential recovery to some arbitrary multiple of their already lower incomes marginalizes women's work by increasing the unjust impact of wage disparities. One opponent of a federal statute restricting non-economic damages testified about the negative consequences to women:

> Two people suffer exactly the same injury. Both find themselves unable to perform life's normal activities. One is a man and one is a woman. The man is a plumber. He receives economic damages that are not affected by this bill. The woman is a homemaker and has suffered little "economic loss," and so the compensation she receives for an injury that has shattered her life could be severely limited by this bill. No one could argue that this is fair.[81]

Non-economic damages, awarded for pain and suffering, are frequently a large proportion of the verdict in cosmetic surgery cases. For example, verdicts compensating for emotional distress caused by the fear of possible future disability from ruptured breast implants or disfigurement from the removal of implants typically include little by way of economic damages. The plaintiff in *Short v. Downs*[82] suffered severe emotional injury from the prospect of future catastrophic health complications resulting from silicone injected directly into her breasts. The reckless physician in this case had introduced industrial-grade silicone directly into her body, despite knowing that the Food and Drug Administration (FDA) had banned this dangerous practice in the early 1960s.[83] With errant lumps of silicone throughout her body that required continuous medical monitoring, the plaintiff had to face the rest of her life with the possibility that she might develop cancer from the silicone "spills" inside her body.[84]

§3.6. *His and Her Tort Reforms*

[A] His Tort Remedies

Males suffer far more industrial accidents than women because of occupational stratification. Awards for workplace accidents in factories and assembly lines are overwhelmingly "his" tort remedy. Asbestos-related diseases were the product of unprotected exposure to asbestos dust in male-centered workplaces such as ships, shipyards, and railroads. In our study of punitive damages in products liability, all of the plaintiffs prevailing in cases against asbestos manufacturers were males.[85] Male plaintiffs predominated in almost every product category outside of medical and household products.

Ninety-four percent of all people killed at work are male, a direct result of occupational patterns. A typical example was the case of a mechanic in Remer, Minnesota, who suffered catastrophic brain damage from an exploding tire rim.[86] Another example is the case of a male assembly-line worker whose hand was amputated in an accident involving a forty-five-ton punch press.[87]

Male farmers, rather than farm wives, are disproportionately the victims of defective power mowers, unguarded grain augers, and unnecessary injuries caused by tractors lacking standard rollover protection. A twelve-year old agricultural worker lost a leg to a defectively designed shield on a grain auger. A protruding screw that revolved at high speed severed his limb, acting much like a "fly-cutter on a lathe."[88]

Males are also over-represented in litigation involving defective recreational products, such as boats, motorcycles, and all-terrain vehicles. The world of firearms is typically a male province, so it is not surprising that males are six and a half times more likely than females to die as the result of a firearm accident.[89] In our research, every punitive damages award arising out of a defective firearm accident involved a male plaintiff.

Many of the accidents that led to tort awards were based upon the risky behaviors of young males. Males are twenty-nine times more likely than females to be injured by a fall from a scaffold or ladder,[90] and five times as many males as females die in drowning accidents.[91] Females suffer only one-fourteenth as many fatal boating accidents as males,[92] so it is not surprising that a male was the plaintiff in a case arising out of a boating accident caused by a dangerously defective interlock device.[93] In every motorcycle product case that led to punitive damages, male plaintiffs were involved. The failure of customized brake handles caused an accident resulting in the paralysis of a young male that led to punitive damages in a Florida case.[94]

Males are more aggressive drivers and are nearly three times more likely than women to die in motor vehicle accidents. The disparity is even higher among younger males: four times as many males as females between the ages twenty and thirty die in motor vehicle accidents.[95] When women were injured by recreational vehicles, males were generally the drivers and women the injured passenger or bystander. In *Leichtamer v. American Motors Corp.*,[96] a young male driver injured his wife as well as another female passenger. Tort law needs to take into account the different social roles played by women and men to understand the impact of gender on tort damages.

[B] Her Tort Remedies

As women assume traditionally male jobs in ever increasing numbers, his and her tort worlds will converge, as illustrated by the famous lawsuit filed by Karen Silkwood for radiation exposure she suffered at Kerr-McGee's nuclear fuel processing plant in Oklahoma. An Oklahoma jury awarded Silkwood's estate $10 million in punitive damages for this callous and wanton disregard of worker safety. The plaintiff's punitive damages award was based upon inadequate plant security, inadequate workers' training, and the company's inability to account for 10.4 kilograms of plutonium.[97]

An expert witness testified that the Atomic Energy Commission had cited the plant approximately seventy-five times for violations of federal regulations. A former director of the Health Physics Program at the Oak Ridge National Laboratory testified that he "could not imagine . . . such a lackadaisical attitude . . . to the health and safety of the people."[98] Karen Silkwood suffered great emotional distress from being contaminated by plutonium. Witnesses in her lawsuit testified that she was fearful of a slow death from cancer. Silkwood died in an automobile accident while driving alone to a meeting with a *New York Times* reporter at which she was to present evidence of safety violations at the Kerr-McGee plant. Her ordeal became the subject of the film *Silkwood,* starring Meryl Streep.

The Karen Silkwood nuclear contamination case is atypical because she was injured in a non-traditional job setting. Most product injuries sustained by women plaintiffs in punitive damages cases still occur in traditionally female spheres. Women are far more likely than men to be injured by home appliances, exploding bottles, flammable clothing, household chemicals, or beauty and medical products. The tens of thousands of plaintiffs suffering from valvular heart disease caused by the diet drug fenfluramine-dexfenfluramine ("fen-phen") are almost all women. Females have been awarded punitive damages for injuries caused by skin creams containing mercury and by highly flammable artificial fingernail glue. These hazards are directly correlated with the gendered nature of American society.

Cases involving defective medical products were responsible for nearly half of the punitive damages awards made to women in products liability between 1965 and 1990. Most of these remedies redressed injuries to women's reproductive functions or damages they suffered from botched cosmetic surgery. The Dalkon Shield, Copper-7 IUDs, Bendectin, Varidase, super-absorbent tampons, and breast implants are all examples of dangerously defective products exclusively used by women. In these cases, the FDA's regulation of medical products and devices has provided little or no protection against injury. The FDA has also failed to protect American women from injuries or deaths from L-Tryptophan, Norplant, and DES. Tort law punished the producers of these needlessly hazardous products.

[1] The Dalkon Shield

The FDA enacted the Medical Devices Amendments of 1976 as a direct response to the Dalkon Shield debacle.[99] A. H. Robins began selling its

Dalkon Shield at the beginning of the 1970s in the midst of the sexual revolution.[100] The company marketed the shield as a "modern, superior and safe" birth control method, and advertised that the IUD had the "lowest pregnancy rate . . . 1.1%," that it was "safe," and that it "would prevent pregnancy without producing any general effects on the body."[101] Relying on A. H. Robins's sales pitch and literature attesting to the safety of these devices, doctors implanted the Dalkon Shield in some 2.2 million American women.[102] But the company knew otherwise.

A. H. Robins's own tests revealed that the true pregnancy rate for women using the Dalkon Shield was more than 5 percent and that the shield posed serious health risks to the user.[103] In August 1971, the company was informed that the quality control supervisor at a subsidiary performed a test on the shield that proved that its string tail could "wick" fluid into the uterus, allowing bacteria to infect this normally sterile area. The resulting infection often caused permanent reproductive injury and, in some cases, death. A. H. Robins's failure to employ adequate testing and research, and its concealment of known data about the shield, led to the company's commercial success: it beat its competitors to the IUD market.[104] A. H. Robins's sales revenues from the Dalkon Shield were greater than $11 million.

Even after receiving scores of notices of serious adverse reactions, the company continued to market its birth control device aggressively. A. H. Robins's former quality control director testified that the company knew of the dangers of infection but issued no warning.[105] This delay led to more than 200,000 infections, including seventeen that were fatal. The court in *Tetuan v. A. H. Robins* summarized the misconduct justifying the punitive damages award in the Dalkon Shield litigation:

> There was substantial evidence to conclude that Robins fully compre-
> hended, by 1974 at the latest, the enormity of the dangers it created but
> that it deliberately and intentionally concealed those dangers; that it put
> money into favorable studies; that it tried to neutralize any critics of the
> Dalkon Shield; that it consistently denied the dangers of the Dalkon Shield
> for nearly 15 years after it originally marketed; that it commissioned stud-
> ies that it dropped when they turned out unfavorable; [and] consigned
> hundreds of documents to the furnace.[106]

To give the Dalkon Shield disaster a human face, consider the case of Mrs. Carrie Palmer, a twenty-four-year-old woman who was fitted with a Dalkon Shield in January 1973. By August, Palmer had become pregnant despite wearing the intrauterine device. Her physician decided not to remove the Dalkon Shield, fearing that the procedure might trigger a spontaneous abortion. As the pregnancy progressed, Carrie Palmer became violently ill. Within hours of her admission to a hospital she suffered a spontaneous abortion and nearly died. In order to save her life, doctors were forced to remove her uterus, fallopian tubes, and ovaries.[107]

Judge Myles Lord castigated A. H. Robins's leaders for their deadly misdeeds:

> Gentlemen, the results of these activities and attitudes on your part have been catastrophic. Today, as you sit here, attempting once more to extricate yourself from the legal consequences of your acts, none of you have faced up to the fact that more than nine thousand women have made claims that they gave up a part of their womanhood.... Your company has in fact continued to allow women, tens of thousands of them, to wear a device—a deadly depth charge in their wombs, ready to explode any time.... The only conceivable reasons you have not recalled this product are that it would hurt your balance sheet. [Y]ou have taken the bottom line as your guiding beacon and the low road as your route. This is corporate responsibility at its meanest.[108]

Women suffered injuries including infection, loss of reproductive organs, infertility, stillbirth, and septic abortions from using this IUD.

A. H. Robins received more than three hundred reports of spontaneous septic abortions while the Dalkon Shield was still in place. By 1984, there were tens of thousands of lawsuits against the company, with injured plaintiffs arguing that the manufacturer was liable for fraud for failing to disclose the known dangers of the Shield. Trapped in a difficult litigation stance, Robins finally removed the Dalkon Shield from the market.

A. H. Robins filed for bankruptcy in 1986. In a final insult to the plaintiffs, both those who had died from complications of using the Dalkon Shield and those who were forced to live with physical and emotional pain and disfigurement, the reorganization plan excused the company from paying any punitive damages.

[2] The Copper-7 Intrauterine Device

On February 25, 1974, Monsanto's subsidiary G. D. Searle received FDA approval to market the Copper-7 IUD.[109] The company promoted the contraceptive by selling a pendant in the shape of the Copper-7 IUD. Presumably, the necklace was to be worn by young women to indicate their sexual availability.[110] One advertisement, in *Playgirl* magazine, read: "The 'In' Necklace Shows Your Independence NOW!" Marketing in this way seems especially reprehensible due to the fact that evidence presented by the plaintiffs showed that the device was particularly hazardous to women who had never borne children. Thousands of women sought redress for serious injuries resulting from their use of this IUD, arguing that Searle had placed millions of American females at "risk of serious infection, loss of fertility and surgery for removal of internal organs."[111]

The physical injuries caused by the Copper-7 included pelvic inflammatory disease, ectopic pregnancy, perforation of the uterus and small bowel, and hysterectomies.[112] The only punitive damages award was a $7 million dollar verdict in *Kociemba v. G. D. Searle and Company*,[113] which was predicated upon the company's intentional misrepresentation of its birth control device.

Searle's defense of the Copper-7 was a classic example of trying to sway the jury by blaming the victim. Searle argued that the pelvic inflammatory disease could have been caused by the plaintiffs' promiscuous sexual practices—a legally irrelevant fact, particularly since the company had specifically marketed the product to sexually active women. Discovery extended to include third parties that had engaged in sex with women who filed lawsuits against Searle.[114]

G. D. Searle eventually withdrew the Copper-7 IUD from the market, after reaping $80 million in profits from the sale of this device. Searle's spokes-man contended that the company was removing the device from the market despite the lack of any "medical or scientific reasons for it."[115] For public consumption, the company claimed that women were being denied a desirable product because of the "high cost of defending unwarranted litigation" and the company's "inability to find product insurance at any reasonable cost."[116] Out of the glare of publicity, the company made thousands of out-of-court settlements, rather than risk further litigation.[117]

[3] Toxic Shock Syndrome

Several brands of tampons, including Kotex, Playtex, and Tampax, were composed of polyacrylate fibers, which can serve as a breeding ground for staphylococcus-aureus bacteria. The bacterial toxins can infect and poison the user, producing a condition that became known as "toxic shock syndrome" (TSS). Symptoms include nausea, vomiting, sore throat, a rash, and a high fever. Within forty-eight hours, blood pressure can drop to a dangerous level and, in some cases, TSS can cause liver and kidney failure.[118] More than two thousand women suffered from toxic shock syndrome caused by their use of super-absorbent vaginal tampons. At least a hundred deaths resulted from the use of this dangerously defective product.

Female plaintiffs won several punitive damages verdicts for injuries arising from toxic shock syndrome.[119] In *West v. Johnson and Johnson Products*,[120] a twenty-year-old college student suffered abnormalities in the functioning of her liver and kidney, low blood pressure, and other life-threatening symptoms from toxic shock syndrome caused by using a super-absorbent tampon. Evidence at trial revealed that Johnson and Johnson Products had received complaints about TSS as early as the mid-1970s.[121] Between 1975 and 1980, the company had received 150 complaints of a "more serious" nature about its tampons.

Despite mounting evidence of serious medical complications, the company performed no additional testing.[122] The resulting punitive damages award was based on the company's knowledge that "during menstruation, a vagina is potentially a breeding ground for pathogenic bacteria, but despite such knowledge, Johnson and Johnson Products did not conduct adequate testing of the o.b. tampon [and] . . . having received continuing complaints from consumers about infections . . . did not conduct further studies to determine whether use of the tampon could promote such infections."[123]

[4] Silicone and Saline Breast Implants

More than two million women have had silicone gel–filled breast implants surgically inserted in their bodies.[124] An estimated 80 percent of the breast-implant surgeries were performed to enlarge healthy breasts.[125] The other 20 percent were inserted to correct congenital defects or as part of post-mastectomy reconstruction surgery.[126] Hundreds of thousands of women claim that they have suffered serious problems from leaking or ruptured silicone breast implants.

Tens of thousands of breast-implant product cases are currently pending in state and federal courts nationwide.[127] Most of these claims have been consolidated into global settlements. The vast majority of these cases involve virtually identical claims for punitive damages based upon evidence that manufacturers marketed the implants with prior knowledge of design, manufacturing, and warning defects.[128] On September 1, 1994, a federal district judge approved a settlement providing for a $4.25 billion fund to satisfy thousands of breast-implant claims.[129] Many of the claimants received a settlement that was modest when compared to the severe health problems caused by the implants. Litigation is continuing because many breast implant victims have refused to join in the settlement.[130]

As illustrated by the Mohney breast-implant litigation discussed in Chapter 2, defense counsel frequently uses "good girl–bad girl" gender stereotypes to deflect attention away from the ruptured implants, the true issue of the case.[131] This trial strategy has proven highly effective. Breast cancer survivors receiving reconstructive surgery are far more likely to obtain redress than are women undergoing elective cosmetic surgery.[132] Topless go-go dancers and entertainers have never won a single dollar from juries, even though they have suffered many of the same health problems from ruptured implants as claimants employed in more traditional occupations. Apparently their lifestyles render them "less than equal" before the law.

A federal court of appeals affirmed a $7.34 million award in *Hopkins v. Dow Corning Corp.*,[133] litigation involving a woman who developed mixed connective tissue disease from the silicone that escaped from her ruptured breast implants. The plaintiff had received the implants as part of her reconstructive surgery after undergoing a bilateral mastectomy. The punitive damages verdict was based upon evidence that Dow allegedly concealed clinical studies on the debilitating effects of silicone on the immune system.[134] A key "smoking gun" document in *Hopkins* was a 1975 Dow memo indicating corporate knowledge of a "high rate of rupture—several devices had ruptured as a surgeon was trying to put them in."[135] Another internal memo "noted that after the mammaries had been handled for a while, the surface became oily; [indeed] some were bleeding on the velvet in the showcase"[136] from leaking silicone. As a result, the sales staff was instructed to "be sure samples are clean and dry before customer dealing: wash with soap and water in nearest washroom, dry with hand towels."[137] The Ninth Circuit U.S. Court of Appeals found ample support for punitive damages based upon the trial record:

> Dow's conduct in exposing thousands of women to a painful and debilitating disease, and the evidence that Dow gained financially from its conduct, may properly be considered in imposing an award of punitive damages. Moreover, given the facts that Dow was aware of possible defects in its implants, that Dow knew long-term studies of the implants' safety were needed, that Dow concealed this information as well as the negative results of the few short-term laboratory tests performed, and that Dow continued

for several years to market its implants as safe despite this knowledge, a substantial punitive damages award is justified.[138]

The potential for future punitive damages claims by thousands of additional women was crucial in motivating other breast implant manufacturers to join the global settlement of breast implant litigation claims. Dow Corning has filed for bankruptcy and has effectively insulated itself from joint and several liability for punitive damages awards as a member of the Dow corporate family.

§3.7. The FDA Defense and Gender Injustice

[A] Food, Drug and Cosmetic Act

In 1938 Congress passed the Food, Drug and Cosmetic Act in order to monitor the safety of food and drugs. However, the FDA did not regulate devices such as breast implants until 1976, when the Medical Device Amendment was enacted. Consequently, the Dalkon Shield, breast implants, and other medical devices that were on the market before this legislation are beyond the FDA's jurisdiction. Even after it was given jurisdiction, the FDA has been reluctant to use its authority to police products that adversely affect women's reproductive health. The agency's inaction has directly damaged the health of hundreds of thousands of women. For example, G. D. Searle's Copper-7 IUD caused serious pelvic infections, loss of fertility, and required remedial surgery in thousands of women. Similarly, high-estrogen contraceptives manufactured by Ortho Pharmaceutical Company caused renal failure precisely because of their unnecessarily high estrogen content. Nonetheless, Ortho continued to promote the use of high-estrogen contraceptives, not even warning doctors of the growing evidence of risk. Estrogen levels were lowered only after a jury awarded $2.75 million in punitive damages for failing to warn of the danger.

[B] FDA Defense against Liability

A controversial tort reform, the FDA defense, would increase the harm caused by the FDA's inaction.[139] The FDA defense immunizes manufacturers from all punitive damages for any injury resulting from a drug or device approved by the FDA.[140] If inadequate labeling or warning causes a plaintiff's harm, no punitive damages may be awarded against a seller if the labeling or packaging was FDA-approved. The product suppliers argue that an FDA defense is necessary in order to protect American industry from a flood of litigation from mass tort claimants. There are two exceptions to this defense, but it is extremely hard to prove either of them: (1) that the company intentionally and wrongfully withheld from or misrepresented the safety of the drug or device to the agency, or (2) that the company bribed an employee of the FDA to gain approval of the drug or device in question.

The FDA defense insulates the manufacturer from all punitive liability for its reckless indifference. The tort reformers' argument for an FDA defense is that it is necessary to "improve the climate for innovation in medical technology"[141] and to lower the cost of insurance.[142] Already, five states have granted immunity to companies that market products that have FDA approval.[143] These states have, essentially, abandoned the consuming public to the self-monitoring of the medical-industrial complex.

The granting of such immunity takes *caveat emptor* to a new level. Manufacturers, by the nature of their business, are profit-driven enterprises. With a government-issued immunity shielding them from the consequences of their own actions, they are less motivated to act in the interest of the general public. The race to the marketplace or the reluctance to remove products from the shelves is too frequently shaped by impermissible cost–benefit equations.

The FDA defense, on its face, seems to bring common sense to the common law. After all, isn't the government already protecting us by devising safety standards? However, the FDA defense makes good sense only if the agency vigilantly polices clinical trials of drugs and medical devices. The FDA approval process itself is, unfortunately, no guarantee that a medical product is safe.

The FDA does not have a staff of independent scientists to conduct its own tests or even the ability to oversee corporate clinical trials; it is overworked and understaffed. The Reagan Administration stripped the FDA's budget, forcing the agency to reduce its staff by more than one thousand employees between 1979 and 1989. Tests on some medical devices, including heart defibrillators and a home test for ovulation, were so deficient that the FDA's chief at the Center for Medical Devices commented that they were "not up to the level of fifth-grade science."[144]

The U.S. General Accounting Office report on the FDA's drug review process concluded that more than half of the nearly two hundred drugs approved by the FDA between 1976 and 1985 manifested post-approval risks so serious that the drug was either withdrawn from the market or the medical product had to be relabeled.[145] Defective medical products have already caused serious harm to the public, despite FDA approval. As one consumer advocate noted: "History clearly demonstrates that despite the appearance of a thorough and extensive regulatory regime, the FDA has not been able to adequately protect the public from manufacturers who knowingly or recklessly market dangerous medical devices. There are far too many examples of instances where the FDA could not by itself adequately protect the public from dangerous, defective medical devices."[146]

As with many regulatory agencies, high-level FDA officials circulate between government service and employment with pharmaceutical or drug companies, potentially undermining their loyalty to the public interest. The FDA should be the first line of defense, not the only defense.

Our empirical analysis of a quarter century of products liability cases suggests that the FDA defense would disproportionately hurt women. Most mass torts affecting women involve injuries from defective products placed inside their bodies, whereas men are seldom injured in this fashion. "Her" punitive damages tort world centers on harms from medical products that are now regulated by the FDA: drugs, contraceptives, breast implants, pharmaceutical products, and medical devices.

The vast majority of high-stakes mass tort cases that have led to punitive damages awards involved products used exclusively by women. Government approval should not give free license to manufacturers who fail to take prompt remedial action in withdrawing drugs and medical products they know to be dangerous. At minimum, the FDA defense would be yet another barrier making it more difficult for women to find redress for products that damage their bodies.

The typical products liability case costs $250,000 to $1 million to litigate. Without the prospect of punitive damages, an attorney may not be willing to file a lawsuit involving what the law considers largely non-economic injuries, such as disfigurement or the loss of fertility. As proposed, the immunity provided by the FDA defense would likely prove an insurmountable obstacle to many women's recovery for injuries that are due to defective products.

Under the proposed FDA defense, a host of new products designed for insertion into women's bodies would be immunized from punitive damages.[147] Female condoms would receive immunity from punitive damages, even though the FDA sped up review and approved the product in spite of tests that showed a high pregnancy rate among users.[148] The FDA defense tacitly assumes that the agency is doing its job, but the history of medical products is one of benign neglect. Companies aggressively market their products and earn profits while the FDA passively learns of a profile of adverse reactions—after the fact and usually too late to avoid completely preventable injuries.[149]

The FDA's failure to withdraw the Dalkon Shield, once it gained jurisdiction, is a case study of agency delay and inaction. The FDA's reluctance to act in the silicone-gel breast implant debacle provides another illustration of its laxity in protecting women's health. Between 1977 and June 1992, reports of approximately 14,250 problems associated with silicone breast implants were filed with the FDA. The FDA failed to monitor breast implants, even after many scientists and physicians had expressed serious concerns about their safety.

In *Wooderson v. Ortho Pharm. Corp.*,[150] the Kansas Supreme Court upheld the $2.75 million punitive damages award to a woman who suffered acute renal failure as a result of using the Ortho-Novum 1-80 contraceptive. The court ruled that the defendant's failure to warn women in the face of an accumulating body of medical and scientific evidence of blood-vessel wall damage, acute renal failure, malignant hypertension, and hemolytic uremic syndrome (HUS) warranted punitive damages. There were twenty-one other cases of HUS in women using oral contraceptives, yet the company continued marketing the product without an adequate warning. The FDA defense is a corporate subsidy that will have the cumulative effect of increasing corporate profits at the expense of women's health.

§3.8. Medical Malpractice as Gender Justice in Disguise

Traditional tort law upholds family values by recognizing that women are chiefly responsible for family and home. Non-pecuniary damage awards, for example, compensate the family for the loss of the mother's key role in raising children. Tort reform that limits non-economic damages diminishes the value of women's roles in our society. Formal equality without recognition of occupation stratification is gender injustice in disguise.

Non-sexual intentional torts by health care providers are another source of injuries to female patients. In our study of medical malpractice verdicts, fifty-eight of the punitive damages awards involved some intentional tort other than sexual abuse.[151] Sixteen of the cases stemmed from aggravating circumstances that occurred in the course of committing intentional torts,

including the intentional infliction of emotional distress, false imprisonment, and assault and battery. Fraud was the basis for another twenty-two
verdicts. Spoliation or alteration of medical records to conceal negligence
accounted for another twenty punitive damages awards.

In *Johnson v. Woman's Hospital*,[152] the plaintiff miscarried and gave
birth to an infant who lived for only an hour. In a subsequent visit to the
hospital, the mother inquired about the burial of her baby's remains. She
"was led to a section of the hospital where a freezer was opened and she
was handed a gallon jar of formaldehyde with the discolored and shriv-
eled body of her child floating inside."[153]

The callous misconduct of this hospital employee caused the plaintiff
to suffer severe emotional distress. In this case, a note in Mrs. Johnson's
file from her pathologist with instructions that the baby's body was "not
to be disposed of as a surgical specimen"[154] led to a punitive damages
award. If there had not been this smoking gun, the awarding of punitive
damages would have been highly unlikely.

Our research has found that females were more likely than males to be
victimized by extreme breaches of fiduciary duty in medical malpractice actions. In *Austin v. Methodist Hospital, Inc.*,[155] a hospital released confidential
medical records showing that the plaintiff had given birth out of wedlock.
This outrageous invasion of her privacy caused the plaintiff to suffer gastri-
tis, intestinal difficulties, humiliation, and psychological pain.

In *Banks v. Charter Hospital of Long Beach*,[156] a twenty-one-year-old female received punitive damages for having suffered severe emotional pain
when her name and photograph appeared in an advertising brochure for the
hospital's substance-abuse treatment unit. The injury in this case was purely
an infliction of mental distress, involving little or no economic loss as the
law defines these terms. Women are most affected by tort reforms that limit
recovery for non-economic damages in medical malpractice lawsuits.[157]

Since the medical profession is male-dominated, it is not surprising
that some of its worst excesses are perpetuated against females.[158] Two-
thirds of punitive damages verdicts in our study of medical malpractice
cases nationwide between 1963 and 1993 arose out of bad medicine rendered to women.[159]

Two-thirds of the thirty-four punitive damages awards against hospitals were in favor of women, and female plaintiffs also predominated in
the cases alleging sexual abuse by a health care provider. These verdicts
cluster around specialties related to women's distinctive biological, de-
mographic, and social characteristics.

Female plaintiffs predominated in every age category for punitive damages awarded in medical malpractice from 1963 to 1993. Neglect and abandonment in nursing homes disproportionately injure elderly women because they live longer than men; twenty of the thirty-one punitive damages verdicts against nursing homes were awarded to female residents. Gender differentials were also pronounced among plaintiffs between thirteen and thirty-five years of age. Grossly substandard acid peels, tummy tucks, breast implants, and other cosmetic surgical procedures victimized women in this age group. Delays in performing caesarian sections, which resulted in brain-damaged infants, also disproportionately affected women in the years of greatest fertility. Our study uncovered sixteen punitive damages awards against gynecologists or obstetricians.

Non-economic damages are the principal source of compensation for reproductive injuries and miscarriages—intangible injuries that cannot be measured in terms of lost wages or imputed earnings. In contrast, more than 70 percent of the male plaintiffs receiving punitive damages suffered total disability (at least temporarily) or death from bad medicine. Male injuries typically involve substantial economic damages, while many of the females suffered no severe physical injury. More than three in four medical malpractice punitive damages verdicts based upon purely psychological injuries were awarded to female plaintiffs. Emotional injuries are the most likely to be remedied through non-economic damages, since there are often few direct economic losses.

Medical malpractice verdicts in favor of the women in our sample were almost three times more likely to include a pain-and-suffering component than those awarded to men. This finding is consistent with past research showing that male victims receive more in economic damages but less in non-economic damages than do their female counterparts.[160] The typical pain-and-suffering verdict awarded to a female in our sample was twice as large as that given to a male. The median pain-and-suffering award for the ninety-six women who received punitive damages was exactly $100,000, while the median for the thirty-three men was $50,000. This disparity suggests that tort law revisions that limit non-economic damages will adversely affect more women than men.

The explanation for the disproportionate number of non-economic damage awards for women lies in the gendered nature of injuries. Nearly nine out of every ten victims of sexual abuse by medical providers were female.[161] The only compensable injury in most of these sexual abuse cases was emotional pain and suffering. While not constituting a readily computable economic loss, such pain and suffering is real and a significant loss suffered by the victim.

Pain and suffering, mental anguish, and loss of consortium verdicts are disproportionately awarded to women in order to compensate them for reproductive injuries. The loss of consortium includes "not only the loss of support and services, but also the loss of love, companionship, affection, society, sexual relations and solace."[162] A woman may suffer emotional injury from the prospect of future catastrophic health complications resulting from defective medical products. Awards for the emotional distress caused by the fear of possible future disability from breast implants or permanent disfigurement from the removal of implants typically include little in economic damages.

Uncapped non-economic damages awards, like punitive damages, will frequently be the difference between obtaining legal representation and being denied a day in court. Non-economic damages are a critically important incentive in nursing home lawsuits because "life expectancy" and "work life" tables minimize the economic value of elderly residents' lives and well-being. Because they are elderly, "nursing home residents have little value in cold monetary terms."[163] Defining a person's "worth" solely by his or her earning potential is clearly unjust.

In one psychiatric sexual exploitation case, the plaintiff's attorney stated that his client suffered post-traumatic stress disorder from the therapist having sexual relations with her.[164] Although it was projected that she would need several additional years of therapy, the severity of her economic injury was hard to judge since, at the time of trial, she had not suffered any loss of income. In fact, she had achieved much greater professional success since the incident in question. It was only the prospect of non-economic and punitive damages that provided sufficient incentive to bring suit in "the first case of a patient against a therapist tried in North Carolina."[165] These landmark cases are critical in order to vindicate the rights of women and to send a message to institutions or individuals that are tempted to abuse their authority or economic power.

§3.9. Conclusion

Only since World War II has the law redressed mental injuries, prenatal injuries, and reproductive injuries in her world of tort recovery. Tort reform would reduce or eliminate remedies for many gender-based injuries because of limitations on non-economic damages, joint liability, and punitive damages. Without a clear understanding of the gendered nature of tort remedies, women's voices are unlikely to be heard above the din of corporate stakeholders.

Tort reform is diverting the path of law from the direction of liability toward that of immunity and irresponsibility. As we show in Chapter 4, punitive damages awards are becoming increasingly necessary to counter impermissible cost–benefit calculations made by managed care bureaucrats. The rise of the health maintenance organization (HMO) has created new forms of patient abuse, which must be controlled by powerful tort remedies.

4

In Defense of Patients' Rights

§4.1. Introduction

In the 1997 movie *As Good As It Gets*, Melvin Udall (played by Jack Nicholson) is an obsessive-compulsive novelist. Carol Connelly (Helen Hunt) is a waitress at a diner. One of the principal themes of the movie is Carol's ongoing struggle with her Health Maintenance Organization (HMO) over treatment for her son. Melvin's obsessive-compulsive routine of eating the same meal at the same table, served by Carol, is interrupted when her son, Spencer, is unable to receive adequate medical treatment for his chronic lung disorder because the HMO has denied him a referral to a specialist. Melvin ends up paying for Spencer's private respiratory therapy so that Carol can return to work.[1]

This movie is unrealistic because it ends happily when a wealthy benefactor provides an alternative to the HMO. Many Americans fear that they will be denied crucial treatment because the HMO's accountant will override their physician's best judgment, trading health for wealth.[2] Fifty-five percent of HMO members are at least somewhat convinced that if they were sick their "health plans would be more concerned about saving money than about what is the best medical treatment."[3] HMO members want expanded rights to seek specialists outside of the network and the right to "sue their health plans for denials of care."[4]

[A] Why Americans Want a Right to Sue Their HMOs

The era of Dr. Marcus Welby–like independent physicians is coming to a close as individual private practices are being replaced by corporate managed care.[5] "If current trends continue, the number of major parties involved in the health care enterprise will be reduced to only two. The new first party will be the governmental or business purchaser of health care, and the new second party will be the nationwide suppliers of health care—the mega-corporate health care delivery systems."[6]

Managed care represents a wide array of approaches to organizing the delivery of health care.[7] Fifty-one million Americans are currently enrolled in HMOs and another 50.2 million are in Preferred Provider Organizations (PPOs).[8] Two-thirds of insured employees are in managed care plans.[9]

An HMO is efficient because it is an integrated, prepaid health care delivery system.[10] Managed care has its "McDonalds of medicine," including for-profit multi-hospital chains such as Hospital Corporation of America, American Medical International, Humana, Inc., National Medical Enterprises, Charter Medical Corporation, and Republic Health Corporation. Millions of Americans are members of mega-HMOs such as Kaiser Foundation Health Plans, MetLife-Travelers, U.S. Health Care, and Prudential Health Care Plans.

Mergers and the consolidation of hospitals and nursing homes are creating more health care giants. In 1996 alone, there were 196 hospital mergers involving 370 hospitals.[11] Hospital Staffing Services, Inc., provides medical staff for hundreds of hospitals across the nation.[12] This concentration of medical power creates the potential for abuse.

HMOs reduce costs, but not by economizing on their executives' compensation packages. More than two-thirds of HMOs are for-profit organizations.[13] The twenty-five highest paid HMO executives received annual salaries that ranged from $2,104,414 to $29,061,550 in 1996.[14] In addition to these large sums, the average unexercised stock option for each of the twenty-five executives was $13.5 million, for a total of $337.4 million in 1996 alone.[15] The average compensation of a CEO of one of America's 574 HMOs was $3.9 million.[16] If HMOs are truly concerned with costs, "they might look at the amount of HMO premium dollars reallocated from patient care to its well-heeled executives."[17]

Consumer dissatisfaction with managed care is skyrocketing.[18] A class action suit was filed against Kaiser Permanente, the largest HMO, for requiring members to split prescription pills, which results in misdosages.[19] One in two Americans believes that managed care has decreased the quality of medical services.[20] State officials report that "health care complaints have grown 50% over the last one to three years, far faster than HMO enrollment has increased."[21] Only 30 percent of patients in HMOs are satisfied with their ability to choose their own doctor.[22] An October 1998 poll of Indiana residents found that 70 percent agreed that the government should do more to regulate HMOs.[23]

A widely aired HMO advertisement states that the "basic premise of managed care is simple: give members the right care, at the right time and in the right setting."[24] However, many Americans perceive the HMO as actually being indifferent to their well-being[25] Dissatisfaction is endemic to all types of managed care plans, from HMOs to PPOs to point-of-service plans.[26] United Health Group has responded to negative opinion by granting its affiliated doctors final authority on decisions about patient care.[27]

[B] History of Medical Malpractice

Whatever the shortcomings of the HMO, Americans today enjoy far better protection from medical malpractice than in the past. Nineteenth-century doctors operated "with virtual impunity" and were not held accountable even for medical treatment based on "myth, irrationality, and deception."[28] Quacks and "snake oil" salesmen traveled from town to town, touting amazing products that allegedly cured chronic ailments ranging from baldness to heart disease.[29] Prior to the passage of the Food and Drug Act in 1906, "there were approximately 50,000 patent medicines being sold," some of which contained dangerous opiates and cocaine.[30]

Tort verdicts to compensate for medical malpractice were extremely difficult to win in the period before the Civil War. For example, a "doctor in America as late as the 1860s gave a patient a drug to induce contractions, which caused her uterus to rupture." The doctor then "dissected and removed the fetus to save the mother, inadvertently removing some of the woman's intestines."[31] His patient died a few hours later. The doctor offered the dead woman's husband a pittance of $300 in compensation.[32] No one would wish to return to "the good old days" before the rise of medical accountability.

Medical malpractice was a touchy topic with pre–Civil War doctors even though plaintiffs were unlikely to prevail. Physicians expressed dismay at the "alarmingly frequent prosecutions for malpractice," and some doctors even closed their surgical practices because of the threat of malpractice verdicts.[33]

In 1879, the Maine Medical Association attacked "vexatious" lawsuits filed against physicians by "pettifoggers."[34] Medical malpractice litigants were described as the "ignorant and vicious poor who were aided by meddlesome lawyers and doctors; the former for the fees which they may get by pushing the doctor to the settlement of a vexatious affair; the latter to avenge fancied wrongs and gratify a rankling and cankerous jealousy and envy."[35]

Unqualified practitioners and itinerant quacks were rarely charged with criminal malpractice when unorthodox treatments resulted in the death of their patients. A reformer of the period argued that "the quack, the pill vendor, the life-elixir compounders, the panacea concocter . . . may permanently injure health, or even steal the breach from man's nostrils without being charged with misdemeanor or felony."[36] One self-styled doctor "testified that the arterial and venous circulation were on opposite sides of the body."[37]

Punitive damage awards in medical litigation were almost nonexistent before the 1970s. Courts required plaintiffs to prove punitive damages by a standard functionally equivalent to that of criminal manslaughter. Medical malpractice cases in general were rare because of a "conspiracy of silence" in which doctors refused to testify against each other, no matter how substandard the medicine.[38] A dissenting judge in a medical malpractice case observed that "[a]nyone familiar with cases of this character knows the so-called ethical practitioner will not testify on behalf of a plaintiff regardless of the merits of his case. This is largely due to the pressure exerted by medical societies and public liability insurance companies."[39]

Prior to World War II, even the rare punitive damages judgments that were assessed against grossly incompetent practitioners were frequently overturned on appeal.[40] Punitive damages were rarely recovered, even if the patient was killed by substandard medical procedures, because of the difficulty of proving malice.[41] To survive the appeals process, a verdict had to be predicated upon extreme misbehavior. One of the earliest punitive damage awards to be upheld in an American medical malpractice case was an 1882 case in which an attending physician accidentally amputated an infant's penis rather than his umbilical cord.[42] The Texas court rejected the doctor's defense that a neighbor assisting in the birth gave him the "wrong thing to tie," finding that the doctor was criminally indifferent to the welfare of his patient.[43]

[C] Patient's Right to Sue

At present, 125 million Americans cannot sue their managed care organization directly for medical malpractice because the federal Employment Retirement Insurance Security Act (ERISA)[44] preempts tort and contract lawsuits by patients.[45] ERISA immunizes HMOs from lawsuits for medical negligence or the denial of needed medical services. This means that most Americans have no legal remedy if their HMO arbitrarily denies needed treatment.

Corporate medical stakeholders defend the ERISA preemption by asserting that runaway medical liability awards would cause premiums to skyrocket and lead to costly and unnecessary "defensive medicine." Consumer groups, in contrast, argue that expanding the patient's right to sue would increase accountability. In 1998, Congress scuttled a true HMO Patient's Bill of Rights after a well-funded opposition campaign by managed care lobbies.[46] The Business Roundtable paid for television advertisements that claimed that if patients were allowed to sue their insurance plan, they "would swamp the system, drive up costs and deny health care to millions more."[47] Medical insurance lobbyists successfully argued that lawsuits would result in a substantial rise in "insurance costs, effectively swelling the ranks of the uninsured."[48] The greatest fear of HMO executives is that their organizations might be subject to uncapped punitive damages.

The health care debate is characterized by misleading labels. The Republican-sponsored Patient Protection Act, for example, actually was a restrictive bill that precluded lawsuits for an HMO's decision to deny or delay treatment that results in injury or death. The Act also restricted an HMO patient's right of recovery for the cost of services denied and would have precluded the patient from seeking compensatory, non-economic, or punitive damages.[49]

The managed care industry is continuing its "expensive campaign to defeat consumer protection legislation."[50] In 1999, the insurance industry championed the Medical Malpractice Rx Act (HR 2242), which would have further restricted patients' right to recovery by capping non-economic damages at $250,000 and imposing limitations on joint and several liability,[51] periodic payments,[52] and the collateral source rule.

A true patients' bill of rights would permit enrollees to sue their health maintenance organizations in state courts for punitive damages. The HMOs oppose such rights, however, and have banded together to lobby against them. "The American Association of Health Plans, a Washington-based advocacy group representing 1,000 HMOs, believes that the patient's bill of rights would clog up the courts, break the banks of health insurers and benefit only trial lawyers."[53] President George W. Bush has threatened to veto a bill sponsored by Senator Edward Kennedy and John McCain because it would permit patients who were "wrongfully denied treatment to sue for punitive damages of up to $5 million, a figure the president's aides said . . . was far too high."[54]

A few courts have held HMOs liable for malpractice under an ostensible agency theory.[55] In 1999, Aetna U.S. Health Care was assessed a $120 million jury award in California for a provider's denial of essential medical treatment.[56] The supporters of a patient's right to sue HMOs argue for permitting such lawsuits on the grounds that "it [is] only fair for health maintenance organizations and other managed-care companies to be held liable for errors, just like doctors and hospitals."[57]

[D] Malpractice Awards against Individual Physicians

Medical malpractice is a failure to meet generally accepted professional standards of medical practice that causes injury to a plaintiff. Medical malpractice claims are based upon diverse grounds, including misdiagnosis, failure of diagnosis, delay of treatment, incompetent surgical procedures, nursing home neglect, failure to obtain informed consent, and allowing untrained personnel to treat patients. Until about fifty years ago, a locality rule was applied that held that it was unfair to compare the country doctor to "sophisticated doctors practicing in large urban centers."[58] Now, however, physicians are held to a more national standard, being expected to have the same knowledge and skills of other medical specialists.[59]

Tort reformers have placed heavy burdens in the path of plaintiffs seeking a medical malpractice recovery. In Massachusetts, for example, an injured plaintiff may not even file a medical malpractice case unless an arbitration tribunal consisting of a judge, a physician, and an attorney find a sufficient basis for a claim.[60] No punitive damages or prejudgment interest may be recovered against a medical provider that is classified as a government agency or entity.[61] Massachusetts limits the total recovery for non-economic damages in cases where there is no permanent disability.[62]

All but a few states have enacted restrictive tort reform laws.[63] These state statutes were enacted as a response to a punitive damages crisis that never existed. Punitive damages awards have also been extremely rare or nonexistent in all jurisdictions. Eleven states did not have a single punitive damages verdict in a medical malpractice case over a thirty-year period between 1963 and 1993, and nineteen states had three or fewer punitive damage awards in the same period.[64] Punitive damages are generally reserved for truly shocking cases of lethal medicine.[65] To recover punitive damages in most jurisdictions, the plaintiff must prove conduct roughly analogous to criminal manslaughter or reckless disregard of patient welfare.

A punitive damages award was assessed against Dr. Glenn C. Millar, who practiced medicine as an obstetrician and gynecologist in Sierra Vista Hospital in Martinez, California. Dr. Millar married Debbie Crandall, a woman twenty-seven years his junior, but the couple was not happy. When Mrs. Crandall-Millar checked into the Sierra Vista Hospital for a hysterectomy in September 1983, Dr. Millar's colleague, Dr. Tatreau, performed the surgery.[66] Dr. Millar, then estranged from his wife, secretly arranged to assist with the surgery and was charged with deliberately sewing his wife's vagina shut in retaliation for a suspected extramarital affair.

Mrs. Millar sued Dr. Millar, Dr. Tatreau, and Sierra Vista Hospital jointly and severally for medical malpractice. Dr. Millar denied deliberately injuring his estranged wife, but the surgeon performing the subsequent corrective surgery testified that the damage to Mrs. Millar's vagina could not have resulted from mere negligence. Mrs. Millar testified that her husband told her: "I've fixed it so you'll never screw around on me again."[67] An attending nurse confirmed this testimony, stating that Dr. Millar boasted about the damage that he had caused to his wife's vagina.[68]

A jury in Fresno, California, awarded Debbie Crandall-Millar $1 million for pain and suffering and $5 million in punitive damages. She has since remarried and had reconstructive surgery, which did not lead to a complete recovery. "She can have sex, but it hurts her a lot."[69] California's Board of Medical Quality Control placed Dr. Glenn Millar on probation for sixty months for negligent medical care. The Board based its disciplinary action solely on the doctor's failure "to inform the patient she had sustained a bladder injury during surgery."[70]

Another example of outrageous medical misconduct was the case of Dr. E. Philip Nuernberger, who administered biofeedback therapy to a young female patient, Barbara Marston, who suffered from chronic headaches. In one of the first treatment sessions, Dr. Nuernberger asked Marston to lie down in deep relaxation and then reached over and kissed her. He told her that this was the kiss that "sealed" the trust between them. During their fourth session, he again kissed her and asked, "That's not so bad is it?" He next administered a neck and shoulder massage, unbuttoned her blouse, and engaged in heavy petting with her. Marston reported the actions of Dr. Nuernberger to the Minneapolis clinic where he was employed and filed a lawsuit.

In a consolidated case, Dr. Nuernberger caressed and kissed Nancy Williams while she was in therapy. He urged Williams to move out of her parents' home and get her own apartment so that he could conduct nude body massages and other intimate "therapy." He told her that she was his favorite patient and that he would see her anytime, even if she could no longer afford to pay his usual hourly rate. Williams testified that she requested Dr. Nuernberger to cease his sexual advances and that she was severely depressed and chemically dependent during this period. A Minnesota jury found this deceitful physician guilty of malice and in violation of the rules of the medical profession, which forbid sexual activity with patients under any circumstances.[71] The Minnesota Supreme Court upheld the $50,000 punitive damages award against Dr. Nuernberger, finding that he had fraudulently committed sexual assaults on his patients under the guise of treatment.[72]

Dr. John Nork performed at least thirty-seven unnecessary back operations to finance his drug habit.[73] This physician was practicing at the local Veteran's Administration Hospital despite the fact that twenty-five medical malpractice lawsuits were pending against him.[74] He admitted in court that he had been addicted to "uppers and downers" and that he had performed negligent surgery,[75] including an unnecessary laminectomy that caused a patient to suffer partial paralysis. Dr. Nork was assessed punitive damages for his grossly negligent surgeries, coupled with his fraudulent misrepresentations.[76]

In a bizarre Texas case, the sexual abuse of a child led to punitive damages against two physicians and the medical clinic where they practiced.[77] The child's father, who was involved in a homosexual relationship with his family doctor, forced his three-year-old son to engage in numerous sexual acts with the physician under the charade of medical treatment. The child also watched while his father and the doctor engaged in sexual conduct. The father allowed his son to be sexually exploited each week for several years in order to secure the physician's favorable testimony in an upcoming workers' compensation trial. The twin brother of the abusive doctor was also found liable because he failed to stop the sexual abuse of the child, which he knew was occurring at their clinic.

The child suffered physical pain as well as severe emotional injuries that required hospitalization and long-term therapy. A Texas jury assessed $5 million in punitive damages jointly and severally against the medical clinic and another $2 million against the abusive physician and his twin brother. Such moral monsters are a vanishing breed because modern managed care facilities have instituted measures to screen out unfit physicians.

[E] Corporate Medical Liability

A hospital's duty is to comply with national standards of care set by accrediting organizations. A managed care facility will also have vicarious liability for the negligence of its physicians.[78] The oversight of health care providers has eliminated many of the substandard or slipshod procedures previously followed in hospitals. Newly devised protocols prevent foreign objects from being left inside of patients during surgery. Nurses, too, have higher standards for record-keeping and patient monitoring as a response to nursing malpractice lawsuits.[79]

Many of these improved practices were the result of "providers' admissions of inadequacy in some aspect of care. Examples include incident reports, medication control systems, bed rails, and identification bracelets. . . . The informed consent procedure has been improved greatly as well, including a written record of the process and more frequent attempts by practitioners to provide their patients with information about procedures, including their potential risks."[80]

Hospitals were first held vicariously liable for the negligence of an affiliated physician in the 1965 case of *Darling v. Charles Memorial Community Hospital*, in which a nurse's failure to test for circulation caused a college football player to have his leg amputated.[81] New protocols for testing for circulation in broken legs were instituted after this case.

Hospitals have enacted new risk-management protocols to reduce the probability of unnecessary surgeries, fraudulent billing practices, anesthesia errors, and post-surgical infections. Many of these improved policies came as the direct result of medical malpractice lawsuits. Hospitals have improved protocols for credential checks after having been assessed punitive damages for hiring grossly incompetent, criminal, or impaired physicians.[82] The Southern California Hospital was the defendant in a lawsuit for failing to "monitor properly and actively and to actively intervene" against Dr. Nork's grossly substandard back surgeries.[83] The California hospital had violated its duty to properly select and regularly renew this physician's visiting privileges. Another health care facility was found liable for failing to investigate the credentials of an affiliated physician who falsely stated that he had privileges at other hospitals. This patently unqualified doctor could not have harmed patients if the hospital had performed even a minimal background check.[84] Extreme cases like this clearly warrant punitive damages.

The debate over punitive damages in medical cases revolves around assertions that these awards are routinely given for minor medical mistakes or for bad outcomes. In the next section, we test these claims with hard empirical data and show that the fears of runaway punitive damages in medical malpractice are unfounded. Even if punitive damages were stricken from the legal landscape, this reform would have little or no impact on overall health care costs. Increased medical bills are the result of increased health care costs by providers, not of excessive litigation. Prescription drug sales alone have accelerated each year since 1993, when sales were $50.6 billion, to 1998 when sales reached $93.4 billion.[85]

§4.2. Empirical Studies of Medical Malpractice Lawsuits

Medical malpractice is defined as liability for health care procedures where the standard of conduct falls below "good medical practice, which is to say, what is customary and usual in the profession."[86] The guidelines of the Joint Commission on the Accreditation of Health Care Organizations are used as benchmarks for determining whether a hospital has met its standard of care. Few topics in health care policy generate more heat, and less light, than punitive damages in medical malpractice.[87]

When President Bill Clinton proposed the National Health Security Act to "ensure individual and family security through health care coverage for all Americans,"[88] the American Medical Association (AMA) complained that the plan failed to cap punitive damages.[89] The "Big Four"—hospitals, doctors, insurance companies, and drug manufacturers—have an army of lobbyists waging an aggressive and well-financed war to deny patients the right to sue managed care organizations for medical negligence or breach of contract. This "medical-industrial complex"[90] has great political influence, consisting as it does of as many as 650 groups that "spent more than $100 million from January 1993 to last March [1994] to influence the outcome of health care legislation, according to a recent study by the Center for Public Integrity, a nonprofit Washington group that examines public issues. There is no issue of public policy in which the sheer strength of those special interests has so overwhelmed the process as in the health care reform debate."[91] The spending has only increased since then.

Despite the hue and cry from the medical-industrial complex, medical malpractice lawsuits are actually filed in only a very small percentage of the instances of actionable medical negligence.[92] Lawsuits against the medical establishment are notoriously difficult for plaintiffs to win.[93]

§4.3. Fact and Fallacy in Medical Malpractice

Our research is the first to provide systematic nationwide data on the quantitative and qualitative dimensions of punitive damages in medical liability cases. The database we constructed includes all punitive damages verdicts resulting from misconduct by doctors, nurses, technicians, hospitals, nursing homes, and every other type of medical provider.[94] The medical-liability verdicts were located through searches of appellate state and federal law reporters, trial verdict reporters, court records, and through interviews with hundreds of practitioners.[95]

The following empirical findings are based on a nationwide sample of verdicts handed down in courts between 1963 and 1993. This data base is more than ten times larger than the next largest empirical study. Our major finding was the sharp discrepancy between how punitive damages in medical liability cases are portrayed by tort reformers and the underlying factual foundations of these awards. Most of the popular beliefs about punitive damages in medical malpractice are simply wrong, as the next section will show.

[A] Research Findings: Fact Replaces Fallacy

[1] FALLACY: Juries Regularly Award Punitive Damages in Medical Malpractice Actions
     FACT: Punitive Damages Have Increased over Time, But from a Minuscule Base, and Punitive Damages Account for Less Than One-Thousandth of One Percent of Health Care Costs

The Health Care Liability Alliance argues that huge medical malpractice awards are up dramatically, which it claims highlights the desperate need for reform of medical liability at the federal level.[96] This assertion is misleading because it ignores the question, Up from what? Contrary to the claim that there are too many punitive verdicts, the data show that punitive damages are awarded in fewer than 5 percent of all successful American medical malpractice cases. We found only 270 punitive

TABLE 1
Punitive Damages Awards in Medical
Malpractice, 1963–93

Year	No. of Awards	% of 30-Year Total
1963–73	8	3%
1974–78	16	6%
1979–83	37	14%
1984–88	93	34%
1989–93	111	41%

damages awards in medical malpractice cases nationwide over a thirty-year period of 1963–1993.

As Table 1 shows, the number of punitive damages awards in medical malpractice has been steadily increasing since the 1960s, but from an extremely low base. The rising number of awards in recent years is the result of the expansion of managed care. Over the thirty-year period, liability has shifted from individual physicians to health care organizations.

Punitive damages were almost never awarded in medical malpractice verdicts prior to the early 1960s. In the first decade of medical liability awards, between 1963 and 1973, the typical defendant was an individual physician in a for-fee services setting rather than a corporate entity, and 70 percent punitive damages awards during this period were against individual doctors. By the late 1980s, health care corporations were primary defendants in two-thirds of the verdicts. This shift reflects the fact that most Americans are now enrolled in managed care organizations and that punitive damages are an important weapon against impermissible cost cutting by health care bureaucracies.

In medical malpractice litigation, there are definite punitive damages hot spots and cold spots. The Southern Atlantic states led the nation with nearly a quarter of the punitive damage verdicts, while New England accounted for only 3 percent of the awards. Five states accounted for almost half of the total punitive damages verdicts nationwide: Texas (35), California (35), Alabama (30), Georgia (17), and Florida (14). Eleven states did not have a single punitive damages verdict in medical malpractice over the entire thirty years. Nineteen additional states had three or fewer punitive awards from 1963 to 1993.[97] Even the hot-bed jurisdictions are relatively chilly, averaging only about one punitive damage award per year. If a litigation crisis exists, it is definitely not due to punitive damages in medical malpractice.

Medical malpractice cases are very difficult to win, so it should not be surprising that punitive damages are so rare. New York plaintiffs in medical malpractice cases had a success rate that ranged from a high of 40 percent to a low of only 30 percent from 1988 to 1997.[98] Punitive damages are awarded in less than 1 percent of all medical malpractice verdicts. In 1988, the most active year for medical malpractice punitive damage awards, there were only thirty-three punitive verdicts nationwide.

The Health Care Financing Administration (HCFA) estimates that the nation's total health care bill for medical expenditures was more than $176.5 billion in fiscal year 1998.[99] Health care costs have increased by an average of $7 billion per month during the 1990s. All medical liability combined accounts for about 1 percent of national health care expenditures.[100]

[2] FALLACY: Multimillion-Dollar Punitive Damages Awards in Medical Malpractice Are Awarded for Trivial Injuries
FACT: Punitive Damages Awards Are Reasonably Proportional to Actual Damages in Medical Malpractice Awards

In the rare instance when punitive damages are awarded, the amount is typically modest and proportional to actual damages.[101] Median punitive damages awards in medical malpractice cases were only slightly higher than actual damages.[102] Less than one-fourth of the punitive awards were in excess of $1 million; only 4 percent of the verdicts were $10 million or greater. A total of less than $5.6 billion in punitive damages has been awarded against health providers in three decades, less than the nationwide increase of total health care costs in a typical month. The reality of punitive damages is that there is no tort wheel of fortune.[103]

[3] FALLACY: Judicial Controls over Punitive Damages in Medical Malpractice Are Lax
FACT: Judges Frequently Vacate, Remit, or Reverse Punitive Damages Awards

Media accounts of the few large punitive damages verdicts are misleading because they highlight the large sums awarded at trial, but rarely report post-trial reversals or reductions. Many awards are never collected because of judicial reversals, post-trial settlements, or the insolvency of the defendant physician.[104] Only 42 percent of punitive damages verdicts survived the appeals process intact. Even some of the most egregious cases were reversed or remitted by appellate courts. In Alabama, for example, a punitive damages award against a mental hospital for the reckless release of a homicidal maniac who "scalped his victim to the ears"[105] was overturned on appeal. The typical victim of medical malpractice receives a net recovery "in the range of 39 to 44 cents on the [original verdict] dollar."[106]

Most states have enacted tort reforms "reducing awards to plaintiffs, limiting frequency of claims, or raising procedural barriers affecting potential malpractice plaintiffs."[107] Jurors are never informed that the awards they give may be automatically scaled back because the amounts exceed their state's cap. The Fourth Circuit U.S. Court of Appeals, for example, upheld the reduction of a $1,850,000 verdict to $750,000 in a wrongful death case in order to comply with Virginia's cap on recovery in medical malpractice actions.[108] In a Texas case, the trial court reduced a punitive damages verdict from $950,000 to $200,000 so that the award would comply with that state's cap on punitive damages.[109] The 1995 round of Texas tort reforms, instituted under the leadership of Governor George W. Bush, limits punitive damages awards to two times compensatory damages in all tort verdicts.

Punitive damages were assessed against an Idaho hospital when a patient died after having his oxygen supply disconnected so that he could be conveniently wheeled to another room. The two attending nurses did not want to take the additional time to hook him up to a portable oxygen unit. The decedent's wife and daughter testified that they warned the nurses "not to do it that way."[110] The hospital's defense was that the nurses' actions were consistent with a hospital-wide policy of moving patients from room to room without oxygen. Hospital employees testified that the patient would have soon died from his lung disease anyway. The plaintiff's counsel noted that "the jury was very put out about this attitude and awarded $180,000 in punitive damages against Twin Falls Clinic and another $300 against the nurse who was in charge." When the punitive damages award was reversed on appeal,[111] the attorney observed that "appellate courts do not like punitive damages. . . . I'll think twice before I ask for punitive damages again in a medical malpractice case."[112] Plaintiffs will frequently trade away the punitive damages portion of the award in a settlement because courts are so active in striking down these awards.

Punitive damages were a bargaining chip in settlement negotiations in *Menaugh v. Resler Optometry*.[113] In *Menaugh*, a twenty-seven-year-old court reporter was injured by an optometrist's gross negligence in permitting his unlicensed son to fit her with extended-wear contact lenses. The optometrist's son falsely claimed that he was licensed to practice optometry. In fact, the young man had no formal training in the safe use or care of contact lenses. The son gave the woman inaccurate instructions on how to store and clean her extended-wear lenses, which led to the development of a painful corneal ulcer. The victim was awarded $150,000, including $25,000 in punitive damages. After the Missouri appellate court reversed the punitive damages, the case settled for $65,000.[114] In our sample, 42 percent of the punitive damages verdicts reviewed posttrial were reduced or reversed.

[4] FALLACY: *Hospitals Face the Problem of Overkill from Multiple Punitive Damages Awards*
FACT: *Very Few Defendants Are Assessed Multiple Punitive Damages*

Overkill may make good newspaper headlines or a good law school hypothetical, but it is not a real issue in medical malpractice litigation. The issue of "overkill" is of long-standing concern in the field of products liability. Mass torts such as the asbestos, tobacco, and handgun litigations have the potential for multiple punitive damages verdicts arising out of the same course of wrongdoing. In *Roginsky v. Richardson-Merrell, Inc.*,[115] Judge Henry Friendly feared that companies could be destroyed by "multiple punitive awards running into the hundreds."[116] Judge Friendly had "the gravest difficulty in perceiving how claims for punitive damages in such a multiplicity of actions throughout the nation can be so administered as to avoid overkill."[117]

A tort reform advocate testified as follows in favor of restricting multiple punitive damages in medical malpractice litigation:

> In the context of medical liability reform, some defendants may be charged with a multiplicity of punitive damage claims for what is, in essence, one act or course of conduct, e.g., a hospital is negligent in maintaining a doctor, or a health care provider is negligent in having the doctor on a recommended list. It would be sound social policy to address this problem—it can only be addressed at the federal level. Multiple imposition of punitive damages can put a hospital out of business before some injured people receive compensatory awards. There should be reasonable limits on the multiple imposition of punitive damages for what is the same or similar conduct.[118]

Underkill is the real concern because plaintiffs so rarely receive punitive damages against physicians even where there is extreme negligence.

Dr. Nork had at least twenty-five pending malpractice claims against him in the early 1970s for unnecessary and incompetently performed back surgeries. Despite clear evidence that he endangered the health and safety of hundreds of patients, he was assessed punitive damages only twice.[119] More than twenty cases were filed against an Oklahoma osteopath who caused untold suffering with numerous incompetent back surgeries,[120] but only two punitive damages awards were imposed. No hospital, clinic, or managed care organization has been driven out of business due to multiple punitive damages for the same course of conduct.

[5] FALLACY: *Punitive Damages Awards Have a Negative Social Impact* FACT: *Punitive Damages Litigation Has Resulted in Improved Medical Practices*

The American Medical Association (AMA) argues that tort liability needlessly drives up the cost of medical care. Numerous anecdotal reports suggest that doctors are leaving litigation-prone specialties such as obstetrics due to medical malpractice concerns. The hidden face of medical malpractice is that legal accountability has improved American health care. An estimated 36 million Americans are treated by incompetent physicians each year.[121] The tort system gives plaintiffs the opportunity to expose wrongdoing by acting as private attorneys general.[122]

Our study revealed a large number of cases in which safety measures were instituted after a successful tort verdict. A hospital in Springfield, Massachusetts, initiated a sponge-count and surgical instruments inventory after a tort verdict in favor of a fifty-nine-year-old patient who had a nine-inch forceps inadvertently left inside his chest after heart surgery.[123] The U.S. Air Force instituted a foreign-object protocol after a doctor forgot to remove an eleven-inch ribbon from an officer's abdomen following gall bladder surgery.[124]

The standard protocol for diagnosing the source of chest pain associated with heart attacks has dramatically improved at certain hospitals since the resolution of lawsuits in the late 1980s.[125] A number of victims of heart disorders sued a U.S. Air Force Hospital for negligent diagnoses occurring in the emergency room. Patients were misdiagnosed as suffering from indigestion despite displaying symptoms of heart attacks, including obvious chest pain, nausea, sweating, and severe radiating pain into the neck, arm, and jaw. Two military personnel suffered fatal coronary infarctions within days of their hospital release because of this misdiagnosis. A third patient died from a heart attack weeks later after being misdiagnosed by the same faulty procedure. Stringent requirements for diagnostic testing in coronary cases were introduced at all Air Force medical facilities worldwide in the wake of a lawsuit.

Nursing homes have adopted numerous safety measures as a response to tort litigation. After a large punitive damages verdict resulting from the case of an Alzheimer's patient who drowned while left unattended in a bathtub, an entire nursing home chain adopted a revised protocol for supervising vulnerable elderly patients. The improved protocol based the degree of supervision required on the patient's physical and mental condition. In another nursing home case, a patient died as a result of substandard care due to inaccurate records. The punitive damages award was the spur that led to improving staff training programs and correcting many violations of California's safety code.[126]

A patient suffered massive brain damage from a misplaced catheter in another case. To avoid further litigation, new protocols were implemented to ensure that catheters are properly placed.[127] A psychiatric hospital was assessed punitive damages for failing to monitor a suicidal patient. A new protocol for suicide watches was adopted after a punitive damages verdict.[128]

Tort damages provide a wake-up call to medical providers to change their practices or face the consequences. Hospitals are learning to avoid liability by error-proofing their practices and procedures.[129] Sometimes it takes tragic cases and litigation to "overhaul equipment and policies."[130] The Franciscan Children's Hospital in Boston developed "revised procedures for handling drug overdoses" after the "death of a two-and-a-half-year-old who slowly suffocated after her breathing tube became disconnected."[131] Our study provides evidence that hospitals are enacting failsafe measures partially as a response to litigation.

Restricting patient's rights though tort reform has not lowered medical bills. Indiana's 1975 Medical Malpractice Reform Act capped all damages at $500,000 and eliminated punitive damages to lower malpractice outlays. Yet, the mean payment for larger malpractice claims turned out to be substantially higher than in neighboring states that did not have these restrictions. Mean and median payments in Indiana were 18 and 42 percent higher than in Michigan and Ohio, respectively—states that did not cap damages.[132]

An empirical study of Texas insurance rates concluded that the promised savings from tort reforms have not materialized.[133] Caps on medical damages have had little or no impact on insurance rates and primarily limit the awards of the most severely injured plaintiffs. On the other hand, tort reforms have already had unanticipated negative consequences.

The Government Accounting Office (GAO) studied medical malpractice verdicts handed down in the mid-1980s in Arkansas, California, Florida, Indiana, New York, and North Carolina. The GAO found that after tort reforms were instituted, every state experienced increases in the number of claims, the amount of payment per claim, and insurance premiums.[134]

The Office of Technology Assessment (OTA) found little evidence that preventive law significantly raises the cost of medical treatment.[135] The OTA concluded that tort reform probably would have a negligible impact on defensive medicine:

> Traditional tort reforms—particularly caps on damages and amendments to the "collateral source" rule—reduce malpractice insurance premiums, but their effects on defensive medicine are largely unknown and are likely to be small. To the extent that these reforms do reduce defensive medicine, they do so without differentiating between defensive practices that are medically appropriate and those that are wasteful or very costly in relation to their benefits.[136]

[6] FALLACY: *Doctors Are Victimized by Malcontent Patients Who File Frivolous Lawsuits* FACT: *Unfit Physicians and, Increasingly, Cost-Cutting HMOs Victimize Patients*

Juries are often portrayed as irrationally generous, routinely handing out millions of dollars to plaintiffs suffering from only minor harm.[137] The presumed rising tide of tort damages is attributed to the belief that lawsuits are a way for greedy plaintiffs to pick the deep pockets of corporations. In fact, medical malpractice verdicts are rare even when there is clear and convincing evidence of negligence. An estimated 1 out of 156 surgeries involves a significant mishap, but these mistakes rarely lead to medical malpractice claims.[138]

By no stretch of the imagination could the cases we studied be called frivolous. The typical victim of medical malpractice in our study died or was permanently disabled as the result of reckless misconduct. All too often, the medical wrongdoing that led to punitive damages was indistinguishable from the legal standard for criminal manslaughter.

The lack of proper medical treatment at an unlicensed alcohol treatment center led to a manslaughter conviction in addition to a punitive damages award in one recent case. A patient died after repeatedly being bound, gagged, and force-fed liquor as part of a crackpot version of aversive therapy. The staff at the clinic attempted to conceal the death by dragging the patient's body outside and sitting him in a chair next to a pay phone "to make it look like he walked up there and died."[139] In another case, an infant died because of a doctor's failure to perform a caesarean section despite electronic monitors showing fetal distress for a three-hour period. The infant died shortly after delivery, a result preordained by the physician's failure to observe that the fetus was in danger.[140]

One in four plaintiffs in our study suffered a permanent disability as a result of medical malpractice. Fourteen of these plaintiffs suffered irreversible brain damage. A thirty-five-year-old salesman entered a hospital for a tonsillectomy and died after suffering from hypoxic brain damage due to a negligent medical procedure. The improper administration of the anesthetic caused the patient to lapse into a coma.[141] Twenty-four percent of the cases involved plaintiffs who suffered severe emotional trauma arising out of medical mishaps, such as the forty-five-year-old man who suffered impotency because of the hospital's unsafe use of a re-sterilized disposable arterial catheter that broke off during an angiography.[142]

The failure of physicians to follow standard practice guidelines accounted for 29 percent of the punitive damages verdicts. As part of a routine diagnostic test, a Massachusetts hospital medical team was injecting a colorless and odorless dye into a patient's artery. No one on the medical staff checked to see if the dye was loaded into the injector. When the physician pushed the button to administer the dye, air was injected, causing an embolism. The bubble of air quickly traveled to the patient's brain and he died instantly: "Before and during the procedure, the staff was gossiping and talking about who had an affair over the prior holiday weekend. The nurse, who was supposed to make sure that the proper procedure was followed, saw bubbles coming out of the tube at the connection closest to the power injector. . . . She assumed that this meant that the dye had been loaded into the injector. . . . The empty bottle from the previous procedure was still in the injector . . . The hospital imposed strict protocols about the procedure after this case."[143]

In a nursing malpractice case, punitive damages were assessed against a nurse who improperly injected steroids into a patient's arm instead of the buttocks, causing the patient to suffer excruciating pain and permanent disability.[144] Punitive damages are only awarded if there is such an entire lack of care to raise a presumption that the medical provider is indifferent to the danger of injury to the patient.[145]

Many of the punitive damages awards stemmed from gross surgical errors amounting to recklessness or wanton misconduct. A podiatrist's misplaced incision resulted in excruciating pain and permanent disability to the plaintiff in *Strauss v. Biggs*.[146] The podiatrist had a high-volume practice with many elderly patients. This assembly-line medicine was evidenced by the fact that the defendant performed the surgery in his office at 1 A.M. with a waiting room full of elderly patients. Punitive damages were also based upon substandard surgical technique. The physician's "misplaced incision was far away from where it needed to be."[147] Doctors who were guilty of serial medical negligence were by far the most likely to be assessed punitive damages. A fifty-three-year-old man suffered an above-the-knee amputation of his right leg caused by an infection after an aortic graft. Punitive damages against the hospital were based upon evidence that it was aware of the surgeon's incompetence and knew that he was the subject of several malpractice lawsuits, but took no action.[148] A pharmacy with a long history of misfiling and mislabeling prescription drugs was assessed punitive damages when another mistake caused a plaintiff to suffer severe ulcers and bleeding.[149]

"Traditionally, a claim of lack of informed consent focuses on disclosures regarding treatment or surgery, the risks and the alternatives."[150] As the court in *Canterbury v. Spence*[151] stated, "every human being . . . of adult years and sound mind has the right to determine what shall be done with his own body." Ten percent of the cases we studied involved extreme violations of informed consent. In *Wong v. Garcia-Lavin*,[152] an unlicensed and inexperienced cosmetic surgeon failed to warn the plaintiff of the known risks of a face-lift procedure.[153] The plaintiff suffered facial scarring and deformed lower eyelids from the botched procedure.

Punitive damages were imposed on medical providers who participated in "ghost surgery," where unqualified personnel replace the scheduled physician. Such was the case of a breast reduction performed in *Vitali v. Bartell*.[154] The plaintiff was scheduled for a breast-reduction mammoplasty with Dr. Bartell, a board-certified cosmetic surgeon, but instead, a less qualified surgeon performed the procedure with poor results.

The abandonment or neglect of patients was an aggravating circumstance in 16 percent of the cases in our study. Abandonment occurs when a physician leaves a helpless patient in a position of peril in settings that range from nurseries to nursing homes. The neglect in nursing homes frequently rises to the level of abandonment. In many of the cases, over-worked nurse's aides failed to provide adequate supervision.

A million-dollar punitive damages award punished a nursing home that hired an uncertified and unqualified assistant who then assaulted a ninety-seven-year-old resident. The decedent suffered a swollen jaw and severe bruising and died shortly after the attack.[155] In another nursing home case, an Alzheimer's patient slipped, fell, and subsequently drowned in a bathtub because of faulty supervision.[156] After a punitive damages award was im-posed, the defendant nursing home installed safety strips in bathtubs and instituted closer supervision of its elderly patients.[157] The adverse media publicity from the case led to the passage of a Florida statute to protect the health and safety of nursing home patients.[158]

Sexual abuse of patients by medical providers led to punitive damages in 13 percent of the cases, while sexual abuse by doctors accounted for about 2 percent of the offenses for which disciplinary sanctions were imposed by medical boards in 1989.[159] At least 140 of a California gynecologist's pa-tients charged him with sexual abuse before the medical authorities finally revoked his license to practice.[160] Nearly half of all malpractice insurance claims that were paid on behalf of psychiatrists and psychologists resulted from sanctionable psychotherapist–patient sexual contact.[161] Self-reported survey data reveal that "six to thirteen percent of psychotherapists admit to having had sexual contact with their patients."[162]

Courts have increasingly held that a physician occupies a position˙ of trust and confidence.[163] This fiduciary relationship results, in part, from a patient's need to share potentially embarrassing or damaging information with his or her physician.[164] Sexual relations are a *prima facie* violation of the fiduciary relationship between a doctor and patient. The intensity of the therapeutic relationship "may tend to activate sexual and other needs and fantasies on the part of both patient and therapist, while weakening the ob-jectivity necessary for control."[165] Psychiatrists who make sexual contact a part of the treatment for a patient are abusing transference.[166]

Inappropriate sexual contact was a factor in punitive damages handed down against a psychiatrist who entered into a sexual relationship with his sixteen-year-old patient.[167] A Texas jury punished a physician for seducing a fashion model patient who was being treated for sagging breasts.[168] In many of these cases, the physician overprescribes or misprescribes drugs to facilitate the sexual exploitation of his patient.

The victims of sexual abuse by a medical provider frequently suffer from extreme emotional distress requiring long-term therapy. A thirty-five-year-old woman suffered post-traumatic stress disorder, feelings of distrust for therapists, and severe emotional distress following episodes of sexual abuse by her therapist. She originally sought help from her therapist to treat her inability to establish normal relationships with men. Following one therapy session, the plaintiff and her therapist engaged in sexual intercourse. Her sexual encounters continued as she sought therapy from a colleague of her lover.[169]

The plaintiff sued her ex-therapist, arguing that he was professionally negligent for failing to manage transference and countertransference.[170] The defense counsel portrayed this case as "sex for money" or prostitution in his closing statement.[171] The plaintiff received a $100,000 punitive damages award based upon evidence that the counselor had illicit sexual encounters with three other patients.[172] The therapist was not licensed by any regulatory body and quit before his employer could fire him.[173]

In 8 percent of our cases, physician fraud led to punitive damages awards. Unnecessary surgeries to enhance the physician's income were the most prevalent example of this variety of fraud.[174] The plaintiff in a "dental assembly line" case underwent twenty unnecessary root canal procedures,[175] and was one of 135 victims suing the same dentist for similar misbehavior. The profit-hungry dentist ground teeth nearly to the gum line as a "short cut," and had claimed that his mass-market root canal procedure was a sound preventive measure. His self-serving reasoning was that the teeth might need a root canal procedure some time in the future, so why not perform prophylactic root canals now? The jury's punitive damages award was based upon testimony that the dentist was acting out of greed rather than his patients' welfare.[176] Two dental school professors testified that these so-called "prophylactic" root canal procedures were unnecessary, poorly performed, and would cause serious dental difficulties in the future.

Alteration of medical records or spoliation of evidence to cover up misdeeds was the primary aggravating circumstance in twenty punitive damages verdicts. Concealment of medical negligence coupled with neglect led to punitive damages against a California surgeon accused of substandard surgery. Stephanie Kinzel, a forty-one-year-old manager in Los Angeles, was experiencing chronic pain in her knees and was treated by Dr. Messieh.[177] Dr. Messieh and a colleague performed Mrs. Kinzel's knee operation at Los Angeles Doctors' Hospital. During the surgery, one of the doctors accidentally punctured the posterior capsule, nearly severing an artery in her leg. Mrs. Kinzel showed no palpable pedal pulse, yet the surgeons went into the waiting room and told the plaintiff's husband: "We nicked a vein, but everything is ok." Dr. Messieh left the hospital and the nurses began calling him, reporting that Mrs. Kinzel's foot was blue and cold, and that there was no pedal pulse. Dr. Messieh did not return to the hospital for several hours, and only then did he consult with a vascular surgeon.

The vascular surgeon recommended an angiogram, but Dr. Messieh refused to approve the procedure. By the time the angiogram was ordered, there was no one at the hospital qualified to administer it. The plaintiff was then transferred to Centinela Hospital, where an angiogram confirmed total blockage of the popliteal artery. Her foot had to be amputated. The jury found Dr. Messieh liable for punitive damages in the sum of $2 million.

Fraudulent concealment was also a predicate to punitive damages in a number of nursing home cases. A seventy-nine-year-old Alzheimer's patient died after being administered fifty times the recommended dosage of Thorazine on three separate occasions in a Kentucky nursing home.[178] Punitive damages were awarded to the plaintiff based upon evidence that nursing home personnel altered the decedent's medical records in an attempt to hide their errors. Falsification of medical records also led to punitive damages in a New York case where the physician concealed his failure to diagnose a case of spinal meningitis.[179]

Fraudulent alteration of medical records also led to punitive damages against a Maryland hospital. Testimony at trial showed that in cases of potential litigation the hospital's routine practice was to "deep-six" pertinent records to obstruct discovery of its negligence. The hospital would remove the records from their normal places of storage and conceal them in a separate filing cabinet by the order of the director of medical records. When litigants made requests for records, most clerks in the medical records department would be unable to locate the pertinent files.[180] These verdicts were the product of extreme deviation from professional standards of care rather than ordinary negligence.

[7] FALLACY: *Criminal and Civil Penalties Frequently Punish Doctors* FACT: *Medical Boards or Criminal Courts Rarely Prosecute the Conduct Leading to Punitive Damages*

The tort system is particularly important because state medical boards have been notoriously ineffective in detecting and punishing incompetent physicians.[181] All too often, tort law is the only line of defense against a physician's reckless misconduct because medical boards routinely fail to revoke the licenses of doctors who chronically commit criminal offenses or engage in grossly substandard medical practices. State medical boards are notoriously lenient in punishing doctors "found guilty of sexual abuse, substandard care, criminal offenses, prescription violations and drug or alcohol abuse."[182] Less than a third of the 1,715 Medicare doctors disciplined at the federal level for fraud were also sanctioned by their respective state's licensing boards.[183] Less than one half of one percent of the nation's doctors face state sanctions.[184]

Government regulators seldom discipline doctors, even when the physicians treat patients with clearly harmful medical techniques. The Texas Board of Dental Examiners only briefly suspended a dentist who performed unnecessary and incompetent root canal procedures on more than one hundred patients.[185]

A rare instance of government prosecution of medical fraud was *United States v. Jacobson*.[186] In *Jacobson*, a fertility doctor used hormone therapy as a means of convincing infertile women that they were experiencing bodily changes due to pregnancy. He falsified pregnancy tests by creating false positives and "managed" their pseudo-pregnancies for months, even administering fake ultrasound tests. He went so far as to take fetal measurements of these phantom babies. As outrageous as this misbehavior was, it was his impregnating of an estimated seventy-five unsuspecting women with his own sperm that led to a five-year prison sentence. Unlike the *Jacobson* case, the questionable doctors in our study were never imprisoned and few ever lost their medical licenses.

The penalties levied by medical boards were generally quite mild compared to the punishment resulting from a punitive damages award. Several defendant physicians voluntarily left the practice of medicine after being assessed punitive damages, perhaps in an attempt to forestall regulatory sanctions. The Board of Medical Quality Control suspended the license of the physician who secretly performed surgery on his former wife.[187] An unqualified doctor in Florida who practiced cosmetic surgery was fined $2,500 for permitting unlicensed persons to perform chemical face-lifts. The Board of Medical Examiners placed a California doctor on probation for engaging in sexual relations with his patient over many years.[188] These cases, however, were rare exceptions.

The multiplicity of state disciplinary boards often allows physicians to reestablish their practices simply by moving across state borders. A podiatrist who had been successfully sued many times surrendered his Delaware license and moved to Pennsylvania, where he was already licensed.[189] Some state medical boards do not report offenses, so there is no way to determine prior misdeeds in other states. Few medical boards take a proactive investigative role in uncovering sexual abuse of patients. The National Practitioner Data Bank requires insurance companies to report all malpractice payments made on behalf of physicians. Although this data bank potentially serves as a "flagging system" to protect against incompetent doctors, it is not accessible to patients.[190] Punitive damages punished and deterred many physicians who were not sanctioned by regulatory bodies.

[8] FALLACY: *Medical Malpractice Liability Does Not Benefit Society*
     FACT: *Punitive Damages Have Evolved to Protect the Most*
     Vulnerable American Patients

As the sections that follow will amply demonstrate, punitive damages in medical malpractice lawsuits serve the interests of health care consumers. Punitive damages provide remedies for the victims of egregious breaches of medical ethics. Medical malpractice vindicates patients' "rights to determine what can be done to their own bodies."[191]

§4.4. *Protecting Economically Disadvantaged Patients*

The potential liability of the HMO for impermissible cost containment has become the subject of a national debate. At its best, the HMO is an efficient institution that renders the finest medical care in the world. The HMO can provide patients with a variety of medical services performed by many specialized professionals and technicians. There is an inherent conflict of interest, however, between corporate cost containment and a hospital's statutory and moral duty to provide emergency health care for the impoverished.[192]

Frequently, economically disadvantaged patients do not belong to an HMO and lack medical insurance, which can leave them without medical care.[193] Punitive damages have been awarded against physicians who discharged patients from a hospital even though they were in desperate need. The earliest reported case of failing to treat disadvantaged patients was a Rhode Island verdict in which the physician discharged a woman with an obstructed bowel despite knowing that her death was a certainty.[194] The physician failed to finish the surgery, making an "unskillful opening into the abdomen and without attempting to do anything to relieve the obstructed bowel, sewed up the wound."[195] Punitive damages were based upon the physician's outrageous act of discharging his patient from the hospital coupled with his bad judgment in failing to complete the required surgery.

The failure of a Texas obstetrical clinic to maintain facilities for performing caesarian sections and its mistreatment of an indigent Mexican patient led to punitive damages.[196] The clinic shipped the patient to another hospital by ambulance, but by the time she arrived, the infant was dead. The second hospital refused to extract the dead fetus and discharged the woman, to be returned to Mexico. Her nightmarish ordeal did not end until her dead fetus was delivered by caesarian section in Mexico several hours later.

In *LeCroy v. Hughes*,[197] a roofer's assistant slid off the roof of a house, fracturing his left wrist, right elbow, and skull. He was taken to a hospital, where the emergency room physician ordered x-rays. The defendant radiologist then interpreted the x-rays and an orthopedist set the fractures. When the injured man returned one week later, he was referred to a charity hospital in town. One hour after his arrival at the charity hospital, he was diagnosed with severe neurological trauma.[198] As a result of the inadequate treatment at the first hospital, the front left lobe of the roofer's brain became necrotic and had to be removed. The physicians were judged negligent in failing to order a CAT scan or to hospitalize the plaintiff for examination.

This patient's lack of medical insurance was the likely cause of his being classified as a "gomer" ("Get Out of My Emergency Room"). The doctor decided not to administer costly neurological tests on purely economic grounds, with total indifference to his patient's welfare. The jury awarded $2 million in punitive damages to the plaintiff based upon the argument that the doctor "dumped" the impoverished patient rather than provide adequate treatment. After paying a $3.4 million settlement, the hospital changed its policy regarding patients without insurance, as well as its policy of failing to refer patients to specialists.[199] Many other cases demonstrate similar gross failures to care adequately for disadvantaged patients.[200] Punitive damages provide the economically powerless with important leverage to ensure that managed care institutions live up to their responsibilities.[201]

§4.5. Punitive Damages to Protect against Elder Abuse

As health care costs increase, there are greater financial incentives to understaff nursing homes. Punitive damages are one of the few remedies available to deter cost cutting at the expense of the welfare of elderly patients. Nursing home patients are in a particularly vulnerable position, unable to help themselves and frequently incapable of communicating clearly.

In one nursing home case, a physician ordered an external catheter placed on a seventy-six-year-old stroke victim. The patient's hands were bound to prevent him from removing the catheter. Because the catheter was so tight, gangrene of the penis developed, necessitating a radical amputation. The man died three weeks later of unrelated causes after enduring much unnecessary suffering. The jury awarded $125,000 in compensatory and $25,000 in punitive damages against the nursing home for its abject failure to monitor and properly care for this vulnerable patient.[202]

Mistreatment of the elderly residents of our nation's nursing homes is already epidemic. Injuries caused by neglect or intentional omission include: "(1) restraint injuries; (2) decubitus ulcers; (3) severe dehydration and malnutrition; (4) exposure to the elements; (4) falls and fractures; and physical abuse and assault."[203] Punitive damages have been imposed in many nursing home cases in recent years for exploiting patients for financial gain.[204] A recent example was a seventy-seven-year-old nursing home resident who suffered gangrene resulting in the amputation of a limb stemming from improper care in a Florida nursing home.[205] In another example of gross and repeated nursing home neglect, a resident suffered the amputation of his foot because an infected heel blister went untreated.

The plaintiff in *Darblay v. Western Medical Enterprises, Inc.*,[206] received punitive damages from ARA Services, Inc., one of the largest convalescent home chains in the United States. Annie Fern Darblay was admitted to Driftwood Convalescent Hospital to recover from hip surgery. Mrs. Darblay was unable to walk without assistance and needed help getting to the bathroom. She repeatedly pushed her call button but there was no response by attendants for fifteen to twenty minutes. When the elderly woman could wait no longer, she fractured her hip attempting to stand on her good leg while trying to reach the bedpan.

The plaintiff sued the convalescent center, charging that it had prior knowledge of inadequate staffing. Evidence was produced establishing conscious disregard of safety:

> Patients left lying in feces and urine for hours; flies on patients' faces and bodies; incontinent patients left lying with catheters exposed; patients left sitting in cold air, partially undressed; patients left lying on torn, wrinkled plastic sheets because there was insufficient linen; patients not being turned as often as required, with decubiti occurring as a result; patients allowed to have dirty hair, long fingernails, long facial hair and dirty teeth; patients left unattended for hours at a time.[207]

Punitive damages were premised upon numerous health and safety violations as well as understaffing.[208] Documentary evidence was uncovered confirming that substandard conditions were tolerated at the nursing home while ARA was reaping huge profits.[209] Eventually, the nursing home lost its license over "shockingly inhumane, unsanitary and unsafe conditions."[210]

A North Carolina court ordered a nursing home chain to pay $15 million, including $7.5 million in punitive damages, for denying a prescribed painkiller to a cancer patient in the last months of his life.[211] A nursing home's failure to turn and properly position a sixty-nine-year-old woman in a diabetic coma resulted in a punitive damages claim in *Clark v. Clearwater Convalescent Center, Inc.*[212] The nursing home's neglect caused infected bedsores, which necessitated the amputation of her leg. In another case, an eighty-nine-year-old woman suffered a hip fracture and later died after she fell out of her bed.[213]

In 1997, a $92 million verdict including punitive damages was awarded to an elderly patient in a Texas nursing home.[214] In that case, a retired police officer died from untreated bedsores, starvation, and dehydration caused by a nursing home's inadequate staffing. Food and water were placed where the patient could not reach them.[215] In many of these cases, the nursing home's failure to provide sufficient medical attention was the result of impermissible cost cutting.

A few states have expanded the role of tort law in punishing and deterring bad nursing homes. Florida enacted a Nursing Home Residents' Bill of Rights, providing patients with the right to recover punitive damages for neglect and substandard medical treatment.[216] Florida nursing home operators have responded by significantly improving their patient care. Nine in ten nursing homes in Florida currently meet or exceed federal standards.[217]

§4.6. Policing Total Institutions

Nursing homes are one of the largest categories of total institutions, that is, places where residents conduct all of their life activities.[218] Mental hospitals, prisons, and homes for the disabled are other examples of total institutions where the residents are in a vulnerable position. As with the nursing home patients, the abuse of mental patients is difficult to detect because patients frequently are not in a position to report wrongdoing. Punitive damages are an important incentive for total institutions to carefully police employees who care for those in a dependent or vulnerable position.

Punitive damages in nursing home cases send a message to the entire industry that shortchanging of patient care will be punished. In a California case, another patient impregnated an institutionalized, mentally disabled woman. The convalescent home was assessed punitive damages for the failure of supervision, improper prenatal care, and the administering of drugs that damaged the fetus.[219]

Punitive damages of $500,000 were awarded to the family of a mentally disabled child who died from complications that developed after a nurse carelessly gave the child a scalding bath.[220] Federal prisoners have been awarded punitive damages when prison officials fail to provide necessary medical treatment or neglect their welfare.[221] In *Doe v. Swift*,[222] a psychologist who sexually assaulted his client, a mentally ill woman in a state psychiatric hospital, was assessed punitive damages.

In *Doe v. Walker*,[223] a thirty-two-year-old female assault victim received punitive damages.[224] The plaintiff testified that a male patient harassed her on her first day in the hospital, but her complaints were ignored. This patient subsequently raped her. The hospital had prior notice that the stalker was potentially dangerous since "the man asked a hospital admissions officer to have sex with him and made sexual remarks to female patients and hospital workers."[225] The plaintiff suffered from post-traumatic stress syndrome.[226] Punitive damages were based "upon the hospital's negligence in allowing the attack to occur and the willful misconduct for the attempts to cover up the incident after it occurred."[227]

The "smoking gun" was a record of anonymous calls to a rape crisis center and evidence of the hospital's unwillingness to cooperate with the sheriff's investigators, as well as an improper in-house physical examination of the plaintiff.[228] The plaintiff testified that "the hospital refused to let her use a telephone and tried to cover up what happened. The hospital administrator on call that night later pleaded guilty to obstructing justice."[229] The hospital's defense against the charge of cover-up was that they were only protecting "the confidentiality of their patients."[230]

This was a complicated and dramatic case. The defense accused the plaintiff of not informing her attorneys that she had been "raped once before the 1982 incident" by her husband, who allegedly put a gun to her head, forcing her to have sexual intercourse with him.[231] During the trial, the plaintiff had several emotional breakdowns on the witness stand, including one incident where she "let out a chilling scream and ran out of the courtroom."[232]

After a two-week-long trial, the jury awarded $450,000 including punitive damages. The defense filed for a mistrial on the grounds that the jury was left with the image of the plaintiff's chilling scream and emotional breakdown on the stand.[233] The hospital and its insurance carrier paid the award and the state's attorney prosecuted the rape case against the patient.[234]

A Massachusetts mental institution's concealment of negligence led to punitive damages in a highly publicized case.[235] A twenty-year-old woman committed suicide by hanging herself while committed to a state mental hospital. The decedent had attempted suicide three times in the preceding month. Despite these danger signs, one-to-one supervision was reduced to fifteen-minute checks.

On the day of her death, the patient suddenly appeared distraught and anxious at a hospital staff meeting. The patient was turned away by medical personnel and hanged herself within an hour.[236] The jury found the defendant grossly negligent and awarded $190,000 against the woman's psychiatrist. A false entry in the records showing an evaluation immediately prior to the decedent's suicide was the "smoking gun" leading to punitive damages.[237] When the total institution violates its fiduciary duty to protect the helpless, it confirms our "worst fears because there but for the grace of God go I."[238]

§4.7. Policing Unregulated Cosmetic Surgery

Americans spent more than $1.7 billion on cosmetic procedures in 1993. This branch of the medical profession uses Madison Avenue advertising techniques to stimulate demand. Women are targeted by hundreds of cosmetic surgery advertisements such as the following: "Hi, I'm Carol. If you'd like to know how cosmetic surgery changed my life, call me."[239] What Carol doesn't tell you is that these procedures are too often performed by unqualified personnel who willingly trade patient safety for profits. The vast majority of grossly substandard cosmetic surgeries were performed on women.

Cosmetic surgery is a poorly regulated multibillion-dollar business.[240] A Congressional Committee report concluded:

> Traditional peer review of cosmetic surgery is virtually nonexistent, since an estimated 95 percent of these procedures are done in doctor's offices outside of hospitals and the protective eye of surgical review boards. Coast to coast these office practices are touted as institutes, or centers, or clinics of cosmetic surgery in the most expansive ads. But in too many cases, we see one doctor in a Spartan surgical setting with a skeleton crew. Too often they lack the most basic life-support systems found in the smallest hospital emergency rooms . . . even normal government and private audit systems are absent since in most instances these surgeries are covered neither by Medicare nor private health insurance.[241]

Many substandard facelifts, liposuctions, and acid peels are performed in non-hospital settings where health care providers are unlicensed and unobserved.[242]

In *Wall v. Noble*,[243] a plastic surgeon seduced his patient, a twenty-four-year-old fashion model.[244] The plaintiff alleged that the cosmetic surgeon was grossly negligent because: (1) the defendant performed breast surgery using substandard techniques; (2) the defendant failed to inform the plaintiff of the risks attendant to breast implant surgery; and (3) the defendant's sexual relations with the patient violated the surgeon's fiduciary duty. In a California case, a cosmetic surgeon performed negligent surgery by removing too much skin from a patient's face. The plaintiff also claimed that the surgeon touched her vaginal area when she was in the recovery room.[245] A severe chemical reaction from a face peel led to severe hypertrophic scarring in a Florida case in which the defendant was not licensed and failed to test the patient's skin for allergic reaction to chemicals.[246]

A recklessly performed operation to reduce abdominal fat became the basis for punitive damages.[247] The victim of this grossly negligent "tummy tuck" operation died after developing a staph infection. The basis of the punitive damages claim was the cosmetic surgeon's negligent decision to proceed with the operation despite finding active lesions indicating *staph aureus*. The decedent was not an appropriate candidate for cosmetic surgery because she suffered from obesity, asthma, and uncontrolled diabetes.

Trial lawyers are reluctant to pursue elective cosmetic surgery cases because juries are inclined to blame the victim. Undergoing cosmetic surgery is frequently regarded as an indication of undue concern for personal appearance: "Aside from breast implant suits, which are largely products liability cases, cases involving bad results in face lifts, tummy tucks and the like are seldom worth pursuing. Juries muster little sympathy for the sometimes quarrelsome patient; qualified experts are very difficult to locate."[248] Without the possibility of winning punitive damages, few unqualified and incompetent cosmetic surgeons will ever be held accountable for their reckless misconduct.

§4.8. Punishing Medical Quackery

Medical quackery has long flourished in the United States. Quack medicine was already a $3.5 million business by the time of the Civil War. Questionable cures and devices were not purged from the medical profession until the Progressive Age.[249] At the turn of the century, the AMA complained that a "study of the multitude of mail-order medical fakes makes plain one fact: Few of such concerns are owned by the renegade physicians whose names adorn the stationery of the companies. Most companies of this kind are organized and capitalized by shrewd—and often unscrupulous—businessmen. These companies are run solely and only for profit; the health or well being of the victim who seeks their aid is a matter of indifference. . . . The business is a commercial one; pills and tablets bought by the million from pharmaceutical houses . . . these are the stock in trade of mail-order medical fakers."[250]

In the modern period, punitive damages punish physicians, chiropractors, and other health care providers who engage in quackery. Punitive damages are one of the few effective social controls against such outlandish medicine as that involved in *Wolfram v. Stokes*,[251] where doctors forced the plaintiff to consume a quart of eighty-proof liquor each day as part of an "experimental treatment of alcoholism."[252] The trial judge upheld the verdict for punitive damages because the patient did not give her informed consent to participate in the experimental program.[253]

In *Shelton v. Carlton*[254] a widow brought a medical negligence case against a chiropractor and his fasting-based medical facility for causing the death of her husband. William Carlton was seeking relief from a chronic condition of ulcerative colitis.[255] He read several books on fasting, including one by the defendant, Dr. Shelton, titled *Fasting Can Save Your Life.*[256] Dr. Vetrano of the Shelton Health School of San Antonio, Texas, recommended that Carlton quit taking medication and enroll in his experimental fasting program. When Carlton joined the group he weighed 192 pounds. He lost 60 pounds in less than a month and died shortly after being admitted to Baptist Memorial Hospital in San Antonio.[257]

The concept of minimum daily nutrition was ignored and all medication strictly prohibited by officials at Vetrano's fasting school.[258] Mr. Carlton's autopsy report reveals that his death was "caused by severe dehydration, malnutrition and aspiration pneumonitis."[259] There were "at least seven known deaths that occurred at the Shelton Health School with the possibility of two more unreported deaths buried on the premises."[260] In three of these prior fatalities there were "shockingly similar circumstances and from virtually similar causes of death as Mr. Carlton."[261]

Children were victimized by a painful skull-stretching therapy prescribed by quacks in a bizarre California case. The parents of learning-disabled children were awarded punitive damages against the defendant who used a technique based on a bizarre theory for treating retardation:[262]

> The basic tenet of the neuro-organizational technique was that learning-disabled children suffered from improper pressure on their brains and that, by stretching the skull, these learning disabilities would disappear. Also, once the skull was stretched, the chiropractors would cure "ocular lock" by stretching the fascia of the eye muscles of the children. The skulls were adjusted by putting pressure on the tops of the mouths of the children and the fascia of the eye was stretched by pushing with the fingers into the eye sockets. As the treatments progressed, they became more and more painful to the children. Witnesses testified that the children were screaming on the chiropractic table when they were being treated, went into seizures on the table, vomited . . . and would struggle very hard to get away. The chiropractors explained that these seizures and screams were not the result of "pain," but rather the result of the immaturity of the children and were merely an "emotional release" of the children's "hidden fears."[263]

Punitive damages are an appropriate sanction for medical providers whose unorthodox medical treatments endanger patients.

§4.9. The Latent Functions of Medical Malpractice Actions

[A] Punishing Sex in the Forbidden Zone

"Sex in the forbidden zone" by health care providers is almost exclusively a female injury perpetrated by a more powerful male in a fiduciary relationship.[264] Punitive damages awards are the means by which the law, that is, society, punishes the invasion of physical or psychological boundaries by males in positions of trust. Sexual misconduct that can result in punitive damages awards falls into two broad categories: the abuse of transference by those working with the psychologically vulnerable, and conduct that is tantamount to aggravated sexual assault.[265]

Transference is deemed critical to the therapeutic process because the patient "unconsciously attributes to the psychiatrist or analyst those feelings which he may have repressed towards [others]. . . . [I]t is through the creation, experiencing and resolution of these feelings that [the patient] becomes well."[266] In the therapeutic process, a psychiatric patient has a diminished ability to control sexual emotions because of the trust the patient must place in the therapist. Sexual activity between therapist and patient is always presumed to be a misuse of transference.

Abuse of transference mirrors the gendered power differentials in American society. The great majority of these cases involved older, high-status males exploiting their fiduciary position for sexual advantage. Thirteen women, as opposed to only five men, received awards for emotional injuries caused by unethical psychiatrists. Many of these cases also included the misprescribing of drugs for inappropriate purposes.

Such a breach of transference led to a punitive damages award in *Hinkle v. Petroske*, where a psychiatrist had sex with his female patient every week for nearly thirteen years.[267] Evidence at trial revealed that the defendant continued to prescribe Nembutal long after he knew that the plaintiff was emotionally addicted to the drug. The plaintiff contended that her psychiatrist's actions led to her suicide attempt. The award of $1.9 million included $1 million in punitive damages against the psychiatrist, who was also found liable for $1.87 million in damages and lost wages in favor of another ex-patient.

A Virginia psychiatrist sexually abused a teenage schizophrenic patient beginning when she was fifteen years old. The physician admitted to engaging in sixty incidents of sexual relations with the girl but argued that there was no harm, since her condition had not worsened. Several expert witnesses testified that if the patient had been treated properly, she could have progressed to an outpatient status. The plaintiff dropped her claim for punitive damages because of doubts about whether the defendant's insurance policy would indemnify against a punitive award.[268] Another psychiatrist defended his sexual relationship with a sixteen-year-old female patient by contending he and his patient were simply a man and woman in their private capacities.

A thirty-five-year-old woman suffering acute organic brain syndrome sued her physician, who had been sexually abusing her for six years under the masquerade of therapy.[269] The plaintiff first consulted the defendant, an osteopath, when she was twenty-five. The osteopath, who had no formal training in counseling or psychiatry, began treating the plaintiff for "harried housewife" syndrome with Ritalin. Within the first six months of treatment, she was having sexual relations with the osteopath in his office in order to "fill her emptiness." He injected her with amphetamines and hallucinogens similar to LSD. He even administered sodium amytal, an obsolete drug last used for shell-shocked veterans in World War I.

The patient attempted suicide, repeatedly slashing her wrists and then calling her physician. The defendant stitched her wounds without the benefit of anesthesia. After four years, the patient attempted to leave the defendant's care and consulted a psychiatrist, who admitted her to a hospital for detoxification. However, the osteopath refused to send her medical records to her new doctor. The abusive osteopath visited her while she was in the detoxification unit and persuaded her to run away from the hospital with him.

After this incident, the plaintiff's marriage broke up and she moved in with the defendant and continued her intimate "therapy" for two additional years. When she attempted to stave off the osteopath's sexual advances one night, he beat her severely, fracturing her skull. No criminal charges were filed because the frightened woman fled the state. She eventually filed a medical malpractice lawsuit against the abusive osteopath, receiving a $300,000 punitive damages award.

Doctors engaging in sexual abuse or other sexual misconduct were far more likely to be punished by punitive damages than by public authorities in many states. In a typical case, twenty-two-year-old Audrey Jean Chanley began a sexual relationship initiated by her psychiatrist that continued until she was in her late twenties. In her lawsuit against the psychiatrist, she contended that Dr. Prastka had seduced her through manipulation, domination, and mood-altering drugs. The psychiatrist's defense was that Ms. Chanley initiated the sexual relationship and that it occurred after the termination of the physician–patient relationship. It is worth noting that, prior to the verdict, Dr. Prastka offered Chanley a structured settlement of $250,000 over fifteen years, provided that she would testify for him in his efforts to regain his medical license prior to the verdict. The jury awarded Chanley a punitive damages award to punish the sexual abuse by her psychiatrist.[270]

An Illinois psychotherapist began seeing a couple for marriage counseling in 1990. When the couple separated, the wife continued individual sessions. The therapist soon began having sexual contact and, later, sexual intercourse with her. When this relationship ended, the estranged wife reported the therapist to the Illinois Department of Professional Regulation, which discovered that he was having sexual intercourse with other patients as well. The husband and wife filed separate lawsuits alleging malpractice and intentional or negligent infliction of emotional harm. The couple's children also sued the therapist.[271]

The claim that breach of transference caused post-traumatic stress disorder and aggravated the plaintiff's preexisting borderline personality disorder led to a $7 million verdict against a California doctor.[272] The plaintiff was a former schoolteacher who suffered from serious psychological problems and had attempted suicide numerous times. She asked her psychiatrist whether he would have sex with her during her third visit. For nine years, the psychiatrist abused the transference process by engaging in sexual relations with his patient. The plaintiff also contended that her therapist-lover committed medical malpractice by addicting her to diet pills. The doctor's defense was that that his patient's psychological problems were preexisting and had not been worsened by his "intimate therapy."

In *Mould v. Leggett*, a twenty-four-year-old unmarried woman became involved in a sexual relationship with her treating psychiatrist.[273] The plaintiff suffered from serious depression and eating disorders and had attempted suicide. In April 1987, the plaintiff entered a mental institution for inpatient treatment of her severe emotional disorders. During her hospitalization, Dr. Leggett made sexual overtures to his patient, including kissing, hugging, and fondling. Based in part upon their personal relationship, Dr. Leggett arranged for her early release, after which the plaintiff continued therapy as an outpatient of the hospital.

When Mould revealed the relationship to a friend, it was reported to hospital officials. She also told her brother, who gave her an answering machine, which she used to tape Dr. Leggett's intimate telephone calls. In the lawsuit filed by the plaintiff against both the hospital and the psychiatrist, the court found the hospital vicariously liable for failing to discover Dr. Leggett's prior history of improper relationships with young female patients. The basis for the hospital's *respondeat superior* liability was the negligent retention of an unfit physician.

Punitive damages have frequently been assessed against physicians who exploit their prescription-writing power for sexual advantage. A thirty-two-year-old woman brought an action against her family physician, charging that she received sample medications and excessive prescription drugs in exchange for weekly sexual intercourse. The defendant argued that it was a consensual relationship, not within the physician–patient relationship, and not consummated in exchange for drugs. Utilizing the same "blame the victim" tactic so successfully employed by corporate tort defendants, he questioned the emotional stability and character of the plaintiff, noting in particular her prolific sexual history. In this case, however, the jury gave his defense no weight and awarded the plaintiff $300,000 in punitive damages.[274]

[B] Punishing Intentional Torts

Non-consensual sexual contact with patients is a crime as well as an intentional tort. The victimized patient in these cases is likely to have been in some vulnerable position, often drugged or unconscious. In *Sciola v. Shernow*,[275] the plaintiff visited her dentist's office to have a molar filled, for which procedure the dentist administered nitrous oxide. To her horror, the plaintiff, upon awakening, felt the defendant's tongue in her mouth and experienced severe pain in her breasts from his fondling while she was unconscious. In another case, an osteopath plied his female patient with a number of illegal drugs in the course of seducing her. Few of these egregious medical malpractice cases resulted in criminal prosecution. Not one defendant served a day in jail for such egregious misconduct. Tort awards are the last defense against sexual predators who masquerade as doctors and medical providers. All too often, a suit for punitive damages is the last and only means for redress by the injured and abused.

[C] Policing the Failure of Informed Consent

The concept of informed consent evolved in the 1960s and 1970s to vindicate a patient's right to be informed of the risks and comparative advantages of treatment options. The failure of informed consent is highly correlated with gender. Twenty-one of the twenty-six punitive damages verdicts based on the extreme failure of informed consent were awarded to female plaintiffs.[276] In 1993, American women were awarded more than $1.7 billion for damages arising from negligent cosmetic procedures.[277] The vast majority of grossly substandard cosmetic surgeries were performed on women. Not surprisingly, these "sunrise profit centers of the medical profession" were a major contributor to punitive damages litigation involving women. Punitive damages have been awarded for grossly substandard chemical face peels, as well as for fatalities that occurred during routine procedures like tummy tucks and liposuction. Cosmetic surgery is subject to minimal state and federal regulation, and some physicians pursue profits at the expense of good treatment.[278]

[D] Uncovering Gross Incompetence

It is reasonable to expect medical personnel to exercise the superior knowledge, skill, and care ordinarily possessed and employed by reputable members of the medical profession in good standing.[279] The improper practice of medicine that results in injury to the plaintiff may be the basis of punitive damages only if there is an extreme departure from accepted professional standards.[280] Although women were injured in non-gendered ways as well, many cases of substandard medical care involved injuries to a woman's reproductive system[281] or disfigurement suffered at the hands of cosmetic surgeons.[282] Punitive damages in *Vitali v. Bartell*[283] stemmed from a botched breast-reduction surgery. Obstetrical malpractice amounting to reckless indifference to patient safety was proven by the plaintiff in *Olsen v. Humana, Inc.*,[284] in which a hospital's gross failure to monitor a fetus and improper administration of a drug during delivery caused an infant to suffer severe brain damage. A physician is liable for punitive damages only for recklessly or intentionally harming the patient.

[E] Investigating and Punishing Neglect and Abandonment

Women constitute a substantial majority of nursing home residents because, while men have higher rates of life-threatening diseases that can lead to serious disability or premature death, women suffer from higher rates of acute but non-fatal chronic conditions, such as arthritis. Nursing home mistreatment is particularly serious for women because their potential for injury is heightened by a greater vulnerability to fractures. Absent the punitive damages remedy, plaintiffs' attorneys have little incentive to prosecute cases on behalf of nursing home residents or indigent patients since these persons have almost no economic value under American tort law. Elderly nursing home residents will typically have no medical bills or lost earnings to claim as damages. Nursing homes residents and their attorneys act on behalf of the public in correcting the inhuman conditions they encounter.[285]

In many hospital neglect cases, the patients involved are disadvantaged not only by their gender, but by their social class as well. The neglect of an indigent female patient led to punitive damages in *Jones v. Hospital for Joint Diseases*.[286] In that case, the plaintiff was an impoverished forty-one-year-old black woman from Harlem with an infected knee. She remained in the hospital for seven days but received no treatment; she was then discharged because she did not have a medical payment card. Her knee infection worsened and finally her leg had to be amputated at the mid-femur level because of gangrene.

[F] Controlling Corporate Health Care Providers

The law of medical malpractice fulfills "a forward-looking goal of deterring the defendant and others from acting that way in the future."[287] Managed care organizations help protect the public against unnecessary surgeries, but their drive for cost control increases "the potential for harm, and consequently, the potential for liability arising out of the utilization review program."[288] Under mechanical formulas designed to lower costs, cookbook medicine will inevitably displace physician autonomy, resulting in substandard care. Medical diagnosis and treatment are too indeterminate to permit standardized cost–benefit formulas to guide medical decisions. The president of the AMA has proposed legislation that will make it illegal to dismiss a doctor who places "the patient's interests ahead of the health plan's bottom line."[289]

Tort remedies create a necessary deterrent in the managed care environment, where there are tempting financial incentives to trade patient welfare for profits. Tort remedies that serve the purpose of deterrence are needed in those situations in which the defendant has obtained ill-gotten gains.[290] Health care entities expose patients to different risks than do individual physicians. Corporate managers have no incentive to perform fraudulent or unnecessary surgeries and are in the best position to expose those medical personnel who would intentionally harm patients. The growing dangers to medical consumers are institutional neglect, impermissible health care rationing, and the withholding of treatment to maximize profits. A health care advocacy group recently uncovered an Aetna training video that suggests that patients who have a right to sue get better care.[291]

One of the big, unfinished battles facing Congress is whether patients will have adequate legal protection against the misdeeds of the medical establishment. The present law does not even ensure that doctors and nurses can report unsafe practices or bad medicine without fearing reprisals. Nurses, for example, have been disciplined for violating gag orders by speaking to the press about inadequate childbirth practices.[292] Some managed care organizations require that their affiliated medical personnel contractually agree not to disclose the full range of treatment options available to the patient.

One HMO requires its physicians "not to take any action or make any communication, which undermines or could undermine the confidence of enrollees, their employers, their unions or the public in the [managed care organization]."[293] Another HMO requires its doctors to sign a so-called "disparagement clause" that "prevents a physician from alerting the public to unsafe medical practices."[294] These practices are calculated to prevent patients from discovering medical negligence or impermissible cost containment. Our empirical study of medical malpractice awards suggests that patients need punitive damages to punish those who mistreat them. Tort reform will have unanticipated negative effects on the remedies necessary to make corporate medicine accountable.

§4.10. Conclusion

The latent function of medical malpractice is to provide a grievance mechanism against substandard doctors and medical providers. The most vulnerable Americans—the poor, women, the elderly, and those in total institutions—rely on tort remedies to protect themselves against uncaring, incompetent, and exploitative medical personnel. At least thirty states are currently considering legislation providing patients with the right to sue their HMOs for claims of medical malpractice, breach of the insurance contract, and inadequate quality of medical care. Texas recently permitted patients to sue their HMO.[295]

Corporate medicine has been the target of a recent wave of medical malpractice lawsuits for negligent supervision, medically inappropriate treatment, and bad faith cost-containment.[296] Five separate class action lawsuits have recently been filed charging a number of HMOs with violations of the Racketeer Influenced and Corrupt Organizations Act (RICO) and the Employee Retirement Security Act (ERISA) for placing corporate financial health above patient treatment.[297]

A few courts are carving out exceptions to the ERISA immunity. A federal judge in New Orleans recently ruled that ERISA did not preempt all state tort claims in a misdiagnosis case that resulted in the death of a nine-year-old boy.[298] Another federal judge ruled that an HMO could be sued in state court over a doctor's decision denying mental hospital care to a teenage schizophrenic who later killed himself.[299] As the HMOs come under increasing pressure to cut costs, patient welfare will inevitably suffer unless tort law provides sufficient countervailing power. The right to sue medical providers should be expanded, not further limited.

5

In Defense of Products Liability and Safety

> I saw the pale student of unhallowed arts kneeling beside the thing he had put together. I saw the hideous phantasm of a man stretched out, and then, on the working of some powerful engine, show signs of life and stir with an uneasy, half-vital motion.
>
> —Mary Wollstonecraft Shelley, *Frankenstein*

§5.1. Introduction

In Mary Wollstonecraft Shelley's celebrated novel *Frankenstein*, Dr. Frankenstein's goal is to create a perfect being. Instead, the unfortunate Dr. Frankenstein accidentally produces a monster that seeks to destroy him. Reformers argue that the tort system is like that. They maintain that torts have mutated into an untamed monster, which is causing self-inflicted wounds to our collective well-being. Businesses claim that they "are being handcuffed by the threat of frivolous litigation."[1] Manufacturers assert that "[e]ngineers can't design innovative products without looking over their shoulders."[2] Believing the myth that torts strike randomly has diverted companies from practicing preventive corporate law that would reduce the risk of costly litigation.

Businesses see tort remedies, especially punitive damages, as a monster that must be destroyed. Ninety percent of chief executive officers of major companies agree that it is "extremely important or very important" for Congress to pass federal tort reform.[3] Sixty-one percent of the chief executives surveyed stated that their companies have lobbied or contributed to lobbying for tort reform.[4] The tort reform movement is largely funded by contributions from large corporate interests ranging "from tobacco companies to carmakers."[5]

Big business has always resisted the expansion of tort remedies because it raises the price of wrongdoing. Tort reform has become a multi-million-dollar industry chiefly benefiting public relations companies, law firms, lobbyists, and lawmakers.[6] Print and broadcast advertisements promulgate the message of "Tort Reform Now."[7] The unintended negative consequence of the tort reform battles is to distract corporate America from the more fruitful endeavor of using preventive law to uncover needlessly hazardous practices. Tort remedies will be necessary so long as unwary American consumers are placed in unnecessary peril.

[A] Tort Horror Stories

The general public is amused, angered, and perplexed by accounts of loony tort filings publicized by tort reformers. Bart Simpson was forced to write on a classroom blackboard "I will not file frivolous lawsuits" in *The Simpsons'* 1998 season premiere.[8] Tort reformers frequently cite the case of a woman who received $2,699,000 in punitive damages after injuring her back opening a pickle jar. The tale of the customer of a steak house who sued because his meat was overcooked symbolizes a civil litigation system apparently out of control.[9] The tort reformers publish unusual tort filings that highlight "the lunacy that lawsuit abuse has caused"[10] on April Fool's Day. Tort horror stories create the impression that Fortune 500 companies routinely pay settlements to whiners who refuse to take responsibility for the consequences of their reckless actions.

Marc Galanter found that many of the tort horror stories highlighted by the tort reformers were either false or presented in highly misleading ways.[11] In the pickle jar case, for example, the defendant was assessed punitive damages for an illegal course of conduct over a five-year period. The convenience store employer violated state and federal law by refusing to accommodate the disability of his employee, assigning her to tasks he knew she could not perform. He retaliated against the plaintiff and fired a manager who testified on her behalf in a workers' compensation hearing.

Wacky warnings are presented as emblematic of lawsuit abuse. The popular assumption is that bizarre warnings came in the wake of a ridiculous jury verdict. The Michigan Lawsuit Abuse Watch sponsors a contest on Wacky Warning Labels. One of the finalists was a warning on a cartridge for a laser printer that warned: "Do not eat toner." Another warning label advised users of hair dryers: "Never use while sleeping."[12] The American Tort Reform Association (ATRA) reported how a milk-a-holic sued the dairy industry for failing to warn him that whole milk clogged his arteries. ATRA added the editorial note that the label should have read: "WARNING: TOO MUCH MILK CAN MAKE YOU A FRIVOLOUS-LAW-SUIT FILING MORON."[13] ATRA does not report the outcome of the milk-a-holic case, which was an early dismissal of the complaint.

The tort reformers use anecdotes and horror stories to falsely imply that consumers generally sue for injuries caused by their own stupidity.[14] One all-too-typical example of the half-truths characteristic of this mis-information campaign is the story reported by *USA Today* in which a "manufacturer offered a settlement of $7.5 million in a suit over the color of its tricycles."[15] The color was not the basis for the lawsuit. In the actual case, a toddler suffered a devastating brain injury caused by a defectively designed tricycle. The twenty-month-old boy was riding his tricycle, which had a wire metal basket over the handlebars. The tricycle tipped over and an exposed metal prong on the basket penetrated the boy's skull through the nostril, causing permanent disabilities. One of several dan-gerous design features was that the color of the basket was the same as that of the tricycle, concealing the potentially lethal nature of the metal prong.[16] This illustrates how actual cases are distorted, first, to catch the reader's attention with sensational headlines, and then, to mislead the public with facts that are selectively reported, or "rearranged," to further the position of the tort stakeholder.

A widely circulated urban myth concerns an Alabama woman who was supposedly awarded $250,000 in punitive damages even though she was not injured or even present when a gas heater malfunctioned. In the ac-tual case, four family members were overcome by carbon monoxide while they slept because of a Sears gas water heater that was designed without a safety shut-off device or a common carbon monoxide sensor. A seven-teen-year-old girl died and three others incurred serious injuries. It was true that one of the plaintiffs was not present the evening of the tragedy, but she had spent prior weeks breathing in harmful vapors.[17] Phantom injuries were not at issue in this case.

Another popular legal legend tells of an elderly woman who sued a soft drink company after being blinded by a bottle cap when she opened the container with pliers. In the actual case, Mae Roberts suffered a complete loss of sight in her left eye as a result of the aluminum twist-off cap being forcibly ejected from the bottle. Punitive damages were based upon the bottler's prior knowledge of a large number of similar accidents without taking steps to protect the public.[18]

The media frequently distort the public's view about tort law by uncritically parroting these misleading narratives. Jay Leno, for example, included the milk-a-holic case in his monologue on June 10, 1997: "A man in suburban Seattle is suing the dairy industry because he's become addicted to milk and it has raised his cholesterol to dangerous levels."[19] The mere fact that a frivolous lawsuit has been filed does not mean that the civil justice system is in need of radical reform any more than a single aberrant criminal jury verdict means that our criminal law system ought to be abandoned. The early dismissal of marginal tort cases proves that the American civil justice system has well-established mechanisms to screen out questionable lawsuits quickly and effectively. Judges have the power to impose sanctions and assess costs if a case is deemed frivolous.

The public's sympathy is now with well-heeled Fortune 500 companies rather than the victims of defective products because of the success of the tort reformers' public relations campaign. The misplaced focus on bizarre cases deflects attention from the true basis for products liability cases. Dangerous products, not moronic consumers, account for the vast majority of these lawsuits. The deterrence of unsafe products and practices is the latent function of tort liability, though the general public remains largely unaware of this fact.[20]

[B] Why Juries Impose Punitive Damages against Corporations

High-stakes personal injury tort verdicts are not random acts of redistributive justice by runaway juries but rather stem from extreme corporate misbehavior. A forty-eight-year-old housewife was maimed and blinded when a can of Drano exploded in her face. The explosion was caused by a defective design that permitted water to seep into the granular chemicals, causing a chemical reaction that produced intense heat, which in turn converted the water to steam. The screw-top lid allowed pressure to build up, causing an explosion. Prior to this litigation, there were several other lawsuits claiming damages for injuries caused by similar Drano can explosions. After being assessed punitive damages, the manufacturer of Drano redesigned the can with a flip-top lid that would release before pressure in the can built up to explosive levels.[21]

Products liability lawsuits have exposed many hazards undetected by government regulators. Many workplace product injuries occur in establishments regulated by the Occupational Health and Safety Administration (OSHA). OSHA, which is understaffed and overworked, has contributed very little to overall injury prevention.[22] Empirical research has been "unable to find any significant aggregate effect [that OSHA has] on injury rates."[23] An "average-sized company or job site is less likely to see an OSHA inspector than to witness the passage of Halley's Comet."[24]

Similarly, the Consumer Product Safety Commission (CPSC) has a legacy of three decades of underenforcement.[25] The agency has promulgated few safety standards and has not played a significant role in protecting American consumers.[26] The Food and Drug Administration (FDA) has also been criticized for its failure to set priorities and for promulgating pro–drug company regulations.[27] The tort system ensures that Americans need not depend solely upon the government to enforce product safety.

Federal agencies such as the CPSC lack the staff and resources to monitor all foreign and domestic manufacturers. The CPSC claims that it "saves lives and keeps families safe," but it is a toothless tiger.[28] It has jurisdiction over 15,000 types of consumer products but has issued mandatory safety standards for fewer than fifteen items. No government agency has the independent scientists or research staff necessary to protect the public, so government regulators are dependent on industry research for evidence of adverse reactions. The CPSC is powerless to meaningfully enforce its safety standards against foreign manufacturers who do not follow American product safety practices. In many instances, it is tort law, not government regulatory bodies, that protects the public.

Preventive vigilance, motivated by the fear of liability, has been a key incentive for corporations to improve product safety and risk-management procedures. Tort law's economic function of deterrence creates incentives for allocating resources to safety.[29]

§5.2. The Social Utility of Products Liability

"[W]e've yet to find a harmful life form." . . . "What kind of place is this? No disease, germs, no lice, no flies, no rats, no—"

"No whiskey or red light districts." Hall straightened up. "Quite a place . . ."

". . . I'm wondering whether this is the Garden of Eden our ancestors fell out of."

Hall wandered over to the window of the lab and contemplated the scene beyond. He had to admit it was an attractive sight. . . . [Hall was alone in his lab, examining life-forms under the microscope when he was c]hoked off because the two eyepieces of the microscope had twisted suddenly around his windpipe and were trying to strangle him. . . . He kicked it loose and drew his blast pistol. . . . Hall fired. It disappeared in a cloud of metallic particles.[30]

Philip K. Dick's science fiction story "Colony" occurs on the distant Planet Blue, an apparent utopia where there are no obvious hazards or diseases. The utopia is destroyed when deadly shape-shifting beings begin to disguise themselves as normal, everyday objects. A space traveler is practically strangled by his belt when it metamorphoses into a furious metal snake. Another colonist is almost crushed to death by his favorite armchair when it suddenly closes around him.[31] A young husband is nearly killed by a red-and-white scatter rug that wraps around his legs like a python. In shock, he explains to his fellow colonists how his favorite rug turned on him: "My wife gave it to me. I—I trusted it completely."[32] At the end of the story, these harmless-looking objects kill all of the space travelers. This scenario may seem absurd, but it makes a critical point. We need to know that our consumer products will not harm us. Business prosperity depends on safety because it creates consumer confidence in a product.

We are disinclined to believe that consumer products can turn on us. Yet, a retired cement finisher was killed by his runaway 1972 Ford F-100 pickup truck in *Alexander v. Ford Motor Co.*[33] The unlucky driver stepped out and faced the rear of his truck. The pickup suddenly self-shifted into reverse, knocking him to the ground and crushing his leg. The victim died from his injuries and hypothermia resulting from all-night exposure to inclement weather. Punitive damages were based upon a "smoking gun" memorandum from Ford executives revealing that the company had prior consumer complaints about its trucks self-shifting from park to reverse.[34] American consumers had no advance warning about this deadly defect. We live in a safer society because of preventive and remedial measures instituted by corporations that fear products liability.

Personal injury verdicts send the deterrent message that "tort does not pay."[35] Justice Benjamin Cardozo stated the rationale for the modern law of products liability in his 1916 opinion in *MacPherson v. Buick Motor Co.*:[36]

> If the nature of a thing is such that it is reasonably certain to place life and limb in peril when negligently made, it is then a thing of danger. Its nature gives warning of the consequences to be expected. If to the element of danger there is added knowledge that the thing will be used by persons other than the purchaser, and used without new tests, then, irrespective of contract, the manufacturer of this thing of danger is under a duty to make it carefully.[37]

Justice Roger Traynor's concurring opinion in *Escola v. Coca-Cola Bottling Co.*[38] stated that "public policy demands that responsibility be fixed wherever it will most effectively reduce the hazards to life and health inherent in defective products that reach the market."[39]

§5.3. Punitive Damages in Products Liability

Punitive damages in products liability were first judicially recognized in the mid-1960s in the infamous MER-29 scandal. Richardson-Merrell's concealment of the numerous dangerous side effects of this anti-cholesterol drug led juries to award the first punitive damages for a defective product.[40] MER-29 was thought to reduce the risk of heart attacks and strokes. Richardson-Merrell began animal testing of MER-29 in 1957. All of the laboratory rats that ingested the drug suffered immediate abnormal blood changes.[41] Richardson-Merrell had evidence of a profile of developing danger, which was made even clearer after a second rat study uncovered abnormal blood changes caused by MER-29.

An extended test of MER-29 was conducted on laboratory monkeys in early 1959. The technicians observed that the monkeys were falling off the exercise bars because the drug blinded them. The scientist directing the monkey study ordered a Richardson-Merrell laboratory technician "to falsify a chart of this test by recording false body weights for the monkeys."[42] (Body weights were a significant indication of the side effects of MER-29.) When the lab technician protested, a Richardson-Merrell official told her: "You do as he tells you and be quiet."[43] The MER-29 records were further altered, showing ersatz positive results long after the monkeys were killed. Richardson-Merrell produced a brochure for the medical community, employing the falsified test results and excising any reference to the high correlation between MER-29 and abnormal blood conditions.[44] The company submitted wholly fictitious body and organ weights and blood tests for dead rats to fool the FDA into believing that the test animals had survived.[45]

The FDA reviewers informed Richardson-Merrell that its new drug application was incomplete and ordered an additional two-year study of rats and a three-month study of dogs. Nine out of the ten rats in the study soon developed eye opacities from the effects of MER-29. Richardson-Merrell concealed the severity of the problem by reporting that eight out of the twenty rats that took MER-29 developed mild inflammation of the eye.[46] The company's examination of the rats was conclusive: twenty-five out of thirty-six rats developed opacities as a result of ingesting MER-29. Richardson-Merrell completed its study of dogs in February 1960. One dog in the test group suffered total blindness from the drug. Again, the results of these tests were withheld from the FDA.

The misinformed FDA granted Richardson-Merrell's application to market MER-29, and the drug was launched onto the market with an unprecedented promotional and advertising campaign. Doctors were provided with more promotional literature on MER-29 than any previous medical product. Richardson-Merrell's brochures claimed that "MER-29 was . . . virtually nontoxic and remarkably free from side effects even on prolonged clinical use."[47]

Two months after the drug was approved, the FDA received an unsolicited whistle-blowing letter from Dr. Loretta Fox, a Richardson-Merrell scientist. Dr. Fox reported that in her experiments with MER-29 on rats, she had personally observed corneal eye opacities caused by the drug. The FDA passed the scientist's letter on to Richardson-Merrell and solicited its comments.

Richardson-Merrell's top officials told a different story. The head of the company's toxicology department responded that MER-29 was used on thousands of rats and that only one group showed any eye changes.[48] The Richardson-Merrell memorandum to the FDA falsely asserted: "We have no evidence from our experience or from the literature that MER-29 would, in itself, produce such changes."[49] Yet, Richardson-Merrell's pathologist further tested the long-term effects of MER-29 and found that the laboratory rats were blinded by low as well as high dosages of MER-29.

Richardson-Merrell received the first adverse reaction reports from humans taking MER-29 as early as January 1961. A patient complained of a film over his eyes after using MER-29 for a short period.[50] The company's highest officials were told of eye lesions in humans as well as in animals, yet continued to claim that there were no adverse reactions to the drug.[51] A field report submitted to the company noted that a doctor taking MER-29 suffered deterioration in eyesight from the drug. Still, physicians continued to be told by sales representatives that MER-29 was a proven drug and that there was no question of its efficacy or of its safety.[52]

By March 1961, the company had received more than fifty reports of thinning hair from persons taking MER-29. Richardson-Merrell's vice president made a corporate decision not to inform the sales department about adverse reaction reports because of a concern that the test data would "discourage efforts in promoting sale of the drug."[53] By late 1961, the Mayo Clinic reported two case studies of patients developing cataracts and suffering hair loss and skin irritation after taking MER-29. A Richardson-Merrell official telephoned the FDA in late 1961, reading a proposed reassurance letter that the company hoped to send to the medical profession. The misleading letter gave an anemic warning of the then-known side effects of "skin trouble, falling hair and cataracts, but advising doctors that they could continue use of the drug."[54]

FDA officials met with Richardson-Merrell's president in November 1961. The FDA concluded that MER-29 should be immediately recalled from the market. Richardson-Merrell was reluctant to suspend sales even after the FDA seized its records and uncovered the misreported research findings.[55] MER-29 was administered to approximately 400,000 consumers, injuring at least 50,000 patients, in its short time on the market.[56] Consumers developed serious problems after using the drug for periods of less than three months.[57] The company's president argued that MER-29 was the "biggest and most important drug in Richardson-Merrell history . . . and vowed to defend it at every step."[58]

A New York jury awarded $100,000 in punitive damages based upon evidence that Richardson-Merrell had lied to the FDA, the medical profession, and consumers about the safety of MER-29.[59] This episode was the first time in the history of Anglo-American jurisprudence that a company was assessed punitive damages for marketing a dangerously defective product. The Second Circuit U.S. Court of Appeals reversed the punitive damages, observing that there was the potential for punitive damages overkill, since the New York litigation was the first of some seventy-five similar cases to be tried. The court's concern about overkill proved to be unfounded because the MER-29 disaster resulted in only three punitive damage awards.[60] William Merrell, the founder, and several other Richardson-Merrell executives were fined for submitting false animal data to the FDA. In the next section, we examine the factual foundation for the punitive damages awards that came after the MER-29 litigation.

§5.4. Empirical Data on Punitive Damages in Products Liability

The widespread corporate belief that large tort awards are random "lightning strikes" that hurt the innocent and guilty alike leads many companies to neglect preventive law. Too often, companies apply their resources to tort reform lobbying rather than investing in safer products and practices. According to a survey of 529 manufacturing companies with at least $50 million in annual sales, corporations often lack a risk management department, which would prevent many dangerous defects that lead to serious injury and tort litigation.[61] Companies need to be more diligent in conducting legal audits of issues such as quality control, product literature, product design, and product testing in order to avoid lawsuits. The message of tort liability is to screen and supervise employees closely or bear the consequences. A review of the empirical studies of punitive damages shows that these verdicts are patterned and avoidable.

Michael Saks's 1992 review of tort litigation concluded that "every empirical study of the [punitive damages] question has reached conclusions that, to say the least, fail to support" the claim that "punitive damages have grown dramatically in both frequency and size."[62] Researchers have now completed nine empirical studies on the pattern of punitive damages in the United States:[63]

1. The Rand Institute for Civil Justice study of jury verdicts in two counties (Rand I)
2. The American Bar Foundation study of jury verdicts in eleven states (ABF I)
3. The GAO *Report on Verdicts in Five States* in 1983–1985
4. Landes and Posner's study of federal and state appellate cases published in the West law reporters
5. Rustad and Koenig's study of twenty-five years of punitive damages awards in products liability
6. Rustad and Koenig's study of three decades of punitive damages awards in medical malpractice
7. The Department of Justice, National Center for State Courts, and Cornell University Civil Justice survey of 1992 verdicts
8. The Rand Institute of Civil Justice's follow-up study of punitive damages (Rand II)
9. The American Bar Foundation follow-up study of punitive damages (ABF II)

These studies, which constitute a reliable baseline for studying punitive damages, unanimously conclude that the tort reformers are simply wrong. There is no nationwide crisis. Far from it. Punitive damages are rarely awarded. No empirical support was found in any of the nine studies for the claim that the size of punitive damages in medical malpractice or products liability is excessive.

The most recent American Bar Foundation study (ABF II) supports the earlier research studies, confirming that plaintiffs are rarely successful in obtaining punitive damages.[64] Punitive damages in medical malpractice claims were awarded in less than 3 percent of plaintiff verdicts. Products liability litigants fared somewhat better, receiving punitive damages in almost 9 percent of the successful claims. Plaintiff success rates also closely tracked the findings of the earlier study: 32 percent for malpractice and 39 percent for products liability, compared to 31 percent and 38 percent, respectively, in the earlier study.[65]

The Justice Department study also confirmed that punitive damages awards in products liability and medical malpractice were rare.[66] Plaintiffs received punitive damages awards in only 6 percent of the successful verdicts in all substantive fields of the law; punitive damages in products liability were even rarer. In 1992, juries disposed of 360 products liability cases;[67] plaintiffs prevailed in only 142 of these cases.[68] Punitive damages were awarded in only three instances,[69] accounting for only about 10 percent of all money awarded to plaintiffs during that period.[70] Despite the rarity of these verdicts, the proposed federal revisions seek to restrict the rights of consumers injured by dangerously defective products and faulty medicine. There are no proposals to contain, much less restrict, the ability of businesses to sue other businesses.

Rand found that 50 percent of all punitive damages awards arose out of litigation involving intentional torts.[71] The rate of punitive damages ranged from a low of only about 2 percent in personal injury litigation to a high of 23 percent in intentional tort cases.[72] Nearly one-third of the punitive damages awards (32 percent) arose out of commercial, business, or contract cases;[73] only 19 percent arose out of personal injury cases.[74] Punitive damages were awarded most frequently in intentional tort cases and in business and contract disputes rather than in personal injury litigation.[75] Rand researchers attributed the changing proportions of punitive damages awards in business contract cases to doctrinal developments, not to out-of-control juries.[76]

The Rand II study concluded that eight out of ten punitive damages arose out of litigation involving intentional torts and business contracts.[77] One in five successful verdicts in business and intentional tort cases also included punitive damages. Products liability lawsuits accounted for less than

5 percent of all punitive damages awards; medical malpractice accounted for only 2 percent.[78]

The American Bar Foundation (ABF) researchers reported similar findings. Most punitive damages awards were assessed in business contract cases or where plaintiffs suffered physical injury. The ABF concludes that "[f]ew [punitive damages awards] arise in those cases involving property damage or emotional or reputation harm."[79] Plaintiffs, however, rarely received punitive damage verdicts in medical malpractice or products liability cases, the focus of the tort reform controversy.

Economic loss cases, not personal injury, have produced the largest punitive damages awards in recent years.[80] In 1994, the vast majority of $100 million-plus punitive damages awards arose out of business disputes.[81] Examples include the $1.5 billion punitive damages award assessed in an Arizona business tort case,[82] the $221 million awarded in a lender liability action,[83] and a $220 million award in a fraud and environmental contamination verdict.[84] Large punitive damages verdicts have also been awarded in patent infringement actions where there has been an independent tort such as fraud or breach of fiduciary duty.[85] Many of the largest punitive damages settlements in recent years arose out of commercial losses from fraud or disputes over business contracts.[86]

The $145 billion punitive damages award made in July 2000 to a class of five hundred Florida smokers against the tobacco industry is the largest civil jury award in history.[87] The next largest punitive damages award was the environmental loss claim against Exxon for spilling 11 million gallons of crude oil in Prince William Sound.[88] The third largest punitive damages award was the $4.8 billion awarded in a products liability case.[89] The fourth largest award resulted from a business dispute over control of Getty Oil, where Texaco allegedly induced Getty to breach a contract to sell its shares to Pennzoil. A Texas jury awarded Pennzoil $7.53 billion in actual damages along with punitive damages of $3 billion in *Pennzoil Co. v. Texaco, Inc.*[90] As Rand studies indicated, these large verdicts are emblematic of the trend toward large awards in business contract cases.

Our analysis of twenty-five years of punitive damages in products liability cases has shown these verdicts to be rare, proportionate to the wrongdoing, and based on avoidable patterns of corporate recklessness.[91] Texas led the nation with fifty-one punitive damages verdicts in products liability, followed by California with thirty-five, Florida with thirty-four, Missouri with twenty-two, and Illinois with twenty-one. Six states—

Louisiana, Michigan, Nebraska, New Hampshire, North Dakota, and South Dakota—awarded no punitive damages in any personal injury or products liability case from 1965 to 1990. Ten other states had only one punitive award over the same period.

Medical malpractice punitive awards cluster in jurisdictional hot spots. Five states account for almost half of all punitive damages awarded in medical malpractice litigation. The medical malpractice hot spots tend to be the same jurisdictions in which products liability punitive damages are more common; punitive damages in medical malpractice are rare or non-existent in the remainder of the states. In fact, eleven states did not have a single punitive damages verdict in a medical malpractice case over the thirty-year period of the study; nineteen additional states had three or fewer punitive damages awards.

The Department of Justice study of 1992 verdicts in the seventy-five most populous U.S. counties found a similar pattern.[92] Texas ranked first in punitive damages with eighty-three, followed by California with seventy. Georgia was third with sixteen awards, followed by New York (nine), Kentucky (eight), Florida (seven), Illinois (seven), and Virginia (seven). Fifty percent of the jurisdictions surveyed by Jury Verdict Research had twenty-two or fewer punitive damages in all areas of the law for the period 1987 to March 1995.

The business community is ill served by the myth that punitive damages are a product of casino-style random verdicts. Our analysis of the factual foundations of every punitive damages award in products liability from 1965 to 1990 convinces us that the legal sting of punitive damages is avoidable. The key to the successful punitive damages case is the effective use of "smoking gun" evidence, which indicates that a corporation had knowledge of a developing or known substantial product hazard but failed to protect the consumer.[93] The remainder of this chapter gives managers practical tips on how to avoid punitive damages in products liability based upon an empirical study of the aggravating circumstances that led to a quarter century of products liability awards.

§5.5. Ten Commandments for Preventive Law

As Oliver Wendell Holmes once noted:

> When you get the dragon out of his cave on to the plain and in the daylight, you can count his teeth and claws, and see just what is his strength.

But to get him out is only the first step. The next is either to kill him, or to tame him and make him a useful animal.[94]

Empirical data on the factual foundation of three decades of punitive damages awards in products liability reveals that litigation is patterned and predictable. The Ten Commandments of punitive damages are designed to serve as a template for risk managers to avoid the circumstances that expose a manufacturer to the possibility of punitive damages. "Accident prevention . . . is even better than accident compensation. . . . 'A fence at the top of the cliff is better than an ambulance in the valley below.'"[95] In the typical punitive damages cases we studied, a company violated several of our Ten Commandments for avoiding punitive damages. In the MER-29 case, for example, almost every one of the Commandments was breached. In many of the other featured cases, several Commandments were violated.

FIRST COMMANDMENT: Thou Shalt Comply with Product Safety Standards

A corporation's knowing violation of a government or industry safety standard, statute, or regulation is frequently a foundation for the finding that it has been recklessly indifferent to consumer safety.[96] An industry or governmental standard sets the floor (but not the ceiling) on product safety. If a corporate defendant disregards a known safety standard where there is obvious risk, punitive damages will very often follow.

Borom v. Eli Lilly[97] was a wrongful death action against the manufacturer of Oraflex, a drug associated with sixty-one deaths in England. Punitive damages were based upon evidence that Eli Lilly marketed the drug despite knowledge that it could cause serious kidney problems. The plaintiff's opening statement argued that the company withheld reports of adverse reactions from the FDA:

> [T]he defendant in this case, Eli Lilly and Company, learned of this unique death syndrome some months prior to Mrs. Jones even receiving her first Oraflex tablet. The evidence is going to be that the company, notwithstanding the knowledge of this disease, did not report these deaths to the Food and Drug Administration, which they were required to do. The evidence is going to be that the company knew of the deaths of patients in its own internal records. You will see that the company knew of the death of as many as thirty people associated with the taking of benoxaprofen before Mrs. Jones ever received a single Oraflex tablet.[98]

A corporation that sold surgical bandages to hospitals without complying with an industry standard of eliminating potentially deadly rhizopus bacteria was assessed punitive damages. The plaintiff had to undergo painful debridement to the bone in order to destroy the bacteria introduced by the tainted bandages. The company had prior knowledge of other incidents of bacterial contamination and had been previously warned by the FDA to take preventive measures against the bacteria.[99]

A corporation was assessed punitive damages for violating an industry standard for the safe handling of potentially deadly chlorine gas canisters in *Leslie v. Jones Chemical Co.*[100] The chlorine tank was used as a water purifier in a swimming pool at the Sahara Hotel in Las Vegas, Nevada.[101] The plaintiffs were injured when the chlorine tank suddenly exploded, spewing poisonous gas over the patio area. Punitive liability was predicated upon evidence that the company deliberately evaded procedures for the safe handling of chlorine tanks.[102]

A natural gas leak caused an explosion in the plaintiff's farmhouse in another case involving excessive preventable danger.[103] The homeowners did not detect the leak because of the defendant's failure to use a malodorant despite the fact that the company's corporate safety committee required it to do so.[104] A natural gas industry expert testified that the inclusion of malodorants in natural gas had been an industry standard since the 1960s.[105]

A company's failure to cooperate with a CPSC-mandated recall of gas water heater valves, produced by another corporation, led to punitive damages against the marketer of natural gas in another case.[106] The defendant propane retailer volunteered to mail recall notices to its 60,000 potentially affected customers, but failed to honor its promise. The punitive damages arose out of an explosion that resulted from the lack of notice about the defective gas fitting.

The company's violation of an industrial safety standard was key to the punitive damages awarded in *King v. Kawaguchi Ltd.*[107] A worker suffered the traumatic amputation of three fingers while attempting to free foreign material from assembly-line machinery. The top guard on the machine was not fixed or interlocked, contrary to standards developed by the American National Standards Institutes (ANSI). The warning on the front of the machine conveyed the impression that the machine would not operate while the guard was open, lulling a worker into suffering a traumatic injury.

Adherence to state-of-the-art safety standards will mitigate, if not obviate, punitive damages. One of the latent functions of tort law in protecting the public is to set a high standard of care on the manufacturer in the field of product safety and development. The manufacturer has a virtual monopoly of knowledge about non-obvious product hazards and is therefore in a far better position to understand the need for remedial measures than are government regulators. The government-compliance defense is a perverse incentive to do nothing more than what is required by regulators. Products liability holds the manufacturer accountable for adequate testing in the research laboratory rather than after an epidemic of injuries in the marketplace.

SECOND COMMANDMENT: Thou Shalt Not Misrepresent
Product Safety

The manufacturer that fraudulently proclaims the safety of its product despite knowing there are hidden dangers may be punished through punitive damages. In *Leichtamer v. American Motors Corp.*,[108] a jeep manufacturer was held liable for misrepresentation in advertisements showing that its CJ-7 Jeep was suitable for "off-road" use on rugged terrain.[109] Television advertisements depicting youthful motorists driving jeeps up and down steep hills were used to sell this recreational vehicle.[110] The Ohio Supreme Court upheld a punitive damages award against the defendant based upon evidence that the manufacturer's advertisements encouraged youthful drivers to take unnecessary risks in a vehicle that lacked adequate rollover protection.[111]

The manufacturer failed to test its jeep for pitchover and provided a grossly inadequate roll bar that did little more than add "rugged good looks."[112] Two persons were killed and two others injured in the accident that led to the *Leichtamer* litigation. An American Motors engineer had warned the company that its failure to retrofit CJ jeeps would inevitably result in rollover accidents, subjecting the company to tort liability. Even so, the CJ jeep was not redesigned until punitive damages were awarded.

A worker was permanently injured on August 29, 1985, by a chemical drum that exploded due to vapors from a chemical mixture made and sold under the brand name Electro Kleen.[113] Even after being emptied of all usable chemicals, the drum was highly flammable, contrary to its label, which stated that Electro-Kleen was "non-flammable and would not burn." Larry Achord was directed by his supervisor to use an acetylene torch to cut the drum in half. After reading the label, Achord applied the acetylene torch to the container. The chemical drum exploded, nearly severing his leg. Punitive damages is a highly probable consequence if a company intentionally or negligently misrepresents the safety of a potentially deadly product.

THIRD COMMANDMENT: Thou Shalt Not Conceal a Known Danger

A company that conceals dangers rather than promptly taking remedial measures to protect the public faces substantial exposure to punitive damages if its wrongdoing is uncovered. Zora Gillham turned her Admiral television set off and returned fifteen minutes later to find it on fire, with flames shooting to the ceiling.[114] Mrs. Gillham was seriously burned trying to quell the fire, resulting in an eighteen-month hospital stay.[115] The fire in Gillham's television set was caused by the spontaneous ignition of its defectively designed high-voltage transformer.

Admiral had received ninety-one complaints about exploding televisions prior to the fire that injured Gillham. The hazard was so extreme that the defective transformer sometimes kindled fires after Admiral television sets were turned off. Some of the Admiral sets even caught on fire in dealers' showrooms before they were sold.[116] Punitive damages were based upon Admiral's knowledge that the transformer was dangerous and its failure to protect the public, even after numerous reported fires.[117]

The Colt Gun Company marketed a replica of its Wild West revolver without a safety catch in order to preserve the gun's historical authenticity. The pistol could discharge when dropped if the user did not follow the company's precise instructions. The only safety step taken to protect the public was a weak warning in the instruction booklet that the safest way to carry the Wild West revolver was with five cartridges in the chamber and the hammer on the sixth chamber. The victim of a drop-fire accident in Kansas received punitive damages when his gun accidentally discharged, shooting him in the bladder and rendering him permanently impotent.[118] The Tenth Circuit U.S. Court of Appeals upheld the verdict based on evidence of Colt's failure to install an effective safety device on the gun after gaining knowledge of previous accidents. The defendant manufacturer had filed a patent application in 1850 with the United States Patent and Trademark Office for a design change that would have eliminated the drop-fire hazard.

A young girl suffered the traumatic eradication of her right breast accompanied by serious burns and scarring from a sulfuric acid drain cleaner in *Cloroben Chemical Corp. v. Comegys*.[119] Cloroben's drain cleaner was marketed in a plastic container that was not child-resistant. During discovery, the company consistently denied the existence of any prior claims filed against it seeking compensation for injuries caused by the accidental spillage of its product, "Drain Snake." Prior claims against Cloroben were uncovered only after a protracted battle over the scope of discovery.[120] Punitive damages were based in part upon the company's suppression of documents and its delay in producing claim files. A reasonable alternative design change would have been to market Drain Snake "in a childproof package, especially since the product was ultra-hazardous."[121] A risk manager who attempts to cover up a hazard or a dangerous condition does so at the company's peril.

FOURTH COMMANDMENT: Thou Shalt Not Downplay a Known Danger

A "conscious business decision" to expose the consuming public to excessive preventable danger creates the risk of punitive damages. Manufacturers, distributors, and retailers often have a monopoly of knowledge about a product's hidden dangers or latent defects. The manufacturer is in the best position to know how to design, test, market, distribute, and monitor its products. A manufacturer acquiring knowledge of a developing profile of danger has a duty to protect the public even if it might depress sales.[122] Product defects are to be "scrapped in the laboratory, not ducked in the environment of use."[123]

Valerie Lakey, a five-year-old North Carolina girl, was playing in a community wading pool. The pool's drain cover, which constrains the strong hydraulic vortex, was missing and Valerie became lodged in the opening.[124] The pool's suction created a vortex so strong that it literally eviscerated the child. Seventy-five percent of her bowels were pulled out of her anus and her life was saved only by heroic efforts of the medical personnel at a North Carolina hospital.[125] The little girl ultimately survived but endured years of surgeries, hospital stays, and consultations with specialists.

Valerie's parents sued Sta-Rite Industries, a Wisconsin pool equipment manufacturer, the owner of the suction pump, and the owner of the pool.[126] Sta-Rite had more than a dozen prior complaints of injuries caused by broken or missing pool drain covers, yet did not issue warnings or make design changes until mid-1987.[127] A Sta-Rite internal report acknowledged that such "accidents were more common—the pressure from open drains tearing rectums and disemboweling small children. Without the grate, the suction is unimpeded and can exert considerable force."[128] The jury verdict settlement was directly based upon Sta-Rite's failure to warn consumers of the dangers of suction and entrapment in open drains.[129] The jury awarded Valerie $25 million and was scheduled to consider punitive damages when the case was settled for the amount of compensatory damages. In addition, the other defendants settled for $5.9 million prior to trial.[130]

The manufacturer changed its warnings and instructions on the safe use of its drain covers only after the case was filed. The State of North Carolina also passed statutes requiring wading pool covers due to this litigation.[131] Reports of the settlement led the entire swimming pool industry to recall its drain covers. Valerie's parents helped to change North Carolina law "to close all wading pools with single drains."[132] The CPSC published extensive guidelines to help pool operators avoid similar entrapment injuries in the future.[133]

In *Wahl v. McDonnell*, punitive damages were assessed against the manufacturer of a U.S. Air Force jet whose pilot died when his aircraft was unable to recover from a dive because the flight controls jammed.[134] The pilot ejected at 400 miles per hour from 2,000 feet and was instantly killed. The defective IE9 Escapac ejection seat in the jet caused him to twist and turn in the air until his neck snapped and his spinal cord severed. There were prior incidents with injuries and deaths caused by the malfunctioning of the parachute. After the punitive damages award, the manufacturer made design changes to the flight controls in all Air Force jets to eliminate the possibility of similar accidents.

Mulligan v. Lederle Laboratories involved a woman who was injected in 1960 with Varidase, a blood-clot-dissolving drug.[135] By 1962 she developed chronic mouth sores from the drug. She suffered microscopic hematuria in 1967 and severe kidney disease in 1976 from long-term use of the drug. The drug manufacturer had learned about the hazardous side-effects of Varidase, but did not issue warnings. The company's "failure to heed evidence of prior injuries caused by [the] product and modify [the] product accordingly" was the predicate of punitive damages.[136]

In *Willis v. Floyd Brace Co.*,[137] the supplier of a leg brace for polio victims was repeatedly asked by a user to repair a defective brace. The seller told the polio victim that there was nothing wrong with his brace, even though the device was malfunctioning. The plaintiff broke his leg owing to a fall caused by the failure of his leg brace to lock into place. Punitive damages stemmed from the company's flagrant indifference to the victim's safety, as demonstrated by its reckless dismissal of consumer complaints.[138]

A manufacturer of heavy equipment had reports of an electrocution hazard in its industrial power shovels. Prior electrocutions resulting from the faulty design of its equipment did not motivate the company to take steps to protect workers:

> At least one electrocution prior to ours occurred. The company did finally send out warning signs to be posted on the face of the guard prior to the accident in question but the owners could not post them because they were too large to fit on the smaller, inadequate [machine] guards. Testimony at trial revealed that the president of the company was recklessly indifferent to public safety. The president was reported to have said when the defective guard was pointed out to him: "Bring me ideas that save us money, not ones that cost us money." There was a letter in the defendant's files documenting that an electrical engineer for the company had recognized in the field the danger to men working around these machines, especially the easy access to the high voltage collector. He recommended a design change many years before the accident.[139]

A $3 million punitive damages award was imposed against the manufacturer in *Airco v. Simmon First National Bank*.[140] Airco marketed an artificial breathing machine that malfunctioned for several minutes, causing the plaintiff to suffer serious lung injury and irreversible brain damage. The breathing apparatus employed a confusing system of similar black hoses that provided a continuous mix of gases. Air traveled in a circuit and entered the patient through a mask equipped with valves. When the air left the patient's lungs, it returned to the mask and traveled through a different hose back to the anesthesia machine, which removed the carbon dioxide.[141]

Airco's ventilator was so inefficiently designed that technicians had to switch back and forth from the bag to the ventilator during surgical procedures. This practically assured that someone would attach a wrong hose, with deadly consequences. The inevitable happened when an operating-room nurse wrongly connected another hose in the middle port. The misplaced hose pumped air into the patient's lungs, but without a way for the air to escape. The buildup of air pressure burst the patient's lungs. The resulting deprivation of oxygen caused the patient to suffer a catastrophic brain injury.[142]

The danger in the ventilator's design could easily have been averted had the maker substituted a particular selector valve for either of two alternatives: a manual system for which the ventilator was designed or a selector valve having two rather than three ports.[143] The ventilator ports lacked adequate labels and warnings. The company's own records documented its growing awareness that its ventilating machine could kill. The company also knew of a research article about a substantially similar prior accident with the device.

A company's failure to warn consumers of the known hazards of rental trailers being hooked up to inappropriate bumper flanges led to an award of punitive damages in *Chatagnier v. U-Haul International, Inc.*[144] The decedent's U-Haul trailer accidentally disconnected from his pickup while he was crossing a bridge. The decedent and his wife left their automobile to reconnect the trailer and were struck by another vehicle, hurling them off a highway overpass to the concrete twenty-six feet below. The equipment rental company settled before trial. The case against the manufacturer of the trailer hitch proceeded to trial, ending with a punitive damages verdict based upon evidence that the lessor had conducted tests establishing the danger of connecting trailers to the thick bumper flanges of most cars and trucks. Risk managers must document the steps taken to warn the public of known or developing dangers. The burden will be on the manufacturer to prove that warnings were sufficient to protect the public.

FIFTH COMMANDMENT: Thou Shall Not Trade Safety for Profits

Punitive damages are appropriate when a manufacturer's profits are attributable to its willingness to recklessly market an unnecessarily hazardous product.[145] In 1997, 2.3 million Americans suffered disabling injuries and an additional 43,200 lost their lives in motor vehicle accidents.[146] In *Durrill v. Ford Motor Company*,[147] Devary Durrill was driving her Ford Mustang II on a four-lane highway when she had car trouble. After she pulled over to the shoulder of the road, her Mustang II was struck from behind, rolled over, and burst into flames. Her burns were so devastating that her rescuer was initially unable to determine whether she was a male or female. Eighty percent of Durrill's body was covered by second- and third-degree burns.

Durrill survived another week in excruciating pain. Her nurse described her condition: "Her hair had all been burned off, like she was bald-headed. . . . You lose a lot of fluids from the burns, and it would crust up on her face. It was kind of red and black and swollen and horrible. Her arms, legs and chest were simply charred. Her kidneys quit and her heart failed. She was agitated and in constant pain and thrashing around."[148] Durrill's parents heard her scream and ask for her boyfriend and for family members. She died in misery.

As early as 1968, more than fifteen years before the *Durrill* case, Ford was aware that 600 to 2,200 persons suffered fatal burns from post-collision fires in its vehicles. As we saw in Chapter 2, Ford Motor Company had prior knowledge that its entire line of vehicles was prone to fuel-fed fires. Moreover, Ford's vice president testified that his company expected its fuel tanks to rupture at closing speeds of only twenty-five miles per hour. Ford's Chassis Research Department had advocated inexpensive changes that would have substantially reduced the risk of a fire hazard: bladder tanks, flak suits, and breakaway filler pipes. However, Ford's chief executive officer, Lee Iacocca, personally lobbied President Richard Nixon to convince him to roll back proposed safety regulations.

The evidence that Ford saved $200 million over a three-year period by delaying implementation of modifications to its fuel integrity system demonstrated its indifference to public safety. Ford had essentially the same fuel-integrity system in the Mustang II as in the Pinto, but Ford chose not to warn Mustang II owners at the time it was notifying Pinto owners of the danger. When a manufacturer's profits are attributable to its willingness to market a product with a known defect, then punitive damages are appropriate.

In a Texas case, a 1977 Ford LTD automobile self-shifted from park to reverse due to a defect in the transmission, killing a fifty-two-year-old housewife who left the vehicle to close a gate behind the car.[149] Ford had definite knowledge of hundreds of prior complaints of its cars self-shifting from park to reverse due to vibration.[150] Eighty-nine prior similar self-shifting accidents resulted in serious injuries or death.[151] Punitive damages were also based upon interoffice communications showing that Ford received approximately six letters per month complaining about its defective transmissions, yet failed to take remedial steps to protect consumers.[152]

In *Braatz v. Rockwell-Standard Corp.*,[153] a fourteen-year-old Minnesota farm boy received a $3,880,000 jury verdict including punitive damages for amputation injuries suffered when he fell into the unguarded shaft of a grain auger. A non-standard, square-headed screw that protruded from the shaft was the design defect that caused the farm accident. Testimony showed that the full cost of compliance with the accepted industrial standard of shielding the protruding screw was a mere $2.38 per grain auger. The company's failure to implement this low-cost safety feature, combined with management knowledge of many prior injuries, elicited punitive damages.

Punitive damages "are intended to inject an additional factor into the cost–benefit calculations of companies who might otherwise find it fiscally prudent to disregard the threat of liability."[154] Punishment and deterrence can be attained only if the defendant is "stung" by taking the profits out of its wrongdoing.

SIXTH COMMANDMENT: Thou Shalt Promptly Protect the Public

Punishment and deterrence are appropriate where a manufacturer knows of a product's defective design and makes a conscious decision not to take prompt remedial measures. When a product manufacturer knows its product is inherently dangerous and that its continued use is likely to cause death or serious injury, a jury may find that it is consciously indifferent to public safety.[155] In *Saupitty v. Yazoo Manufacturing Co.*,[156] a riding lawn mower's drive wheel locked, causing the plaintiff to be thrown from the mower and to sustain amputation injuries.[157] A jury returned a verdict of $560,000 compensatory and $440,000 punitive damages. The punitive portion of the award was based upon "evidence of numerous prior accidents causing serious injuries to other individuals" and "the manufacturer's total refusal to retrofit or repair or warn of the dangerous design of the machine."[158] Yazoo had no safety program and no engineering department, and it failed to change its tractor's design after receiving notice of several similar accidents.[159] After the verdict, the defendant attempted to recall the lawn mowers in order to correct the condition.

A corporation's inexcusable delay in implementing safety improvements despite knowledge of a dangerous defect will generally support an inference that the company is recklessly indifferent to consumer safety. In *Connell v. Cessna Aircraft Corp.*, a 402B Cessna airplane crashed due to power loss, killing the three airline personnel on board.[160] The manufacturer placed these small airplanes on the market despite knowing of dozens of instances of engine failure due to defective magnetos. The maintenance policy was to wait until there were 1 to 2 percent failures before taking corrective action. This financially driven decision resulted in the airplane crash that led to a $100,000 punitive damages award.[161] No safety steps were taken until after the verdict of $10.5 million was rendered. Only then was a detailed inspection procedure issued to mechanics to prevent future magneto failures.[162]

In *Cupp v. Fleetwood Enterprises, Inc.*,[163] a fifty-eight-year-old company owner suffered permanent paralysis when the undercarriage of a mobile home he was transporting collapsed on top of him, crushing his vertebrae. The manufacturer of the mobile home disregarded the advice of its employee to replace defective parts and to warn the public about the dangers posed by overloading. The safety manager's annual bonus was based upon sales, not safety steps taken to protect America's consumers. The jury awarded $8 million in punitive damages to punish the defendant for failure to take remedial measures upon learning of a dangerous condition.

A manufacturer that acquires knowledge of a dangerous defect must undertake prompt remedial measures to recall products or give proper warnings. A seller may be liable for a post-sale failure to recall a defective product if there were prior occurrences and the defendant failed to protect the public.

SEVENTH COMMANDMENT: Thou Shalt Not Rest upon the State-of-the-Art Defense

When corporate documents indicate a need for safety improvements, the fact that no government agency mandated these improvements is a weak defense against a punitive damages claim. Compliance with industry safety standards is also no defense against punitive damages.[164] A company may be deemed recklessly indifferent and even grossly negligent despite complying with industry standards or accepted industrial safety practices. Section 295A Comment c of the Restatement (Second) of Torts states:

> No group of individuals and no industry or trade can be permitted, by adopting careless and slipshod methods to save time, effort, or money, to set its own uncontrolled standard at the expense of the rest of the community. If the only test is to be what has always been done, no one will ever have any great incentive to make any progress in the direction of safety.[165]

The U.S. Supreme Court in *Silkwood v. Kerr-McGee*[166] reviewed a tort action brought by Karen Silkwood's estate against an Oklahoma nuclear facility to recover for plant contamination. A jury awarded the plaintiff $505,000 in compensatory damages and $10 million in punitive damages.

The Tenth Circuit U.S. Court of Appeals reversed the awards, arguing that they were preempted by federal nuclear regulations. The U.S. Supreme Court reversed and remanded, holding that even though the Nuclear Regulatory Commission (NRC) had exclusive control over nuclear safety, a state could permit a tort lawsuit if the plant's safety did not conform to state tort law standards.

The Oklahoma jury imposed punitive damages against Kerr-McGee for radiation injuries as a consequence of plutonium escaping a nuclear fuel processing plant in Cimarron, Oklahoma. There was expert testimony that Karen Silkwood's contamination included genetic damage and the risk of lung cancer. It was uncontested that Karen Silkwood was contaminated by plutonium at home in her apartment, an estimated twenty miles from the nuclear plant site.[167] During the nuclear plant's five years of operation, there were approximately seventy-five violations of NRC standards. Kerr-McGee's argument was that the company substantially complied with federal regulations despite the contamination incidents. Moreover, NRC standards would still permit the escape of small quantities of plutonium.[168] Kerr-McGee claimed that it "had no common law duty to contain plutonium within the walls of their facility and . . . could not be held liable merely for permitting plutonium to escape."[169]

Karl Morgan, Director of the Health Physics Program at Oak Ridge National Laboratory, testified that Kerr-McGee's safety program was "very weak and inadequate."[170] Dr. Morgan stated that the Cimarron plant "was the worst facility he had encountered in 35 years as a consultant to the nuclear industry."[171] He testified that Kerr-McGee displayed a "don't care" attitude reflected in the company's poor plant security, inadequate worker training, and feeble radiation detection efforts. Dr. Morgan's expert opinion was that the Cimarron facility should receive an "F" or failing grade. Even the defense expert conceded that the facility would in his judgment receive only a "C."[172]

Kerr-McGee's inventory system was so lax that more than 18,160 grams of plutonium could not be located after the plant was closed. There were 574 reported contamination incidents during the five years the plant operated. The whole community was placed in jeopardy. "One-half gram of plutonium is enough to give 35 million people a lifetime lung burden."[173]

Following the jury's verdict awarding Silkwood's estate $10 million in punitive damages, the defendant argued that punitive damages were preempted because Kerr-McGee's conduct was in substantial compliance with NRC regulations. The district court ruled that there was ample evidence to support punitive damages. Even if the company substantially complied with federal nuclear regulations, it could still be held recklessly indifferent to the public welfare.[174] The Tenth Circuit U.S. Court of Appeals reversed the verdict, holding that the award was preempted by NRC regulations. The U.S. Supreme Court reversed and remanded, ruling that an award of punitive damages to the Silkwood estate did not conflict with the Atomic Energy Act of 1954, or with the 1957 Price Anderson Act.[175] The U.S. Supreme Court remanded the case back to the U.S. Court of Appeals for the Tenth Circuit.

In July 1985, the U.S. Court of Appeals reversed the plaintiff's award, holding that Oklahoma's workers' compensation act precluded Silkwood's recovery for personal injury.[176] The *Silkwood* case is an example in which traditional rules of tort law provide greater protection than if a nuclear plant operator is only required to comply with lax federal safety regulations.[177]

In 1983, after Betty O'Gilvie used Playtex tampons during her menstrual period, she developed first a sore throat and later a vaginal infection. Mrs. O'Gilvie's temperature skyrocketed to 105 degrees, at which point she lapsed into unconsciousness and died of toxic shock syndrome (TSS). In *O'Gilvie v. International Playtex, Inc.*,[178] the Tenth Circuit U.S. Court of Appeals found that International Playtex had willfully and wantonly injured the plaintiff. The punitive damages award in *O'Gilvie* was based upon evidence that Playtex advertised that its tampons were safe and effective, despite the company's knowledge that other manufacturers were reducing the absorbency of their products to guard against TSS.[179]

An internal memorandum by a Playtex employee acknowledged that "in being obsessed with 'absorbency' we lost sight of the fact that 'leakage' complaints did not decrease as the tampon absorbency potentials [were] increased."[180] The Tenth Circuit U.S. Court of Appeals reinstated a jury award of $10 million in punitive damages. Playtex stopped making tampons containing polyacrylate fibers, a decision attributed to its desire to avoid further punitive damages.[181] The TSS litigation is a case study of how a company can comply fully with FDA labeling requirements, while at the same time failing to protect the health of consumers.

A products liability action was brought against Honda for the negligent design of its sub-compact automobile in *Dorsey v. Honda Motor Co.*[182] Glen Dorsey, an engineer, suffered severe brain damage when he struck his head on the A-pillar post at the left of the windshield after colliding with a full-sized automobile.[183] The district court determined that Honda's compliance with federal safety standards precluded punitive damages.[184] The U.S. Court of Appeals for the Fifth Circuit reversed this finding,[185] ruling that Honda's compliance with governmental regulatory standards was admissible but that such compliance did not give the defendant a license to market a car that it knew to be uncrashworthy.[186]

The manufacturer is in a better position than regulators to know how to protect the public because it is generally the first to uncover a profile of developing danger. Justice Larsen of the Pennsylvania Supreme Court, in *Lewis v. Coffing Hoist Division*,[187] stated: "[W]e have made it clear that a manufacturer cannot avoid liability to its consumers that it injures or maims through its defective design by showing that 'the other guys do it too.'"[188]

Compliance with weak federal regulations was also the issue in *Gryc v. Dayton-Hudson Corp.*[189] The manufacturer in this case fully complied with Federal Fabrics Act standards even though the material was dangerously flammable. In *Gryc*, a four-year-old girl was severely burned when her cotton pajamas burst into flames as she reached across an electric stove to shut off a timer. Her scars were permanent and required several skin grafts. The Minnesota Supreme Court upheld a $1 million punitive damages award based upon evidence that the children's pajamas were made of flannelette that burned at a rate only slightly slower than newsprint. Punitive damages settlements, rather than government regulators, helped to remove the dangerous flannelette product from the marketplace. After this case, the CPSC enacted more stringent flammability standards for children's pajamas.

Internal documents proved that the company knew the federal standards were inadequate but continued to market the pajamas with reckless disregard of the known risk.[190] Mere compliance with government safety standards does not immunize a company when it knows that the product nevertheless poses an unreasonable chance of injury to the consuming public. As the Minnesota Supreme Court stated: "The punitive damages remedy merely serves to impose a higher duty on the manufacturer. . . . Congress did not expressly intend to preempt state private remedies by its preemption provisions."[191]

The tort system is the last defense when government standards are weak, outdated, or set by the regulated industry. Product manufacturers undermine proposed government regulations through lobbying and lawsuits. The National Association of Manufacturers challenged an OSHA regulation requiring lock-out or emergency devices such as circuit breakers for industrial equipment.[192] The Pharmaceutical Manufacturers Association filed a lawsuit against FDA regulations that governed the wording of package inserts, alerting patients to the dangers of estrogen drugs. The

CPSC has managed to enact only a handful of safety standards, and even those have been weakened by industry lobbyists. The fact that a company has complied with regulations is no assurance that the product does not contain excessive preventable dangers.

EIGHTH COMMANDMENT: Thou Shalt Adequately Test Products

Defendants may be assessed punitive damages for the inadequate testing of their products.[193] A $27 million jury verdict was awarded to two developmentally impaired infants whose injury was a consequence of consuming a baby formula.[194] The defendant omitted sodium chloride, an essential nutrient for brain development, from its product without assessing what impact that decision would have on neurological development.[195] Thousands of infants ultimately suffered cognitive deficits and brain damage resulting from the inadequately manufactured infant formula.[196] The jury rejected the company's self-serving defense that it removed the salt and substituted salt water to protect the infants from the hazards of high blood pressure. According to the plaintiff's attorney, the decision was profit-oriented and saved the company $14,000 a year.[197] The FDA sought criminal sanctions against the defendant, but the U.S. Department of Justice declined to prosecute. Concerns about the unregulated baby food industry led Congress to pass the Infant Formula Act of 1980.

The defendant in *Batteast v. Wyeth Laboratories, Inc.*,[198] was assessed $13 million in punitive damages for failing to warn physicians that prescribing aminophylline to infants could result in permanent brain damage.[199] The primary basis for the punitive damages award was grossly inadequate testing. The company's research had been limited to five cats, fourteen dogs, and fourteen convicts, with no tests for its effects on infants.[200]

The failure to test for the effects of moisture on a mining machine led to an award of punitive damages in *Shackleford v. Joy Manufacturing Co.*[201] In *Shackleford*, a miner was working in a thirty-inch coal seam,[202] removing rock from a roof fall that had buried the front of the machine, when the boom suddenly activated and struck him. The plaintiff argued that Joy Manufacturing disregarded its own technology in connection with the design of the continuous miner. The failure of the boom switch was caused by moisture in the remote control mechanism. Documents indicated that the defendant knew about moisture and dampness in the mine, yet failed to provide a remote control system to compensate for moisture. Evidence that the designer of the defective boom swing switch was not even an engineer was used to prove the manufacturer's reckless indifference.[203]

In *International Armament Corp. v. King,* an importer of 12-gauge double-barrel shotguns was assessed punitive damages for its conscious indifference to consumer safety.[204] The defendant failed to inspect every shotgun despite having rejected 150 of the first shipment of 700 shotguns due to defects. An accidental gunshot caused by a defect resulted in serious injury to the plaintiff. The court found that the company's failure to inspect and test weapons reflected the defendant's conscious indifference to the rights, welfare, and safety of consumers.[205]

An elderly woman purchased a humidifier that proved to be a breeding ground for bacteria because of a company's lack of testing.[206] If the manufacturer had properly tested the product, it would have discovered that the disinfectant used was far less effective than household bleach.[207] Inadequate testing was also an aggravating factor leading to punitive damages in a medical product case in which a seven-year-old girl suffered severe brain damage as a result of "flow back" caused by the use of a regional anesthetic. The drug seeped out from under the tourniquet into the bloodstream, causing irreversible brain damage. The "flow back" problem when the drug was administered to young children had not been studied sufficiently.

Ninth Commandment: Thou Shalt Give Adequate Warnings

The failure to provide adequate warnings regarding the safe use of a product is considered to be a type of product defect. The labeling of vaccines, for example, must be clear and not false or misleading.[208] Failing to warn consumers of excessive preventable dangers so that they can take steps to avoid the peril is frequently the cause of punitive damages.

A Japanese company marketed a modular telephone knowing that the hand-held model posed a danger of "ear-blasting" and "ear blowouts." Punitive damages were assessed in favor of an unwarned physician who suffered permanent hearing loss. The "smoking gun" in the case was the company's extensive file of prior "ear blasting and blowout cases." The company appeared to consider ear-blasting to be a cost of doing business, not a dangerous condition to be corrected.[209]

A family of four died from carbon monoxide poisoning caused by the use of charcoal briquettes indoors to heat their home. The warning was inadequate to advise consumers of the deadly hazards of using charcoal without sufficient ventilation. The anemic warning on the label read:

"CAUTION—FOR OUTDOOR USE—COOK ONLY IN PROPERLY VENTILATED AREA."[210] Today, all packages contain conspicuous warnings of the deadly consequences of burning charcoal without proper ventilation.

In *Starkey v. Whiteside Motors, Inc.*,[211] the steering locked on a young woman's 1987 Pontiac Grand Am, causing her automobile to crash into an embankment and roll over. She was driving to Whiteside Motors, the defendant, at the time of the accident to determine the cause of a noise in the steering of her automobile. Punitive damages were based upon the claim that certain GM models suffered from a condition known as "morning sickness," which caused a sudden loss of power resulting in hydrostatic lock. The "smoking gun" was evidence that General Motors knew of the problem but discontinued warnings to dealers and vehicle owners.

Cover-ups and concealment were aggravating circumstances in many of the punitive damages verdicts against the manufacturers of asbestos. Asbestos-related diseases are permanent, irreversible, and almost always fatal.[212] An estimated 21 million American workers were exposed to asbestos fibers in the workplace starting in 1930.[213] Workers handled asbestos without protective equipment or even a warning about the serious consequences of unprotected exposure.

A woman whose husband died of asbestosis after being exposed for more than a decade filed the first successful product lawsuit against the manufacturer.[214] The court found the defendants strictly liable for the failure to warn workers. Johns-Manville Corporation's medical personnel were instructed not to inform workers about the results of medical tests that confirmed that they were suffering from asbestosis. The president of an asbestos company wrote a letter to its legal director stating "the less said about asbestos, the better off we are."[215] In *Menne v. Celotex Corp.*,[216] the plaintiff suffered from chronic lung disease caused by exposure to asbestos dust while working as a pipe fitter in a shipyard from 1942 to 1948.[217] Punitive damages were based upon the defendant's "knowledge of hazards of asbestos since 1930" and its failure to warn workers of these known hazards.[218]

Even an inadequate warning of product dangers may provide a punitive damages safe harbor in some jurisdictions. In *Kritser v. Beech Aircraft Corp.*,[219] a court refused to submit a punitive damages claim to the jury even though the company's inadequate warning did not exhibit the appropriate level of concern for public safety. However, there are a great number of other cases where punitive damages were predicated upon an inadequate warning. In *Mason v. Texaco, Inc.*, the U.S. Court of Appeals for the Tenth Circuit upheld punitive damages for the defendant's inadequate warning of the known carcinogenic risk from unprotected exposure to benzene fumes.[220] The decedent developed leukemia and died after being exposed to benzene that the defendant produced and marketed without providing a warning.

The fiery deaths of the plaintiff's husband and two children in a Toyota Corona station wagon, which was rear-ended and burst into flames, led to a $44.2 million award in *Adegbite v. Toyota*.[221] The force of the rear-end collision punctured the gas tank, engulfing the passenger compartment in flames. Punitive damages were based upon the company's failure to warn consumers about the fuel-integrity problems, despite its knowledge of previous similar accidents. The vulnerability of this model to fuel-fed fires was open and obvious, yet Toyota marketed the model without correcting the problem or warning motorists.

Inadequate warning claims are often coupled with design defect causes of action in automobile products liability litigation. On June 27, 1973, Patricia Rinker went to a Ford dealership in Clay County Missouri.[222] A salesman showed her three used Ford LTDs and took Mrs. Rinker on a test drive in each vehicle. The third automobile was a 1969 Ford LTD with a V-8 engine. While driving back to the dealership, she pressed the accelerator to the floor to test the car's pick up.[223] The second time she checked the acceleration, she removed her foot from the pedal, but the car continued to accelerate. As she approached the intersection at high speed, she crashed into a concrete median divider. The LTD became airborne, striking another vehicle. Mrs. Rinker suffered permanent disfigurement with scars on her face, head, and on both knees. Ford Motor Company was assessed punitive damages based upon evidence that the company had twenty-nine prior reports of incidents of broken fast-idle cams causing accidents, but took no steps to warn its dealers.

An inadequate warning may be deemed "heedless" and "reckless," justifying punitive damages. The product manufacturer that fails to warn, or gives an inadequate warning of a known danger, does so at its own peril. Saving money by failing to warn the public is a false economy.

Tenth Commandment: Thou Shalt Do Complete Remedial Measures

An automobile manufacturer's incomplete remedial measures in the face of a public danger may create a basis for punitive damages. Failure to aggressively recall malfunctioning valves in the braking systems of semitrucks led to punitive damages in *Davis v. Velan Enterprises*.[224] In *Davis*, a nineteen-year-old truck driver was killed when his brakes failed. The defendant manufacturer had knowledge of a number of prior brake failures attributable to malfunctioning of the brake valve. The defective valve had been subject to a previous inquiry by a regulatory agency.[225] "The manufacturer . . . made a 'running' manufacturing change; that is, it used up all the defective valves before installing a new valve. It was one of the [defective] valves installed during the 'manufacturing' change that malfunctioned causing our accident."[226]

Punitive damages were assessed against a car dealer because of its improper repair of an automobile's wiring.[227] The "smoking gun" in *Petrus Chrysler-Plymouth v. Davis* was an independent contractor's testimony that the defendant had instructed him to do the incomplete repair of a potentially dangerous condition:

> [The] independent contractor testified that Defendant instructed him not to repair the wiring but simply to rig it so that the air conditioner and radio would work. The Defendant told the independent contractor they would repair it later if the Plaintiff complained. . . .
>
> [The] vehicle burst into flames while being driven by . . . the [purchaser's] wife with young children as passengers. They just barely escaped before flames completely engulfed the vehicle.[228]

Punitive damages were based in part upon the dealer's concealment of the danger, which led to the family's injuries.[229]

Concealment of a product defect from dealers led to a $15 million punitive damages award in *General Motors Corp. v. Johnston*.[230] On August 12, 1987, Ford Lewis was driving a 2500 series Chevrolet pickup truck. Lewis had purchased the truck two days earlier and had driven it less than 200 miles. His seven-year-old grandson, Barton Griffin, was riding in the passenger seat. Lewis stated that as he attempted to drive through a highway intersection, the engine of his pickup stalled. A tractor-trailer truck, driving through the intersection, struck the pickup truck, injuring Lewis and killing Barton. A defective computer chip had caused the truck to stall. This programmable read only memory chip (PROM) failed to properly relay commands to the engine.

Punitive damages were based on General Motors' prior knowledge of defects in the computer chip placed in its pickups. The company issued a "silent" or "unpublished" recall whereby it informed all of its dealers to replace the PROM with a newly designed computer chip only if a customer complained. The plaintiffs offered into evidence 268 internal reports of stalling problems with the pickups caused by defective chips. The jury awarded $75,000 in compensatory damages and $15 million under Alabama's wrongful death statute.

The Alabama Supreme Court reduced the award by half but found a sufficient basis for punitive damages because of General Motors' business decision to risk the public rather than to recall or replace the defective computer chips. The court observed that "this is not a case where the death occurred as a result of mere inadvertence or even where wanton conduct occurred on a single occasion. Here General Motors placed hundreds of thousands of its customers' lives at risk in order to save money and increase its profits."[231] It would have cost $42 million to recall the 600,000 pickups. This figure did not take into account the lost sales that General Motors would have suffered from the adverse publicity of the nationwide recall.

In *Cantrill v. Amarillo Hardware Co.*,[232] a company was assessed punitive damages when it delayed making changes to a ladder that violated a safety standard developed by Underwriters Laboratories, an industry standards–setting organization. Underwriters threatened to remove its certification if modifications were not made. Punitive damages were awarded because the company continued to sell its stock of defective ladders after learning of the need for a design change, exposing the public to excessive preventable dangers.[233]

In *Collins v. Interroyal Corp.*,[234] the defendant's continued marketing of a stool known to be defective was evidence of its "conscious disregard for the safety of others." The stool was unreasonably dangerous because it did not possess a reliable locking mechanism. As in *Cantrell*, punitive damages were based upon evidence that the company changed its product design, yet continued to sell the old defective stools. A company must take all practical steps to reduce excessive preventable dangers or face the consequences. A manufacturer risks punitive damages when it uses up its defective inventory before stocking newly designed products. Just as an inadequate warning may trigger punitive damages, so will inadequate remedial measures.

$5.5. Conclusion

Preventive law anticipates and resolves problems before they become full-blown personal injury cases. The lesson of three decades of punitive damages awards is that these verdicts are patterned and therefore preventable. Promptly discovering and reporting hazards will mitigate punitive liability. Without centralized safety oversight, a company may not spot a pattern of developing dangers until there is an epidemic of consumer injuries. Liability audits may help a company take early corrective action. Environmental reviews, for example, help companies "identify inappropriate or unlawful environmental practices. By taking early corrective action, a company can avoid even greater liability for penalties or response costs in subsequent years, and can reduce the possibility of shutdowns."[235] Preventive law may be the basis for challenging unnecessarily burdensome laws and regulations, resulting in improved public relations and more effective management.[236] Having completed a legal audit is a mitigating circumstance and may refute a plaintiff's claim that the company was recklessly indifferent to the public interest.[237]

Ford Motor Company is an example of a company that has enacted preventive law measures in the wake of several punitive damages awards. In 1980, Ford appointed a new president, Donald Peterson, who championed improved safety oversight.[238] In 1982, Ford implemented significant improvements in fuel-system integrity. The company instituted the most advanced air-bag program of any American manufacturer.

As with Ford Motor Company, punitive damages may be the impetus for changes in corporate policies that turn out to be good for business in the long run. Tort reform is a distraction that undermines preventive vigilance. Companies court disasters such as the mass torts of thalidomide, toxic shock syndrome, and silicone breast implants when they do not make product safety a priority. The minimal, reactive approach advocated by tort reformers is a poor substitute for preventive measures. A company is far more likely to be bankrupted by the loss of public trust in its products than by a sizable punitive damages award.

6

A Tort Law for the Twenty-First Century

> Forecasting the "future of tort law," the bridge from now into a generation hence will arch three areas: an area of stable doctrine; an area of assault upon, possible retreating from, and retrenchment of existing gains; and the largest sector, steady progress and continued breakthrough in the area impinging on the liberty and security of the individual. —Thomas F. Lambert, Jr., "Law in the Future: Tort Law: 2003," *Trial* (July 1983): 93

§6.1. Introduction

The outset of a new millennium is a good time to speculate on the future of tort law. Tort law historically has provided important consumer protections for average citizens "against entities too powerful to be restrained by lesser remedies."[1] It continues to fulfill its latent function of providing a grievance mechanism for the most vulnerable members of American society.[2] Torts provide individual compensation while policing corporate malfeasance. Women, consumers, workers, and the elderly are just a few of the groups that have benefited from this private law with a public vision. Those who pursue torts act as private attorneys general, playing an important role in filling the enforcement gap against reckless misconduct.

This chapter argues that by employing private law for a public purpose, tort law will continue to be vital in the twenty-first century. Tort law is an effective form of social control to vindicate "ideas and institutions which are central to our civilization (the dignitary interest of the individual) . . . bodily integrity, freedom of speech, family rights, right to privacy, reputation, emotional tranquility, the right to enjoy property and to do business, the protection of the honest business . . . from the despoiler and the cheat."[3]

The most important latent function of tort law is the "business of interstitial legislation," that is, of compensating for wrongs that are rarely punished through criminal law.[4] Private attorneys general fulfill the latent function of expressing grievances in areas where government enforcement is lax or nonexistent.

§6.2. Tort Law's New Collective Justice

Despite two decades of retrenchment, new vistas for tort remedies are emerging. Islands of tort expansion include new rights to redress for substandard health care, nursing home abuse, hate groups, human rights violations, tobacco products liability, poorly tested medical products, and Internet-related wrongdoing.

[A] Patients' Rights

The continuing vitality of tort law is evidenced today in the patients' rights movement to redress abuses by managed care organizations. Individual lawsuits against Health Maintenance Organizations (HMOs) are giving way to class action litigation for "patterns of pain" caused by impermissible cost cutting, for gag clauses that penalize physicians who discuss treatment options with patients, and for limiting access to specialists.[5] Aetna was recently sued for instituting concealed policies that place the company's profits above the goal of delivering quality health care.[6]

Cost cutting by managed care organizations has alienated doctors as well as patients. Physicians in California, New Jersey, and Pennsylvania have filed class actions against HMOs for payment delays and for the failure to reimburse them for services rendered.[7] Joinder of claims is the only practical means for patients and physicians to make managed care providers accountable for profit-driven decisions that violate the public interest.[8]

[B] Elder Abuse in Nursing Homes

The elderly in nursing homes are particularly vulnerable to substandard medical treatment. In recent years, class actions have been filed against nursing home chains that engage in impermissible cost cutting leading to inadequate staffing, safety code violations, patients left in feces and urine for hours, and other deplorable conditions. Nursing home patients rarely file individual cases. As Richard Epstein observes, elderly "victim/patients are not good candidates for sizable verdicts. . . . Many of them are old and sickly."[9] Only the joinder of claims, coupled with the prospect of punitive damages, permits these plaintiffs to file suit. Florida governor Jeb Bush has proposed a tort reform that would limit the size of awards against nursing homes.[10]

[C] Torts against Hate Groups and Hated Individuals

The congregation of a black church in South Carolina obtained tort damages when arsonists burned their house of worship as part of "the Christian Knights practice of promoting white supremacist goals through violent means."[11] The Ku Klux Klan in Texas was the defendant in a punitive damages lawsuit filed by private attorneys general.[12] The Southern Poverty Law Center won $1 million in punitive damages against the Church of the Creator, a racially motivated group.[13]

The Aryan Nations was assessed $6.3 million for negligent supervision of its guards, who assaulted a couple outside its headquarters.[14] The multimillion-dollar punitive damages award was based on the pattern of "outrageous conduct" of Aryan Nations' founder Richard Butler in encouraging a climate of hate and hiring unstable individuals with a propensity for violence.[15] Unable to pay the verdict, the defendants filed for bankruptcy. The sheriffs seized their assets, including the group's headquarters and Internet website. The organization was even required to transfer the intellectual property rights to the name "Aryan Nations" to the plaintiffs.[16]

Punitive damages have also been assessed against hated individuals who are beyond the reach of the criminal law. The Ninth Circuit U.S. Court of Appeals upheld a $1.2 billion punitive damages award against the estate of the former president of the Philippines, Ferdinand Marcos, to punish a pattern of human rights violations.[17] Punitive damages were also awarded to the victims of a "campaign of torture, arbitrary imprisonment and summary executions against perceived enemies of the government" at the hands of an Ethiopian dictatorship.[18] O. J. Simpson was assessed $25 million in punitive damages by a civil jury for the aggravated circumstances surrounding the murder of Nicole Simpson and Michael Goldman. The size of the verdict was calibrated to have the proper punitive effect in light of O. J. Simpson's wealth and imputed future earnings.[19]

[D] Tobacco Liability

The catastrophic economic costs of tobacco-related illnesses fell on the smoker, the health care provider, and the taxpayer until class actions were filed against the tobacco industry. Rather than face the possibility of unlimited punitive damages awards, the cigarette companies agreed to a $246 billion settlement. In 1998, Congress expanded the tobacco settlement to $516 billion over twenty-five years.[20] In addition to this payment, a Florida jury awarded a $144.8 billion punitive damages award in a class action consisting of 500,000 victims of lung cancer and other diseases caused by smoking.[21]

[E] Poorly Tested Medical Products

Thousands of women joined a class action against the American Home Corporation on the grounds that its "fen-phen" diet drug combination caused heart-valve damage and other injuries. Under a class action settlement, those suffering from heart-valve disease caused by this poorly tested drug combination will receive settlements whose size will depend on their age and the severity of their injury. Another 6 million former users of this medication, who currently demonstrate no symptoms, will be paid the costs of medical monitoring.[22]

§6.3. Pursuing Collective Justice

Class actions are a mechanism to overcome the difficulties of "one individual bringing a sole action prosecuting his or her rights."[23] The private attorney general employs joinder of claims to permit victims of mass torts to redress harms through collective justice. The court must determine that the claims or defenses of the represented parties are typical of the class and that the group's representatives will fairly and adequately protect the interests of the class.[24]

Class action lawsuits may be subject to abuse, especially in so-called "coupon settlements" in which consumers receive only a small discount if they purchase additional products or services from the defendant vendor.[25] While the victims collect a pittance, the plaintiffs' attorneys may receive millions of dollars. Such one-sided deals do nothing to vindicate the "rights of groups of people who individually would be without strength to bring their opponents into court at all."[26]

Corporations stand accused of encouraging such settlements as a way of protecting themselves against damaging verdicts. John Coffee argues that the class action is in danger of being turned from a plaintiffs' weapon into a defense shield: "Some corporations welcome and even seek out class action litigation and settlements as quick routes out of costly courtroom battles resulting directly from their misdeeds."[27]

Judges have the power to reject settlements that contain disproportionately large attorneys' fees or that shortchange the consumer. The court vetoed a settlement of the Ford Bronco II class action in which Ford proposed to provide consumers with a video on how to drive, a road atlas, a flashlight, and an opportunity to purchase high-priced cellular service from the company. The plaintiffs' attorneys were to receive $4 million in return for accepting Ford's liability-limiting proposal. The court also rejected a class action settlement involving Nissan vans sold between 1987 and 1990 in which the company offered vehicle owners only a $500 discount coupon for future purchases while the plaintiffs' attorneys were to receive $1.5 million.[28]

[A] The Joinder of Private and Public Attorneys General

The most controversial types of class actions are those filed jointly by private and public attorneys general. The line between private and public has blurred in the past three years as state and city governments have begun to hire private attorneys to prosecute class action lawsuits against industries whose hazardous products create a financial burden that is borne by the taxpayers. Forty-six states have joined in a $206 billion Master Settlement Agreement over twenty-five years to pay for the public health costs of tobacco-related illnesses.[29] Two dozen states have already received hundreds of millions of dollars in payment to reimburse them for medical costs arising from smoking-related injuries. The Master Settlement Agreement was the first time the tobacco industry was held responsible for the costs of health problems due to tobacco use.[30]

A number of municipalities are suing handgun manufacturers to recoup the public health and other costs arising from the negligent marketing of these weapons. The plaintiffs contend that areas with weak gun control regulations are being provided with more weapons than the local market can absorb, knowing that the surplus will be resold through illegal channels. State attorneys general are joining forces with private lawyers in prosecuting these cases in New Orleans, Atlanta, and Newark. The plaintiffs argue that the manufacturers irresponsibly sell their guns in a manner that makes it particularly easy for the weapons to end up in criminal hands.[31] These claims of negligent marketing and distribution of handguns have largely been dismissed.[32]

Rhode Island's attorney general has retained a prominent South Carolina plaintiffs' law firm to prosecute lead paint manufacturers for marketing a product that can produce mental retardation in children.[33] Plaintiffs' attorneys in these public/private lawsuits are paid for their work through contingency fees. The firms do not receive any money unless the state collects a judgment. If the plaintiffs win, the payment to the private law firms can be enormous.[34] Rhode Island, for example, has agreed to remit 17 percent of any proceeds from its class action to the private attorneys.

Corporate America favors curbing the use of private attorneys general in public interest litigation. As governor of Texas, George W. Bush signed a bill limiting the authority of that state's attorney general to retain private companies to aid in class action lawsuits.[35] At the federal level, the Interstate Class Action Jurisdiction of 1999 is the most recent in a series of bills proposing limits on consolidated lawsuits, products liability suits, medical malpractice awards, and punitive damages. The bill passed the House, but was not enacted by the Senate.[36] Congress is considering legislation to require all large class actions to be filed in federal court unless the plaintiffs are residents of a single state.[37] This will have the effect of preventing class actions from being pursued in states chosen for their relatively pro-plaintiff courts.

This expansion of tort law has been criticized as "a form of regulation through litigation in that attorneys general not only seek payments for government programs that help those who have been injured but also seek changes in the business practices of the industries being sued."[38] These public/private alliances are controversial because, despite the fact that the government initiated the lawsuits, defendants are not accorded the procedural protections provided in criminal trials.

[B] The Struggle over Capping Punitive Damages

Punitive damages are a key incentive for filing lawsuits against corporations because they allow private attorneys general to defray the considerable expenses of uncovering corporate wrongdoing by providing a bounty beyond the amount necessary for compensation. Keeping punitive damages in the hands of private attorneys general evens the playing field between claimants and corporations. The possibility of receiving a share of a punitive damages verdict was key to private trial attorneys agreeing to fund the war chest necessary to tackle the tobacco industry.[39] Immunity and limited liability breed indifference and irresponsibility. Optimal deterrence requires that punitive damages strip the defendant of the potential gain of wrongdoing and, perhaps, "sting" the defendant as well.

[C] New Threats to Private Attorney General Lawsuits

[1] The High Price of Secrecy

The private attorney general role in unmasking hidden dangers is being undermined by a disturbing trend toward court-approved protective orders classifying certain documents as confidential. Sealed court records undermine the latent function of tort law by allowing the company to continue to conceal problems from potential victims. More than three years before Firestone's recall of 6.5 million tires, a college football player was killed "after the tread on an ATX tire peeled away and the vehicle rolled over."[40] Firestone quickly settled the case confidentially, and hundreds of documents pertaining to the case were sealed "at Firestone's demand."[41] Firestone had settled at least eighty similar tire lawsuits since 1991, each under a secrecy agreement.[42]

A young father was paralyzed from the neck down and now requires a twenty-four-hour personal care attendant, because of the catastrophic injuries he suffered when using a yard toy called Slip 'N Slide. After filing suit against the manufacturer of the toy, the plaintiff's attorney learned of seven prior accidents in which consumers suffered broken necks while using it.[43] A videotape detailing substantially similar prior accidents had been sealed by court order as the result of prior confidential settlements. The plaintiff and his attorney hoped to issue a press release alerting consumers about the hazards of the Slip 'N Slide, but the defendant manufacturer told them that if they publicized the danger, there would be no settlement. The company eventually stopped manufacturing the Slip 'N Slide after additional lawsuits were filed against the manufacturer of this treacherous toy.

Confidential settlements should be restricted on public policy grounds. The case studies in Chapter 2 provide illustrations of the social hazards of permitting sealed settlements. In the 1992 case involving a sixty-seven-year-old farmer who was killed when his Kubota B-7100 tractor rolled over on top of him,[44] the family rejected a $10 million settlement with Kubota that would have precluded the disclosure of information about the tractor's defective design to the public as well as other potential litigants.

In the Kentucky school bus case, also discussed in Chapter 2, Ford offered the plaintiffs a confidential settlement that would have allowed the company to put the public relations disaster behind it by sealing the records. In fact, most of the victims' families settled their claims against Ford Motor Company and Sheller-Globe Corporation confidentially within a few weeks after the accident. But the Fairs and the Nunnallees refused to accept Ford's settlement offer. The resulting lawsuit exposed the problem of Ford's school buses to the public, saving the lives of schoolchildren nationwide.[45]

In our empirical studies of products liability and medical malpractice verdicts, we found a disturbing trend toward sealing court records. In products liability cases involving punitive damages decided after 1986, almost a third had confidential settlements concealing "smoking gun" evidence of dangerous defects. Confidential settlements were also found in approximately a third of the punitive damages medical malpractice cases. Secrecy agreements deprive private attorneys general, government regulators, and consumers of their most potent weapon against corporate misconduct—public knowledge of the defective product or impermissible corporate policy.

Secrecy agreements make it more difficult for other victims to obtain compensation for their injuries and result in additional preventable injuries and deaths. These settlements deprive the public of information about health, safety, and environmental hazards that is essential in making intelligent purchasing decisions. The social costs of secrecy far exceed the largely theoretical costs of overkill and bankruptcy of defendants who injure large numbers of persons.

[2] Capping Punitive Damages Is Capping Social Justice

Tort reformers seek to cap punitive damages, but caps on tort liability severely limit the remedy's efficiency in deterring corporate misconduct. Capping tort recoveries makes it possible for a corporate entity to accurately predict its punishment in advance and to incorporate that cost into the price of the consumer product or practice. The potential of unpredictable multiple punitive damages "forces a prudent manufacturer intent on max-imizing profits to hesitate before marketing a known defective . . . or an untested product."[46]

Caps on damages will hurt the interests of a variety of vulnerable Americans, such as brain-damaged infants injured by medical negligence. A federal court in Colorado reduced a $1 million non-economic damages award to $500,000 due to that state's tort reform statute. The capped award was for the family of an infant permanently disabled because of medical negligence in delivery.[47] Negligence during childbirth typically involves large awards of non-economic damages to compensate the child for a lifetime of misery. Pain-and-suffering awards also typically com-pensate the child's mother, who often must either leave the workforce or hire professional care for her invalid child. Limiting awards for pain and suffering to brain-damaged infants and their families sends a message that undermines traditional family values.

One critical issue is whether large punitive damages awards against corporations are constitutional. Defense lawyers have been successful in applying the Reconstruction Era's Fourteenth Amendment to protect corporations against excessive awards, arguing that large punitive dam-ages verdicts are a redistribution of the company's wealth without due process.[48] As Justice Sandra Day O'Connor warned in *Haslip v. Pacific Mutual Life Ins. Co.*,[49] punitive damages permit juries to target or penal-ize unpopular defendants or redistribute wealth.[50]

The Court has revisited the issue of how to determine if a punitive dam-age award is excessive several times during the last decade. In *Haslip*,[51] the Court found a punitive damages award with a ratio of greater than four times actual damages was close to the line of constitutional impropriety. In *TXO Production Corp. v. Alliance Resources Corp.*,[52] the Court stated that a key factor in determining the constitutionality of punitive damages was whether there was a reasonable relationship between punitive damages and compensatory damages. In *BMW of N. Am. v. Gore*,[53] the Court found a 500-to-1 ratio between punitive damages and compensatory damages to be grossly excessive.

The Court's emphasis on the ratio between punitive and compen-satory damages is misplaced and undermines the latent function of puni-tive damages. Under state law, it has long been established that punitive damages could consider the wealth of the defendant, because the amount of financial punishment necessary to deter a defendant of limited means is less than the sum required to sting a defendant with substantial assets.

Corporations are almost always assessed larger tort damages than individuals not because of blind redistributive impulses on the part of juries, but because of the nature of the harm they inflict. As William Prosser observed, "it is the corporation's capacity to absorb or avoid losses, rather than a predisposition against wealth that accounts for larger awards."[54]

Tort law's positive role in accident prevention is the result of successful lawsuits by private attorneys general equipped with the weapon of punitive damages. The threat of uncapped liability has inspired corporations to redesign their products and revise their policies to protect the public. Still, the role of the private attorney general is under unremitting attack. Tort reformers have successfully convinced legislatures, the press, and much of the public that juries are victimizing corporations by awarding "too much" to injured plaintiffs.[55]

The boundary between a tort defendant justly assessed a large sum for outrageous misconduct and a jury acting with improper "passion or prejudice" is a narrow one. As with so many legal reforms, the true answer to the concern about possible misuse of tort law lies in implementing sufficient procedural and evidentiary safeguards to ensure its proper use, not in discarding this flexible and essential tool.[56]

Capping punitive damages to two or three times actual damages will permit unscrupulous companies to engage in "strategic behavior" at the expense of all Americans. Some companies will find it cheaper to pay capped punitive damages than to alter dangerous, unethical, or risky business practices. A cap will lessen the deterrent function of punitive damages by allowing firms to trade public safety for profits on the basis of cost–benefit analyses. Caps will also make it more difficult for the elderly and other groups to bring lawsuits, resulting in heinous conduct going unpunished. Caps enacted at the state level reallocate the cost of suffering beyond an arbitrary amount of money from the wrongdoer to the victim, the family, and the taxpayers.

[3] Attacking Wealth-Based Tort Damages

Perhaps the most controversial aspect of tort law is taking a corporation's net worth or income into consideration in assessing punitive damages.[57] Punitive damages, unlike the criminal law, vary the punishment depending upon the economic circumstances of the defendant. Of the forty-five states that permit punitive damages, thirty-seven allow evidence of the defendant's wealth.[58]

Restricting punitive damages to a given ratio or cap is a disguised attack on the use of corporate wealth in setting punishment. Considering wealth in assessing the amount of punishment seems at first to be out of synch with the core American value of fair play. Anglo-American jurisprudence generally treats all individuals alike, at least in theory. The *Laidlaw v. Sage*[59] court succinctly stated the "cardinal principle" of American law is that the "rich and the poor stand alike in courts of justice, and that neither the wealth of the one nor the poverty of the other shall be permitted to affect the administration of the law."[60]

However, despite the fact that all comers are formally and procedurally equal in the American judicial system, there are numerous instances where wealth, or more often the lack of wealth, determines one's qualification or standing in the courts. The party with few legal resources is at a decided disadvantage when litigating against a national corporation. The possibility of punitive damages can be a significant bargaining chip that helps to level the playing field and thus to promote a fair settlement of the claim.

Wealth has long been considered relevant in many areas of the law. Numerous government regulations that take into account one's earnings are not considered denials of due process or impermissible unequal treatment before the law. Federal income tax rates are higher for individuals with large incomes, for example. Wealth is taken into consideration for taxation of Social Security benefits. These payments are taxed only when a recipient's income exceeds a certain level. Upper-middle-class families whose income exceeds a given level may be ineligible for or have restricted access to government-funded student aid and other programs. The Sherman Antitrust Act exacts fines of up to $10 million for corporations, but caps individual fines at $350,000. Wealth-based civil punishment is employed in civil forfeiture litigation, antitrust enforcement, and whistle-blower cases. The federal criminal code recognizes wealth-based payments and fines; the federal sentencing guidelines base corporate fines on the company's pecuniary gain from the offense and impose large fines to achieve deterrence.[61]

§6.4. The Historical Dispute over Wealth-Based Punitive Damages

The concept of punitive damages has always been particularly controversial because it is the only American legal remedy that explicitly takes into account the power imbalance created by the superior wealth and social

status of a defendant. In representing a rich man who was assessed punitive damages for an aggravated assault, Abraham Lincoln argued that the
defendant's wealth and power should not be admissible because of the
possibility of unfair prejudice against the rich. In 1845, the Illinois Appeals Court rejected Mr. Lincoln's argument:

> It is the policy of the law to protect the persons and property of the poor.
> The consequences of an assault upon a poor man, who has a family depen-
> dent upon his labor for support by which he is maimed for life, are surely
> more serious than they would be to a man in affluence. There is nothing
> more abhorrent to the feelings of the citizens of a free government than
> oppressing the poor and distressed under the forms and color of, but in re-
> ality in violation of, the law.[62]

Despite Lincoln's argument, the use of wealth in determining the size
of punitive damages remains a well-established principle of Anglo-American common law.[63] As recently as the early decades of this century, tort
litigants routinely made references to the defendant's wealth and the
plaintiff's poverty.[64] Appellate judges frequently referred to the social and
economic inequality between the parties in a lawsuit as a justification for
civil punishment.[65] But as a counterbalance, defendants were protected
by evidentiary and procedural safeguards against the misuse of evidence
of their assets. Trial lawyers who deliberately made references to corporate wealth in order to create populist outrage risked having their awards
set aside by the court on the grounds that the verdict was an improper result of the jury's "passion and prejudice."[66] The remedy recognizes that
the amount necessary to punish a major corporation must be greater
than that for a local business or individual, but that a defendant has the
right to a judicial review of the size of the punitive damages in order to
ensure that the penalty is not excessive.[67]

The contemporary critics of wealth-based punitive damages argue that
since the "wealthy defendant derives no greater benefit than a poor defendant, then both will be equally deterred (or equally undeterred) by the
threat of [compensatory] tort liability."[68] A prominent tort reformer
maintains that "[t]he wealth of the defendant bears no obvious relationship to deterrence goals. If the diminishing utility of money reduces the
rich defendants' 'real' liability costs, it equally reduces the risk-prevention
costs the defendant would need to incur."[69] Although such assertions are
theoretically elegant, they defy common sense.

An illustration of the potential role of wealth-based punishment in preventing a corporation from calculating the price of wrongdoing on a cost–benefit basis is the practice of a major package delivery service, whose trucks routinely ignore the parking regulations of Boston's Beacon Hill, with its quaint—and very narrow—historic streets and byways. The company treats the frequent tickets it receives as a result of its parking violations as simply a predictable and reasonable cost of doing business.

Punitive damages against this company would not be appropriate because no significant social harm results from its parking policy. However, if these delivery vans began leaving their trucks where they would block ambulances and fire trucks, punitive damages might be an optimal remedy because they could be calibrated to the amount necessary to deter a practice that endangers the public welfare. Caps on tort penalties allow defendants to calculate the long-term profit from their misbehavior and include such limited fines in their cost–benefit calculations as a routine cost of doing business.

When public well-being is at stake, wealth is a necessary ingredient in the punitive damages equation because of the vast assets of America's giant corporations.[70] As Justice Louis Brandeis warned:

> Through size, corporations, once merely an efficient tool employed by individuals in the conduct of private business, have become an institution—an institution that has brought such concentration of economic power over those so-called private corporations that are sometimes able to dominate the State. . . . Such are the Frankenstein monsters which states have created by their corporate laws.[71]

Punitive damages have long been awarded as an "impressive lesson" to powerful companies that abuse their position of authority.[72]

In the vast majority of states, punitive damages are based upon the wealth of the defendant as well as the actual and potential harm caused by its misdeeds.[73] This is good public policy. In a products liability action, a single defective item may cause catastrophic harm to hundreds of thousands of consumers. Corporations will not be deterred from externalizing large-scale risks unless punishment is proportional to their means.[74] If potential wrongdoers know that their total exposure is limited to a fixed amount, the deterrent effect is limited. As the *Goddard v. Grand Trunk Railway* court stated, "When it is thoroughly understood that it is not profitable to employ careless and indifferent agents, or reckless and insolent servants, better [employees] will take their places, and not before."[75] If wealth can be taken into account in setting punishment, even a multibillion-dollar corporation will think twice before subjecting the public to needless hazards.

$6.5. Why We Still Need the Private Attorney General Role

Those advocating tort reforms do not offer alternative forms of corporate punishment.[76] Although the jailing of company officials is sometimes mentioned as an effective deterrent to corporate wrongdoing, the imprisonment of executives is very rare, due to the complex structure and vast legal resources of large corporations. Punitive damages awards, when they have no cap arbitrarily imposed on them, function to create a "socially efficient level of expenditure on precautions."[77]

It is unclear how tort law will make the transition as the American economy is transformed from a durable goods–producing economy to one based upon intellectual property, information, and services.[78] Emerging technologies create new legal dilemmas to be policed by tort sanctions. The amazing malleability of old torts permits causes of action and remedies to evolve to counter new threats. In every historical epoch, tort law has quickly adapted to new social and technological conditions.

At early common law, torts punished the wrongdoer who violently assaulted his neighbor or seduced his neighbor's wife. In the age of the railroad, the law of negligence evolved to provide remedies for accidents caused by faulty trestles, careless maintenance, or reckless engineers. In the first half of the twentieth century, privacy-related torts developed along with the rise of the telephone, nationwide media, and electronic eavesdropping devices. In the 1960s, the law of products liability emerged to protect consumers against expanded dangers from destructive products, chemicals, and medical devices. Medical malpractice evolved to provide patients with protection against health care providers employing impermissible forms of cost cutting. Tort law is again evolving, this time to meet the new hazards presented by the information revolution.

$6.6. Torts in the Information Age

In only two decades, software publishing has grown from an infant industry to become America's third-largest industrial sector.[79] The U.S. software industry now consists of more than eight thousand companies selling products and services worldwide.[80] The information technology revolution has launched the networked personal computer that dominates the consumer market, as well as the worldwide system of interconnected computers that comprise the Internet.

Emerging technologies create new legal dilemmas that must be resolved by evolutionary developments in the law of torts. Data packets do not report to customs when they cross national borders on the virtual highway; routers do not pause to consider whether trade secrets are being misappropriated. Treaties defining cybercrimes have not yet been negotiated, making international law enforcement extremely difficult.[81]

[A] Gaps in Cybercrime Enforcement

Tort law plays a key role in punishing emergent forms of wrongdoing because criminal sanctions inevitably lag behind in times of rapid technological change. The greater flexibility of tort law gives it advantages over the criminal law in controlling harmful conduct in cyberspace. A fundamental principle of criminal law is that there must be "some advance warning to the public as to what conduct is criminal and how it is punishable."[82] This is an almost impossible burden to meet at a time when emerging technologies give rise to novel forms of socially harmful behavior. Tort law, on the other hand, does not require that defendants receive advance warning that some specific conduct is punishable by punitive damages.

Tort law has no death penalty or ability to incarcerate a defendant. However, a large tort award sends a social message that the victim deserves to be compensated at the perpetrator's expense. Companies know that they must control the online torts of their employees or risk being stung with substantial monetary damages.

Criminal laws must be carefully crafted to avoid constitutional challenges based on vagueness and other First Amendment concerns. An overly broad statute may have a chilling impact on the development of the Internet by criminalizing legitimate as well as socially destructive acts. The State of Washington's anti-"Spam" (unwanted e-mail) statute, the Washington Unsolicited Electronic Mail Act, was recently overturned for violating the U.S. Constitution's Commerce Clause.[83] California's anti-"Spam" law was similarly struck down because it "unconstitutionally subjects interstate use of the Internet to inconsistent regulations."[84]

Even when criminal statutes are clearly being violated, law enforcement against cybercrimes is unlikely to be effective. Federal, state, and local enforcement agencies lack the financial, technical, and scientific expertise necessary to investigate and punish many Internet-related harms. Every state has enacted a computer crime statute that criminalizes the invasion another's computer without authorization, but this form of lawbreaking is seldom prosecuted. Law enforcement funds for high-technology crimes are not a priority when compared to traditional crimes such as street violence, illegal use of drugs, or burglary.

Even if a high-technology crime unit is able to gather the evidence necessary to prosecute a cybercriminal, the trial is likely to be expensive and the outcome is uncertain. The burden of proof in a criminal prosecution is "beyond a reasonable doubt," a standard difficult to satisfy for Internet crimes because of the complexity of this high-technology environment. In the prosecution of a cybertheft of trade secrets, for example, there is often a need for an information security expert to reconstruct e-mails or other electronic "smoking guns."

[B] Torts in Cyberspace: The New Frontier

As the result of the difficulty of obtaining a criminal conviction, the victims of Internet-related torts are far more likely to seek civil redress. As one computer forensics expert advises: "First you find out who did it. Then get legal advice. And if you can't get it stopped, file a civil suit."[85] Today, tort-like remedies that are so new that they have not even been named are developing to deter cyberstalking, e-mail threats, online impersonation, identity theft, and secret monitoring of websites.

Justice Oliver Wendell Holmes, Jr., observed that "legal obligations that arise but cannot be enforced are ghosts that are seen in the law, but that are elusive to the grasp."[86] Internet torts are similarly elusive because, unlike traditional torts, they are not committed face-to-face. Tort law began as a body of law that chiefly protected bodily integrity and property, but it has now evolved to control Internet misdeeds that do not involve injuries as clear-cut as bodily damage or harms to tangible property. In the eighteenth century there was no doubt that an assault occurred when a defendant on horseback attempted to run down his neighbor. When a nineteenth-century railway conductor threw a passenger from a moving train, there was no problem of causal connection or of identifying the parties. In sharp contrast, the commission of torts on the Internet can be subtler and yet more damaging than the same acts committed in a traditional fashion.

Old tort principles are already being employed to police wrongdoing committed anonymously and seamlessly on the "global super-network of over 15,000 computer networks used by over 30 million individuals, corporations, organizations, and educational institutions worldwide."[87]

[C] Gender Justice in Cyberspace

Online stalking of women by males is a new threat created by the Internet.[88] The Federal Bureau of Investigation (FBI) has the resources and expertise to investigate cyberstalking of the U.S. president or other high governmental official, but not to protect the estimated hundreds of thousands of women stalked by predatory males, which is increasingly occurring on the Internet.[89]

In one recent example, a woman was systematically humiliated in an Internet "chat room" over a six-month period.[90] Her stalker posted "detailed personal information and a doctored pornographic photograph with her likeness" on a website.[91] He enlisted a network of Internet contacts to spread rumors that the victim was a drug addict looking for sex. This type of misbehavior is unlikely to be prosecuted by criminal law but nevertheless causes serious emotional injury to the plaintiff, and thus exposes the wrongdoer to the possibility of a large punitive damages award. Techno-tort remedies are developing to deter cyberstalkers, online impersonators, impostors, identity thieves, and sexual harassers. A female pilot working for Continental Express received a large punitive damages award from the company after several male co-pilots superimposed her face on pornographic pictures and posted them on a computer bulletin board.[92]

In *Coniglio v. City of Berwyn*, a female city employee filed a hostile workplace claim under Title VII of the Civil Rights Act of 1964 as well as an action for the intentional infliction of emotional distress arising out of her supervisor's habit of viewing pornography on the Internet in full view of her at work.[93] The plaintiff testified that her supervisor often printed out pictures of naked women on glossy paper and kept them in binders in his office. The plaintiff charged that she was terminated shortly after complaining about her supervisor's behavior as "wasting company time." The U.S. district court denied the defendant's motion to dismiss the plaintiff's hostile workplace and retaliation claims, but held the tort action to be preempted. The tort of outrage may be employed in future cases, provided that the facts give rise to a tort independent of the federal and state civil rights statutes.

Cyberstalking and e-mail harassment tend to be gender-linked injuries in which most perpetrators are men and most victims are women. The typical cyberstalking case involves an ex-husband, spurned lover, or distant admirer who uses anonymity to perpetrate threatening acts.[94] In a recent workplace harassment case, a male used anonymous remailers to harass a female co-worker in a plot to extort sexual favors from her by threatening to disclose her past sexual history.[95] Racism is also a factor in cyberstalking. The first conviction for online hate speech came in May 1998 against a California college student who e-mailed death threats to fifty-nine Asian classmates.[96]

A growing number of jurisdictions are considering updating the criminal law to punish online stalking.[97] California became the first state to enact a specific anti-cyberstalking statute in 1999. Michigan used its general anti-stalking law in 1996 to convict an e-mail harasser.[98] The Stalking Prevention and Victim Act of 1999 was introduced in Congress to strengthen federal laws against this rapidly growing form of misbehavior.[99] Because of the criminal law's "light penalties and the confusing, immature nature of state laws on cyberstalking, these cases are difficult to prosecute."[100]

Maryland recently enacted a statute punishing harassment by e-mail as a direct response to the inadequacies of existing legal sanctions for such conduct.[101] A New York court's dismissal of an Internet assault claim led to the passage of the law.[102] In that case, a University of Maryland graduate teaching assistant and writer answered a website advertisement soliciting writing samples from aspiring authors. The young woman received a letter in reply from an online literary agency that praised her writing and asked her to forward a full manuscript accompanied by a seventy-five-dollar "reading and market evaluation fee." To determine the authenticity of the agency, she sent a different sample of her writing to them using her maiden name. The agency responded to this second sample by sending the plaintiff a letter identical to the first response but this time soliciting a one-hundred-fifty-dollar fee.[103]

The graduate student concluded that the online agency was nothing more than a scam for soliciting bogus fees. When the plaintiff posted various notices on Internet bulletin boards denouncing the defendant and warning others not to pay for its "services," the company responded by launching a campaign of harassment against her on the Internet. The agency posted messages that falsely claimed that the plaintiff was the author of hard-core pornography, "mail-bombed" her e-mail account, and sent offensive messages to third parties about her. The plaintiff's name, address, and telephone numbers were posted on newsgroups specializing in sadomasochism.[104] False postings in the plaintiff's name were transmitted to electronic bulletin boards. For example, postings were made in her name on bulletin boards for beer lovers in which she appeared to denounce beer drinkers as drunks and morons. The company sent crank messages, posing as the plaintiff, to insult her co-workers.[105]

The online agency was discovered to be the harasser when "it slipped up and left her name and e-mail address in one of the literary agency's Internet ads." The victim filed a lawsuit charging that the agency deliberately placed her in danger of imminent sexual assault by posting Internet messages in her name containing crude sexual propositions.[106] She sought to recover damages for personal and professional injury including the cost of therapy. Despite the egregious circumstances of this case, the plaintiff's lawsuit was dismissed for failure to state a claim upon which relief could be granted. She had no remedy for the Internet harassment other than to close her e-mail account. The Maryland criminal prosecutors declined to prosecute the ersatz literary agency since there was then no state or federal criminal statute against using e-mails to intentionally harass others.[107]

[D] Tort Immunities in Cyberspace

Lawrence Lessig's book *Code and Other Laws of Cyberspace* argues that the producers and owners of information technologies have economic interests that may conflict with the public good. Legal rules must be developed, whether in tort law or through public regulation, that constrain commercial power on the Internet.[108] In the field of intellectual property, for example, information-producing and -distributing corporations seek special protections for business method patents, computer software, and Internet-related rights to distribute music, streaming video, and other information products.

Congressionally enacted tort immunities are a subsidy to the Internet-related economy in the same way that nineteenth-century courts subsidized the growth of the railroads by constructing liability-limiting defenses such as the fellow servant rule and contributory negligence. These immunities raise difficult questions of social policy. On one hand, the use of legal doctrine to protect infant industries may breed irresponsibility. A provider that has an absolute immunity from torts or infringements committed by its subscribers is less likely to develop safeguards against misuse and abuse of the Internet. On the other hand, excessive liability may hamper the valuable flow of information on the Internet. The following cases illustrate that well-intentioned immunities may produce unintended negative consequences.

The best-known statutory immunity granted to high-technology companies was the enactment of the Year 2000 Information and Readiness Act, which made it more difficult to file tort lawsuits for damages suffered because of "Y2K" related computer failures. This statute, which was enacted over President Bill Clinton's veto, requires that plaintiffs provide defendants with a ninety-day notice period in which to fix the problem before a tort can be prosecuted. The law also requires that punitive damages be assessed under the standard of clear and convincing evidence, and it caps punitive damage verdicts against small business. Class actions involving more than a hundred plaintiffs and $10 million in damages can only be filed in federal court. This law turned out to have relatively little impact since the widely predicted Y2K disasters did not occur.

Broad statutory immunities have been enacted to protect interactive computer service providers from tort claims based on damaging information posted by third parties. In the late nineteenth century, courts held that telephone companies, telegraph operators, and other communication carriers were not liable for defamatory statements made over their lines. Newspapers, on the other hand, were held strictly liable for defamation as publishers. The Communications Decency Act of 1996 (CDA) applies similar principles to Internet service providers (ISPs) by granting them immunity from lawsuits for defamatory and other tortious activities occurring on their services.

Section 230 of the CDA states: "No provider or user of an interactive computer service shall be treated as the publisher or speaker of any information provided by another information content provider."[109] By defining the ISP as a mere conduit rather than a publisher, the federal statute was originally designed to limit liability for defamation by third-party postings on its service. The rationale was that the ISP lacked the resources to monitor millions of e-mail messages, postings, and other electronic communications on its service.

Congress recognized the threat that tort-based lawsuits "posed to freedom of speech in the new and burgeoning Internet medium."[110] Prior to the enactment of the CDA, the courts were sharply divided as to whether a provider could be charged with defamation for materials third parties posted on its service. Courts were divided as to whether an ISP was more like a publisher with traditional editorial functions or a conduit of information like a newsstand or bookstore.[111]

The courts have extended this statutory immunity far beyond its original intent of protecting the ISP in its publisher's role.[112] In *Zeran v. America Online*,[113] an anonymous person posted an Internet advertisement on an America Online (AOL) bulletin board offering "naughty Oklahoma t-shirts" for sale. The caption on the shirts indicates support for the bombing of the federal court building in Oklahoma City. Customers were given the home telephone number of the plaintiff to call if they wished to order the tasteless merchandise.

In fact, the Oklahoma bombing t-shirt advertisement was a hoax calculated to cause the plaintiff extreme emotional distress. Angry AOL subscribers threatened to kill Zeran. To make matters worse, an Oklahoma City radio station announced Zeran's telephone number on the air and he was "inundated with death threats and other violent calls." AOL was notified of the deception but refused to let the plaintiff post a retraction.

Zeran filed a lawsuit against AOL and the radio station but was unable to serve process on the primary perpetrator because of his inability to discover who had committed the cruel hoax. The *Zeran* court ruled that AOL could not be held culpable, interpreting Section 230 as creating an absolute "immunity to any cause of action that would make service providers liable for information originating with a third-party user of the service."[114] The court ruled that "Congress considered the weight of the speech interests implicated and chose to immunize service providers to avoid any restrictive effect."[115] This broad immunity left the plaintiff without any remedy for the harm he had suffered.

In *Blumenthal v. Drudge*,[116] AOL was sued for defamation arising out of the online edition of a political gossip column. Matt Drudge had an exclusive contract with AOL, which paid him royalties of $3,000 a month to publish his "Drudge Report" on its computer system. In August 1997, Drudge wrote and transmitted a defamatory statement about White House senior aide Sidney Blumenthal, falsely alleging that Blumenthal had a history of spousal abuse.

Blumenthal filed suit against Drudge and AOL, arguing that Section 230(c)(1) did not immunize AOL because Drudge was in a contractual relationship with AOL rather than being a mere poster. The court disagreed, ruling that Section 230 granted AOL immunity despite the licensing relationship. This interpretation of the statute strips the ISP of a major incentive to protect the public. AOL benefits from the traffic and advertising revenues produced by Drudge but bears no responsibility for his misdeeds.

The District of Columbia Court rejected Drudge's contention that it lacked jurisdiction over defamatory statements in the Drudge Report because the deed had taken place in cyberspace rather than in Washington, D.C. The court ruled that because Drudge's interactive website specifically focused on D.C. political gossip, and because the columnist regularly distributed his writings to D.C. residents, the lawsuit could proceed.[117]

The immunity granted under Section 230 has also been extended to include an ISP's chat rooms. In *Jane Doe v. America Online, Inc.,*[118] a child pornographer used an AOL chat room to contact young boys for sexual purposes. The plaintiff and two other youths engaged in sexual activity with the defendant and with each other. The defendant photographed and videotaped these sexual encounters and used the chat room to sell the obscene pictures. The plaintiff argued that AOL had violated Florida's Computer Pornography and Child Exploitation Prevention Act of 1986 by allowing the defendant to offer child pornography for sale on the website.

AOL moved to dismiss this and other causes of action based upon the immunity granted by the CDA. The trial court agreed with AOL's position that the broad immunity applied to the anti–child pornography statute as well as to the common law of torts. The Florida court of appeals affirmed, ruling that the CDA preempts Florida law on these causes of action.[119]

In another case, an anonymous user of an ISP posted messages falsely charging that the plaintiffs were performing satanic rituals on children. The plaintiffs sued the provider for negligence as well as for the intentional infliction of emotional distress. The court held that these causes of action were barred under the safe harbor provision of the CDA, leaving the plaintiffs with no recourse against the ISP.[120]

The stalker-murderer of a New Hampshire woman obtained personal information about his victim by employing an Internet research service. The killer had been infatuated with the woman since high school. Prior to murdering her, he had threatened her on several web pages and had used the personal information provided by the research service to track her movements. The ISP is immunized, but it remains an open question whether the court will extend this immunity to the Internet research service.

The downside of broad immunities is that the ISP has less of an incentive to make its service safe for the consuming public. ISPs with a tort safe harbor may delay development of the technologies needed to prevent wrongdoing.

[E] John Doe in Cyberspace

Anonymous wrongdoers are being unmasked by private attorneys general with little help from ISPs. Tort litigants are using John Doe subpoenas to compel the ISP to disclose the identity of anonymous wrongdoers. Compaq filed a John Doe subpoena against an ISP, ordering it to disclose the identity of anonymous posters of false information that might affect Compaq's stock price.[121] A Seattle financial education company filed a slander lawsuit against ten users of Yahoo! message boards who were identified through the use of a subpoena.[122] An Emory University professor used a John Doe subpoena to identify the author of an anonymous libelous posting on a website. The Virginia jury awarded the plaintiff $350,000, the first punitive damages award for online defamation.[123]

A John Doe subpoena may be the only viable way to unveil the identity behind an anonymous harasser or a "Spam"-transmitting website. However, forcing ISPs to disclose the identity of posters may have a chilling effect on free expression.[124] It is unclear whether a provider would be immunized by Section 230 if it refused to respond to John Doe subpoenas. A court recently held that E-Bay was immune under Section 230 for an unfair competition lawsuit for bootleg musical recordings sold on its website.[125] As a result of these court decisions, major Internet firms are immune for unlawful sales or postings. In order for tort liability to arise, the provider must have actual knowledge of illegal sales and take some affirmative action to facilitate the wrongdoing. John Doe subpoenas raise troubling privacy issues when corporations use them to unmask whistle-blowers who criticize company policies in online forums.[126]

[F] Online Privacy

Tort law is evolving as ISPs develop new technologies to investigate anonymous attacks on subscribers. In *John Does v. Franco Productions*,[127] a number of intercollegiate athletes were secretly videotaped in various states of undress by hidden cameras in restrooms, locker rooms, and showers. The videotapes were sold to a number of websites, including Genuity.net and TIAC.net, which transmitted still images of the nude or partially clothed athletes on the Internet. The court dismissed the plaintiffs' complaint against the web host, finding that it was immune from liability for invasion of privacy and other torts associated with the distribution of the tapes on the Internet.

An ISP is able to trace third-party identities provided that the victim reports the online misconduct promptly. The FBI's computer crime unit employs new tracing and tracking technologies to investigate cyber-crimes. The FBI presented "419 computer crime cases to federal prosecutors in 1998, an increase of 43 percent from 1997."[128] While the partnerships among law enforcement, ISPs, and customers in tracing wrongdoing are socially useful, such activities raise obvious privacy issues.

The erosion of privacy has accelerated with the rise of the global Internet. Data are sold, transferred, retransmitted, and manipulated as the lifeblood of e-commerce. "Big businesses gather customer data with 'vacuum cleaner'–type processes and store the data."[129] Litigation over who has the rights to various types of information gathered by corporations will be occupying the courts for years.[130] The CVS drugstore chain, for example, is currently facing a lawsuit for selling confidential information about the purchases of its customers to pharmaceutical manufacturers.[131] Health Net, a California insurance company, compromised the privacy of 12,000 patients when it transmitted sensitive medical records to the wrong doctors.[132]

Cookies are text files saved in a "Netscape Communicator or Microsoft Internet Explorer (the major browsers) directory or folder and stored in RAM while the individual's browser is running."[133] Because "cookies" permit companies to trace online activity, they invade the user's privacy. Many of the major corporations have voluntarily agreed not to send e-mail to the browser's address or sell personal information to third parties without the user's consent.[134] It is an unsettled question as to what tort remedies Americans have for the misuse of information collected on corporate websites. A variety of other difficult issues are emerging, as the Internet increasingly becomes part of everyday life.

[G] Online Privacy in the Workplace

The Fourth Amendment prohibits unreasonable searches and seizures by government entities, but it does not apply to the private workplace. The law protects government workers from unreasonable searches by their employer, but employees in private workplaces do not enjoy similar protection.[135] An estimated 45 percent of large U.S. companies currently monitor their employees' electronic communications.[136] Private businesses are free to secretly monitor their employees' Internet usage and e-mails, even if the company has assured the workers that their communications are confidential.[137]

The courts have uniformly held that computer systems are the property of the employer and that, therefore, the employee has no reasonable expectation of privacy in e-mail communications.[138] In a Massachusetts case, a C.E.O. spent eight hours reading his employees' e-mail messages and then fired those workers who had made disparaging, albeit accurate, comments about his sexual liaison with a co-worker. The court rejected the employees' claim that the secret monitoring violated the wiretap statute or the common law right of privacy.[139]

Employers often monitor the e-mail and Internet usage of their employees in order to prevent the misuse of these technologies and to ensure that employees do not jeopardize a company's trade secrets or proprietary information by careless use of e-mail or postings in Web chat rooms.[140] A Microsoft employee was terminated for sexual harassment based upon evidence gathered through secret monitoring of his e-mail. A court rejected his claim of invasion of privacy, holding that because the e-mail messages were stored on a company computer, they were not the employee's personal property.[141] Even if the employee had a reasonable expectation of privacy, Microsoft would have been privileged to access his e-mail messages to find relevant evidence in its investigation of sexual harassment. The court ruled that the company's interest in preventing inappropriate sexual comments outweighed the plaintiff's claimed privacy interest in those communications.

Corporations may be held vicariously liable for allowing racist or sexist misuse on their e-mail systems, which gives them a strong justification for monitoring the messages of their employees. Electronic networks are often set up with screening systems that red flag the use of harassing terms. Dow Chemical Company fired dozens of employees who transmitted pornographic or violent e-mails.[142] The corporation felt that it had no choice but to terminate the employees because of the risk that their activities would expose Dow to sexual harassment lawsuits.[143]

Employers may be tempted to fire workers for even minor e-mail misuse because an electronic "smoking gun" in an employee's inbox could be interpreted as evidence of a hostile work environment. Once placed on notice, employers may be subject to an Equal Employment Opportunity Commission investigation, or worse, a punitive damages lawsuit for failing to take prompt remedial measures against the harassment.[144]

The National Labor Relations Board (NLRB) has intervened in two recent cases to protect workers who had been fired for misuse of the company's e-mail system.[145] In one of these cases, a worker was dismissed for sending e-mail critical of the company's vacation policies.[146] In the second case, an engineer was fired for sending an e-mail containing union-organizing materials. Employees in the non-union environment are not likely to benefit from NLRB's intervention. Unless the employee is fired for using the Internet for union-related communications, e-mail monitoring would be outside the jurisdiction of the NLRB. As the use of e-mail in the workplace grows, tort law will increasingly be called upon to balance the competing interests of the employee's privacy rights and the employer's need to know. The field of workplace privacy is an area in which new tort remedies are needed.

§6.7. Old Torts in New Actions

Classic tort doctrines are being applied successfully to Internet wrongdoing. An example is the use of tort law to punish and deter unwanted e-mail or "Spam." "Spamming" is the practice of sending unsolicited e-mail, a tactic akin to flooding the postal service with junk mail. Although the practice is widely condemned in the Internet community, e-mail addresses are mined by junk mailers "who send out millions of messages over and over again."[147] An estimated 25 million junk e-mail communications are transmitted every day.[148]

The ancient tort of trespass to chattels has been extended to punish the purveyors of junk e-mail.[149] Plaintiffs argue that the defendants' continued transmission of e-mail messages through their computer equipment is actionable because it interferes with computer resources, which is the trespass to chattels. This flood of unwanted messages is not merely irritating to the recipient. The crushing weight of junk e-mail can clog a computer system and cause delay in scheduled upgrades.[150]

Hotmail, a Silicon Valley ISP, filed a trespass to chattels action against a Spammer who sent hundreds of thousands of unsolicited e-mails to its subscribers, advertising pornographic materials and get-rich-quick financial schemes.[151] The court found that the Spammer intentionally invaded Hotmail's computer system by creating accounts that exceeded the terms of service,[152] and held that it had trespassed upon the ISP's computer space by causing tens of thousands of misdirected and unwanted e-mail messages to appear to be authorized. In one of the very few criminal prosecutions for "Spamming," two defendants each received a two-year prison sentence for transmitting 50 million unsolicited junk e-mails.[153]

[A] Remedies for Fraudulent Concealment or for Spoliation of Electronic "Smoking Guns"

The new information technologies make it easy to destroy or alter evidence with a click of the mouse. *Fraudulent concealment of evidence* involves the alteration of electronic "smoking guns" that relate to existing or pending litigation. *Spoliation of evidence* is the deliberate destruction of, or the failure to preserve, essential evidence.[154] A corporation's intentional deletion of incriminating e-mail may create liability for the tort of spoliation. In New Jersey, a court imposed a $1 million sanction to punish a company's failure to preserve key documents in litigation.[155] New tort remedies will be needed to prevent individuals and organizations from covering the tracks of their wrongdoing as technological developments provide new means of digital deception.

[B] Liability for Computer Viruses

Electronic viruses are destructive computer codes that contain instructions to alter or destroy computer-based data files. These viruses infect "executable files or the system area of hard and floppy disks" and then damage other computer functions.[156] Viruses pose serious threats to companies, which may lose invaluable information from the unleashing of malicious code. Computers throughout the world were infected with the CIH virus activated on April 26, 1999; in March 1999 the "Melissa Virus" caused untold numbers of computers to crash worldwide.

Negligence is the failure to exercise the due care expected of a reasonable person under the circumstances. Applying negligence to computer viruses is difficult because the malicious code is introduced anonymously.[157] Once the infection begins, viruses are transmitted and then retransmitted accidentally by unaware parties. Because of this problem, consumers are increasingly demanding a warranty of "virus-free software."[158] A question for tort law is whether innocent parties should be held strictly liable for transmitting computer viruses.

Destructive computer viruses have caused widespread harm, but their authors have rarely been criminally prosecuted because of the expense of investigative work. State and federal computer crime statutes have been utilized on a few occasions to punish those who release viruses, but this is more the exception than the rule. The author of the Melissa computer virus pled guilty to violating New Jersey and federal law by causing $80 million in damage through unleashing this destructive code.[159] This is regarded as a landmark case because "[f]or the first time, we . . . have a legal precedent that sends a strong message to computer virus writers that they will be held accountable for their crimes."[160]

The inability of criminal law to deal effectively with new threats to the common good was illustrated by the dismissal of all charges against the author of the "Love Bug," the "most destructive computer virus to attack the Internet."[161] Although 45 million computers were infected by this computer virus, Philippines law enforcement authorities were powerless to prosecute the perpetrator since no criminal statute had been violated.

The software industry has sought to limit its liability for the risk of transmitting viruses, a proposal successfully opposed by consumer advocates.[162] An early draft of a software-licensing provision would have imposed a negligence-based standard in allocating responsibility for transmitting viruses.[163] This standard would make either the licensor (vendor) or licensee (user) liable for viruses introduced into a computer system after it leaves the software vendor's control. Future cybertort cases will focus on whether a software developer or programmer is liable for creating computer programs that are unusually susceptible to the introduction of viruses.

A closely related issue that has not been resolved by the courts is the software vendor's right to disable its product through "electronic repossession." Electronic repossession of software may be achieved through active or passive programs written into the software by the manufacturer. An active restraint impacts the licensee's ability to access his or her own information, whereas a passive restraint prevents unauthorized use but does not lock the owner out of his or her own computer. Installing an active disabling routine into software might subject a software vendor to intentional tort liability for spreading a potentially destructive computer virus.

[C] Fraud in Cyberspace

Tort liability for fraud may occur on the Internet when a seller misleads potential purchasers about the value of goods or services. A person selling fake sports memorabilia such as a forged Ted Williams autographed bat or golf clubs supposedly used by Tiger Woods may be punished for online fraud. Misrepresentation in online transactions encompasses a broad range of commercial activities and may occur with the sale, licensing, lease, rental, exchange of goods, or rendering of services. Whether Internet auction sites such as E-Bay can be held liable when sellers misrepresent items is unclear.[164]

The collapse of the public/private distinction is illustrated by the policing of private Internet transactions by the Federal Trade Commission (FTC). The FTC filed an action for deceptive trade practices in connection with an online auction in which computer products were paid for but never delivered.[165] In that case, the FTC entered into a settlement agreement with the online seller, barring him from ever conducting Internet commerce.[166]

[D] Identity Theft

Companies as well as individuals are vulnerable to being victimized by "identity fraud" on the Internet, since its anonymity allows users to make false claims.[167] The Internet makes it easy for imposters to assume false personas, making cyberspace a haven for identity theft. When an imposter used the plaintiff's Social Security number to apply for credit, the California federal court held that the credit-reporting agency needed to prove that it had used reasonable procedures to assure maximum accuracy.[168] The agency failed to meet this burden because it did not notice that the credit application information provided by the imposter included a name that was not identical to the plaintiff's.[169]

[E] Failure to Protect Internet Security

It is an open question whether a website must comply with an industry standard of care for network security. To date there are few cases dealing with whether a website may be sued for negligent security when it permits hackers, intruders, or other unauthorized third parties to misappropriate personal information or trade secrets. If a website does not have a firewall or an audit of intrusion attempts, is this negligent security? If a firewall is defectively designed and permits intrusions, is the software engineer liable for computer malpractice? If a company has a certified security system to protect third-party data but does not monitor intrusions, is it liable? If an intruder or virus destroys or alters data belonging to third parties, does the company's failure to have a contingency plan make it liable? These and many other questions about Internet security will shape the negligence law of cyberspace.

[F] Liability for Hate Speech in Cyberspace

The Internet has become a haven for hate groups. Racism and anti-semitism have spawned "more than 2,100 websites," mostly in the United States.[170] Germany had 330 registered hate websites in 1999, a number that doubled to 800 in 2000.[171] The Anne Frank Foundation estimates that the number of websites advocating racist violence could run as high as 8,000.[172] A typical website seeks to "destroy and banish all Jewish thought and influence," echoing Hitler's call for a "final solution."[173]

There are thousands of websites dedicated to advancing the cause of white supremacy. The *National Observer on the Internet* is an example of a racist Internet publication that "advocates biological terrorism and regularly celebrates 'lone wolves' such as Oklahoma City bomber Timothy McVeigh and Buford Furrow, accused in the 1998 attack on a Jewish preschool in the San Fernando Valley."[174]

A tort lawsuit was recently filed against a hate group that posted online threats. The Pennsylvania state attorney general sought an injunction against the group because its website contained threats of violence against specific members of the state's Human Relations Commission.[175] The site warned that "[t]raitors like this should beware, for in our day, they will be hung from the neck from the nearest tree or lamppost."[176] This is a clear example of the increasing role of torts in policing activities on the borderline between crime and tort.

Yahoo! was recently ordered by a court to prevent any French citizen from purchasing Nazi memorabilia on its online auction site. The case raises the issue of whether any court has jurisdiction to restrain hate speech in cyberspace.[177] Legal dilemmas such as these will shape the future path of Internet torts.

§6.8. Conclusion

Tort law's remarkable quality of continually adapting old causes of action to new threats and dangers makes it an important institution of social control.[178] The Maryland cyberstalking and workplace abuse cases are perfect illustrations of the continuing vitality of the law of torts. Tort law needs to be strengthened, not diminished, if it is to control abuses made possible by the Internet and other new information technologies. Tort law plays a key role in holding wrongdoers responsible for their misdeeds.

A strong tort regime ensures that not even multibillion-dollar corporations operate beyond the reach of the law. Tort remedies, such as punitive damages, teach even the most powerful actors that "tort does not pay."[179] Optimally, punitive damages are used to punish and deter wrongdoers when the "probability of detection is very low and the probability of harm is very high,"[180] which is often the case with Internet torts. To keep defendants from having an unfair competitive advantage, we must ensure that the price of wrongdoing significantly exceeds the gain.[181] Tort law is, as it always has been, forward-looking, with the ability to adapt to new social problems and conditions. Progressive tort law brings common sense to the common law.

Notes

NOTES TO THE PREFACE

1. William L. Prosser, *Handbook of the Law of Torts*, 3d ed. (St. Paul, Minn.: West Publishing Co., 1964), 14.

2. The term "civil wrongs" was coined by Lawrence Friedman is his study of how nineteenth-century tort law became a legal system for denying compensation to torts victims. Lawrence Friedman, "Civil Wrongs: Personal Injury Law in the Late 19th Century," *American Bar Foundation Research Journal* (1987): 351. Our book updates Friedman's thesis by examining how the tort reform movement is attempting to frustrate victims' rights to recovery. This book is also inspired by Roscoe Pound's *Social Control through Law* (1942; reprint, Hamden, Conn.: Archon, 1968).

3. W. Page Keeton et al., *Prosser and Keeton on the Law of Torts*, 5th ed. (St. Paul, Minn.: West Publishing Co., 1984), 5.

4. We are using the perspective of critical functionalism to uncover the hidden face of tort law. Robert Merton created the sociological concepts of manifest and latent functions. Robert Merton, *Social Theory and Social Structures* (Glencoe Ill.: Free Press, 1968). Herbert Gans employed structural functional analysis in his critical study of poverty. Herbert Gans, "The Functions of Poverty: The Poor Pay All," in John B. Williamson, Jerry F. Boren, and Linda Evans, eds., *Social Problems: The Contemporary Debates* (Boston: Little, Brown, 1974), 140–46; see Michael L. Rustad, *Women in Khaki: The American Enlisted Woman* (New York: Praeger, 1982) (applying "critical functionalism" to the increased recruitment of women in the all-volunteer military of the mid-1970s).

5. Government regulators were ineffective at uncovering the corporate misconduct that led to these cases. Despite these serious threats to the public safety, corporate defendants rarely received official sanctions. Few corporate defendants are ever fined or otherwise sanctioned, even when they recklessly endanger the American public. From 1965 to 1990 only one company was criminally sanctioned for wrongdoing that led to punitive damages in a products liability case. Few defendants even received civil penalties for conduct that led to an epidemic of deaths and catastrophic injuries. No civil penalties were imposed on these products liability defendants by the Consumer Product Safety Commission, the Food and Drug Administration, or any other federal or state regulator.

6. John G. Fleming, *An Introduction to the Law of Torts* (Oxford: Clarendon Press, 1967), 1.

7. *Neal v. Newburger Co.*, 154 Miss. 691, 700, 123 So. 861, 863 (1929).

8. By private attorney general, we are referring to both the plaintiff and his or her attorney.

9. *Janssens v. Johns-Manville Co.*, 463 So.2d 242 (Fla. 1984).

10. Id.

11. *Prudential Ins. Co. v. U.S. Gypsum*, 828 F. Supp. 287 (D.N.J. 1993).

12. *Medical malpractice* is a cause of action arising out of an injury or death caused by the negligence of a medical care provider. Medical malpractice considers prevailing standards of care in a given medical specialty. The level of care, skill, and treatment must also take into account surrounding circumstances. See, e.g., Fla. Stat. 766.102 (2000). If a physician is certified as a specialist, the standard of care becomes those specialists with similar training and skill.

13. "The contingent fee arrangement does not encourage lawyers to accept nonmeritorious cases with a low probability of winning just because the possible recovery is large." Stephen K. Dietz, C. Bruce Baird, and Lawrence Berul, "The Medical Malpractice Legal System," *Report of the Secretary's Commission on Medical Malpractice* (Washington, D.C.: U.S. Department of Health, Education and Welfare, January 16, 1973), 87, 154.

14. Charles Laurence, Film Review, "Crusader in High Heels," *The Mirror* (April 5, 2000): 22–23.

15. Renee Sanchez, "Fear of Toxins in Tap Water Rocks California Town," *Washington Post* (December 8, 2000): B1.

16. This phrase adapts Louis Brandeis, *Other People's Money and How the Bankers Use It* (New York: A. M. Kelly, 1971), 92.

17. Adam Cohen et al., "Are Lawyers Running America? Their Lawsuits Are Setting Policy on Guns, Tobacco and now HMO's, Who Elected Them?" *Time* (July 17, 2000): 22.

18. Gary T. Schwartz, "Tobacco, Liability, and Viscusi," *Cumberland Law Review* 29 (1999): 555.

19. Thomas F. Lambert, Jr., "NACCA—Rumor and Reflection," *Harvard Law Record* (September 1956): 1.

20. Steven McGready, Intel Corp., Keynote Address: "The Digital Reformation: Total Freedom, Risk, and Responsibility," in *The Harvard Conference on Internet and Society* (Cambridge, Mass.: O'Reilly and Associates, 1996) (quoting the late poet Allen Ginsberg).

21. Our colleague Tom Lambert wrote of the hypocrisy unleashed by tort reform lobbyists "who steamroll 'reform' statutes through the legislatures. . . . [T]he hypocrites responsible were the kind of lobbyists who would cut down a redwood tree and then mount the stump and make a speech for conservation."

Thomas F. Lambert Jr., "Editorial," *Journal of the American Trial Lawyers Association* 27 (1984): 438.

22. William Glaberson, "Damage Control: A Special Report; Some Plaintiffs Losing Out in Texas' War on Lawsuits," *New York Times* (June 7, 1999): 1.

23. Another form of tort reform is to limit appellate bonds securing verdicts before there is a final resolution to a case. Florida, for example, recently enacted a statute that "limits appellate bonds to $100 million or 10 percent of a company's net worth, instead of having to post bonds that cover the full amount of punitive damages." Lloyd Dunkelberger, "State Officials Doubt Award Will Stand Up," *Sarasota Herald-Tribune* (July 15, 2000): 1.

24. Litigation designed to intimidate and even bankrupt corporate critics has been labeled SLAPP (Strategic Litigation Against Public Participation) suits by professors George Pring and Penelope Canan of the University of Denver. George Pring and Penelope Canan, *SLAPPS; Getting Sued for Speaking Out* (Philadelphia: Temple University Press 1996).

25. Carl Deal and Joanne Doroshow, *The CALA Files: The Secret Campaign by Big Tobacco and Other Major Industries* (New York: The Center for Justice and Democracy and Public Citizen, NY: 2000).

26. Michael L. Rustad, "Nationalizing the Tort Law: The Republican Attack on Women, Blue Collar Workers, and Consumers," *Rutgers Law Review* 48 (1995): 673.

27. *Johnson v. Girdwood*, 7 Misc. 651, 28 N.Y.S. 151 (1894), aff'd. 39 N.E. 21 (1895).

28. Keith Bradsher, "A Study of Ford Explorer's Design Reveals a Series of Compromises," *New York Times* (December 7, 2000): C1.

29. Id.

30. "Feeding Frenzy over Firestone," *National Law Journal* (September 11, 2000): A-1.

31. Id.

32. Ricardo Alonso-Zaldivar, "Unlimited Fines Sought for Car Safety Violations," *Los Angeles Times* (September 12, 2000): A-1 (reporting attempts to raise the level of fines that could be imposed by regulators for auto safety violations).

33. Larry Kramer, "Firestone Hit by New Suit on '500' Tires," *Washington Post* (September 22, 1978): F1.

34. Id.

35. Joan Claybrook and David Bollier, "Regulations that Work: Ten Rules That Have Made Our Lives Better," *Washington Monthly* 18 (April 1986): 47.

36. The trial by water was conducted by requiring the defendant to plunge his arm in boiling water. If he escaped harm, he was innocent; if he was scalded, he was guilty. James A. Ballentine, *Ballentine's Law Dictionary*, 3d ed. (Rochester, N.Y.: Lawyers Co-operative Publishing Co., 1969), 1269.

37. See Robert Bartlett, *Trial by Fire and Water* (New York: Oxford University Press, 1986).

38. *State v. Henderson* 226 Kan. 726, 735, 603 P.2d 613, 620 (1979) (describing medieval courts of Inquisition).

39. Robert S. Peck, "Ohio's Tort Reform Measure Overturned," *Trial* (November 1, 1999): 35 (pointing out that the McDonald's hot coffee case was used as evidence for the need for tort reform in the 1995 Ohio tort bill that abolished joint and several liability, modified comparative negligence, increased the statute of limitations and repose, and limited tort damages).

40. In *State ex. Rel Ohio Academy of Trial Lawyers v. Sheward*, 86 Ohio St.3d 451 (Ohio 1999) (declaring tort reform statute to be an unconstitutional violation of Ohio's separation of powers doctrine and that state's "one subject" provision) and *Best v. Taylor Machine Works*, 689 N.E.2d 1057 (Ill. 1997) (declaring Illinois tort reform statute as an unconstitutional violation of the right to jury and other state constitutional grounds) (citing tort reformers misuse of hot coffee case as described in Rustad, "Nationalizing Tort Law").

41. "Courting Justice: Caps on Damages," *New Jersey Lawyer* 9 (April 3, 2000): 680 (citing cases provided by the Association of Trial Lawyers of America successfully challenging tort reforms).

42. Keith Marder, "Hopping on the Bandwagon to Parody Simpson Case," *Times Union* (October 1995): C-8 (describing Seinfeld hot coffee episode).

43. Full-thickness burns are serious burn wounds, which pose a serious risk of infection and may also require skin substitutes or transplants. New products have been developed that permit tissues to be grown outside the body. Gail Naughton, Interview with President, Advanced Tissue Sciences, CNBC-Dow Jones, *Business Video* (Transcript 0628Ccby-b53) (June 28, 2000).

44. Michael Rustad bases this account of the McDonald's hot coffee case on a telephone interview with plaintiff's counsel, Reed Morgan.

45. The defense of comparative negligence reduces recovery according to relative fault of the plaintiff in contributing to her own injury.

46. *BMW of N. Am. v. Gore*, 517 U.S. 559, 568 (1995) (holding that punitive damages award was grossly excessive, exceeding the due process clause of the Fourteenth Amendment in that none of the aggravating factors associated with particularly reprehensible conduct was present and that the award was five hundred times the amount of actual damages).

47. See *Liebeck v. McDonald's Restaurant, Inc.*, No. CV-93-02419 (Banally County Court, New Mexico, November 1994).

48. Keith Bradsher and Matthew L. Wald, "More Indications Hazards of Tires Were Long Known," *New York Times* (June 6, 2000): 1.

49. National Commission on Product Safety, Hearings Before the United States Senate Committee on Commerce, 91st Congress, 2d Session (1970), 91–92 (statement of Thomas F. Lambert, Jr.).

50. Margaret Cronin, Fisk, "Net Libel Verdict Is Upheld," *National Law Journal* (December 25, 2000–January 1, 2001): A19.

51. *Dennis v. United States*, 341 U.S. 494, 564 (1951) (J. Frankfurter).

NOTES TO CHAPTER 1

1. William E. Nelson, "From Fairness to Efficiency: The Transformation of Tort Law in New York, 1920–1980," *Buffalo Law Review* 47 (1999): 117, 117.

2. Id.

3. The concept of tort law in the process of becoming was frequently used by Professor Thomas Lambert to describe the flexibility of tort doctrines in adapting to social change.

4. William L. Prosser, *Handbook of the Law of Torts*, 3d ed. (St. Paul, Minn.: West Publishing Co., 1964), 1.

5. James Dudley and Edwin Baylies, *Addison on Torts*, American ed. (Boston: C. C. Soule, 1876), 11.

6. Fowler Vincent Harper, *A Treatise on the Law of Torts: A Preliminary Treatise on Civil Liability for Harms to Legally Protected Interests* (Indianapolis: Bobbs-Merrill, 1933), 12.

7. James A. Ballentine, *Ballentine's Law Dictionary*, 3d ed. (Rochester, N.Y.: The Lawyers Co-operative Publishing Co., 1967), 223.

8. Id.

9. William M. Landes and Richard R. Posner, "New Light on Punitive Damages," *Regulation* (October, 1986): 33.

10. Joseph Story, "Court of Legal Study," in *The Miscellaneous Writings of Joseph Story*, ed. William W. Story (Boston: Little, Brown, 1852), 70–71.

11. Marcus L. Plant, Foreword to William L. Prosser, *Selected Topics on the Law of Torts* (Ann Arbor: University of Michigan Law School, 1955).

12. Marshall S. Shapo, "In the Looking Glass: What Torts Scholarship Can Teach Us about the American Experience," *Northwestern Law Review* 89 (1995): 1567 (observing that torts are a "looking glass" reflecting the values of society).

13. "Furthermore, as the conditions of life are never static, law, which is the expression of those conditions, to fulfill the functions of its existence must be a body of rules continuously subject to modification and change." 1 American Law Institute, *Principles of Corporate Governance: Analysis and Recommendations* XXII (Philadelphia: American Law Institute, 1995).

14. Thomas F. Lambert, Jr., "The Jurisprudence of Hope," *American Trial Lawyers Journal* 31 (1965): 29.

15. Kermit L. Hall, ed., *Tort Law in American History* (New York: Garland Publishing Co., 1987), xiii.

16. William L. Prosser, "*Res Ipsa Loquitur* in California," *Selected Topics on the Law of Torts* (Ann Arbor: University of Michigan Law School, 1953), 306.

17. Robert L. Rabin, "Some Reflections on the Process of Tort Reform," *San Diego Law Review* 25 (1988): 13.

18. Id.

19. Thomas F. Lambert, Jr., "Seeing the '70's—Anticipations in Automobiles Law in the '70's," *Journal of the American Trial Lawyers Association* 34 (1972): 60, 62.

20. "Some critics decry the expansive nature of tort doctrine that has brought on a crisis, for example, in medical malpractice insurance." Id.

21. Thomas Koenig and Michael Rustad, "The Quiet Revolution Revisited: An Empirical Study of the Impact of Tort Reform on Punitive Damages in Products Liability," *Justice System Journal* 16 (1993): 23 (citing tort reform statutes).

22. Torts evolve by courts carving out remedies for new injuries. Common law courts permitted recovery for outrageous conduct leading to severe emotional distress before there was a formal tort of the intentional infliction of emotional distress. Courts are applying traditional causes of action for new injuries such as trespass to chattel to remedy "Spam" e-mail. When these old causes of action prove to be inadequate to punish and deter Internet wrongdoing, new torts will be born.

23. *Black's Law Dictionary*, 7th ed. (St. Paul, Minn.: West Publishing Co., 1999), 1496.

24. A defendant is liable for battery if "(a) he acts intending to cause a harmful or offensive contact with the person of the other or a third person, or an imminent apprehension of such a contact, and (b) a harmful contact with the person of the other directly or indirectly results." *Restatement (Second) of Torts* §13 (1965). The *Restatement* defines intend as when the "actor desires to cause consequences of his act, or that he believes that the consequences are substantially certain to result from it." Id. at §8A.

25. A defendant is liable for assault if "(a) he acts intending to cause a harmful or offensive contact with the person of the other or a third person, or an imminent apprehension of such a contact, and (b) the other is thereby put in such imminent apprehension." *Restatement (Second) of Torts* §21 (1965).

26. A defendant is liable for false imprisonment if "(a) he acts intending to confine the other or a third person within boundaries fixed by the actor, and (b) his act directly or indirectly results in such a confinement of the other, and (c) the other is conscious of the confinement or is harmed by it." *Restatement (Second) of Torts* §35 (1965).

27. Intentional torts to the person include battery, assault, false imprisonment, and the intentional infliction of emotional distress. Intentional torts to property include trespass to land, trespass to chattels, and conversion. Finally, there are intentional torts against businesses, such as fraud, the intentional interference with contract, and the interference with prospective advantage.

28. Trespass to chattels is committed by intentionally "(a) dispossessing another of the chattel, or (b) using or intermeddling with a chattel in the possession

of another." *Restatement (Second) Torts* §217 (1965). A trespass to chattel occurs when a defendant takes property belonging to another but does not impair its value or condition in a significant way.

29. John H. Wigmore, "A General Analysis of Tort-Relations," *Harvard Law Review* 8 (1894): 377, 378.

30. The term *intent* means to deliberately bring about a result by invading the interests of another. As employed in intentional torts, it means "that the actor desires to cause consequences of his act, or that he believes that the consequences are substantially certain to result from it." *Restatement (Second) Torts* §8A (1965). The *Restatement* uses the word "act" to "denote an external manifestation of the actor's will and does not include any of its results, even the most direct, immediate, and intended. *Restatement (Second) Torts* §2 (1965).

31. Oliver Wendell Holmes, Jr., *The Common Law* (Boston: Little, Brown, 1881), 4.

32. Stephan Landsman, "The History and Objections to the Civil Jury Systems," in Robert E. Litan, ed., *Verdict: Assessing the Civil Jury System* (Washington, D.C.: Brookings Institution, 1993).

33. 34 Eng. Rep. 722 (K.B. 1366).

34. James Barr Ames and Jeremiah Smith, *A Selection of Cases on the Law of Torts* (Cambridge: Roscoe Pound, 1917), 1 (noting that case was reported in Year Book, at the Assizes, Coram by Thorpe, CJ. in 1348 or 1349).

35. 80 Eng. Rep. 284 (K.B. 1616).

36. Weaver, the plaintiff, was accidentally injured by a musket shot fired by another militiaman during a military exercise. Victor E. Schwartz et al., *Prosser, Wade and Schwartz's Torts*, 10th ed. (New York: Foundation Press, 2000), 5.

37. *Smith v. Stone*, 82 Eng. Rep. 533 (1647).

38. The "conditional threat" was: "If it were not for assize-time, I would not take such language from you." *Tuberville v. Savage*, 1 Modern Rep. 3 (1669).

39. Schwartz, *Prosser, Wade and Schwartz's Torts*, 5.

40. *Cole v. Turner*, 87 Eng. Rep. 907 (Nisis Prius 1704).

41. *Huckle v. Money*, 95 Eng. Rep. 768 (C.P. 1763).

42. *Genay v. Norris*, 1 S.C. L. 6 (1784).

43. *Cruden v. Fentham*, 170 Eng. Rep. 496 (1799).

44. 101 Eng. Rep. 1337 (K.B. 1799).

45. *Baker v. Bolton*, 170 Eng. Rep. 1033 (K.B. 1808).

46. See, generally, Lanni P. Tama, "Recovery for Loss of Consortium in Wrongful Death Actions," *Brooklyn Law Review* 49 (1983): 605, 607.

47. 103 Eng. Rep. 926 (1809).

48. Id. at 927.

49. 128 Eng Rep. 761 (C.P. 1814).

50. *Joel v. Morrison*, 172 Eng. Rep. 1338 (1834) (holding that the master was liable for injuries caused by his servant unless he was on a frolic).

51. *Longridge v. Levy*, 150 Eng. Rep. 863 (1837) (holding that seller was liable for exploding gun caused by latent defect on theory of fraudulent misrepresentation).

52. *Vaughan v. Menlove*, 132 Eng. Rep. 490 (1837).

53. The defense of the ignorant farmer was rejected in favor of an objective standard for negligence. The standard for due care in negligence is what a reasonable person would do in the circumstances. Since *Vaughan*, a few exceptions have evolved adjusting the negligence formula for children, invalids, and persons with disability.

54. *Priestly v. Fowler*, 150 Eng. Rep. 130 (1837).

55. 152 Eng. Rep. 588 (1842) (holding that a plaintiff might recover despite his contributory negligence if the defendant could have avoided the accident and had the "last clear chance"). Prosser argued that the "last clear chance" created undue complexity in the negligence doctrine and referred to it as the "jackass doctrine." Prosser, *Handbook of the Law of Torts*, 437 n. 99 (discussing *Davies v. Mann*, 152 Eng. Rep. 588 (1842). In *Davies v. Mann*, 152 Eng. Rep. 588 (1842), a plaintiff tied his donkey at the side of a highway and it was killed by a team of horses riding down the highway at high speed.

56. *Day v. Woodworth*, 54 U.S. 363 (1851) (stating that punitive damages was "smart money" to punish wanton and malicious conduct).

57. *Thomas v. Winchester*, 6 N.Y. 307 (1852).

58. *Blyth v. Birmingham Waterworks, Inc.* 156 Eng. Rep. 1047 (1856) (holding that there was no negligence in installing water mains in the streets of Birmingham, England, that could not withstand the effects of an unprecedented frost).

59. Prosser, *Handbook of the Law of Torts*, 21.

60. Id.

61. The plaintiff relied on the *res* (the thing itself) to raise an inference of negligence. The court ruled that the act of a barrel of flour rolling out of a warehouse window and striking a pedestrian would not have occurred unless the person in charge was at fault. *Byrne v. Boadle*, 159 Eng. Rep. 299 (1863) (stating the doctrine of *res ipsa loquitur*, which may be roughly translated as "the thing speaks for itself"). The plaintiff's burden was to prove only that the barrel fell on his head and that it fell from the window of the defendant. *Lloyde v. West Midlands Gas Board*, 2 All ER 1240 (1971) (discussing *Byrne v. Boadle*).

62. "Circumstantial evidence means that from facts in evidence other facts may reasonable be inferred. The *res ipsa loquitur* case is a circumstantial evidence case which permits the jury to infer negligence from the mere occurrence of the accident itself." Prosser, "*Res Ipsa Loquitur* in California," 314.

63. Id at 304 (citing *Scott v. London & St. Katherine Docks Co.*, 159 Eng. Rep. 665 (1865)).

64. *Sioux City & P. R.R. v. Stout*, 84 U.S. 677 (1873); see also *Sioux City v. Pacific R.R. Co.*, 21 Minn. 207 (1875) (permitting children to recover despite the general rule of no duty of care owed to trespassers).

65. *Phillips v. Barnet*, 1 Q.B.D. 436 (1876).

66. 138 Mass. 14 (1884).

67. *Bennett v. Bennett*, 116 N.Y. 584, 23 N.E. 17 (1889).

68. 2 Q.B.D. 57 (1897).

69. Oliver Goldsmith, "The Traveller," in *The Traveller, The Deserted Village, and Other Poems by Oliver Goldsmith* (London: Samuel G. Goodrich, 1819), 48.

70. A writ was a legal process commanding the arrest of a person or seizure of his property.

71. "The element of damages seems to have been the chief invigorating force between the origin and development of trespass, and also the main cause of that remarkable development of writs and the forms of action which took place in the thirteenth century and included much less in addition to trespass." George E. Woobine, "The Origins of the Action of Trespass," *Yale Law Journal* 33 (1924): 799, 801.

72. John H. Langbein, Introduction to *Private Wrongs*, volume 3 of William Blackstone, *Commentaries on the Law of England* (1768) (facsimile of the First Edition) (Chicago: University of Chicago Press, 1979), iv.

73. See, e.g., Sir George Tucker, *Blackstone's Commentaries with Notes of Reference to the Constitution and Law of the Federal Government of the United States and of the Commonwealth of Virginia* (Philadelphia: William Young Birch and Abraham Small, 1803).

74. "The English editions which were exported just did not meet the demand, so that in the years 1771–1772 Robert Bell, the Philadelphia publishers, was able to sell an American edition of 1,400 copies at 3 pounds a set, and then print a second edition barely a year later at a slightly increased price. In the new American Law Schools of Harvard, Yale and Columbia, Blackstone's *Commentaries*, edited and annotated by a succession of editors, had become the popular text book and served to educate generations of students in the principles of the common law." Gareth Jones, "Sir William Blackstone," in George S. Grossman, ed., *The Spirit of American Law* (Boulder, Colo.: Westview Press, 2000), 66–67.

75. Morton J. Horwitz, *The Transformation of American Law: 1780–1860* (Cambridge, Mass.: Harvard University Press, 1978), 4.

76. Id.

77. Norman E. Cournoyer, *Hotel, Restaurant and Travel Law: A Preventive Approach* (Albany, N.Y.: Delmar Publishers, 1998), 6.

78. Langbein, *Introduction to Volume III of Blackstone's Commentaries*, 3:v.

79. George E. Woodbine, "The Origins of the Action of Trespass," *Yale Law Journal* 33 (1924): 799, 814–15.

80. William Blackstone, *Commentaries on the Law of England*, vol. 3 (1768; reprint, Chicago: University of Chicago Press, 1979), 119.

81. A trespasser was also absolutely liability for transgressing his neighbor's land boundaries, but even in this there were exceptions for hunting and other activities.

82. *Baker v. Bolton*, 170 Eng. Rep. 1033 (K.B. 1808).

83. Lanni P. Tama, "Recovery for Loss of Consortium in a Wrongful Death Action," *Brooklyn Law Review* 49 (1983): 605.

84. Harper, *A Treatise on the Law of Torts*, 2.

85. Prosser, *Handbook of the Law of Torts*, 3 (quoting Frederic Pollock, *Law of Torts*, 5th ed. (1951)).

86. Prosser, *Handbook of the Law of Torts*, 29.

87. Id.

88. Id.

89. John G. Fleming, *An Introduction to the Law of Torts* (Oxford: Clarendon Press, 1967), 4.

90. Prosser, *"Res Ipsa Loquitur* in California," 305 (citing case in which the axle of a stagecoach broke, injuring the passenger, *Christie v. Griggs*, 170 Eng. Rep. 1088 (1809)).

91. William L. Prosser, "The Borderland of Tort and Contract," *Selected Topics on the Law of Torts* (Ann Arbor: University of Michigan Law School, 1953), 389.

92. Blackstone, *Commentaries*, 3:20.

93. Id.

94. Id.

95. Id. at 121.

96. Many of the intentional torts survive in modern law and some have even been adapted to Internet wrongdoing. All intentional torts require that the defendant desires the consequences of his or her act or knows that the result is substantially certain to occur.

97. Id.

97. Id.

98. Id. at 127–28.

99. Id.

100. Id.

101. Id.

102. By balancing the social utility of a land use against its probable or known harm, courts often permitted activities such as pollution or excessive noise, which would have not permitted under an absolute rights approach.

103. Nuisance developed into two branches: private and public. A private nuisance lawsuit could be filed by a private individual, whereas a public nuisance could only be filed by public authorities.

104. Id.

105. Id. at 164.

106. Blackstone, *Commentaries*, 3:127.

107. Prosser, "The Borderland of Tort and Contract," 406.

108. Id.

109. Id.

110. *R.R. Co. v. Lockwood*, 84 U.S. 357 (1873).

111. Prosser, "The Borderland of Tort and Contract," 406.

112. Id. at 165.

113. The concept of merchantability evolved out of the law merchant tradition of medieval fairs. Law merchants were informal courts consisting of merchants who dispensed speedy justice. Goods sold in these markets had to comply with an implied warranty of being at least fit for ordinary purposes or they were not merchantable.

114. Prosser, "The Borderland of Tort and Contract," 409.

115. Blackstone, *Commentaries*, 3:122.

116. Id.

117. Id.

118. Prosser, "The Borderland of Tort and Contract," 409.

119. Blackstone, *Commentaries*, 3:123.

120. "The essence of the tort of libel is the publication of a statement about an individual that is both false and defamatory. Since falsity is a *sine qua non* of a libel claim and since only assertions of fact are capable of being proven false, we have consistently held that a libel action cannot be maintained unless it is premised on published assertions of fact." *Brian v. Richardson* 87 N.2d 46 (1995).

121. Blackstone, *Commentaries*, 3:123.

122. Id.

123. Id.

124. Id. at 122–23.

125. Id. at 125.

126. Id.

127. Id.

128. Id. at 138.

129. Thomas F. Lambert, Jr., "The Jurisprudence of Hope," *American Trial Lawyers Journal* 31 (1965): 29, 33 (critiquing the interspousal immunity defense with the rhetorical question: "if a husband mutilates his wife, how much conjugal tranquility is there to protect?").

130. Blackstone, *Commentaries*, 3:130-39.

131. Id.

132. Id.

133. Id.

134. Id.

135. Id.

136. Id. at 140.

137. Id.

138. Id.

139. Id.

140. Blackstone, *Commentaries*, 1:161.

141. Id. at 462.

142. Blackstone, *Commentaries*, 3:140.

143. Id.

144. The *trespass per quod consortium amisit* was an action, which applied where the defendant assaulted or otherwise abused the wife so that the husband was deprived of her society. *Trespass per quod servitum amisit* was an action of trespass, which applied if the defendant assaulted or abused a servant so that the master was deprived of his services. James A. Ballentine, *Ballentine's Law Dictionary*, 3d ed. (Rochester, N.Y.: Lawyer's Cooperative Publishing House, 1967), 1298 (citing Blackstone's *Commentaries*).

145. Blackstone, *Commentaries*, 3:140.

146. Id. at 144.

147. Goods wrongfully taken could be recovered through *replevin*. *Detinue* was used to regain custody of wrongfully detained goods that were originally in the lawful possession of the defendant.

148. Blackstone, *Commentaries*, 3:145.

149. Prosser, *Handbook of the Law of Torts*, 76.

150. Bryan A. Garner, *A Dictionary of Modern Legal Usage*, 2d ed. (New York: Oxford University Press, 1995), 271.

151. Id. at 152–53.

152. Tom Lambert used this example to demonstrate that the popular misconception about the "one bite rule" was bad dog law. See Harper, *A Treatise on the Law of Torts*, 368 (citing *Smith v. Pelah,* 2 Strange 1264 (1764*)*.

153. Blackstone, *Commentaries*, 3:167.

154. Id. at 208.

155. Id. at 209.

156. Id. at 213.

157. This is Latin for "a trespass from the beginning." Ballentine, *Ballentine's Law Dictionary*, 1298.

158. Trespasses were divided into two writs depending upon whether the injury was direct or indirect. *Trespass on the case* was filed when the injuries were indirect and a trespass was committed without force. *Trespass vi et armies* applied in cases where the trespass was inflicted with direct force. Garner, *A Dictionary of Modern Legal Usage*, 889.

159. Id.

160. *Black's Law Dictionary*, 4th ed. (St. Paul, Minn.: West Publishing Co., 1951), 467.

161. Blackstone, *Commentaries*, 3:139.

162. See Linda L. Schluetter and Kenneth R. Redden, *Punitive Damages*, 2d ed. (Charlottesville, Va.: Michie Co., 1989), 1:3 (noting that punishment by multiple damages is documented as early as 2000 B.C.); see also James Sales and Kenneth Cole, "Punitive Damages: A Relic That Outlived Its Origins," *Vanderbilt Law*

Review 37 (1984): 1117, 1119 (noting the statutory remedy of multiple awards in the Hindu Code of Manu and the Code of Hammurabi).

163. Schluetter and Redden, *Punitive Damages*, 3 n. 1.

164. Sales and Cole, "Punitive Damages." 1119.

165. Id.

166. Mohammed Abdul Malek, "A Study of the Qur'an B: The Universal Guidance for Mankind" (visited October 17, 1999) <http://members.aol.com/mamalek/index.htm> (quoting the Qur'an) (visited October 17, 1999).

167. Note, "Vindictive Damages," *American Law Journal* 4 (1852): 61, 75.

168. S. P. Scott, *Corpus Juris Civilis: The Civil Law* (1932), 4:320 (translating XVII Enactment of Justinian tit. 2). The *Corpus Juries Civilis* is the codification of the law of ancient Rome, comprising constitutions, juristic law, and writings compiled under the orders of the Emperor Justinian in the sixth century A.D. The Justinian Code provided multiple damages against defaulting debtors: "If I commit the transaction of my business to a party who is liable to me in an Action for quadruple damages (within a year), and, after the lapse of the year, for only simple damages; even though I should begin suit against him on mandate. After the year has elapsed, he will be bound to pay me quadruple damages; because a party who undertakes the management of another's business is required to pay him what he would have been compelled to pay others." Id. at 320.

169. Barry Nicholas, *An Introduction to Roman Law* (Oxford: Oxford University Press, 1962), 245.

170. Id. at 209.

171. The corporate defendant cited the Medieval English doctrine of amercements as evidence for the presence of due process guarantees for the modern remedy of punitive damages in the U.S. Supreme Court case of *Browning-Ferris Indus. v. Kelco Disposal, Inc.*, 492 U.S. 257 (1989).

172. Frederick Pollock and Frederic W. Maitland, *The History of the English Law*, 2d ed. (London: Cambridge University Press, 1923), 514.

173. Oliver Goldsmith, "The Traveler," in *The Deserted Village: A Poem*, ed. Samuel G. Goodrich (New York: Sidney's Press, 1819).

174. See Thomas A. Street, *The Foundations of Legal Liability: A Presentation of the Theory and Development of the Common Law* (1916; reprint, Littleton, Colo.: Fred B. Rothman, 1989) (discussing the role of ancient Roman *legis actiones* in history of remedial law), 3:13–16.

175. 98 Eng. Rep. 489 (K.B. 1763).

176. 95 Eng. Rep. 768 (K.B. 1763).

177. 98 Eng. Rep. 489, 489–99 (K.B. 1763).

178. Id.

179. Id.

180. Id.

181. The King's Bench's independence in these rulings prefigured our separa-

tion of powers. In this case, even King George III was subject to the Magna Carta and the law of the land.

182. *Wilkes v. Wood*, 98 Eng. Rep. at 490.

183. *Huckle v. Money*, 95 Eng. Rep. 768, 768 (K.B. 1763).

184. Id. at 768–69.

185. The police were assessed punitive damages for shooting an innocent bridegroom in the buttocks and trying to cover-up their activities in *Butcher v. Krause*, 200 F.2d 576 (7th Cir. 1952). Marshall S. Shapo, "Note on Police Brutality," in *Tort and Injury Law*, 2d ed. (New York: Bender, 2000), 53.

186. The word "intent" means that an actor "desires to cause the consequences of his act or believes that the consequences are substantially certain to result from it." *Restatement (Second) Torts*, §8 (2000).

187. William Blackstone, *Commentaries on the English Law*, ed. William C. Jones (1916), 3:1607–8, 1647–48, 1655–56, 1699–1700, 1782–83, 1804–5 (referring to the imposition of exemplary damages for intentional torts against the person and property).

188. Note, "Vindictive Damages," American Law Journal 4 (1852): 61, 75.

189. Marshall S. Shapo, *The Duty to Act—Tort Law, Power and Public Policy* (Austin: University of Texas Press, 1977), xiii (stating that the central role of tort law has been with moderating relations of power).

190. William B. Willcox and Walter L. Arnstein, *The Age of Aristocracy: 1688 to 1830*, 5th ed. (Lexington, Mass.: D. C. Heath, 1988).

191. *Tullidge v. Wade*, 95 Eng. Rep. 909, 909 (K.B. 1769).

192. Id.

193. *Praed v. Graham*, 24 Q.B.D. 53 (1889).

194. *Benson v. Frederick*, 97 Eng. Rep. 1130, 1130 (K.B. 1766) (assessing exemplary damages against militia colonel for whipping a common soldier out of personal animus).

195. *Forde v. Skinner*, 172 Eng. Rep. 687, 687 (Horsham Assizes 1830).

196. Id.

197. *Emblen v. Myers*, 158 Eng. Rep. 23, 23-24 (Ex. 1860).

198. Id. at 24–25.

199. See, e.g., *Randleman v. Johnson*, 187 S.W.2d 626, 627 (Ark. 1916) (upholding $2,000 in punitive damages for false accusations where actual damages were only nominal); *Redfield v. Redfield*, 39 N.W. 688, 691 (Iowa 1888) (upholding $1,000 in punitive damages to a plaintiff unable to rise for a short period after a beating); *Davis v. Chicago, R.I. & P.R. Co.*, 182 S.W. 826, 829 (Mo. 1916) (upholding $1,520 punitive damages award against a railroad for its wrongful exclusion of a passenger); *Mueller v. St. Louis Transit Co.*, 83 S.W. 270, 271 (Mo. 1904) (upholding $500 punitive damages award against a street car company for conductor's misconduct in forcibly resisting a passenger's effort to leave a street car); and *Craker v. N.W. Railway Co.*, 36 Wis. 657, 661 (Wisc. 1875) (awarding a

school teacher $1,000 in punitive damages for the indignity of being kissed against her will by a train conductor).

200. *Merest v. Harvey*, 128 Eng. Rep. 761, 761 (C.P. 1814).

201. Id.

202. The U.S. Supreme Court in *BMW of N. Am. v. Gore*, 517 U.S. 559, 575 (1995), stated that reprehensibility of the defendant's conduct is given the greatest emphasis in determining the constitutionality of a punitive damages award.

203. Id.

204. Id.

205. Id.

206. Prosser, *Handbook of the Law of Torts*, 11.

207. *Edwards v. Leavitt*, 35 Vt. 135 (1873) (emphasis in original).

208. *Milwaukee and St. Paul R.R. Co. v. Arms*, 91 U.S. 489, 492 (1875).

209. W. Page Keeton et al., *Prosser and Keeton on the Law of Torts*, 5th ed. (St. Paul, Minn.: West Publishing Co., 1984), 1071.

210. 1 S.C. L. (1 Bay) 6 (1784).

211. Id.

212. 63 Ill. 553 (1872).

213. The definition of offensive bodily contact continues to use the standard that "it offends a reasonable sense of personal dignity." *Restatement (Second) of Torts* §19 (1965). "In order that a contact be offensive to a reasonable sense of personal dignity, it must be one which would offend the ordinary person and as such one not unduly sensitive as to his personal dignity." Id. at §19, cmt (a).

214. See, e.g., *Shaffer v. National Can Corporation*, 565 F. Supp. 909 (E.D. Pa. 1983) (holding that supervisor's use of his authority to gain sexual favors and retaliatory behavior states cause of action for intentional infliction of emotional distress).

215. *Reed v. Davis*, 4 Pick. 212 (Mass. 1826).

216. Id. at 218.

217. *Luther v. Shaw*, 147 N.W.2d 18, 20 (Wis. 1914).

218. The court cited *Restatement (Second) of Torts*, §46 cmt. e (1979) for the proposition that the relationship between the parties was a significant factor in determining the imposition of liability. Id.

219. Dan B. Dobbs, *The Law of Torts* (St. Paul, Minn.: West Publishing Co., 2000), 3.

220. 7 Kan. App., 2d 603, 645 P.2d 916 (1982).

221. See, e.g., *Daffenbaugh-Williams v. Wal-Mart Stores*, 188 F.3d 278 (5th Cir. 1999).

222. The intentional infliction of emotional distress did not develop as an independent tort until the middle of the twentieth century. Emotional injuries could be recovered if attached to another independent tort such as assault, battery, or false imprisonment. Justice Roger Traynor's landmark opinion in *State*

Rubbish Collectors Association v. Siliznoff, 38 Cal.2d 330, 240 P.2d 282 (1952), recognized the right to be free from "serious, intentional, and unprivileged invasions of emotional and mental tranquility." The *Siliznoff* case was the first U.S. appellate case to permit recovery for severe emotional distress even if there were no physical manifestations. *Restatement (Second) of Torts* §46 (1965) cited *Siliznoff* in recognizing a cause of action for the tort of outrage. Section 46 makes a defendant liable for this tort if, by extreme and outrageous conduct, he intentionally or recklessly causes severe emotional distress to another. In general, the conduct must be "so outrageous in character, and extreme in degree, as to go beyond all possible bounds of decency, and to be regarded as atrocious, and utterly intolerable in a civilized community." Id. at §46, cmt. d (1965). The tort of outrage "does not extent to mere insults, indignities, threats, annoyances, petty oppressions, or other trivialities." Id. Today, there are jurisdictional differences in whether a plaintiff may recover in the absence of showing a physical manifestation of severe emotional distress caused by the defendant's outrageous misconduct.

223. *Conteras v. Crown Zellerbach Corp.*, 88 Wash. 2d 735, 565 P.2d 1173 (1977).

224. Id. at 741.

225. Roscoe Pound, *My Philosophy of Law* (New York: Wm. Gaunt and Sons, 1941), 249.

226. William Blackstone, *Commentaries*, 3:19

227. *Black's Law Dictionary*, 7th ed. (St. Paul, Minn.: West Publishing Co., 1999), 1056.

228. Id.

229. Fleming, *An Introduction to the Law of Torts*, 4.

230. Id.

231. Borgna Brunner, ed., *The Time Almanac 2000* (Boston: Information Please, 2000), 602.

232. Id.

233. Id.

234. Id.

235. *Tooley v. Ry. Passenger Assurance*, 24 F. Cas. 53 (Cir. Ct. S.D. Ill. 1873).

236. *R.R. Co. v. Lockwood*, 44 Cal. 71 (Cal. Sup. Ct., 1872).

237. Id.

238. *Negligence* is an act or omission by which the defendant fails to exercise the due care of a reasonable person in the circumstances.

239. Prosser, "The Borderland of Tort and Contract," 411.

240. Lawrence M. Friedman, *A History of American Law*, 2d ed. (New York: Simon and Schuster, 1986), 467.

241. Knowledge of the risk is critical to a finding that the plaintiff knowingly and voluntarily assumed it. *Cincinnati, N.O. & T.P.R. Co. v. Thompson*, 236 F. 1, 9

(6th Cir. 1916). In order for there to be assumption of risk, there must be knowledge and apprehension of the specific risk and a voluntary choice to assume it. When the defense was originally conceived, workers only choice was to assume the risk of workplace hazard or lose their job.

242. G. Edward White, *Tort Law in America: American Intellectual History* (New York: Oxford University Press, 1980), 61.

243. Id.

244. 45 Mass 49 (1842) (holding that the railroad was not liable for injuries suffered by a railway engineer at the hands of a switch tender employed by the same company in the absence of a showing that the railway knew of the employee's incompetence or retained an unfit employee).

245. *Brown v. Kendall*, 60 Mass. 292 (1850).

246. *Small v. Howard*, 128 Mass. 131, 136 (1880) (stating that "[i]t is a matter of common knowledge that a physician in a small country village does not usually make a specialty of surgery. . . . He would have but few opportunities of observation and practice in that line such as public hospitals or large cities would afford").

247. *Heaven v. Pender*, 11 Q.B.D. 503 (1883).

248. *Beckwith v. Oatman*, 43 Hun. 265 (N.Y. 1887) (finding pharmacy liable for defective compounding of prescription drug).

249. 80 Wis. 523, 50 N.W. 403 (1891).

250. Samuel D. Warren and Louis D. Brandeis, "The Right to Privacy," *Harvard Law Review* 4 (1890): 192 (describing privacy as a right to an "inviolate personality").

251. *Booth v. Rome, W. and O.T.R.R. Co.*, 140 N.Y. 267, 35 N.E. 592 (1893).

252. 151 N.Y. 107, 45 N.E. 354 (1896).

253. *Kimberly v. Howland*, 55 S.E. 778, 780 (N.C. 1906) (ruling that blasting resulted in "greatly shocking her nervous system" despite lack of impact).

254. *Ives v. South Buffalo, Railway*, 94 N.E. 431 (N.Y. 1911).

255. *Wilson v. Faxon*, 208 N.Y. 108, 101 N.E. 799 (1913).

256. *Thornhill v. Carpenter-Morton, Co.*, 220 Mass. 593, 108 N.E. 474 (1915) (holding manufacturer liable for highly flammable floor stain).

257. 217 N.Y. 382, 111 N.E. 1050 (1916). Judge Cardozo stated that "if the nature of the thing is such that it is reasonably certain to produce loss of life and limb in peril when negligently made, it is then a thing of danger." This case extended doctrine first recognized in *Thomas v. Winchester* for poisons to other consumer products.

258. *New York Central R.R. Co. v. White*, 243 U.S. 188 (1917).

259. *Lipman v. Atlantic Coast Line R.R. Co.*, 93 S.E. 714 (S.C. 1917).

260. 162 N.E. 99 (N.Y. 1928).

261. Id.

262. American Law Institute, *Restatement (First) of Torts*, §270 (1929).

263. Lambert, "Seeing the '70's."

264. *Reingold v. Reingold,* 115 N.J.L. 532 (1935).

265. 24 Cal.2d 453, 150 P.2d 436 (1944).

266. The majority opinion applied doctrine of *res ipsa loquitur,* ruling that a soda bottle does not "ordinarily explode if property precautions are taken." Prosser, "*Res Ipsa Loquitur* in California," 317 (discussing case).

267. *Ulm v. Keesport Tin Plate Co.,* 263 Pa. 327, 106 A. 639 (1919).

268. *Philadelphia & Reading R.R. Co. v. Buyer,* 97 Pa. 91 (1881) (reporting case in which plaintiff was killed in a collision between trains caused by negligent act of driving a railway car without stopping, looking, and listening).

269. *Kirtley v. Chicago, Minneapolis and St. Paul Ry. Co.,* 65 F. 386, 392. (W.D. Mo. 1895).

270. *Payne v. Chicago and Alton R.R. Co.,* 129 Mo. Reports 405 (Sup. Ct. Mo. 1895).

271. *Neal v. Gillett,* 23 Conn. Reports 437 (Sup. Ct. Conn. 1855).

272. *Richmond Traction Co. v. Martin's Administrator,* 102 Va. 209, 213 (1903).

273. Id. at 49.

274. Id. at 550.

275. *The Baltimore and Ohio S.W. R.R. Co. v. Alsop,* 176 Ill. 471, 32 N.E. 253 (1898).

276. *Louisville and Nashville R.R. Co. v. Johnson,* 92 Ala. 204, 9 So. 269 (Ala. 1890).

277. *Black's Law Dictionary,* 4th ed. (St. Paul, Minn.: West Publishing Co., 1951), 151.

278. Prosser, *Handbook of the Law of Torts,* 550.

279. *Western and Atlantic R.R. Co. v. Strong,* 52 Ga. 461 (Ga. Sup. Ct. 1874).

280. 45 Mich. 212, 7 N.W. 791 (1881).

281. Id. at 792.

282. Id.

283. Id.

284. Id. at 794 (reversing $5,000 plaintiff's verdict and remanding case for a new trial).

285. *Union Pacific Railway v. Cuppier,* 51 Kan. 642, 72 P. 281 (1903) (reporting case in which employees did nothing to aid a severely injured accident victim).

286. Id.

287. Id.

288. Id.

289. Id. (discussing *Priestly v. Fowler,* 150 Eng. Rep. 1030 (1837).

290. 45 Mass. 49 (1842) (holding that the railroad was not liable for injuries suffered by a railway engineer at the hands of a switch tender employed by the same company in the absence of a showing that the railway knew of the employee's incompetence or retained an unfit employee).

291. Id.

292. Fleming, *An Introduction to the Law of Torts*, 5.

293. Professor Schwartz argues that the touchstone of the negligence era was economic efficiency rather than subsidy. Schwartz's reading of nineteenth-century tort cases is that the courts "exhibited a keen concern for victim's welfare." Gary T. Schwartz, "Tort Law and the Economy in Nineteenth Century America: A Reinterpretation," *Yale Law Journal* 90 (1981): 1717, 1720; see also, Gary Schwartz, "The Character of Early American Tort Law," UCLA *Law Review* 36 (1989): 641.

294. Horwitz, *The Transformation of American Law*, 70.

295. Id. at 210.

296. Schwartz, "Tort Law and the Economy in Nineteenth Century America" 1720.

297. William L. Prosser, "Comparative Negligence," *Selected Topics on the Law of Torts* (Ann Arbor: University of Michigan Law School, 1953), 7.

298. Id.

299. "Some weakening of the doctrine took place by means of the control exercised by trial court judge and jury over findings of fact. But sympathy for injured workers manifested itself in changes in doctrine." Lawrence M. Friedman and Jack Ladinsky, "Social Change and the Law of Industrial Accidents," *Columbia Law Review* 67 (1967): 170, 181.

300. Monaghan v. Northwestern Fuel Co., 140 Wis. 457, 466 (1909) quoted by William L. Crow, "A History of the Legislative Control of Workmen's Compensation in Wisconsin," *Illinois Law Review* 27 (1932): 101, 102.

301. 66 Me. 420 (1876).

302. Id.

303. Id.

304. 84 U.S. 553 (1873).

305. Id.

306. 162 F. 329 (Cir. Ct. S.D. N.Y. 1908).

307. Id. at 330.

308. Id. at 332.

309. Ballentine, *Ballentine's Law Dictionary*, 710.

310. Prosser, *Handbook of the Law of Torts*, 437.

311. Id.

312. Id. at 439.

313. Id.

314. Id.

315. Keeton et al., *Prosser and Keeton on the Law of Torts*, 458.

316. Allan Sykes, "The Boundaries of Vicarious Liability: An Economic Analysis of the Scope of Employment Rule and Related Legal Doctrine," *Harvard Law Review* 101 (1988): 563.

317. *Ira S. Bushey and Sons, Inc. v. United States*, 398 F.2d 167, 171 (2d Cir. 1968) (finding master liable for his drunken seaman's negligence in causing ship in dry dock to be damaged).

318. Id.

319. Courts carved out a "frolic" exception to the common law rule that a master was vicariously liable for his servant's torts. See, e.g., *Baum v. Schweitzer*, 124 Misc. 516, 208 N.Y.S. 549 (1925) (holding that a master was not liable for his servant's negligent driving committed on a detour seventeen city blocks from his designated route).

320. *Joel v. Morrison*, 172 Eng. Rep. 1338 (1834).

321. Id.

322. See, e.g., *Baum v. Schweitzer*, 124 Misc. 516, 208 N.Y.S. 549 (1925) (holding master not liable for his chauffeur's frolic in stopping for lunch at his home "not within the reasonable contemplation of the employer").

323. *Quinn v. Power*, 87 N.Y. 525 (1882) (holding ferryboat owner liable for an accident caused by his negligent servant during a detour from prescribed duties).

324. 208 A.D. 289, 203 N.Y.S. 634 (1924).

325. Note, "Vindictive Damages," *American Law Journal* 4 (1852): 61, 75.

326. Louis D. Brandeis, *Other People's Money* (New York: Frederick A. Stokes Co., 1932), 22–23.

327. *Goddard v. Grand Trunk Ry. Co.*, 57 Me. 202, 223–24 (1869).

328. Id.

329. *Whipple v. Walpole*, 10 N.H. 130, 132 (1839).

330. 2 Colo. 141 (1873).

331. Id.

332. *McNamara v. King*, Id. at 228.

333. Alfred G. Nichols, Jr., "Punitive Damages in Mississippi: A Brief History," *Mississippi Law Journal* 37 (1965): 135, 138.

334. *Hopkins v. Atlantic & S. L. R.R.*, 36 N.H. 9 (1857).

335. *Missouri Pacific Ry. Co. v. Martino*, 18 S.W. 1066, 1067 (Texas Civ. App. 1892).

336. *Louisville and Nashville R.R. Co. v. Eaden*, 29 Ky. 365, 93 S.W. 7 (1906).

338. 6 Ky. 122, 127 (1877).

339. *Chicago and Northwestern Ry. Co. v. Williams*, 55 Ill. 185 (Ill. 1870).

339. Id. at 190.

340. *Fay v. Parker*, 53 N.H. 342 (1842).

341. Letters to the Editor, *Central Law Journal* (St. Louis) 6 (1878): 74, 74.

342. A number of states have adopted some form of state-sharing in which a portion of the punitive damages award goes to the state.

343. Perry Miller, *The Life of the Mind in America from the Revolution to the Civil War* (London: Gollancz, 1966), 152.

344. See Theodore Sedgwick, "The Rule of Damages in Actions *Ex Delicto*," *Law Reporter* 10 (1847): 49, 53.

345. The American Bar Association formed a committee to study the abuses of contingent fees. A witness testifying before the committee countered the broadside against contingent fees: "The chairman of this committee on Contingent Fees seems to be obsessed with the idea of necessity for such legislation [regulating contingency fees]. . . . I think is more calculated to place a stigma on the profession, than to do business. In my experience in the practice of law, I have never known of a case where there was any controversy between a client and a lawyer where a contingent fee was the subject of discussion, or any account of any contingent fee. Id. at 6.

346. Massachusetts courts treated the contingent fee as void, but it was not treated as a wrongful act *per se*. "In most states there is express authority in decided cases that a contract for a contingent fee is a valid one." Max Radin, "Contingent Fees in California," *California Law Review* 28 (1939–40): 587 589.

347. Michael Napier, "For Many, English Rule Impedes Access to Justice," *Wall Street Journal* (September 24, 1992): A17.

348. Id. at 8.

349. Id. at 589.

350. Report of Committee on Abuses of the Contingent Fee, *Proceedings of the Annual Meeting of the New York State Bar Association* (New York: New York Bar Association, 1910): 325.

351. Id. at 329.

352. "Ambulance Chasers and Their Counterparts in Accident Cases," *Law Notes* (February 1911): 207.

353. Radin, "Contingent Fees in California," 595–96.

354. The term "ambulance chaser" was originally applied to the "unseemly activities of overzealous morticians in too promptly soliciting customers." *Kelley v. Judge of Recorder's Court of Detroit*, 239 Mich. 204, 264 N.W. 316, 318 (1927).

355. *Black's Law Dictionary* (St. Paul: West Publishing Co., 6th ed. 1990), 80.

356. "Instant cases illustrate that the claim agent or adjuster of the defendant arrived at the scene with celerity that would defeat even the efforts of a possible ambulance chaser." Id.

357. *Zdancewicz v. Burlington County Traction Co.*, 71 Atl. Rep. 123, 123 (N.J. 1908).

358. Id.

359. 126 N.W. Rep. 902 (Minn. 1910).

360. Id.

361. "Ambulance Chasers and Defendant Corporations," *Law Notes* (April 1910): 1.

362. Id.

363. *Whitcomb v. Standard Oil Co.*, 153 Ind. 513 (1899).

364. *Boland v. Louisville and Nashville R.R. Co.*, 106 Ala. 641, 18 So. 99 (Ala. 1894).

365. Id. at 746.

366. *Johnson v. So. Pacific Co.*, 1961 U.S. 1 (1904).

367. Id.

368. *Second Employer's Liability Cases v. New York, New Haven and Hartford Railroad*, 223 U.S. 1 (1912) (citing 35 Stat. L 65, Chap. 149).

369. *Wilkerson v. McCarthy*, 336 U.S. 53 (1949).

370. Id at 68 (Douglas, J., concurring).

371. Id. at 421.

372. *Hawkins v. Bleakely*, 220 F. Supp. 378, 378 (S.D. Iowa 1914).

373. Prosser, *Handbook of the Law of Torts*, 555.

374. Lawrence M. Friedman and Jack Ladinsky, "Social Change and the Law of Industrial Accidents," *Columbia Law Review* 67 (1967): 170, 190.

375. Prosser, *Handbook of the Law of Torts*, 555.

376. Every state workers' compensation scheme required industrial workers to give up their tort rights and remedies in return for an exclusive, but limited, tort remedy. The workers' compensation statutes abolished common law tort defenses such as the "assumption of the risk, the negligence of a fellow servant and contributory negligence." William L. Crow, "A History of the Legislative Control of Workmen's Compensation in Wisconsin," *Illinois Law Review* 27 (1932): 137, 141.

377. Id. at 380.

378. *Zancanelli v. Central Coal and Coke Co.*, 25 Wyo. 511, 173 A. 981 (1918) (upholding Wyoming's 1915 Workers' Compensation Act).

379. Id.

380. Keeton et al., *Prosser and Keeton on the Law of Torts*, 584.

381. Fleming, *An Introduction to Tort Law*, 22.

382. Keeton et al., *Prosser and Keeton on the Law of Torts*, 585.

383. Lorelie S. Master, "Punitive Damages: Covered or Not?" *Business Lawyer* 55 (1999): 283.

384. Id.

385. Id.

386. Robert L. Rabin, *Perspectives on Tort Law*, 2d ed. (New York: Aspen Publishers, 1983), 68.

387. *Winterbottom v. Wright*, 152 Eng. Rep. 402 (1842).

388. Roger Traynor, "The Ways and Meanings of Defective Products and Strict Liability," *Tennessee Law Review* 32 (1965): 363.

389. Thomas F. Lambert, Jr., "The Jurisprudence of Hope," *American Trial Lawyers Journal* 31 (1965): 29, 36.

390. "The first onrush to the avalanche burying the privity rule in beyond-

food cases" occurred in the mid-1960s. Thomas F. Lambert, Jr., "Recent Important Tort Cases," *American Trial Lawyers Journal* 31 (1965): 253.

391. William L. Prosser, "Comparative Negligence," *Selected Topics on the Law of Torts* (Ann Arbor: University of Michigan Law School, 1953), 1 (citing The Law Reform Act of 1945).

392. *Bonbrest v. Katz*, 65 Supp. 138 (D.D.C. 1946) (permitting recovery for prenatal injuries).

393. *Restatement (First) of Torts* §46, cmt. d (1948).

394. 159 F.2d 169 (2d Cir. 1947) (noting that the burden of adequate precaution (B) depends upon the probability of injury (P) times the gravity of the injury *(L) or B < PL.)*.

395. 340 U.S. 135 (1950).

396. Prosser, "Comparative Negligence," 1 (citing *Insurance Law Journal* survey).

397. 38 Cal.2d 330 (1952).

398. *Duty v. General Fin. Co.*, 154 Tex. 16, 273 S.W.2d 64 (Tex. 1954).

399. 221 Ore. 86, 342 P.2d 790 (1959).

400. 169 A.2d 69 (N.J. 1960).

401. Ronald Coase, "The Problem of Social Cost," *Journal of Law and Economics* 3 (1960): 1.

402. *Monroe v. Pape*, 365 U.S. 167 (1961).

403. *Millikin v. Jewish Hosp. Ass'n of Louisville*, 348 S.W.2d 930 (Ky. 1961) (following *President & Directors of Georgetown College v. Hughes*, 130 F.2d 810 (D.C. Cir. 1942) (abolishing charitable immunity doctrine for hospital in landmark case).

404. *Battala v. State*, 10 N.Y.2d 237, 219 N.Y.S.2d 34, 176 N.E.2d 729 (N.Y. 1961).

405. 377 A.2d 897 (Cal. 1963).

406. 376 U.S. 254 (1964).

407. Robert Keeton and Jeffrey O'Connell, *Basic Protection for the Traffic Accident Victim* (Boston: Little, Brown, 1965).

408. *Oleksiew v. Weidener*, 207 N.E.2d 375 (Ohio 1965) (holding that medical malpractice expert testimony could be elicited from a defendant doctor called by the plaintiff "as if under cross examination").

409. *Haney v. City of Lexington*, 386 S.W.2d 1 (Ky. 1965) (finding city liable for negligence, abolishing municipal immunity).

410. In *Fisher v. Carrousel Motor Hotel*, 424S.W.2d 627(Tex. 1967), the Texas Supreme Court upheld a remedy for battery when a black mathematician was accosted by a white restaurant employee while waiting in the buffet line at a National Aeronautical and Space Administration luncheon. The restaurant employee seized the plaintiff's plate and shouted in a loud and offensive manner to prevent the plaintiff from dining in an all-white facility. This racist incident and

the use of punitive damages to redress the injury occurred prior to the passage of the 1964 Civil Rights Act.

411. *Gleitman v. Cosgrove,* 49 N.J. 22, 227 A.2d 689 (1967).

412. *Toole v. Richardson-Merrell, Inc.,* 251 Cal. App.2d 689,60 Cal. Rptr. 398 (1967).

413. *Larsen v. General Motors Corp.,* 391 F.2d 495 (8th cir. 1968).

414. 443 P.2d 561 (Cal. 1968).

415. *Spano v. Perini Corp.,* 25 N.Y.2d 11, 250 N.E.2d 31 (1969).

416. *Gelbman v. Gelbman,* 245 N.E.2d 192, 194 (N.Y. 1969).

417. *Beaudette v. Frana,* 173 N.W.2d 416 (Minn. 1969); *Gaston v. Pittman,* 224 So.2d 329 (Fla. 1969).

418. *Streenz v. Streenz,* 471 P.2d 282 (Ariz. 1970).

419. *Nader v. General Motors Corp.,* 25 N.Y.2d 560, 307 N.Y.S.2d 647 (1970).

420. "Nader settled his suit for $425,000 in August 1970, saying he would use the money for a 'continuous legal monitoring of General Motors activity in the safety, pollution, and consumer relations area.'" Marshall S. Shapo, *Tort and Injury Law,* 2d ed. (New York: Matthew Bender, 2000), 9 (quoting *New York Times* article).

421. 439 F.2d 477 (D.C. Cir. 1970).

422. Premises liability verdicts are increasingly based upon a theory of inadequate security where the landowner failed to take reasonable precautions to prevent criminal acts.

423. *Fletcher v. Western Nat. Life. Ins. Co.,* 10 Cal. App.3d 376, 89 Cal. Rptr. 78 (1970). See also *Wetherbee v. United Insurance Co. of America,* 71 Cal. Rptr. 765, 95 Cal. Rptr. 678 (1971) (upholding $200,000 punitive damages award against a disability insurer).

424. *Bivens v. Six Unknown Named Agents,* 403 U.S. 388 (1971).

425. *Hoffman v. Jones,* 280 So.2d 431 (Fla. 1973) (replacing contributory negligence with comparative negligence).

426. 13 Cal. 3d 804, 5432 P.2d 1226 (1975).

427. States have adopted a wide variety of comparative negligence regimes. In a pure comparative negligence state such as California, the liability of the defendant is proportional to his wrong. If a plaintiff were 75 percent responsible for her injury, the defendant would pay only 25 percent of the costs of the injury. In a modified comparative negligence system, a plaintiff may be barred from recovery if the plaintiff's negligence exceeded that of the defendant.

428. 131 Cal. Rptr. 14, 551 P.2d 334 (Cal. 1976).

429. *France v. A.P.A. Transp. Corp.,* 56 N.J. 500 (1970).

430. *Hackbart v. Cincinnati Bengals, Inc.,* 601 F.2d 516 (10th Cir. 1979).

431. *Sindell v. Abbott Laboratories,* 607 P.2d 924 (Cal. 1980).

432. The Comprehensive Environmental Response, Compensation and Liability Act, 42 U.S.C. §9601 et al. (1999).

433. See, e.g., *Lunde v. National Citizens Bank*, 6 N.W.2d 809 (Minn. 1942) (finding for the plaintiff in a case where the employee of a tenant was struck by shattering glass of a door in vestibule); *Watts v. Bacon & Van Buskirk Glass Co.*, 155 N.E.2d 333 (Ill. App. 1958, aff'd 163 N.E2d 425 (Ill. 1959) (holding that it was a jury issue whether landlord should have constructed glass door of tempered rather than plate glass).

434. Thomas F. Lambert, Jr., Editorial, "Products Liability: A Trilogy of Duty-to-Warn Cases," *ATLA Law Journal* 36 (1976): 1.

435. Ralph Nader, *Unsafe at Any Speed: The Designed-In Dangers of the American Automobile* (New York: Grossman, 1965), 22.

436. Id. at 68.

437. Id. at 68, 70.

438. Id. at 76–77.

439. Id. at 100.

440. Nader, *Unsafe at Any Speed*.

441. Id.

442. Id.

443. Id. at 169.

444. National Safety Council, *Accident Facts* (Itasca, Ill.: National Safety Council, 1998), iv.

445. Id. at 78.

446. See, e.g., *Bolm v. Triumph Corp.*, 305 N.E.2d 769 (N.Y. Ct. App. 1973).

447. See, generally, Paul J. Komyatte and James L. Gilbert, "Crashworthiness Litigation: Recognizing the Automotive Design Defect Case," *Reference Materials: ATLA National College of Advocacy* (Chicago: Annual Convention, July 29–August 2, 2000), 81.

448. *Ralph Nader, Beware* (New York: Law-Arts Publishing, 1971), 7 (discussing hearings and Final Report of National Commission on Product Safety).

449. Id.

450. Id.

451. Id.

452. Id. at 8.

453. Michael Rustad, "In Defense of Punitive Damages in Products Liability," *Iowa Law Review* 78 (1992): 1, 80–82.

454. Id. at 82.

455. Id at 81–82.

456. Id. at 81.

457. Id. at 82.

458. There is no specialized body of law covering "products liability" comparable to the Uniform Commercial Code comprehensively governing commercial transactions. Plaintiffs in products liability will typically plead theories of

(1) strict products liability; (2) negligence; (3) breach of implied warranty of merchantability; and increasingly (4) fraud, conspiracy, and intentional torts.

459. Id. at 4.

460. United States Consumer Protect Safety Commission, "Newco Announces Recall to Repair Bunk Bed Assembly Kit," (press release dated March 25, 1999).

461. Id.

462. Comparative negligence permits a plaintiff to recover even if he or she is partially liable for an injury. Contributory negligence, even causing 1 percent of the harm, reallocates the entire burden of compensation back to the plaintiff.

463. Jerry J. Phillips, *Tort Law: Cases, Materials and Problems* (Charlottesville, Va.: Michie Co., 1991), 802 n. 1.

464. The state employers' liability laws were patterned on the Federal Employers' Liability Act, which had an apportionment provision. Comparative negligence was also found in the Jones Act of 1915 and the Merchant Marine Act of 1920. Prosser, "Comparative Negligence," 21–22.

465. Id. at 23.

466. 13 Cal.3d 804, 119 Cal. Rptr. 858, 532 P.2d 1226 (1975).

467. Id.

468. California is one of the nine states to adopt comparative negligence by judicial decree. See Phillips, *Tort Law*, 803 n. 2.

469. Id.

470. Id. at 803 n. 3.

471. Prosser, "Comparative Negligence," 27.

472. Id. at 3 (noting that eighteen states have adopted one form of the modified comparative responsibility defense).

473. Thomas F. Lambert, Jr., "The Common Law Is Never Finished: Comparative Negligence on the March," *American Trial Lawyers Journal* 32 (1968): 741.

474. Id. at 167.

475. Joe R. Greenhill and Thomas V. Murto, III, "Governmental Immunity," *Texas Law Review* 49 (1971): 462, 462.

476. *Salvatierra v. Via Metropolitan Transit Authority*, 974 S.W.2d 179 (Ct. of App. of Tex., 1998) (discussing Texas's waiver of immunity and types of claims that may be brought against a government unit).

477. The Federal Tort Claims Act is found at 28 U.S.C. §1346 (2000).

478. Id. at §2674.

479. Id. at §2680.

480. Id.

481. See 28 U.S.C. §2674 (1999) (permitting tort claims against the government); See also 28 U.S.C. §2680 (2000).

482. *Feres v. United States*, 340 U.S. 135 (1950).

483. Ballentine, *Ballentine's Law Dictionary* , 194.

484. "Developments in the Law—Non Profit Corporations," *Harvard Law Review 105* (1992): 1578, 1680.

485. See, e.g., *Friend v. Cove Methodist Church, Inc.*, 396 P.2d 546 (Wash. 1964); *Flagiello v. Pennsylvania Hosp.*, 208 A.2d 193 (Pa. 1965); *Adkins v. St. Francis of Charleston*, 143 S.W. 154 (W. Va. 1965) (abolishing charitable immunity).

486. Id.

487. Bob Van Voris, "Clinton's a Surprising Tort Reformer," *National Law Journal* (August 7, 2000).

488. The privacy-based torts originated in Samuel Warren and Louis Brandeis, "The Right to Privacy," *Harvard Law Review* 4 (1890): 193 (arguing that the essence of the right of privacy was the right to be left alone).

489. *Restatement (Second) of Torts*, §652A, cmt. a (1965).

490. *Restatement (Second) of Torts*, §652A (1979).

491. Lambert, "The Jurisprudence of Hope," 32–33.

492. Id. at 33.

493. Prosser, *Handbook of the Law of Torts*, 354.

494. 26 A.2d 489 (N.J. 1942).

495. Prosser, *Handbook of the Law of Torts*, 354.

496. Id. at 50.

497. *Battala v. State*, 10 N.Y.2d 237, 219 N.Y.S.2d 34, 176 N.EE.2d 729 (1962).

498. Keeton et. al, *Prosser and Keeton on the Law of Torts* , 365–66.

499. Id. at 366.

500. See, e.g., *Reilly v. United States*, 547 A.2d 894 (R.I. 1988).

501. *Restatement (Second) Torts*, §46.

502. *Black's Law Dictionary*, 6th ed. (St. Paul, Minn.: West Publishing Co., 1990), 1102.

503. *Restatement (Second) Torts*, §46, Cmt. (d) (1965).

504. Id.

505. 217 N.Y. 382, 111 N.E. 1050 (1916).

506. 217 N.Y. at 389, 111 N.E. at 1053.

507. Schwartz, *Prosser, Wade and Schwartz's Torts* , 699 n. 2.

508. 32 N.J. 358, 161 A.2d 69 (1960).

509. 161 A.2d at 76 (describing accident).

510. 161 A.2d at 84 (finding liability against both Chrysler and Bloomfield Motors).

511. See U.C.C. §2-318, Alt. c (2000).

512. Gerry Spence's closing argument in the lawsuit filed by Karen Silkwood against Kerr-McGee made this point. See "Gerry Spence's Closing in the Plutonium Death Suit: *The Estate of Karen Silkwood v. Kerr-McGee, Inc.*," May 14, 1979 (visited October 29, 2000) <http://www.courttv.com/casefiles/bycel/spence.html>

(comparing the escape of plutonium to an escaping lion in the statement "if the lion got away, the defendant has got to pay.").

513. *Products liability* is the branch of tort law that imposes broad duties of care on manufacturers for defective products under the principles of negligence, breach of warranty, and strict products liability.

514. 59 Cal.2d 57, 377 P.2d 897, 27 Cal. Rptr. 697 (1962).

515. See id. at 59, 377 P.2d at 898, 27 Cal. Rptr. At 698 (describing accident).

516. Id. at 64, 377 P.2d at 901, 27 Cal. Rptr. at 701.

517. 59 Cal.2d 51, 377 P.2d 897, 27 Cal. Rptr. 697 (1962).

518. In the few jurisdictions that did not adopt 402A, there were attempts to create functional alternatives. Massachusetts, for example, jerry-rigged its Article 2 of the U.C.C. to offer nearly identical protections. See U.C.C., §2-314, §2-316A, and §2-318 (2000).

519. Marshall S. Shapo, "In Search of the Law of Products Liability: The ALI Restatement Project," *Vanderbilt Law Review* 48 (1995): 631 (1995).

520. Tort law has "progressively expanded the obligation owed by manufacturers to those foreseeably harmed by their products." *Hamilton v. ACTU-TEK*, 1999 U.S. Dist. LEXIS 8264 (E.D. N.Y., June 3, 1999).

521. Id at §2.

522. *Mays v. Ciba-Geigy Corp.*, 233 Kan. 38, 661 P.2d 348, 360 (1983).

523. *Restatement (Third) of Torts*, Products Liability §2 (2000).

524. *Restatement (Third) of Torts*, Products Liability §1, cmt. a (2000).

525. Prosser, *"Res Ipsa Loquitur* in California," 318–19.

526. Jerry J. Phillips, *Products Liability: Cases, Materials, Problems* (Charlottesville, Va.: Michie Co., 1994).

527. 78 So.2d 365 (Miss. 1928).

528. *Corum v. R. J. Reynolds Co. v. Lofton*, 205 N.C. 213, 171 S.E. 78 (1931).

529. See, generally, 36 A.L.R. 5th 541 (1996).

530. *Hazelton v. Safeway Stores, Inc.*, 12 Kan. App.2d 377, 749 P.2d 309 (1987) (reversing defense verdict in case in which a plaintiff swallowed a needle that was in bread sold by Safeway).

531. Rodents preferred Coke to Pepsi by a large margin, judging from a survey of the major law reporters. See, e.g., *Simmons v. Wichita Coca-Cola Bottling Co.*, 181 Kan. 35, 309 P.2d 633 (1957).

532. Larry Kramer, "Firestone Hit by New Suit on '500' Tires," *Washington Post* (September 22, 1978): F1.

533. The consumer expectation test is drawn from *Restatement (Second) of Torts*, §402A, cmt. i (1965); *Sperry-New Holland, Div. of Sperry Corp. v. Prestage*, 617 So.2d 248 (Miss. 1993).

534. The *Restatement (Third) of Torts* has eliminated the "consumer expectation" test against the negligence-based standard of risk-utility. Courts adopting the risk-utility approach consider a product to be defectively designed "when the

foreseeable risks of harm posed by the product could have been reduced or avoided by the adoption of a reasonable alternative design." *Restatement (Third) of Torts*, Product Liability §2 (2000). The *Restatement (Third)* would require the Firestone plaintiffs to produce expert testimony that would show that the tread separation could have been prevented with a reasonable alternative design.

535. Phillips, *Products Liability*.

536. See, e.g., *Lindsay v. Ortho Pharmaceutical Corp.*, 481 F. Supp. 314 (E.D. N.Y. 1979) (upholding verdict for plaintiff in a products liability action for a stroke suffered by plaintiff as a result of taking oral contraceptive, based upon breach of the duty to warn physicians of the hazard); see also *Witherell v. Weimer*, 396 N.E.2d 268 (Ill. App. 1979).

537. *Karns v. Emerson Electric Co.*, 817 F.2d 1452 (10th Cir. 1987).

538. See, e.g., *City of Philadelphia v. Beretta U.S.A. Corp.*, 2000 U.S. Dist. Lexis 18392 (E.D.Pa., December 20, 2000) (dismissing all claims of city against gun manufacturers).

539. Premises liability historically depended upon the status of the entrant. Trespassers were owed the lowest level of care, whereas invitees were owed the highest duty of care. Licensees were accorded a middle level standard of care. Since 1970, the status categories have gradually been replaced by a standard of care that depends upon the circumstances.

540. See, e.g., *King v. Trans-Sterling, Inc.*, No. A219783 (Dist. Ct. of Clark Cty. Nev. 1985).

541. Association of Trial Lawyers of America, *Cases That Made a Difference* (Washington, D.C.: ATLA Press, 1993), 15.

542. Non-economic damages are often referred to as pain-and-suffering damages, whereas punitive damages are awarded to punish and deter the defendant.

543. Most states have eliminated the common law doctrine of joint and several liability. However, many states have retained joint and several liability for specified categories. Idaho, for example, eliminated the common law doctrine of joint and several liability for causes of action accruing on or after July 1, 1987. Idaho replaces joint and several liability with comparative fault except in cases where the defendant is engaging in concerted action or has violated toxic or hazardous waste statutes. The joint and several doctrine has not been eliminated in medical device cases. See Idaho Code §6-803(3) (2000).

544. *Johnson v. Girdwood*, 7 Misc. 651, 28 NYS 151 (1894), aff'd 39 N.E. 21 (1895).

545. 174 Cal. Rptr. 348 (Cal. App. 1981).

546. 543 F. Supp. 198 (S.D. Tex. 1981). The court found that Klan members carried guns and rode in shrimp boats to intimidate the Vietnamese fishermen. However, the court dismissed the assault charge, since there was no imminent apprehension of immediate harm.

547. 192 Cal. Rptr. 857, 665 P.2d 947 (1983).

548. N.H. Rev. Stat. Ann. 507: 16 (1986).

549. Since 1986, the American Tort Reform Association has led a quiet revolution in the states, leading to joint and several liability restrictions in thirty-five states, restrictions on the collateral source rule in twenty-two states, punitive damages limitations in thirty-two states, caps on non-economic damages in thirteen states, limitations on prejudgment interest in fifteen states, products liability limitations in fifteen states, and class action reform in three states. See American Tort Reform Association, *2000 Tort Reform Record* (visited November 11, 2000) <http://www.atra.org/atra/record>.

550. 525 A.2d 287 (N.J. 1987).

551. 707 F. Supp. 1517 (D. Minn. 1989).

552. Steven Morris, "Searle Reaches Settlement in Copper-7 Suits," *Chicago Tribune* (June 16, 1989): 1.

553. 984 F.2d 1416, 1421–22 (5th Cir. 1993).

554. 983 F.2d 1130, 1132–37 (1st Cir. 1993).

555. *Potter v. Firestone Tire & Rubber Co.*, 863 P.2d 795 (Cal. 1993) (finding that it was unclear whether toxic dumper's actions were deliberately directed at plaintiffs).

556. *TXO Production Corp. v. Alliance Resources Corp.*, 509 U.S. 443 (1993).

557. 113 S.Ct. 2786 (1993).

558. 512 U.S. 415 (1994).

559. A statute of repose may, for example, eliminate a cause of action for personal injury or wrongful death against designers and builders ten years following construction. In the field of products liability, a statute of repose may eliminate a cause of action twenty years after a product is sold. Statutes of repose are legislative limitations that redefine the period in which a cause of action may be pursued.

560. A growing number of states have found statutes of repose to violate due process, equal protection, access to the courts and other state constitutional grounds. A number of states have open courts clauses in their state constitutions. Missouri's open court provision states "that the courts of justice shall be open to every person, and certain remedy afforded for every injury to person, property, or character, and that right and justice shall be administered without sale, denial, or delay." *Adams v. The Children's Mercy Hospital*, 832 S.W.2d 898 (Sup. Ct. Mo. 1992). The equal protection argument is that all citizens who sustain an injury are limited to the same damages cap irrespective of the extent of their injury. See, e.g., *Jackson v. Mannesmann Demag Corp.*, 435 So.2d 725 (Ala. 1983); *Turner Constr. Co. v. Scales*, 752 P.2d 467 (Alaska 1988); *Best v. Taylor Machine Works*, 689 N.E.2d (Ill. 1997); *Hazine v. Montgomery Elevator Co.*, 861 P.2d 632 (Ariz. 1993); *Lee v. Gaufin*, 867 P.2d 572 (Utah 1993); *Perkins v. Northeastern Log Homes*, 808 S.W.2d 809 (Ky. 1991); *Nelson v. Krusen*, 678 S.W.2d 918 (Tex. 1985).

561. *BMW of N. Am., Inc. v. Gore*, 517 U.S. 559 (1996) (establishing guidelines

for determining whether high ratio punitive damages awards are constitutionally excessive).

562. See, generally, Kristin M. McCabe, "The Texas Health Care Liability Act: Texas Is the First State to Listen to the Concerns of Its Health Care Consumers, But How Much Has It Hurt?" *Journal of Contemporary Health Law and Policy* 16 (2000): 565.

563. Van Voris, "Clinton's a Surprising Tort Reformer," 1.

564. *Amchem Products, Inc., v. Windsor*, 521 U.S. 591 (1997).

565. *Anderson v. General Motors*, No. BC-116-926 (Cal. Super. Ct., July 9, 1999).

566. *United States v. Philip Morris, Inc.*, No. 99-CV24967 (D.D.C., September 22, 1999).

567. 120 S. Ct. 2143 (2000).

568. The plaintiff in *Pegram* was experiencing pain in her groin. Her physician discovered an eight-centimeter inflamed mass in her abdomen. Despite this inflammation, the physician decided that the plaintiff would have to wait eight days for an ultrasound diagnostic procedure. During the delay, the plaintiff's appendix ruptured, causing peritonitis, which is "an inflammation of the tissues (the peritoneum) that lines the abdominal cavity." See Dr. Allan Bruckheim, "Probing the Peril Called Peritonitis," *Buffalo News* (March 15, 1997): 9A. The plaintiff sued her physician for malpractice. The defense was that the malpractice action was preempted by ERISA. The plaintiff filed a fraud charge based on the claim that physician owners were rewarded for limiting medical care such as the ultrasound diagnostic procedure. The district court dismissed the claim, but the Seventh Circuit held that the plaintiff stated a claim for fraud on a fiduciary theory. The U.S. Supreme Court held that the plaintiff was not a fiduciary and her claim was preempted. The Court held that the fact that there were incentives for reduced care did not make the claimant a fiduciary.

569. The symbiotic relationship between medical provider and insurer in reimbursing malpractice claims led to the tort reform movement in medical malpractice.

570. Paul C. Weiler, "The Case for No-Fault Medical Liability," *Maryland Law Review* 52 (1993): 908, 912 (1993).

571. Id. at 909.

572. Id.

573. Dobbs, *The Law of Torts*, v.

574. *Carlin v. Superior Court*, 13 Cal. 4th 1104, 920 P.2d 1347 (1996).

575. James A. Henderson and Aaron D. Twerski, "A Proposed Revision of Section 402A of the Restatement (Second) of Torts," *Cornell Law Review* 77 (1992): 1512, 1530.

576. Id. at 1529.

577. *Banks v. ICI Americas, Inc.*, 266 Ga. 607, 469 S.E.2d 171 (1996).

578. *Freeman v. Hoffman Roche*, 618 N.W.2d 287 (Neb. 2000).

579. The Reporters observe that under Section 2(b), "consumer expectations do not constitute an independent standard for judging the defectiveness of product designs." *Restatement of Torts (Third)*, Products Liability §2b (1998).

580. Id.

581. Id. at §1, Cmt. (a).

582. American Tort Reform Association, *Tort Reform Record* (June 2000) (reporting tort reforms since 1986).

583. Id.

584. Id.

585. Victor E. Schwartz and Mark A. Behrens, "Federal Products Liability Reform in 1997: History and Public Policy Support Its Enactment Now," *Tennessee Law Review* 64 (1997): 595, 599.

586. Philip H. Corboy, "The Not-So-Quiet Revolution: Rebuilding Barriers to Jury Trial in the Proposed Restatement (Third) of Torts: Products Liability," *Tennessee Law Review* 61 (1994): 1043, 1069 (observing that the 1,400 tort reform bills introduced in 1986 were a product of a special corporate and insurer interests).

587. Henderson and Twerski, "A Proposed Revision of Section 402A," 1529.

588. Richard B. Schmitt, "Planned Veto of Liability Bill Is Business's Loss," *The Wall Street Journal* (March 18, 1998): A2 (quoting President Clinton).

589. Van Voris, "Clinton's Surprising Tort Reformer."

590. Texas and Oklahoma enacted comprehensive tort reforms twice in the past decade. Florida limits punitive damages to three times the amount of compensatory damages. Punitive damages in Colorado are limited to the amount of actual damages. Nevada limits the recovery of punitive damages to $300,000 in cases where the compensatory damages are less than $100,000 and up to three times compensatory damages in awards of $100,000 or more. Defendants in Arizona, New Jersey, Oregon, and Utah have complete immunity from punitive damages so long as their product complied with government-mandated safety standards. Indiana allocates 75 percent of all punitive damages awards to the state's victim compensation fund. Indiana has eliminated joint and several liabilities in products liability cases. Iowa adopted a state-sharing statute, which requires that a plaintiff remit 75 percent of all punitive damages to the state. Kansas allocates 50 percent of all punitive damages in medical malpractice cases to the state treasury. Kansas enacted a statute that requires judges rather than juries to award punitive damages. Missouri, like the majority of states, has increased the burden for proving punitive damages to "clear and convincing" evidence. Many states have enacted caps on the total recovery for pain-and-suffering damages. All of these tort reform measures were enacted to benefit corporate defendants. Tort reforms are decidedly pro-defendant, making it more difficult for plaintiffs to recover tort damages or limiting total recovery. Thomas Koenig and Michael Rustad, "The Quiet Revolution Revisited: An Empirical Study of the Impact of Tort

Reform on Punitive Damages in Products Liability," *Justice System Journal* 16 (1993): 21 (citing tort reform statutes); see, generally, Michael Rustad and Thomas Koenig, "Punitive Damages in Products Liability: A Research Report," *Product Law Journal 3* (February 1992): 85; Michael Rustad, "Unraveling Punitive Damages: Current Data and Further Inquiry," *Wisconsin Law Review* (1998): 15.

591. These limitations in tort remedies are described in the Appendix to Justice Ginsburg's opinion in *BMW of N. Am. v. Gore* 517 U.S. 559 (1995).

592. Id.

593. Id.

594. The standard burden of proof in civil cases in the United States is the preponderance of the evidence. Colorado is the only jurisdiction to require punitive damages claimants to prove their case "beyond a reasonable doubt," which is the criminal law standard.

595. Similar health care providers must regard the level of professional care as acceptable and prudent. See Fla. Stat. §766.102 (2000) (describing medical negligence and standards for recovery).

596. National Center for State Courts, Civil Trial Court Network, *Plaintiff's Win Ratios* (Williamsburg, Va.: National Center for State Courts, 1999).

597. *Horne v. Emerald Valley Day Care Ctr.*, No. 16-88-02863 (Cal. Cir. Ct. Los Angeles County 1991).

598. "Notable Verdicts," *National Law Journal* (January 21, 1991): S7 (quoting Morris Dees, plaintiff's attorney).

599. *Berhanu v. Metzger*, No. A8911-07007 (Oregon County Ct., Mulnomah County October 1990), aff.'d 852 P.2d 974 (Oregon 1992), *cert. denied*, 114 S. Ct. 2100 (1994).

600. Id.

601. W. C. Bruce, *John Randolph of Roanoke, 1773–1833* (1922; reprint, New York: Octagon Books, 1970), 211.

602. David E. Bernstein, "Procedural Tort Reform: Lessons from Other Nations," *Regulation: The Cato Review of Business and Government* (March 1999) (visited on April 2, 1999) <http://www.cato.org/pubs/regulation/reg19nle.html>.

NOTES TO CHAPTER 2

1. The film was based upon Jonathan Haar, *A Civil Action* (New York: Vintage, 1996).

2. 628 F. Supp. 219 (D. Mass. 1988).

3. The corporate defendants were liable under the doctrine of successor liability, which made them liable for the torts of the company they acquired. The defendants "stepped into the shoes" of the predecessor corporations that allegedly dumped the chemicals.

4. Id.

5. The plaintiffs contended that the contaminated water caused harm to their respiratory, immunological, blood, central nervous system, gastrointestinal system, urinary-renal system, and other systems. Expert testimony was required to support the claim that these problems were the result of exposure to contaminated water.

6. The trial court found the emotional injuries not compensable under Massachusetts law, which requires that emotional injuries arise from physical injuries caused by the defendant's conduct. However, the court also struck down the plaintiffs' claim of emotional injuries for witnessing the death of the plaintiffs' children. The plaintiffs were present during the illness and death of their children and were immediate family members. However, the plaintiffs did not witness the traumatic death, but rather a long-term illness fatal decline. Id. at 220.

7. The Massachusetts Wrongful Death Act measures damages on the basis of the defendant's culpability. M.G.L.A. ch 229 §2.

8. Judge Skinner ruled that Massachusetts's law did not foreclose the possibility of applying the discovery rule to this case. Id. at 221.

9. Judge Skinner reasoned that it would be a waste of judicial resources for the jury to consider evidence relevant to damages if no causal connection could be proven.

10. *Bigelow v. RKO Radio Pictures*, 327 U.S. 251, 265 (1946) (J. Stone concurring).

11. W. R. Grace, "The Woburn Story: Background Facts about Woburn," W. R. Grace Website (visited December 30, 1998) <http//www.grace.com/html/woburn.html>.

12. Id.

13. Susan Warren, "Grace Considers Chapter 11 Filing amid Rising Asbestos Litigation," *Wall Street Journal* (January 30, 2001): 1.

14. These headlines were widely distributed by the American Tort Reform Association and its affiliated state chapters and umbrella organizations.

15. Clyde Haberman, "Didn't Win a Lottery? Time to Sue," *New York Times* (November 16, 1999): B1.

16. The tort reformers' idée fixe is the war against punitive damages in products liability and medical malpractice. The tort reformers' obsession is to restrict the rights of Americans to obtain redress for injuries caused by dangerously defective products or substandard medical treatment. If this were a true crusade against lawsuit abuse, the focus would be to limit remedies in business tort lawsuits, which account for the majority of million-dollar punitive damage awards.

17. The American Tort Reform Association membership list consists of corporate actors such as the Business Roundtable, General Aviation Manufacturers Association, National Association of Home Builders, Food Marketing Institute, National Association of Manufacturers, National Paint and Coating Association, Pharmaceutical Manufacturers Association, Sporting Goods Manufacturing As-

sociation, Aetna, American Home Products Corporation, Chrysler Motors Corporation, Clorox Company, Dow Chemical USA, General Electric Company, McDonald's, Pfizer, and Travelers Companies. See, generally, The American Tort Reform Association, Membership List, Steering Committee Members (January 1989).

18. "National Lawsuit Abuse Awareness Week," printed in *Congressional Record*, September 26, 1997; reprinted at <http//thomas.loc.gov/cgi-bin/query/Ck?r105/temp/r105fqbuir>.

19. New Yorkers for Civil Justice Reform, *Tort Informer* (visited November 11, 2000) <http://www.nycjr.org/informer/Tia17.html>.

20. Under the doctrine of privity, there must be a direct contractual relationship between the injured party and the company responsible for the injury. See, e.g., *Greenman v. Yuba Power Products, Inc.*, 377 P.2d 897 (Cal. 1962) (proposing strict liability for the injuries caused by defective products).

21. Robert L. Rabin, "A Sociolegal History of the Tobacco Tort Litigation," *Stanford Law Review* 44 (1992): 853.

22. The advertisements from *Hendrix v. Consolidated Van Lines*, 269 P.2d 435 (Kan. 1954), reprinted in Joanne Doroshow, *The Case for the Civil Jury: Safeguarding a Pillar of Democracy* (Washington, D.C.: Center for Responsive Law, 1992).

23. These advertisements were published in the January 26 and March 9, 1953, issues of *Life Magazine* and the February 14 and March 28, 1953, edition of the *Saturday Evening Post*.

24. The anti-juror advertisements were reprinted in *Hendrix v. Consolidated Van Lines*, 269 P.2d 435 (Kan. 1954).

25. This advertisement is reprinted in Doroshow, *The Case for the Civil Jury*, 639.

26. Id.

27. The St. Paul advertisement was reprinted in id.

28. Id.

29. Allen Posey, "Judges Rule in Favor of Juries," *Dallas Morning News* (May 7, 2000): A1.

30. See *Hendrix v. Consolidated Van Lines*, 269 P.2d 435 (Kan. 1954) (finding that insurance companies were not in contempt for distributing anti-liability literature and advertisements).

31. *Borkoski v. Yost*, 594 P.2d 688, 694 (Montana 1979).

32. David E. Rosenbaum, "Business Lobbyists Cheer Victories in Congress," *Deseret News* (Salt Lake City, Utah) (November 29, 1999): D13.

33. *Chamber of Commerce v. Michael Moore, Attorney General et al.*, No. 3:00-CV-778WS (D. Miss., November 2, 2000).

34. James Bradshaw, "Judicial Ad Critics Hail Mississippi Court Ruling," *Columbus Dispatch* (November 4, 2000): 1C.

35. "HIAA Radio Campaign Blasts New Bi-Partisan Patients' Rights Bill," *Bestwire* (August 19, 1999).

36. Katherine Lemon, "Bush Bought by Phony Grass Roots Groups" (visited August 15, 2000) <http://www.alterive7.org>.

37. Id.

38. Id.

39. "AAHP Calls on Congress to Reject Special-Interest Windfall for Trial Lawyers," *Public Relations Newswire* (September 9, 1999).

40. See R. J. Reynolds memo, "Strategic and Tactical Considerations Concerning Ingredients, Privileged Documents Released" (visited July 25, 2000) <http://www.gate.net/cannon/liggett/fl/index.html>.

41. Id.

42. Rabin, "A Sociolegal History of the Tobacco Tort Litigation," 870.

43. Gordon Fairclough, "Tobacco Executives Break Ranks in Punitive Phase of Florida Trial," *Wall Street Journal* (July 13 2000): B1.

44. Whit Ayers, "A Republican Perspective," *Campaigns and Elections* (October/November 1995).

45. "AAHP Launches New Television Campaign," *Public Relations Newswire* (January 25, 1999).

46. David Wallis, "Biting Back: Some Lawyers Try to Make Nice," *New York Times* (November 28, 1999): 3.

47. Jan Harold Brunvand, *The Mexican Pet: More "New" Urban Legends and Some Old Favorites* (New York: Norton, 1986), 9.

48. Thomas F. Lambert, Jr., "The Case for Punitive Damages (Including Their Coverage by Liability Insurance)," *American Trial Lawyers Journal* 35 (1965): 164.

49. This apt description of the human face of litigation was a favorite saying of Thomas Lambert.

50. Ayers, "A Republican Perspective."

51. Jane Goodman and Elizabeth F. Loftus, "Jurors' Attitudes about Civil Litigation and the Size of Damage Awards," *American University Law Review* 40 (1991): 805.

52. Sean F. Mooney, *Crisis and Recovery: A Review of Business Liability Insurance in the 1980s* (Washington, D.C.: Insurance Information Institute (May 1992).

53. A number of state supreme courts have upheld challenges to state tort reforms. See, e.g., *Adams v. The Children's Mercy Hospital*, 832 S.W.2d 898 (Sup. Ct. Mo., 1992) (rejecting claim that victims of medical malpractice are a "suspect class" and that right to a certain remedy represents a fundamental right in upholding constitutionality of Missouri's medical malpractice tort reform).

54. Equal protection analysis under state constitutional law will often parallel federal equal protection analysis in focusing on whether a statutory classification burdens a "suspect class" or impinges upon a "fundamental right." Suspect classes

are those based upon race, national origin, or illegitimacy, which for historic reasons need special protection from a political process. Fundamental rights include rights such as the freedom of the press, freedom of religion, the right to vote, the right to personal privacy, and other basic liberties. If neither a suspect class or fundamental right are present, a statute will be upheld if it is rationally related to a legitimate state interest. *Adams v. The Children's Mercy Hospital*, 832 S.W.2d 898 (Mo. Sup. Ct. 1992).

55. *Moore v. Mobile Infirmary*, 592 So.2d 156 (Ala. 1991).

56. 627 So.2d 878 (Ala. 1993).

57. *Best v. Taylor Machine Works*, 689 N.E.2d 1057 (Ill. 1997).

58. 86 Ohio St.3d 451 (Ohio 1999) (declaring comprehensive tort reform statute to be an unconstitutional intrusion on judicial power on several state constitutional grounds).

59. State tort reforms have been successfully challenged on various state constitutional grounds in Alabama, Arizona, Florida, Georgia, Illinois, Kansas, Kentucky, Louisiana, New Hampshire, New Mexico, North Dakota, Ohio, Oregon, South Dakota, Texas, Utah, Washington, and Wisconsin.

60. *Salvatierra v. Via Metropolitan Tranit Authority*, 974 S.W.2d 179 (4th Dist. Tex. 1998) (citing Article I, §13 of the Texas Constitution in upholding statute).

61. *Data Processing Services, Inc. v. L. H. Smith Oil Corp.*, 492 N.E.2d 314, 319 (Ind. Ct. App. 1986) (holding that services must be performed in a diligent and reasonably skillful manner).

62. Association of Trial Lawyers of America, "The Other Side of the Story: The Real Frivolous Lawsuits: Businesses Suing Businesses," *ATLA Net* (visited December 31, 1998) <http//www.atlanet.org/cjfacts/other/friolou.t>.

63. Dottie Enrico, "Ads Spur Lawsuits over Accuracy," *USA Today* (November 15, 1995): 1B.

64. See, e.g., "Company News: American Express Sues Chase over Credit Card Ads," *New York Times* (December 23, 1998): 3C; Paul Beckett, "Chase Manhattan Settles Lawsuits Filed by American Express over Card Ads," *Wall Street Journal* (December 28, 1998): B5.

65. Consumers Union of U.S., Inc., *Consumers Report* 63 (December 1998): 12.

66. Enrico, "Ads Spur Lawsuits over Accuracy."

67. Id.

68. Jane Dudman, "Two Leading PC Suppliers in the U.S. Are Locked in a Bitter Legal Battle," *The Independent* (London) (February 26, 1996): 7.

69. Enrico, "Ads Spur Lawsuits over Accuracy."

70. Id.

71. Id.

72. *Texaco, Inc. v. Pennzoil Co.*, 784 F.2d 1133 (2d Cir. 1986), rev'd in part, 481 U.S. 1 (1987).

73. *Dominquez Energy L.P. v. Shell Oil Co.*, No. C736 891 (L.A. Cent. Civ. W., D. Cal., January 11, 1994).

74. *Brookfield Communications, Inc. v. West Coast Entertainment Corp.*, 174 F.3d 1036 (9th Cir. 1999) (noting further that "domain names consist of a second-level domain—simply a term or series of terms followed by a top-level domain, many of which describe the nature of the enterprise").

75. See, e.g., *Hasbro, Inc. v. Clue Computing, Inc.*, 2000 U.S. App. LEXIS 27856 (1st Cir., November 7, 2000) (holding no evidence that defendant infringed or tarnished plaintiff's trademark); *Bancroft & Masters, Inc. v. Augusta Nat'l, Inc.*, 2000 U.S. App. LEXIS 20917 (9th Cir., August 18, 2000).

76. *Mattel v. Internet Host* (N.D. Cal., Filed February 1999) (visited June 18, 1999) <http//www.perkinscoie.com/resource/ecomm/netcase/Cases-08.htm>.

77. *Porsche Cars North America, Inc. v. Porsche*, 51 F. Supp. 2d 707 (E.D. Va. 1999).

78. *The Hearst Corp. v. Goldberger*, 1997 U.S. Dist. LEXIS 2065 (S.D. N.Y., February 26, 1997).

79. John R. Thomas, "The Post-Industrial Patent System," *Fordham Intellectual Property, Media, and Entertainment Law Journal* 10 (1999): 3

80. *State Street Bank and Trust Co. v. Signature Financial Group, Inc.* 149 F.3d 1368 (Fed. Cir. 1998) opened the floodgates for e-commerce business methods lawsuits.

81. Andrew J. Trakman and Robert M. Stern, "Domain Names Surf's Up: Wave of Patent Litigation Is Coming," *E-Commerce* 17 (May 2000): 1.

82. See Scott Killingsworth, "Strategic Licensing: Leveraging Technology through Alliances," *Cyber Lawyer* 3 (September 1998): 13.

83. Brian Sullivan et al. "Boarish Battle: Spam vs. Spa'am," *American Bar Association Journal* 82 (April 1996): 16.

84. Id.

85. Enrico, "Ads Spur Lawsuits over Accuracy."

86. Steven M. Bauer, "Assets and Liabilities in an Intellectual Property Audit," *Boston University Journal of Science and Technology Law* 1 (1995): 8.

87. Association of Trial Lawyers of America, "The Other Side of the Story."

88. Troyen A. Brennan et al., "Incidence of Adverse Events and Negligence in Hospitalized Patients," New *England Journal of Medicine* 324 (1991): 370, 370.

89. Id.

90. Adverse events were avoidable iatrogenic injuries attributable to treatment decisions.

91. Id. at 373.

92. Id.

93. Id.

94. Paul C. Weiler, "The Case for No-Fault Medical Liability," *Maryland Law Review* 52 (1993): 908, 918.

95. Robert Pear, "Protect Patients from Fatal Mistakes, U.S. Urged," *Plain Dealer* (November 30, 1999): 10A.

96. Testimony of Ann Brown, Chair, U.S. Consumer Product Safety Commission, *FY 2000 House Appropriations Subcommittee Testimony, Before the Veterans Administration, Housing and Urban Development*, House Appropriations Committee, February 23, 1999 (visited September 1, 2000) <http://www.cpsc .gov>.

97. Id.

98. Id.

99. Bob Davis and Julie Appleby, "Medical Mistakes 8th Top Killer," *USA Today* (November 30, 1999): 1A.

100. National Safety Council, *Accident Facts* (Itasca, Ill.: National Safety Council, 1998), iv.

101. Id.

102. William Ryan, *Blaming the Victim* (New York: Pantheon Books, 1971), xii.

103. In our study of punitive damages in products liability for verdicts awarded 1965–90, we found cases in which the costs of litigation exceeded $1 million. The recent tobacco litigation required the war chests of numerous prominent plaintiffs' firms and the states.

104. Patricia Munch Danzon, "Contingent Fees for Personal Injury Litigation" (R-2458-HCA) (Santa Monica, Calif.: Rand Institute for Civil Justice, June 1980), viii.

105. A study of Franklin County Ohio verdicts found that only one in five plaintiffs in products liability cases won their cases. Plaintiffs in medical malpractice lawsuits prevailed in only approximately one in three cases. Deborah Jones Merritt and Kathryn Ann Barry, "Is the Tort System in Crisis? New Empirical Evidence," *Ohio State Law Journal* 60 (1999): 355.

106. Professor Rustad authored an *amicus* brief on behalf of the Hunt family in the appeal before the Oklahoma Supreme Court. *Hunt v. Kubota Tractor Corp.*, No. CJ-91-268 (Garfield County, Okla., April 27, 1993). This case study is drawn from the trial record and briefs authored by Professor Rustad and plaintiff's attorneys, Alec and Susan McNaughten of the Enid, Oklahoma, law firm of McNaughten and McNaughten.

107. See also *Barnwell v. Kubota Tractor Corp.*, No. 85-9903 (Duval Cty. Cir. Ct., Fla. 1987).

108. Id.

109. Id.

110. "Kubota Cuts Exports of Used Tractors to U.S.," *Japanese Economics News Wire* (January 23, 1992).

111. Id.

112. Tort reformers may argue that Kubota's decision to warn consumers or withdraw the tractors was not a product of litigation, but for unrelated reasons.

113. *Forrest City Machine Works, Inc. v. Aderhold*, 616 S.W.2d 720, 726 (Ark. 1981) (quoting *Sturm, Ruger and Co.* v. *Day*, 594 P.2d 38, 47 (Alaska 1979)).

114. Our case study is based upon court documents provided to us by plaintiff's attorney, Mark Robinson, who was also counsel in the famous Ford Pinto case.

115. "Man Accused of 27 Counts of Drunk-Driving Murder Takes Stand," *Reuters* (December 24, 1989).

116. Myron Becken, "The Kentucky School Bus Crash and Its Aftermath," *Baltimore Sun* (December 24, 1989): 7A.

117. Danny Brandenburg, "Medical Examiner Overwhelmed by 27 Killed in Drunken Driver Case," *United Press International* (December 8, 1989).

118. "Bus Crash Settled in Kentucky," *PR Newswire* (July 15, 1988).

119. "Plaintiff's Motion to Oppose Ford's *in Limine* Motions," document filed in *Nunnallee v. Sheller-Globe Corp.*, No. 88-CI-099 (Carroll County Ct., Ky., 1988).

120. Id.

121. *Grimshaw v. Ford Motor Co.*, 119 Cal. App. 3d 757 (1981).

122. Id.

123. Attorney Mark Robinson made these arguments in opposition to Ford's Motion *in Limine*, Id.

124. *Grimshaw v. Ford Motor Co.*, 174 Cal. Rptr. 348 (Cal. Ct. App. 1981).

125. Id. at 384.

126. Id.

127. Despite the compelling evidence that Ford had knowingly endangered the safety of the public, an Indiana jury found the company innocent of manslaughter charges. The criminal case was filed as a result of the deaths of three young girls in a fuel-fed fire caused by a defect in their Ford Pinto. See Joseph R. Tybro, "How Ford Won Pinto Trial," *National Law Journal*(March 13, 1980): 1.

128. See James S. Kunen, *Corporate Greed, Government Indifference, and the Kentucky School Bus Crash* (New York: Simon and Schuster, 1994).

129. Id.

130. Plaintiff's Motion to Oppose Ford's Motion *in Limine*.

131. Id.

132. 171 Ga. App. 331, 319 S.E.2d 470 (1984).

133. 171 Ga. App. at 337–338, 319 S.E.2d (1984) at 338.

134. 319 S.E.2d at 341, 319 S.E.2d 1984 at 341.

135. Jay Blanton, "Ford Lawyers Blame Mahoney for Deaths, Deny Slighting Safety," *Courier-Journal (Louisville)* (February 11, 1992): 1B.

136. Id.

137. Id.

138. Frank Smith, "A Tragic Quest for Justice," *Tampa Tribune* (November 13, 1994): 6.

139. Jim De Brosse, "A Pain That Never Ends: 10 Years Ago, the Deadliest Alcohol-Related Crash in U.S. History Killed 27 People on I-71," *Dayton Daily News* (May 10, 1998): 1A.

140. "Could School Buses Be Made to Be Safer?" *Phoenix Gazette* (April 19, 1996): B4.

141. *Ellen Mohney v. Alfred C. Speirs and Baxter Health Care*, No. 93-CA-1750 (El Paso County, Colo., 1986). Professor Rustad was counsel to Ellen Mohney in the appeal of the defense verdict to the Colorado Court of Appeals and Colorado Supreme Court; *Mohney v. Speirs*, 86CV3325 (Dist. Ct., El Paso, Colo., June 25, 1993). The Colorado Court of Appeals affirmed the defense verdict of the lower court. See *Mohney v. Speirs*, No. 93-CA-1750 Colo. App. 1996). The record citations have been deleted to improve the readability of this section.

142. As with our other case studies, the products liability defendant had a very different reading of the trial record. Baxter International, like the defendants in the Woburn contaminated water supply case, was a successor corporation who "stepped into the shoes" of a predecessor through the doctrine of successor liability.

143. Dr. Speirs argued that he provided Ellen Mohney with full disclosure of all of the risks and dangers then known about silicone breast implants.

144. Deposition of Dr. Michael Phillips, Defendant's Medical Expert, *Mohney v. Speirs*, No. 86-CV-3325 (Dist. Ct., El Paso, Colo., June 25, 1993).

145. Id.

146. Deposition of Dr. Linda Huang, Plaintiff's Medical Expert, *Mohney v. Speirs*, No. 86-CV-3325 (Dist. Ct., El Paso, Colo., June 25, 1993).

147. See General and Plastic Surgery Devices; Effective Date of Requirement for Pre-market Approval of Silicone Gel-filled Breast Prosthesis; Proposed Rule, 55 FR 20,568, codified at 21 C.F.R. §878 (proposed May 17, 1990). The FDA's proposed findings based on 128 pieces of medical literature concluded that the "AFDA now believes that the following are significant risks associated with the use of the silicone gel-filled breast prosthesis." The FDA considered fibrous capsular contracture and silicone-gel leakage, migration, and infection to be specific risks associated with mammary prostheses. See 55 Federal Register 568–71.

148. See also 57 FR 10,702 (March 27, 1992) (proposing tracking of medical implants containing silicone, in light of serious adverse health consequences of silicone gel).

149. Rule 35 of the Colorado Rules of Civil Procedure requires that a plaintiff place her mental condition "in controversy," and that "good cause" be shown for the examination. See C.R.C.P. 35 (1995).

150. Assuming *arguendo* that she suffered preexisting depression, the "thin-skull" doctrine requires the injurer, rather than the victim, to absorb the enhanced injury caused by the wrongdoing. See *Dulieu v. White*, 2 K. B. 669, 679 (1901) (defendant may not complain that there would be less or no injury if plaintiff had not had a thin skull or weak heart).

151. "Bankruptcy: *In re Dow Corning*," *Breast Implant Litigation Reporter* 9 (July 24, 2000): 3.

152. *Gonzales v. Surgidev Corp.*, No. CV-88-81 (Taos County District Court, Taos, New Mexico, November 16, 1990). We base our case study upon court records and our interviews with Carolyn Merchant, plaintiff's counsel.

153. This section is drawn from *Gonzales v. Surgidev Corp.*, 120 N.M. 151, 899 P.2d 594 (1995).

154. Id. at 120 N.M. at 158, 899 P.2d at 601.

155. Id.

156. Id. at 120 N.M. at 159, 899 P.2d at 602.

157. Id.

158. Id.

159. See *Kozlowski v. Sears, Roebuck and Co.*, 73 F.R.D. 73, 75–76 (D. Mass. 1976).

160. *Hess v. Pittsburgh Steel Foundry and Mach. Co.*, 49 F.R.D. 271, 273 (W. D. Pa. 1970).

161. See *Doanbuy Lease and Co. v. Melcher*, 83 N.M. 82, 448 P.2d 330 (1971); *Pizza Hut of Santa Fe, Inc. v. Branch*, 89 N.M. 325, 552 P.2d 227 (Ct. App. 1976).

162. *Crist v. Goody*, 507 P.2d 478 (Colo. App. 1972); *Glisan v. Kurth*, 384 P.2d 246 (Colo. 1963).

NOTES TO CHAPTER 3

1. See Thomas Koenig and Michael Rustad, "His and Her Tort Reform: Gender Injustice in Disguise," *University of Washington Law Review* 70 (1995): 1.

2. Richard Abel argues that tort law discriminates on the basis of race, gender, and social class. See Richard L. Abel, "The Real Tort Crisis—Too Few Claims," *Ohio State Law Journal* 48 (1987): 443, 443 (1987) (arguing that tort law reflects social inequality in society).

3. Lucinda M. Finley, "A Break in the Silence: Including Women's Issues in a Torts Course," *Yale Journal of Law and Feminism* 1 (1989): 41, 52.

4. The Gender Bias Task Force of Texas found that women experience bias through hostile or demeaning treatment from attorneys and judges, financial and logistical barriers that limit their access to courts, and self-perpetuating gender inequities within the family law system. Other findings are that women face a loss of credibility through biased behaviors and attitudes at all levels of the judicial system, including in cases of sexual assault, where they are viewed as less credible than victims of other types of assault. "Bias in Judicial System Affects Both Genders," *Southwest Newswire* (March 24, 1994), available in LEXIS, News Library, Wires File (summarizing final report, Gender Bias Task Force of Texas, 1994). Similarly, a New York study of the courts found a pattern of "actions taken because of weight given to preconceived notions of sexual roles rather than upon a

fair and unswayed appraisal of merit as to each person or situation." *New York Task Force on Women in the Courts Summary Report* (1986): 378–79 (documenting that women litigants are denied justice because of such factors as their lack of financial resources, their limited credibility, and the male perspective of the judiciary, id. at 384–405). Similarly, an analysis of wrongful death recoveries in the state of Washington found that women's deaths produced smaller compensatory awards than those of men. Jane Goodman, "Money, Sex and Death: Gender Bias in Wrongful Death Damage Awards," *Law and Society Review* 28 (1991): 263 (reporting that juries awarded males higher amounts in wrongful death actions).

5. Robin West, "Jurisprudence and Gender," *University of Chicago Law Review* 55 (1988): 1 (arguing that women's troubles that are not shared by men, such as date rape, are not taken seriously enough by the legal system); Sylvia A. Law, "Rethinking Sex and the Constitution," *University of Pennsylvania Law Review* 132 (1984): 955 (discussing gender bias embedded in legal assumptions).

6. Jessie Bernard, *The Future of Marriage* (Harmondsworth: Penguin, 1976).

7. Elizabeth Janeway, *Powers of the Weak* (New York: Alfred A. Knopf, 1980), 4.

8. *Postal Telegraph-Cable Co. v. Tonopah and Tide Water R.R. Co.*, 248 U.S. 471, 475 (1919) (J. Holmes).

9. There is a long-standing debate in the social sciences over the degree to which gender is genetically or socially constructed. See, e.g., Eleanor E. Maccoby, *Social Development: Psychological Growth and the Parent–Child Relationship* (New York: Harcourt Brace Jovanovich, 1980).

10. Lenore J. Weitzman, *The Divorce Revolution: The Unexpected Social and Economic Consequences for Women and Children in America* (New York: Free Press, 1985).

11. Eleanor D. Kinney et al., "Indiana's Medical Malpractice Act: Results of a Three-Year Study," *Indiana Law Review* 24 (1991): 1275 (reporting that "[m]en tended to have larger awards than women, received against defendants above and beyond any compensatory damages to punish particularly egregious conduct").

12. Cynthia Grant Bowman, "Street Harassment and the Informal Ghettoization of Women," *Harvard Law Review* 106 (1993): 517, 518.

13. Ronald K. L. Collins, "Language, History and the Legal Process: A Profile of the 'Reasonable Man,'" *Rutgers Law Journal* 8 (1977): 311, 312.

14. W. Page Keeton et al., *Prosser and Keeton on the Law of Torts*, 5th ed. (St. Paul, Minn.: West Publishing Company, 1984), 901–2.

15. *Black's Law Dictionary*, 5th ed. (St. Paul, Minn.: West Publishing Co., 1979).

16. *Black's Law Dictionary*, 7th ed. (St. Paul, Minn.: West Publishing Co., 1999), 1362.

17. However, as seen in Chapter 1, exemplary damages were awarded to a female pauper whose head had been maliciously shaved by the employee of a "poor house." *Forde v. Skinner*, 172 Eng. Rep. 687 (1830).

18. Court referred to damages allowed as an enhancement of compensatory damages as exemplary damages, punitive damages, vindictive damages, or "smart money." The term "vindictive damages" referred to punishing the defendant and vindicating the rights of a party as a substitution for revenge. James A. Ballentine, *Ballentine's Law Dictionary*, 3d ed. (Rochester, N.Y.: Lawyers Co-operative Publishing Co., 1969), 434.

19. 207 N.W. 289 (Wis. 1926).

20. 161 N.W. 290 (Iowa 1917).

21. *Baird v. Biehner*, 42 N.W. 454 (Iowa 1889) (defining seduction as using an artifice or some other fraudulent means to induce a woman to "submit to unlawful sexual intercourse").

22. 1 N.J.L. 77, 77 (1791).

23. *Owens v. Fanning*, 205 S.W. 69 (Mo. Ct. App. 1918).

24. Id. at 72.

25. 198 N.W. 669 (Minn. 1924).

26. 38 Tenn. (1 Head) 209 (1858).

27. *Nyman v. Lynde*, 101 N.W. 163 (Minn. 1904).

28. See also *August v. Finnerty*, 30 Ohio C.C. 433 (1908).

29. *Dix v. Martin*, 157 S.W. 133 (Mo. Ct. App. 1913).

30. *Campbell v. Crutcher*, 224 S.W. 115, 116–18 (Mo. 1920).

31. Id.

32. *Rogers v. Foote*, 84 A. 643 (Me. 1902).

33. *McGee v. Vanover*, 147 S.W. 742 (Ky. 1912).

34. *Thomson v. Portland Hotel Co.*, 239 S.W. 1090 (Mo. App. 1922).

35. *Murphy v. Pettitt*, 251 S.W. 179 (Ky. Ct. App. 1923).

36. *Kohut v. Boguslavsky*, 239 P. 876 (Colo. 1925).

37. However, the Colorado Supreme Court reversed the award, citing "evidence of passion or prejudice" by the jury. Id. at 877.

38. *Flynn v. St. Louis S.W. Ry. Co.*, 190 S.W. 371, 371–72 (Mo. Ct. App. 1917) (upholding $1,500 punitive damages award against conductor found guilty of fondling female passengers' breasts).

39. 18 S.W. 1066, 1066 (Tex. 1893).

40. *Pine Bluff and A.R. Ry. Co. v. Washington*, 172 S.W. 872 (Ark. 1915).

41. *Chicago Consol. Traction Co. v. Mahoney*, 82 N.E. 868, 869–72 (Ill. 1907).

42. *Flynn v. St. Louis S.W. Ry. Co.*, 190 S.W. 371, 371–72 (Mo. Ct. App. 1916).

43. See, generally, Martha Chandlas and Linda K. Kerber, "Women, Mothers and the Law of Fright," *Michigan Law Review* 88 (1990): 814.

44. Post-1968 cases usually benefited mothers obtaining bystander recovery. Thomas F. Lambert, Jr., "Tort Liability for Psychic Injuries: Overview and Update," *American Trial Lawyers Journal* 37 (1978): 1; Thomas F. Lambert, Jr., "Tort Liability for Psychic Injuries," *Boston University Law Review* 41 (1961): 584, 592

(concluding from review of case law that "the feared flood tide of litigation has simply not appeared in states following the majority rule permitting recovery of psychic injuries without impact").

45. *Cusseaux v. Pickett*, 279 N.J. Super. 335, 652 A.2d 789 (1994).

46. Douglas D. Scherer, "Tort Remedies for Victims of Domestic Abuse," *South Carolina Law Review* 43 (1992): 543 (reporting empirical study find that tort actions for domestic abuse are underrepresented in cases decided in the state and federal courts).

47. See, e.g., *Rogers v. Loews L'Enfant Plaza Hotel*, 526 F. Supp. 523 (D.D.C. 1981); *Shaffer v. National Can Corporation*, 565 F. Supp. 909 (E.D. Pa. 1983).

48. Thomas F. Lambert, Jr., "Family Law," *American Trial Lawyers Journal* 37 (1978): 192 (1978).

49. In recent years, women employees have increasingly turned to punitive damages to redress job-related harassment. In *Laughinghouse v. Risser*, 786 F. Supp. 920 (D. Kan. 1992), a plaintiff received $10,000 for the tort of outrage for sexual advances, sexual harassment, and other abusive conduct at work. In *Valdez v. Church's Fried Chicken, Inc.*, 683 F. Supp. 596 (W.D. Tex. 1988), an employee received a $25,000 punitive award from her employer for sexual assault. See also *Pease v. Alford Photo Industries, Inc.*, 667 F. Supp. 1188 (W.D. Tenn. 1987) (assessing punitive damages based upon outrageous sexual harassment). A $50,000 punitive damage award was handed down against an employer arising out of supervisor's four-year campaign of sexual harassment in *Shrout v. Black Clawson Co.*, 689 F Supp. 774 (S.D. Ohio (1986).

50. Jane E. Larson, "Women Understand So Little, They Call My Good Nature 'Deceit': A Feminist Rethinking of Seduction," *Columbia Law Review* 93 (1993): 374 (advocating tort remedies for "sexual fraud").

51. Marianne Wesson, "Girls Should Bring Lawsuits Everywhere . . . Nothing Will Be Corrupted: Pornography as Speech and Product," *University of Chicago Law Review* 60 (1993): 845 (advocating civil remedy for harms causally connected to pornography); See also Catharine MacKinnon, *Feminism Unmodified* (Cambridge, Mass.: Harvard University Press, 1991), 175–95, 200–205 (urging damages for pornography).

52. For example, in *Marlene F. v. Affiliated Psych. Medical Clinic, Inc.*, 48 Cal. 3rd 583, 257 Cal. Rptr. 98, 770 P.2d 278, 285–88 (1989), a psychotherapist was found liable for negligent infliction of emotional distress to the mother of a child he molested. The court acknowledged that the relational aspect of mother–daughter bond that had been injured by the psychotherapist, observing: "The harm was foreseeable; the mother suffered distress (the extent of which is obviously a question for the jury); the injury suffered by the mother is closely, indeed immediately, connected with the therapist's conduct; moral blame plainly attaches to his conduct." Id. at 287.

53. One commentator would extend the reach of tort remedies to punish males who harass females in street encounters. See Bowman, "Street Harassment and the Informal Ghettoization of Women," 517.

54. *Laurie Marie M. v. Jeffrey T. M.*, 159 App. Div. 2d 52, 559 N.Y.S.2d 336, aff.d by77 N.Y.2d 981, 571 N.Y.S.2d 907, 575 N.E.2d 393 (2d Dept. 1990) (assessing $275,000 against defendant for sexually touching his eleven-year-old stepdaughter); *Parsons v. McRoberts*, 123 Ill. App. 3d 1006, 79 Ill. Dec. 495, 463 N.E.2d 1049 (4th Dist. 1984) (assessing a $12,000 punitive damages award against stepfather for forcing his stepdaughter to commit sexual acts with him). See, generally, Jocelyn B. Lamm, Note, "Easing Access to the Courts for Incest Victims: Toward an Equitable Application of the Delayed Discovery Rule," *Yale Law Journal* 100 (May 1991): 2189.

55. In *Deborah S. v. Diorio*, 153 Misc.2d 708, 583 N.Y.S.2d 872 (Civ. Ct. 1992), the victim of an acquaintance rape received $200,000 in punitive damages. The *Diorio* court found the defendant to have undergone a sudden "Dr. Jekyll–Mr. Hyde transformation" after being sexually rebuffed. This reckless behavior justified the large punitive damages award.

56. *Claus v. Lee*, 526 N.W.2d 519 (Iowa 1994).

57. *Weeks v. Baker and McKenzie*, 74 Cal. Rptr. 2d 510 (Ct. of App. Ca., First App. Dist., Div. 1, 1998).

58. Id. at 519.

59. Id.

60. Id. at 522.

61. Id.

62. Lucinda Finley, "Female Trouble: The Implications of Tort Reform for Women," *Tennessee Law Review* 64 (1997): 847, 855.

63. 26 Cal.3d 588, 607 P.2d 924 (1980) (exceptions to waiver of sovereign immunity including claims for "assault, battery, false imprisonment, false arrest, malicious prosecution, abuse of process, libel, slander, misrepresentation, deceit or interference with contract rights").

64. *Hymowitz v. Eli Lilly and Co.*, 539 N.E.2d 1069, 1072 (1989).

65. Market share has been rejected in many states. See, e.g., *Doe v. Cutter Biological*, 852 F. Supp. 909 (D. Idaho 1994) (declining to adopt market share and dismissing products liability action of hemophiliac who contracted HIV from one of two blood suppliers but was unable to determine which company supplied the tainted blood).

66. See, generally, Leslie Bender, "A Lawyer's Primer on Feminist Theory and Tort," *Journal of Legal Education* 38 (1988): 3.

67. Tort reformers label non-economic awards as "soft damages." However, in the case of miscarriage, a woman never simply loses a fetus, just as you never simply lose a limb. Our legal system has long compensated the plaintiff for pain and suffering that results from an injury.

68. David Vogel argues that the corporate community organized chiefly because "[d]uring the second half of the 1960's, the political defeats experienced by business were confined to individual industries. But from 1969 through 1972, virtually the entire American business community experienced a series of political setbacks without parallel in the postwar period. In the space of only four years, Congress enacted a significant tax-reform bill, four major environmental laws, an occupational safety and health act, and a series of additional consumer-protection statutes. The government also created a number of important new regulatory agencies, including the Environmental Protection Agency (EPA), the Occupational Safety and Health Administration (OSHA), and the Consumer Product Safety Commission (CPSC), investing them with broad powers over a wide range of business decisions." David Vogel, *Fluctuating Fortunes* (New York: Basic Books, 1989), 59.

69. Dan Clawson et al., *Money Talks: Corporate PACs and Political Influence* (Amherst: University of Massachusetts Press, 1992), 21–22 (emphasis in original). Clawson et al. argue that a coordinated business community has immense political power: business's vast resources, influence on the economy, and general legitimacy place it on a different footing from other so-called special interests. Business donors are often treated differently from other campaign contributors. When a member of Congress accepts a $1,000 donation from a corporate PAC, goes to a committee hearing, and proposes "minor" changes in a bill's wording, those changes are often accepted without discussion or examination. Id. at 21.

70. Nancy E. Roman, "Verdict in on Political Giving: Spending in State Elections Dominated by Trial Lawyers," *Washington Times* (September 13, 1994): A10.

71. Betsy Hartmann concludes that the key factors impeding contraceptive development are the sexism of the predominately male medical research community, a medical preference for surgical sterilization rather than contraception, and a greater concern for efficiency than safety. Betsy Hartmann, *Reproductive Rights and Wrongs: The Global Politics of Population Control and Contraceptive Choice* (Boston: South End Press, 1987).

72. American Medical Association Council on Ethical and Judicial Affairs, *Gender Disparities in Clinical Decision-Making* (Washington, D.C.: American Medical Association, 1990).

73. The empirical work of Theodore Eisenberg and James Henderson shows a "quiet revolution" that has sharply reduced the success rates of plaintiffs in products liability litigation. They report that plaintiffs' "[s]uccess rates in published opinions fell from 56% in 1979 to 39% in 1989." Theodore Eisenberg and James A. Henderson, Jr., "Inside the Quiet Revolution in Products Liability," *UCLA Law Review* 39 (1992): 731, 793. Such a decline in the fortunes of plaintiffs led Professors Eisenberg and Henderson to "posit that a pro-defendant revolution began in the early to mid-1980s and continued through at least 1989. We base this assertion on declining plaintiffs' successes in product litigation, on pro-defendant

trends in explicit lawmaking in product cases at both trial and appellate levels, and on steadily declining product filings in federal courts." Id. at 741. See also James Henderson, Jr., and Theodore Eisenberg, "The Quiet Revolution in Products Liability," *UCLA Law Review* 37 (1990): 490; and Thomas Koenig and Michael Rustad, "The Quiet Revolution Revisited: An Empirical Study of the Impact of State Tort Reform of Punitive Damages in Products Liability," *Justice System Journal* 16 (1993): 21.

74. The majority of states permit the insurability of punitive damages. As a result, insurance companies have an economic interest in restricting punitive damages. Insurance companies are also primary defendants in punitive damages litigation based upon bad faith actions.

75. Richard Perez-Pena, "U.S. Juries Grow Tougher on Plaintiffs in Lawsuits," *New York Times* (June 17, 1994): 18 (reporting that "in 1992, plaintiffs won 52 percent of the personal injury cases decided by jury verdicts, down from 63 percent in 1989"). Brian Shenker, editorial director of Jury Verdict Research, believes that this phenomenon is the result of "a campaign by the insurance industry, by people like Dan Quayle, saying these big awards are killing our society." Id. See also Neil Vidmar, "Empirical Evidence on the Deep Pockets Hypothesis: Jury Awards for Pain and Suffering in Medical Malpractice Cases," *Duke Law Journal* 43 (1993): 217, 218 (reviewing debate over the law of medical malpractice); Michael Rustad and Thomas Koenig, "The Historical Continuity of Punitive Damages Awards: Reforming the Tort Reformers," *American University Law Review* 42 (1993): 1269, 1277–82 (reviewing debate over the law of products liability).

76. In our study of punitive damages in medical malpractice, we found that the typical medical malpractice case in our sample involved expensive expert testimony. See Michael Rustad and Thomas Koenig, "Reconceptualizing Punitive Damages in Medical Malpractice: Targeting Amoral Corporations, Not 'Moral Monsters,'" *Rutgers Law Review* 47 (1995): 975.

77. Thomas F. Lambert, Jr., "The Case for Punitive Damages (Including Their Coverage by Liability Insurance)," *American Trial Lawyers Journal* 35 (1965): 164, 170.

78. See, generally, Carin Ann Clauss, "Comparable Worth: The Theory, Its Legal Foundation, and the Feasibility of Implementation," *Michigan Journal of Law Reform* 20 (1986): 7; Carol O'Donnell, "Major Theories of the Labor Market and Women's Place Within It," *Journal of Industrial Relations* 26 (1984): 147.

79. Eleanor E. Macoby and Carol N. Jacklin, *The Psychology of Sex Differences* (Stanford, Calif.: Stanford University Press, 1974). In another example, Elaine Draper notes that "[w]omen have usually not been barred from all jobs that entail toxic risks, but only from the relatively high-paying production jobs traditionally held by men." Elaine Draper, "Fetal Exclusion Policies and Gendered Constructions of Suitable Work," *Social Problems* 40 (1993): 90, 94. The sexual division of labor exists not only between job categories, but also within a field. A

"glass ceiling" blocks many women from reaching the highest rungs in a job category. Ann M. Morrison, "Up against a Working Women Glass Ceiling," *Los Angeles Times* (August 23, 1987): 3. Women are the majority of schoolteachers but a small minority of school principals. Law schools that traditionally excluded females and other low-status individuals tend to be at the top of the contemporary prestige hierarchy, and those which were women's law schools tend to track their students into the lower rungs of the profession. Michael Rustad and Thomas Koenig, "The Impact of History on Contemporary Prestige Images of Boston's Law Schools," *Suffolk University Law Review* 24 (1990): 621.

80. Michelle Conlin, "The CEO Still Wears Wingtips," *Business Week* (November 22, 1999): 86.

81. Testimony of Robert Creamer, representing Citizen Action and Illinois Public Action Before House Subcommittee on Commerce, Consumer Protection and Competitiveness of the Committee on Energy and Commerce, U.S. House of Representatives on H.R. 1910, the "Fairness in Products Liability Act," 103d Congress, 2d Session, April 21, 1994.

82. 537 P. 2d 754 (Colo. App. 1975).

83. "Breast Implant Cases May Be Easier Than You Think," *Lawyers Alert* (September 1992).

84. Id.

85. The statistics in this section are drawn from our national study of punitive damages in products liability awards from 1965 to 1990; see Michael Rustad, "In Defense of Punitive Damages in Products Liability: Testing Tort Anecdotes with Empirical Data," *Iowa Law Review* 78 (1992): 1. The U.S. Supreme Court referred to this empirical research as the most "comprehensive study" of punitive damages in products liability. *Honda Motor Co. v. Oberg*, 114 S.Ct. 751 (1994).

86. *Hodder v. Goodyear Tire and Rubber Co.*, 426 N.W.2d 826 (Minn. 1988).

87. *Rush v. Minister Machine Co.*, No. 81-CV-191 (Ohio C.P., Mahoning County, 1984).

88. Interview with David Fitzgerald, Plaintiff's Attorney in *Braatz v. Rockwell Standard Corp.*, No. 23033 (Minn. Dist. Ct., Wright County 1982). See, e.g., *Gruntmeir v. Mayrath Indus.*, 841 F.2d 1037 (10th Cir. 1988) and *Juarez v. United Farm Tools, Inc.*, 798 F.2d 1341 (10th Cir. 1986) (overturning punitive damages award).

89. Susan P. Baker et al., *The Injury Fact Book* (Lexington, Mass.: Lexington Books, 1992): 150.

90. Id. at 20.

91. Id. at 176.

92. Id.

93. *Mulhern v. Outboard Marine Corp.*, 432 N.W.2d 130 (Wis. 1988).

94. *Brogdan v. MTD Products, Inc.*, No. 82-21989 (Fla. Cir. Ct. Dade County 1984).

95. Baker et al., *The Injury Fact Book*, 217.

96. 424 N.E.2d 568 (Ohio 1981).

97. *Silkwood v. Kerr-McGee Corp.*, 769 F.2d 1451 (10th Cir. 1985) (reversing award).

98. Id.

99. Stephen M. Rossoff et al., *Profit without Honor: White Collar Crime and the Looting of America* (Upper Saddle River, N.J.: Prentice-Hall, 1998), 352–53.

100. See, generally, Mary F. Hawkins, *Unshielded: The Human Cost of the Dalkon Shield* (Toronto: University of Toronto Press, 1997).

101. *Palmer v. A. H. Robins Co.*, 684 P.2d 187, 207 (Colo. 1984).

102. Ronald J. Bacigal, *The Limits of Litigation: The Dalkon Shield Controversy* (Durham, N.C.: Carolina Academic Press, 1990); Morton Mintz, "The Selling of an IUD," *Washington Post* (August 9, 1988): 12 (reviewing history of marketing of Dalkon Shield); see, generally, Karen M. Hicks, *Surviving the Dalkon Shield IUD: Women v. the Pharmaceutical Industry* (New York: Teachers College Press, 1994); Morton Mintz, *At Any Cost: Corporate Greed, Women and the Dalkon Shield* (New York: Free Press, 1985); *Marshall Clinard, Corporate Corruption: The Abuse of Power* (New York: Free Press, 1990); John M. Van Dyke, "The Dalkon Shield: A 'Primer' in IUD Liability," *Western State University Law Review* 6 (1978): 1; Susan Perry and Jim Dawson, *Nightmare: Women and the Dalkon Shield* (New York: Macmillan, 1985).

103. *Palmer v. A. H. Robins Co.*, 684 P.2d 187, 196 (Colo. 1984).

104. Telephone interview with Douglas Bragg, Bragg and Dubofsky, P.C., Plaintiff's Counsel in *Palmer v. A. H. Robins Co.*, 684 P.2d 187 (Colo. 1984).

105. *Tetuan v. A. H. Robins Co.*, 241 Kan. 441, 446, 738 P.2d 1210 (1985).

106. Id.

107. *Palmer v. A. H. Robins*, 684 P.2d 187 (Colo. 1984).

108. Note, "Lord's Justice: One Judge's Battle to Expose the Deadly Dalkon Shield I.U.D," *Harvard Law Review* 99 (1986): 875 (quoting U.S. Federal District Court Judge Myles Lord).

109. Peter L. Riley, "The Copper-7 Intrauterine Device: Survey of a Decade of Litigation," *Journal of Health and Hospital Law* 22 (August 1989): 240.

110. See advertisement, *Playgirl* (July 1978): 128.

111. *Kociemba v. A. D. Searle, Inc.*, 707 F. Supp. 1517, 1536 (D. Minn. 1989).

112. *In re G. D. Searle and Co.*, "'Copper 7' IUD Products Liability Litigation," 483 F. Supp. 1343 (J.P.M.L. 1980).

113. 707 F. Supp. 1517 (D. Minn. 1989).

114. Riley, "The Copper-7 Intrauterine Device," 240.

115. Id.

116. Id.

117. Testimony of Bruce Finzen, Partner, Robins, Kaplan, Miller and Ciresi, Minneapolis Minnesota, before Committee on Energy and Commerce, Subcom-

mittee on Commerce, Consumer Protection and Competitiveness, U.S. House of Representatives, Hearings on Fairness in Products Liability Act of 1993, February 2, 1994, reported by Federal News Service, NEXIS (reporting that his company settled 135 Copper-7 cases after winning punitive damages award).

118. Toxic Shock Syndrome, Kidshealth.org (visited on April 2, 1999). <http://www.Kidshealth.org/parent/common/toxic_shock.htm>.

119. See, e.g., *O'Gilvie v. International Playtex, Inc.*, 821 F.2d 1438 (10th Cir. 1987); *Friley v. International Playtex, Inc.*, 604 F. Supp. 126 (W.D. Mo. 1984); and *Wooten v. International Playtex, Inc.*, No. 81-926-3 (D. S.C., June 15, 1982) (awarding punitive damages for injuries caused by the use of Rely, a high-absorbency tampon linked to toxic shock syndrome).

120. 174 Cal. App. 3d 831 (6th Cir. 1986).

121. Id. at 848.

122. Id.

123. Id. at 868.

124. Jack W. Snyder, "Can Emerging Medical Legal and Scientific Concepts Be Reconciled?" *Journal of Legal Medicine* 18 (June 1997): 2.

125. Id.

126. Id.

127. "Implant Makers to Fund Settlement," *New Jersey Law Journal* (February 21, 1994): 8.

128. Plaintiffs' Steering Committee, Source Book for MDL 926: *In Re Silicone Gel Breast Implants Product Liability Litigation*, Northern District of Alabama (May 1993) (citing plaintiffs' claims for "all persons who have had silicone breast implants surgically implanted in their bodies; causes of action listed as negligence, strict liability, failure to warn, negligent misrepresentations, fraudulent misrepresentation, breach of implied warranty, breach of express warranty, intentional infliction of emotional distress, negligent infliction of emotional distress, fear of future product failure, equitable relief including medical monitoring and punitive damages").

129. The global settlement is described *In re Silicone Gel Breast Implant Product Liability Litigation*, 1994 U.S. Dist. Lexis 12521 WL 578353 (N.D. Ala., September 1, 1994). See, generally, Financial Report, "Foreign Women Plan Appeal of U.S. Implant Settlement," *Reuters* (September 16, 1994) (reporting that foreign claimants are appealing compensation schedule which allocated them only 40 and 90 percent of the amount given to U.S. victims).

130. Joanne Wojcik, "Implant Claimants Seek to Pierce Corporate Veil," *Business Insurance* (November 20, 2000): 2.

131. In Denver, for example, the jury decided in favor of Dow Corning Corp. in a products liability action brought by a former exotic dancer who claimed that leaking silicone-gel implants caused her to suffer permanent disability. "Colorado Jury Decides for Dow in Breast Implant Case," *Liability Week* 24 (June 14, 1993): 1.

132. Michael L. Rustad, "Punitive Damages in Breast Implant Products Litigation," *Journal of Massachusetts Academy of Trial Lawyers* 1 (1994): 30.

133. *Hopkins v. Dow Corning Corp.*, 33 F.3d 1116 (9th Cir. 1994).

134. Id.

135. Brief for Plaintiff-Appellee at 5, *Hopkins v. Dow Corning Corp.*, No. 92-16132 (9th Cir. February 1, 1993), aff. 33 F.3d 1116 (9th Cir. 1994).

136. Id. at 6.

137. Id.

138. Id. at 33 F.3d 1116; 1994 U.S. App. LEXIS 23097, *34.

139. Thomas Koenig and Michael Rustad, "His and Her Tort Reform: Gender Injustice in Disguise," 77 (1995): 1, 46–55.

140. An FDA defense was included in a 1993 products liability reform bill. "A Bill to Establish Uniform Products Liability Standards," H.R. 1910, 103d Congress, 2d Session (1993). The FDA defense contained in its companion bill, S. 687, would bar punitive damages in any case where a drug or medical device has received pre-market approval from the FDA, unless the injured party can prove that the manufacturer withheld from or misrepresented to the agency required information that was "material" and "relevant." See *A Bill to Regulate Interstate Commerce by Providing for a Uniform Product Liability Law and for Other Purposes*, S. 687, 103rd Congress, Second Session (1993): 203.

141. "Lack of Life Saving Medical Devices," Hearings Before the Subcommittee on Regulation and Governmental Information of the Senate Committee on Governmental Affairs, 103d Congress, 2d Session (May 20, 1994) (statement of James S. Benson, Senior Vice President Health Industry Manufacturers Association); Bruce N. Kuhlik and Richard F. Kingham, "The Adverse Effects of Standardless Punitive Damage Awards on Pharmaceutical Development and Availability," *Food, Drug and Cosmetics Law Journal* 45 (1990): 693, 695.

142. See, e.g., W. Kip Viscusi et al., "Deterring Inefficient Pharmaceutical Litigation: An Economic Rationale for the FDA Regulatory Compliance Defense," *Seton Hall Law Review* 24 (1994): 1437, 1457.

143. Ariz. Rev. Stat. Ann. §12-701 (1992) (precluding punitive damages for approved drug, unless manufacturer or seller knowingly withholds or misrepresents information to the FDA). New Jersey provides that compliance with FDA-approved warnings is presumptively adequate. Punitive damages are not available if pharmaceutical products are approved by the FDA. N.J. Stat. Ann. §2A: 58C-5 (West 1987); Ohio Rev. Code Ann. §2307.80(C) (Baldwin 1987). Under Oregon's statute, punitive damages may not be assessed against pharmaceutical manufacturers if the drug was manufactured or labeled in conformity with FDA regulations, or generally is recognized as safe and effective pursuant to FDA regulations. Or. Rev. Stat. §30.927 (1993).

144. Philip J. Hilts, "F.D.A. to Toughen Testing Devices," *New York Times*

(March 5, 1993): A18 (quoting Dr. Bruce Burlington, the FDA's Chief of the Center for Medical Devices).

145. U.S. General Accounting Office, *FDA Drug Review: Post-Approval Risks, 1976–1985* (Washington, D.C.: U.S. General Accounting Office, GAO/PEMBD-90-15, April 1990).

146. "Lack of Life Saving Medical Devices," Hearings Before the Subcommittee on Regulation and Governmental Information of the Senate Committee on Governmental Affairs, 103d Congress, 2d Session (May 20, 1994) (testimony of Kristen Rand, counsel on behalf of Consumer's Union).

147. For example, a company may have actual knowledge of the dangerous characteristics of a product and still have FDA approval. Actual knowledge of the dangerous propensities of a medical product is presently a basis for punitive damages. *Wooderson v. Ortho Pharmaceutical Corp.*, 235 Kan. 387, 681 P.2d 1038, *cert. denied* 469 U.S. 965 (1984). Even if fraud cannot be shown, knowingly placing thousands of patients at risk is sufficient basis for punitive damages. In *Kociemba v. G. D. Searle and Co.*, 707 F. Supp. 1517 (D. Minn. 1989), the manufacturer's knowledge that women who had never given birth who used the CU-7 IUD were at high risk for pelvic inflammatory disease resulted in a punitive damages award.

148. Lori Turkel, "FDA Set to Ok Female Condom; But Package to Carry Warning," *Newsday* (April 28, 1993): 6.

149. Companies might argue that the FDA's inaction in the face of a developing profile of danger is "approval by silence."

150. 681 P.2d 1038 (Kan.), *cert. denied*, 469 U.S. 965 (1984).

151. See Rustad and Koenig, "Reconceptualizing Punitive Damages in Medical Malpractice," 975.

152. 527 S.W.2d 133 (Tenn. Ct. App. 1975).

153. Id. at 136.

154. Id. at 139.

155. No. 86-8910 (Fla. Cir. Ct., Duval County 1987).

156. 1992 WL 52109 (Cal. Super. Ct., L.A. County 1992).

157. Computer-aided searches were conducted of the 19,000 cases published in *Medical Malpractice Verdicts, Settlements and Experts*. Finally, we interviewed more than half of the lawyers who tried medical malpractice cases where punitive damages were awarded. We conducted telephone interviews and distributed a questionnaire to a large sample of lawyers specializing in medical malpractice litigation.

158. See, generally, Eileen Nechas and Denise Foley, *Unequal Treatment: What You Don't Know about How Women Are Mistreated by the Medical Community* (Emmaus, Pa.: Rodale Press, 1994).

159. For a discussion of the methodology and findings of this study, see Rustad and Koenig, "Reconceptualizing Punitive Damages in Medical Malpractice."

160. See, e.g., David Leebron, "Final Moments: Damages for Pain and Suffering Prior to Death," *New York University Law Review* 64 (1990): 256.

161. This data was drawn from our study of punitive damages in medical malpractice. See, generally, Rustad and Koenig, "Reconceptualizing Punitive Damages in Medical Malpractice.

162. Lanni, "Recovery for Loss of Consortium in a Wrongful Death Action," *Brooklyn Law Review* 49 (1983): 605, 605 (citing definition of consortium in New York's wrongful death statute).

163. See, generally, Stephen Nohlgren, "Rights Law under Attack," *St. Petersburg Times* (November 22, 1992): 1B.

164. Questionnaire of Seth H. Langson, Charlotte, N.C., Plaintiff's Counsel in *MacClements v. Lafone*, No. 88-CVS-4095 (N.C. Super. Ct., Mecklenberg County February 1990), reported in Jury Verd. Rptr. No. 60442, 1990 WL 4599723 (LRP Jury).

165. Id.

NOTES TO CHAPTER 4

1. Recently, there has been a backlash against HMOs for their policy of discharging patients as early as possible. California, for example, investigates complaints about early discharge from hospitals.

2. See, generally, Customer Complaints, "Where to File a Complaint: Medicare HMOs," (visited August 12, 1999) <http://www.healthscore.org>.

3. Id.

4. Julie Appleby, "Managed Care/HMO," *USA Today* (December 8, 2000): C1.

5. Robert J. Enders, "Antitrust: Payor-Provider Contracting," *Whittier Law Review* 13 (1992): 483, 483.

6. Steve A. Freedman, "Mega-Corporate Health Care: A Choice for the Future," *New England Journal of Medicine* 312 (1985): 579, 580.

7. Stuart Schear, "Overview: Managed Care" (visited August 9, 1999) <http://www.wnet.org/archive/mchc/overview/essay.html>.

8. Stuart Schear, "Your Money and Your Life," Facts About Managed Care (visited August 9, 1999) <http://www.wnet.org/archive/mhc/overview/Sidebar4.html>. CHAMPUS (Civilian Health and Medical Program of the Uniformed Services) and Medicare HMOs are also major players in managed health care. Medicare HMOs "include services for Medicare beneficiaries. These plans exchange the standard Medicare benefits for a plan of coverage in return for which the HMO receives a fixed payment from Medicare." PPOS typically involve networks of physicians and hospitals in which "health care providers agree to reduced health care prices in return for access to a stream of patients provided by an insurer. Often, the PPO also includes various utilization controls."

9. Kaiser Permanente formed the first American HMO in the 1930s. Mayor

Fiorello Laguardia established another early HMO in 1947 for New York City employees. HMOs became institutionalized in the American health care industry in the 1970s. Humana owned more than ninety hospitals throughout the United States by the mid-1980s. The Health Care Financing Agency (HCFA) stimulated the growth of HMOs by providing incentives to enroll medicare beneficiaries. Managed care plans have generally lowered costs and improved medical practice.

10. William A. Chittenden III, "Malpractice Liability and Managed Health Care: History and Prognosis," *Tort and Insurance Law Journal* 26 (1991): 451, 452 n. 2.

11. Damaris Christensen, "Hospital Mergers Seem to Have Little Effect on Outcomes," *Medicine Tribune* (June 18, 1998).

12. See, e.g., Hospital Staffing Services, Inc., *1990 Annual Report to Stockholders* (1991), available in LEXIS, Penben Library, ARS File (reporting that clients include 150 hospitals located in more than 30 states).

13. Schear, "Managed Care Facts" (reporting that 69 percent of HMOs are for-profit).

14. The HMO Page, "Premium Pay: Corporate Compensation in America's HMOs," *Family USA* (April 1998).

15. Id.

16. Id.

17. "HMOs Paying Huge Executive Salaries, But Say Patient Rights Too Costly," *Washingon Report* 38 (May 1, 1998): 1 (visited December 9, 1998) <http://www.uaw.org/publications/wash_report/3808/wr380803.html>.

18. "Consumer Complaints: State Officials See Big Increase," *Health Line* (October 13, 1998).

19. Vivien Lou Chen, "Kaiser Accused of Forcing Members to Split Pills to Cut HMO Costs," *San Diego Union-Tribune* (December 7, 2000) (visited December 10, 2000) <http://PQASB.PQArchiver.com/SanDiego/index.html>.

20. The HMO Page, "Premium Pay: Corporate Compensation in America's HMOs."

21. Id.

22. "Survey: HMO Patients Dislike Lack of Doctor Choice," *Bestwire* (October 14, 1999) (reporting that lack of choice of physicians was the single most important variable explaining HMO dissatisfaction).

23. Courtenay Edelhart and Doug Sword, "Poll Shows Public Wants More Oversight of HMOs: Quality of Care a Major Concern," *Indianapolis News* (October 19, 1998): B-01.

24. CIGNA, "Your HMO Benefits: Make Them 'As Good As They Can Be'" (visited December 8, 1998) <http://www.cigna.com/newsroom/background>.

25. "Referral Denied . . . And It Cost This HMO 1 Million: Health Maintenance," *Medical Economics* 75(October 26, 1998): 53.

26. "More Than One in Five Employees Are Dissatisfied with Their Health-

Care Plans," *Comp. and Benefits for Law Offices* (September 1999). HMOs are structured upon three basic models:(1) The staff model HMO; (2) the Independent Practice Association (IPA) model HMO; and (3) the group model HMO. The staff model HMO directly employs salaried physicians and other providers and often owns or leases its own health care facilities. The traditional IPA model HMO consists of an association that contracts with the HMO to provide medical services to HMO members and, in turn, contracts with private practice physicians who agree to provide health care to HMO members while continuing to treat their non-HMO patients. The group model HMO provides *prepaid* health care for members through contracts with individual medical provider groups, or entities having provider employees. As the industry has developed, the distinction between IPA model HMOs and group model HMOs has faded. Chittenden, "Malpractice Liability and Managed Health Care," 452 n. 2.

27. Gloria Lau, "CMA's Dr. Jack Lewin on United's Return of Control to Doctors," *Investors Business Daily* (November 17, 1999): 1.

28. Leon Jaroff, "What Will Happen to Alternative Medicine?" *Time* (November 8, 1999): 77 (defining medical quackery and unconventional therapies).

29. National Council Against Health Fraud, "Bunko Squad: Quack, Quack?" (visited August 10, 1999) <http://www.___.com/al/altern/bunko/bunko.html>.

30. John Parascandola, "Patent Medicines and the Public's Health," *Public Health Reports* 114 (July 1, 1999): 318.

31. Barry Werth, *Damages* (New York: Simon and Schuster, 1998): 72.

32. Id.

33. Chester R. Burns, "Malpractice Suits in American Medicine before the Civil War," *Bulletin of the History of Medicine* 43 (January–February 1969): 41; reprinted in Kermit L. Hall, ed., *Tort Law in American History: Major Historical Interpretations* (New York: Garland Publishing Co., 1987)

34. Eugene F. Sanger, *Report of the Committee on Suits for Malpractice* (Maine Medical Association, 1879), 1.

35. Id. at 3.

36. Chester R. Burns, "Malpractice Suits in American Medicine," id. at 97.

37. Id.

38. *Smith v. Corrigan*, 126 A. 680, 681 (New Jersey 1924) (characterizing "malice or wrongful motive" as the standard for punitive damages in medical malpractice).

39. *Huffman v. Lindquist*, 234 P.2d 34, 46 (Cal. 1951) (observing that "physicians . . . flock to the defense of their fellow members charged with malpractice and the plaintiff is relegated, for his expert testimony, to the occasional lone wolf or heroic soul, who for the sake of truth and justice has the courage to run the risk of ostracism by his fellow practitioners and the cancellation of his public liability insurance policy").

40. The case of *Braunberger v. Cleis*, 13 American Law Register 587, 594

(Penn. Dist. Ct., 1865), was quite typical of the period. The court denied punitive damages in a wrongful death action against a grossly incompetent surgeon because he was only found to be ignorant, not malicious.

41. See, e.g., *Van Meer v. Crews*, 148 S.W. 40,42 (Ky., 1912) (noting that unskillful surgery did not warrant punitive damages in the absence of a showing of malice).

42. *Brooke v. Clark*, 57 Tex. 105, 113–14 (1882).

43. Id.

44. ERISA supplants all state laws that "relate to" employee benefit plans. State law medical malpractice claims are completely preempted by Section 502(a) of ERISA.

45. Texas enacted the Texas Health Care Liability Act (S. 386), which permits managed care enrollees to sue an HMO for medical malpractice where the HMO fails to employ a reasonable standard of care in denying or delaying medical care.

46. Harry Austin, "Practicing without a License," *Chattanooga Times* (October 14, 1998): A8 (noting that the federal legislation would have given patients the right to sue HMOs for damages for denied care and would have required HMOs to establish and abide by fair appeals procedures and independent arbitration).

47. Id.

48. Id.

49. Patient Protection Act of 1998, 144 *Congressional Record* House Report 6297, H. 6381 (June 26, 1998) (statement of Rep. Patsy Mink, D–Hawaii).

50. The HMO Page, "Corporate Compensation."

51. Under joint and several liability, multiple defendants are responsible for the entire judgment if a co-defendant is insolvent.

52. The periodic payment reform permits defendants to satisfy a judgment for future damages under an installment payment plan. By permitting installment payments, the future judgment payment is spread over an extended period, reducing costs to insurance companies.

53. Melanie Eversley, "Patients' Bill of Rights Looks Poised for Passage," *Atlanta Journal and Constitution* (November 18, 2000): 6A.

54. David Sanger, "Patients' Rights Bill Faulted," *International Health Tribune* (March 22, 2001): 3.

55. See, e.g., *Boyd v. Albert Einstein Medical Center*, 547 A.2d. 1229, 1234–35 (Pa. Sup. Ct. 1988). The doctrine of ostensible agency makes the HMO liable for representing that it is the employer of the physician in its advertising and other literature.

56. Susan R. Huntington, "Can Insurance Protect Plans against Punitive Damages?" *Managed Care* (March 1999).

57. Id.

58. Thomas F. Lambert, Jr., "Comments on Recent Important Cases," *American Trial Lawyers Journal* 31 (1965): 29, 133.

59. W. Page Keeton et al., *Prosser and Keeton on the Law of Torts* (St. Paul, Minn.: West Publishing Co., 1985), 185.

60. M.G.L.A. ch. 231, §60B (2000).

61. M.G.L.A. ch. 231, §60I (2000).

62. Massachusetts has adopted a modified comparative negligence regime, which bars a medical malpractice lawsuit if the plaintiff's negligence exceeds the total negligence of providers. M.G.L.A. ch. 231, §60H (2000). The state enacted the collateral source rule, which has the effect of requiring the trial judge to deduct insurance or premium payments from other sources from the verdict. Massachusetts imposes a statutory cap on attorney's fees that applies specifically to medical malpractice claims. M.G.L.A. ch. 231, §85 (2000). The statutory cap is 20 percent of the recovery unless the attorney's fee is 20 percent or less of the claimant's recovery. The statutory schedule also places limits on attorney's fees for larger awards. As in all other jurisdictions, plaintiffs may not bring medical malpractice claims without expert testimony showing that the defendant failed to provide the accepted standard of care.

63. See, generally, Michael Rustad and Thomas Koenig, "Reconceptualizing Punitive Damages in Medical Malpractice: Targeting Amoral Corporations, Not 'Moral Monsters,'" *Rutgers Law Review* 47 (1995): 975; Thomas Koenig and Michael Rustad, "The Quiet Revolution Revisited: An Empirical Examination of State Tort Reforms of Punitive Damages," *Justice System Journal* 16 (1993): 23.

64. Michael L. Rustad, "Unraveling Punitive Damages: Current Data and Further Inquiry," *Wisconsin Law Review* (1998): 15, 34.

65. Harvey F. Wachsman with Steven Alschuler, *Lethal Medicine: The Epidemic of Medical Malpractice in America* (New York: Henry Holt, 1994), 119.

66. "Ex-Husband, Associate Ordered to Pay $6 Million for Abusive Sex Surgery," *Los Angeles Times* (October 24, 1987): 32.

67. Id.

68. Questionnaire of James McKiernan, Plaintiff's Counsel in *Crandall-Millar v. Sierra Vista Hospital, No.* 59975 (Cal. Cty. Ct. San Obisbo, October 23, 1987).

69. Id.

70. Sidney Wolfe, *13,012 Questionable Doctors: Disciplined by States or the Federal Government*, Public Citizen Health Research Group Report (Washington, D.C.: Public Citizen, March 1996), 90.

71. *Marston v. Minneapolis Clinic of Psychiatry and Neurology, Ltd.*, 329 N.W.2d 306 (Minn. 1982).

72. Id.

73. Abstracts, *New York Times* (November 28, 1973): 24.

74. Id.

75. Id.

76. *Hendrick v. Nork*, No. 200777, (Super. Ct., Sacramento Cty., Calif. November 10, 1972).

77. *Hoffman v. O'Brien*, No. 87-15624 (Harris Cty. Dist. Ct. Tex., July 17, 1989).

78. Dan B. Dobbs, *The Law of Torts* (St. Paul, Minn.: West Publishing Co., 2000), 667.

79. See, generally, Charles C. Sharpe, *Nursing Malpractice Liability and Risk Management* (Westport, Conn.: Auburn House, 1999).

80. Anne M. Stoline and Jonathan P. Weiner, *The New Medical Marketplace: A Physician's Guide to the Health Care System in the 1990s* (Baltimore: Johns Hopkins University Press, 1993), 127, 223–24.

81. 211 N.E.2d 2d 326 (Ill. 1965).

82. Today hospitals have instituted credentials checks to ensure that affiliated doctors have graduated medical school, have completed necessary specialty training, are in good standing with licensing boards and certification authorities, and have no pending legal actions against them.

83. See *Gonzales v. Nork*, No. 228566 (Cal. Super. Ct. Sacramento Cty. 1974); *Hendrick v. Nork*, No. 200777 (Cal. Super. Ct. Sacramento Cty. 1974) (imposing punitive damages for fraudulent and unnecessary back surgeries).

84. Id.

85. "Vital Statistics," *Washington Post* (August 3, 1999) (citing data from HCFA).

86. William L. Prosser, *Handbook of the Law of Torts*, 5th ed. (St. Paul, Minn.: West Publishing Co., 1971), 187.

87. Medical malpractice is "faulty medical management that injures a patient." Randall Bovbjerg and Clark Havighurst, "Medical Malpractice: An Update for Noncombatants," *Business and Health* (September 1986): 38. Joseph King describes medical malpractice litigation as "embrac[ing] all liability-producing conduct arising from the rendition of professional medical services. Negligent medical care does not exhaust all potential sources of professional liability. Liability may also result, for example, from intentional misconduct, breaches of contracts guaranteeing a specific therapeutic result, defamation, divulgence of confidential information, unauthorized postmortem procedures and failures to prevent injuries to certain non-patients." Joseph H. King, Jr., *The Law of Medical Malpractice*, 2d ed. (St. Paul, Minn.: West Publishing Company, 1986), 3; see also W. John Thomas, "The Medical Malpractice 'Crisis': A Critical Examination of a Public Debate," *Temple Law Review* 65 (1992): 459, 460 (noting that "[m]edical malpractice is perhaps the most controversial tort in the American legal system").

88. President William Jefferson Clinton, Address to Congress, "The National Health Security Act" (1993). The National Health Security Act was not enacted by either the House of Representatives or the Senate. The House bill was entitled H.R. 3600, 103d Congress, 1st Session (1993); the Senate bill was S. 1757 103d Congress, 1st Session. See, generally, "The Impact of Managed Care on Doctors Who Serve Poor and Minority Patients," *Harvard Law Review* 108 (1995): 1625,

1625 (noting the "recent failure of the National Health Security Act [and] the current reform effort . . . to state governments and the free market").

89. Health care providers expressed dissatisfaction with the Democratic health care plan because it did not address the concerns doctors had "about malpractice suits, such as the plaintiff's ability to collect unlimited punitive damages." "Trends: Enterprise Liability: Quack Medicine for the Malpractice Mess?" *Health Business* 8 (June 11, 1993): 1. The American Medical Association has been active in the movement to restrict punitive damages in medical malpractice. See "Brief of the Pharmaceutical Mfrs. Ass'n. and the Am. Medical Ass'n. as Amici Curiae in Support of Petitioner," *Pacific Mut. Life Ins. Co. v. Haslip*, 499 U.S. 1 (1991) (No. 89-1279); Martin J. Hatlie, "Professional Liability: The Case for Federal Reform," *Journal of the American Medical Association* 263 (January 26, 1990): 584 (advocating ceiling on non-economic damages and punitive damages in medical negligence cases). The American Bar Association unanimously opposed the American Medical Association's proposal to cap or eliminate non-economic and punitive damages in medical liability cases. Eric Effron and Fred Strasser, "Political Stakes Raised at ABA Meeting," *National Law Journal* (February 24, 1986): 3.

90. Arnold Relman, "The New Medical-Industrial Complex," *New England Journal of Medicine* 303 (1980): 963, 963; Arnold Relman, "Practicing Medicine in the New Business Climate," *New England Journal of Medicine* 316 (1987): 1150 (coining term "medical-industrial complex" to refer to for-profit corporations's rise to power in the medical field).

91. Katharine Q. Seelye, "Lawmakers Feel the Heat from Health Care Lobby," *New York Times* (August 16, 1994): 1.

92. A study of New York State hospital and legal records concluded "we do not now have a problem of too many [medical malpractice] claims. If anything, there are too few." Harvard Medical Practice Study, *Patients, Doctors and Lawyers: Medical Injury, Malpractice Litigation and Patient Compensation in New York* (Cambridge, Mass.: Harvard University Medical School, 1990), 11–4. Few victims of hospital negligence ever file a lawsuit. The Harvard Medical Practice Study concluded that an estimated 23,736 to 31,104 patients suffered injuries at the hands of negligent doctors; 7,000 died as the result of provider negligence. Id. See also A. Russell Localio et al., "Relation between Malpractice Claims and Adverse Events Due to Negligence," *New England Journal of Medicine* 325 (1991): 245–51 (discussing relationship between medical negligence and filed malpractice lawsuits). See also Paul C. Weiler et al., *A Measure of Malpractice: Medical Injury, Malpractice Litigation, and Patient Compensation* (Cambridge, Mass.: Harvard University Press, 1993).

A recent medical negligence study by the Duke University Law School Medical Malpractice Project concentrated on the role of the jury in medical negligence cases. Neil Vidmar, "The Unfair Criticism of Medical Malpractice Juries," *Judica-*

ture 76 (October–November 1992): 118. The Duke researchers analyzed more than one thousand medical malpractice cases filed in North Carolina courts during a three-year period, essentially every malpractice case filed in the state. Plaintiffs won compensation through settlements in 50 percent of the cases and prevailed at trial in another 2 percent. Only 117 cases went to trial.

93. See, generally, Paul C. Weiler, *Medical Malpractice: A Measure of Malpractice* (Cambridge, Mass.: Harvard University Press, 1998) (citing empirical research from the Harvard Medical Practice Study).

94. All punitive damage verdicts awarded through arbitration and jury or judge verdicts were included in this study. Defendants included hospitals, psychiatric hospitals, psychological clinics, nursing homes, medical laboratories, and other institutions rendering medical care. Individual punitive damages defendants were a diverse group, encompassing physicians, psychiatrists, psychotherapists, psychologists, counselors, osteopaths, podiatrists, chiropractors, unorthodox medical practitioners, pharmacists, dentists, nurses, medical auxiliaries, and Christian Science healers.

95. Professor David Baldus of the University of Iowa Law School provided us with his database of 116 medical malpractice actions in which punitive damages were sought. These were the primary data used in David Baldus et al., *Final Report: Improving Judicial Oversight of Jury Damage Assessments: A Proposal for the Comparative Additur/Remittitur Review of Awards for Nonpecuniary Harms and Punitive Damages* (Iowa City: University of Iowa, 1993).

96. Health Care Liability Alliance, "Medical Malpractice Award Median Returns to Decade-High Level: Million Dollar Awards Near Record," 1996 (visited August 7, 1999) <http://www.HCLA.org/html/HCLA/2/595.htm>.

97. Many states do not permit punitive damages; conversely, others do not impose limitations upon them. For example, four states—Louisiana, Massachusetts, Nebraska, and Washington—do not recognize common law punitive damages. New Hampshire has eliminated punitive damages in all actions by statute. In 1985, Illinois abolished punitive damages in all medical malpractice cases. Connecticut only permits plaintiffs to receive punitive damages to reimburse litigation expenses less their taxable costs. Michigan forbids the use of exemplary damages to punish and deter. The remedy of exemplary damages in Michigan is to assuage injured feelings, not for punishment or deterrence.

98. Russ Moran, "Medical Malpractice Win/Loss," *New York Verdict Reporter* (New York: Moran Publishing Company, 1998).

99. Prepared Statement of John Krayniak, Director of New Jersey Medicaid Fraud and Abuse Control Unit, Before House of Representatives, "Oversight Hearing on Medicaid and Fraud and Abuse: Assessing State and Federal Responses," Subcommittee on Oversight and Investigations, May 9, 1999, reported in FDCH Congressional Testimony, November 9, 1999.

100. U.S. Government Accounting Office, "Medical Liability: Impact on Hos-

pital and Physicians Extends Beyond Insurance" (Letter Report, September 29, 1995, GAO/CMP-95-169).

101. The median punitive damages award was an inflation-adjusted $228,600 in 1983 dollars. The median compensatory damage award for all examined cases was $120,120. It is the very few, very large punitive damage verdicts that skew the size of the average award. The mean compensatory award in a medical malpractice case was $592,982, as compared to the mean punitive damages award of $1,724,577. Only a quarter of the punitive damage awards amounted to $50,000 or less. We adjusted the median dollar figures in this section for inflation by the use of constant 1983 dollars. This is the convention in empirical research on jury verdicts. See, e.g., Stephen Daniels and Joanne Martin, "Myth and Reality in Punitive Damages," *Minnesota Law Review* 75 (1990): 1, 22–24.

102. Mean (average) ratios are misleading because of the extremely large or small verdict. For example, in one case, $30,000 in punitive damages and one dollar in compensatory damages were awarded. *Magma Copper Co. v. Shuster*, 575 P.2d 350, 351 (Ariz. Ct. App. 1977). In *Shuster*, a hospital administrator slapped a patient, causing minimal physical damage but great humiliation. Id. at 351–52. Thus, the 30,000 to 1 ratio skews the entire distribution.

103. "Step Right Up, Place Your Bets in Casino-Style Courts," *USA Today* (March 6, 1995): 10A.

104. Reductions of punitive damages were seldom based on a finding that the award was "excessive"; they were generally based upon evidentiary grounds such as the insufficient proof of malicious, intentional, or reckless conduct or the improper admission of evidence. Many punitive damage awards in medical malpractice were not collectible because they were not insured or insurable. For example, in *Crandall-Millar v. Sierra Vista Hospital*, No. 59975 (Cal. Cty. Ct. San Luis Obispo Cty., October 23, 1987), a $1 million pain-and-suffering award was paid to compensate the plaintiff for negligent surgery and intentional torts. However, the $5 million for punitive damages was not covered by insurance and was not paid. Questionnaire of David Sabih, Plaintiff's Counsel in id.

105. Questionnaire of James Hall, Plaintiff's Counsel in *McMillan v. Stuart*, No. CV-85-647 (Tuscaloosa Cty. Cir. Ct., Ala., May 1985).

106. Report to the American Bar Association, *Towards a Jurisprudence of Injury: The Continuing Creation of a System of Substantive Justice in American Tort Law* 2-2 (Chicago: American Bar Association, 1984) (Marshall Shapo Reporter).

107. Neville M. Billmoria, "New Medicine for Medical Malpractice: The Empirical Truth about Legislative Initiatives for Medical Malpractice Reform B Part II," *Journal of Health and Hospital Law* 306 (October 1994).

108. *Boyd v. Bulala*, 877 F.2d 1191 (4th Cir. 1991).

109. *Beale v. Beechnut Manor Living Center*, No. 90-18226, 1992 WL 539187 (Tex. Dist. Ct. Harris Cty. Houston, May 21, 1992).

110. Letter from Kenneth L. Pederson, Plaintiff's Counsel in *Manning v. Twin Falls Clinic and Hospital*, No. 41058 (Twin Falls Cty., Id., April 1987) (February 9, 1994).

111. Id.

112. Id.

113. 799 S.W.2d 71 (Mo. En Banc 1990).

114. Questionnaire of Anthony S. Bruning, Plaintiff's Counsel in *Menaugh v. Resler Optometry*, 799 S.W.2d 71 (Mo. En Banc 1990).

115. 378 F.2d 832 (2d Cir. 1967).

116. Id. at 840.

117. *Roginsky*, 378 F.2d at 839.

118. Testimony of Victor Schwartz, Partner, Crowell and Moring, Before the Subcommittee on Courts and Administrative Practice of the Senate Judiciary Committee, May 24, 1994, reprinted in *Federal News Service*, May 24, 1994.

119. See *Gonzales v. Nork*, No. 228566 (Cal. Super. Ct. Sacramento Cty. 1974); *Hendrick v. Nork*, No. 200777 (Cal. Super. Ct. Sacramento Cty., November 10, 1972), reported in *American Trial Lawyers Journal* 16 (1973): 25 (both cases imposing punitive damages for fraudulent and unnecessary surgery that caused patients to suffer permanent injuries).

120. *Rose v. Chouteau*, No. C-86-39, 1989 WL 389411 (Okla. Dist. Ct., Garfield Cty., February 17, 1989) (assessing punitive damages for unnecessary and unskillful back surgery that left the patient with painful nerve damage).

121. Protecting Medicare and Medicaid Patients from Sanctioned Health Practitioners, Hearing Before the Special Committee on Aging, 98th Congress, 2d Session 6 (1984) (testimony of Dr. Robert C. Derbyshire, author and former president of the Federation of State Medical Boards).

122. *Jackson v. Johns-Manville Sales Corp.*, 781 F.2d 394, 403 (5th Cir.) (stating "punitive damages serve to motivate 'private attorney generals' to bring suit"), *cert. denied*, 478 U.S. 1022 (1986).

123. A medical malpractice case was filed after the patient developed a serious infection from the implement. *Petrangelo v. Engelman*, No. 84-553 (Hamden Cty., Mass. Super. Ct., 1988) cited in Association of Trial Lawyers of America, *Cases That Have Made a Difference* (Washington, D.C.: ATLA Press, 1990), 59.

124. *Nelson v. Steinert*, No. 31522 (Charlton Cty., S.C., May 1988).

125. Association of Trial Lawyers of America, *Cases That Made a Difference*.

126. Id.

127. *Perryman v. Rosenbaum*, 423 S.E. 2d 673 (Ga. Ct. App. 1992) (reporting death of sixty-two-year-old woman from a massive hemothorax caused by improper catheterization). After the award, the radiology department instituted new protocol for verifying proper placement of catheters. Letter from W. Fred Orr III, Plaintiff's Counsel in *Perryman* (April 26, 1994).

128. See Rustad and Koenig, "Reconceptualizing Punitive Damages in Medical Malpractice," 1495 (documenting safety improvements made in the wake of punitive damages awards).

129. Larry Tye, "Patients at Risk: Hospital Errors," *Boston Globe*, March 17, 1999 (visited March 17, 1999) <http://www.globe/metro/packages/hospital_errors/>.

130. Id.

131. Id.

132. See, e.g., William P. Gronfein and Eleanor D. Kinney, "Controlling Large Malpractice Claims: The Unexpected Impact of Damages Caps," *Journal of Health Policy and Law* 16 (1991): 441, 447–48.

133. A 1999 study by the Consumer Federation of America found that the promised consumer savings from Texas tort reforms failed to materialize. J. Robert Hunter, *Texas Tort Reform's Incredible Shrinking "Savings"* (Washington, D.C.: Consumer Federation of America, 1999) (finding that tort reform in Texas has not produced significant reductions in insurance premiums). See also Best Wire Report, "Consumer Group Says Texas Tort Reform Is Overstated," *Best Wire* (December 22, 1999): 1 (reporting Consumer Federation study showing that tort reform had little effect on liability insurance).

134. U.S. Government Accounting Office, *Medical Malpractice: Six State Case Studies Show Claims and Insurance Costs Still Rise Despite Reforms*, GAO/HRD-87-21 (Washington D.C.: U.S. Government Accounting Office, December 4, 1986).

135. Office of Technology Assessment, *Defensive Medicine and Medical Malpractice* (Washington D.C.: Office of Technology Assessment, 1994), 2.

136. Id. at 1.

137. See, e.g., Stephen Chapman, "Odor in the Court: The Great Lawsuit Lottery and How to Close It Down," *Chicago Tribune* (January 29, 1995): C3; Jon Matthews, "Fight Looms on Liability Suits," *Sacramento Bee* (February 6, 1995): A1; "Learning from Baker and McKenzie," *American Lawyer* (October 1994): 83.

138. Nathan P. Couch et al., "The High Cost of Low-Frequency Events: The Anatomy and Economics of Surgical Mishaps," *New England Journal of Medicine* 304 (1981): 634, 635.

139. Antonio Olivo, "Two Sentenced in Death of Alcoholic During 'Aversion Therapy,'" *Los Angeles Times* (September 29, 1998): B3.

140. *Adams v. Golden*, No. CV-87-T-026-N (M.D. Ala., December 16, 1987).

141. *Anderson v. Weisman*, C 98184 (L.A. Cty. Super. Ct., April 15, 1977).

142. *Florida Patient's Compensation Fund v. Mercy Hospital*, 419 So.2d 348 (Dist. Ct. Of Fla., 3d Dist. 1982).

143. Telephone interview with Harry Miles, Plaintiff's Counsel in *Burt v. Meyer*, 508 N.E. 2d (Mass. 1987).

144. *Greer v. Schlegel*, No. 83-CV-616 (Colo. Dist. Ct., Pueblo Cty., May 12, 1987).

145. See also *Anderson v. Weissman*, No. C98184 (Cal. Super. Ct., L.A. Cty., February 11, 1997) (surgeon's gross error causes brain damage).

146. 525 A.2d 992, 994–95 (Del. 1987).

147. Questionnaire of Charles Brandt, Plaintiff's Counsel in *Biggs v. Strauss*, id. at 992.

148. *Clark v. Funk*, No. 84-5946-3 (DeKalb Cty. Super. Ct., March 8, 1985).

149. *Atjuilina v. Thrift Drug Co.*, No. 19760 (Luzerne (Penn.) Cty. Ct., 1987).

150. *Gurr v. Wilcott*, 146 Ariz. 575, 707 P.2d 979 (1985).

151. 464 F.2d. 772 (D.C. Cir. 1972).

152. No. 86-44136CA28, 1988 WL 368460 (Dade Cty. (Fla.) Cir. Ct., April 1988).

153. Id.

154. No. 353 206 (Calif. Super. Ct. Orange Cty. (Calif.) March 2, 1984).

155. This case was reported by Lewis Laska in the May 1998 issue of *Medical Malpractice Verdicts, Settlements and Experts,* Nashville, Tenn. See also Rustad and Koenig, "Reconceptualizing Punitive Damages in Medical Malpractice," 1083 (reporting case).

156. *Beale v. Beechnut Manor Living Ctr.*, No. 90-18826, 1992 WL 539187 (Tex. Dist. Ct. Harris Cty. May 1992).

157. Questionnaire of Vanessa Gilmore, Plaintiff's Counsel in id.

158. *Harmon v. Glisan Care Center*, No. A8111-07086 (Ore. Cir. Ct., Multnomah Cty., August 6, 1982) (awarding $10,000 punitive damages against a nursing home for reckless disregard of patient's health; patient developed stage IV decubitus ulcers, dehydration, and malnutrition while a resident in the nursing home).

159. Ingrid Van Tuinen et al., *9,479 Questionable Doctors*, Id. at 23.

160. Id. at 14.

161. Clifton Perry and Joan Wallman Kuruc, "Psychotherapists' Sexual Relationships with Their Patients," *Annals of Health Law* 2 (1993): 35, 35–37 (citing Judith L. Herman et al., "Psychiatrist–Patient Sexual Contact: Results of a National Survey, II: Psychiatrists' Attitudes," *American Journal of Psychiatry* 144 (1987): 164, 164).

162. Id. at 35.

163. Punitive damages have been assessed in cases involving extreme breaches of fiduciary duty. See, e.g., *Banks v. Charter Hospital*, SOC 9996, 1992 WL 521069 (L.A. Cty. (Calif.) Super. Ct., May 5, 1992) (assessing punitive damages against a hospital that did not have a patient's permission to use her photograph in a brochure advertising mental health services); *Bellard v. Abraham*, No. C406564 (L.A. Cty. (Calif.) Super. Ct. May 10, 1985) (assessing punitive damages against doctor who used patient's medical records to document hospital's substandard program of open heart surgery); *Davison v. Tangari*, No. 85 CV 895 (Shawnee Cty. (Kan.) Dist. Ct. January 13, 1988) (social worker breached fiduciary duty by divulging that his client was seeking psychiatric counseling).

164. See, e.g., *Petrillo v. Syntex Labs, Inc.*, 499 N.E.2d 952, 961 (Ill. App. Ct.), *cert. denied*, 505 N.E.2d 361 (Ill. 1986), *cert. denied*, 483 U.S. 1007 (1987); *Moore v. Webb*, 345 S.W.2d 239, 243 (Mo. Ct. App. 1961); *Kitzmiller v. Henning*, 437 S.E.2d 452, 454 (W. Va. 1993).

165. *St. Paul Fire & Marine Insurance Co. v. Love*, 459 N.W.2d 698, 701 (Minn. 1990) (discussing American Psychiatric Association advisory opinion on phenomenon of transference).

166. See, e.g., *Roy v. Hartogs*, 366 N.Y.S.2d 297 (N.Y. Civ. Ct. 1985).

167. *Chanley v. Pratska*, No. 33-31-88 (Orange Cty. (Calif.) Super. Ct., July 23, 1982) (awarding punitive damages against psychiatrist who entered into sexual relationship with a sixteen- year-old patient).

168. *Wall v. Noble*, No. 34,503 (Harrison Cty. (Tex.) Dist. Ct., First Dist., May 4, 1984) (assessing $625,000 in damages, including $350,000 punitive damages).

169. Telephone Interview with Seth Langston, Plaintiff's Counsel in *Mac-Clements v. Lafone*, No. 88-CVS-4095 (Mecklenberg Cty. (N.C.) Super. Ct., February 12, 1993).

170. Transference occurs when a person under treatment transfers the thoughts and emotions he or she has been having onto the therapist. The process of countertransference occurs when the analyst projects onto his or her patient. See Arthur Robbins, *Between Therapists: The Processing of Transference/Countertransference Material* (New York: Jessica Kingsley Publishers, 1999).

171. Questionnaire of Woody Connette, Plaintiff's Counsel in *MacClements v. Lafone*, No. 88-CVS-4095 (Mecklenberg Cty. (N.C.) Super. Ct., February 1990).

172. Telephone Interview with Seth Langson, Plaintiff's Counsel in *Mac-Clements v. Lafone*, id.

173. Woody Connette, Plaintiff's Counsel, notes that the impact of the case "is that it has created greater awareness of the inappropriate nature of sexual relationships between therapists and patients. The therapist no longer works in field and is now a sales representative for an oil company." Questionnaire of Plaintiff's Counsel, *Woody Connette*, id.

174. Punitive damages were awarded to victims of podiatry malpractice in a number of cases. See, e.g., *High v. Carey*, No. C16108 (L.A. Cty. (Calif.) Super. Ct., March 4, 1974) (awarding $14,180 in general damages and $10,000 in punitive damages for unnecessary operation that left patient with two deformed toes and residual pain); *Strauss v. Biggs*, 525 A.2d 992, 1000–1001 (Del. 1987) (awarding $235,000 in punitive damages against defendant who operated a "[p]odiatric mill [and was] motivated more by money [rather] than by" medical ethics).

175. *Saunders v. Kauffman*, No. 86-447, 1987 WL 229462 (Tex. Dist. Ct. Smith Cty. September 25, 1987).

176. Questionnaire of Craig M. Daugherty, Plaintiff's Counsel in *Saunders*, id. (Questionnaire completed, January 12, 1994); see also *August v. Doerken*, No.

C400447, 1987 WL 230635 (L.A. Cty. (Calif.) Cir. Ct. February 1987) (reporting $10,000 verdict for lack of consent for unauthorized dental work).

177. This case study in drawn in whole from the case of *Kinzel v. Messieh* as described by Plaintiff's Counsel Charles J. Mazursky. Letter to Michael Rustad from Debbie Whitaker, Legal Assistant to Charles J. Mazursky, April 4, 1994.

178. *In re Estate of Sisk v. Consolidated Resources*, No. 85-CI-940, 1988 WL 371055 (Ky. Cir. Ct., McCracken Cty., August 1988).

179. *Scariati v. Flushing Hospital, Malpractice Lifeline* 6 (1981): 3 (awarding $5 million in punitive damages after child contracted spinal meningitis and the treating pediatrician falsified medical records in an attempt to cover up her malpractice).

180. *Franklin Square Hospital v. Laubach*, 569 A.2d 693 (Md. 1990).

181. A study by the Public Citizen Health Research Group found that "[f]ewer than one-half of 1% of the nation's doctors face any state sanctions each year." Van Tuinen et al., *9,479 Questionable Doctors*, 159. Licensing and disciplinary boards often lack the resources to investigate and adequately prosecute incompetent physicians. Public Citizen found that 966 (approximately 17 percent) of the disciplinary actions taken against physicians were the result of enforcement actions in other states. Id. at 15, 23. The next largest category of cited misconduct was a physician's over-prescribing or mis-prescribing drugs (13 percent). Id. at 23. Noncompliance with medical board orders or professional rules accounted for 11 percent of the sanctions, followed by substandard care, which accounted for 9.8 percent.

182. Wolfe et al., *13,012 Questionable Doctors*, 16.

183. Id. at viii.

184. Id.

185. *Saunders v. Kauffman*, No. 86-447, 1987 WL 229462 (Tex. Dist. Ct. Smith Cty. September 25, 1987); see also Rustad and Koenig, "Reconceptualizing Punitive Damages in Medical Malpractice," 1069 (reporting brief suspension of dentist drawn from interview with plaintiff's counsel).

186. 785 F. Supp. 563 (E.D. Va. 1992), aff'd by 4 F.3d 487 (4th Cir. 1993), *cert. denied*, 1145 S. Ct. 1643 (1994).

187. Questionnaire of Jamed McKiernan, Plaintiff's Counsel in *Crandall-Millar v. Sierra Vista Hospital*, No. 59975 (Cal. Cty. Ct. San Luis Obispo, October 23, 1987).

188. See Rustad and Koenig, "Reconceptualizing Punitive Damages in Medical Malpractice," 975.

189. Questionnaire of Charles Brandt, Plaintiff's Counsel in *Strauss v. Biggs*, 525 F.2d 992 (Del. 1987).

190. See 42 U.S.C. §11131(a) (2000).

191. Dobbs, *The Law of Torts*, 652.

192. Maria O'Brien Hylton, "The Economics and Politics of Emergency

Health Care for the Poor: The Patient Dumping Dilemma," *Brigham Young University Law Review* (1992): 971, 972 n. 71.

193. One emergency room physician relates his experience with HMO reluctance to serve the poor: "[G]etting authorization to treat HMO patients in the emergency department and getting HMO physicians to call me back to admit their patients to the hospital is a nightmare. The vast majority of HMOs are incredibly inefficient, as well as remarkably impersonal." Michael C. Thornhill et al., "Research Report," *New England Journal of Medicine* (1985): 579, 580.

194. *Morrell v. LaLone*, 45 R.I. 112, 120 A. 435 (1923).

195. Id. at 437.

196. *Hernandez v. Smith*, 552 F.2d 142 (5th Cir. 1977).

197. No. D-7138 (Fulton Cty. (Ga.) Cty. Ct., February 23, 1989).

198. Telephone interview with Plaintiff's Counsel Robert Goldstrucker in *LeCroy v. Hughes*, No. D-7138 (Fulton Cty. (Ga.) Cty. Ct., February 23, 1989) (Interview completed April 1994).

199. Id.

200. See, e.g., *DeCicco v. Trinidad Area Health Association*, No. 76219 (Pueblo Cty. (Colo.) Cir. Ct., August 3, 1976) (assessing punitive damages against hospital for refusing to dispatch ambulance to carry Hispanic to hospital, though there was no other available ambulance service); *Jones v. Hospital*, 465 N.Y.S.2d 25 (Super. Ct. 1983).

201. Susan Rose-Ackerman proposes that the law require "all HMO's to take a share of the subsidized population." Susan Rose-Ackerman, "Social Services and the Market," *Columbia Law Review* 83 (1983): 1405, 1427. The alternative is to lower the professional standard of care when treating the powerless and dispossessed. See E. Haavi Morreim, "Cost Containment and the Standard of Medical Care," *California Law Review* 75 (1987): 1719, 1724 (positing that "physicians may not always be able to provide customary levels of care, particularly for the poor. Should they nevertheless be held legally liable for the medical consequences of others' economic decisions?").

202. *Jacobs v. Murfreesboro Health Care Center, Inc.*, No. 13,544 (Rutherford Cty. Cir. Ct., Tenn., April 8, 1991).

203. J. Thomas Rhodes III and Juliette Castillo, "Proving Damages in Nursing Home Cases," *Trial* (August 2000): 41, 42.

204. See, e.g., *Davis v. Fairburn Health Care Ctr.*, No. C-97368 (Fulton Cty. (Ga.) Super. Ct., October 1988) (awarding punitive damages against nursing home when seventy-year-old patient died as a result of negligent care); *Hackman v. Dandamudi*, 733 S.W.2d 452, 454, 458 (Mo. Ct. App. 1986) (awarding punitive damages to elderly resident who suffered amputation from infected heel blister); *Baumann v. Seven Acres Jewish Home for the Aged, Inc.*, No. 0059093 (Harris Cty. (Tex.) Dist. Ct., March 23 1990) (assessing $35 million punitive damages award

after an unattended eighty-four-year-old nursing home resident was strangled to death by an improperly used vest restraint).

205. See, e.g., *Frye v. Silver Palm Nursing Ctr., Inc.*, No. CA87-315 (Pasco Cty. (Fla.) Cir. Ct., January 10, 1989) (awarding punitive damages to seventy-seven-year-old nursing home resident who suffered gangrene and amputations from improperly treated decubitus ulcers).

206. No. 129413 (Sonoma Cty. (Calif.) Cty. Ct., October 10, 1984).

207. Letter from Patrick G. Grattan, Plaintiff's Counsel in *Darblay v. Western Medical Enterprises, Inc.*, No. 129413 (Sonoma Cty. (Calif.) October 10, 1984), to Michael Rustad (June 7, 1984).

208. Questionnaire of Patrick Grattan, Plaintiff's Counsel in *Darblay v. Western Medical Enterprises*.

209. Id. at 5.

210. Letter of Patrick Grattan, Plaintiff's Counsel in *Darblay v. Western Medical Enterprises*, to Defendant's Counsel (on file with authors).

211. "Hillhaven Is Ordered to Pay $15 Million to Ex-Patient's Estate," *Wall Street Journal* (November 26, 1990): B7.

212. No. 91-7612-155 (Fla. Cir. Ct. Pinellas Cty. 1991).

213. *Gonzalez v. Camulu Care Center*, No. 13. 61689, 1990 WL 457439 (Bexar Cty. (Tex.) Cty. Ct., January 1990).

214. Frank Stanfield, "Family Sues Nursing Home," *Orlando Sentinel* (November 14, 1998), 1.

215. Id.

216. Id.

217. Id.

218. The concept of total institution was developed by Erving Goffman to refer to settings in which all life activities occur under one roof. Goffman developed the concept to describe mental institutions.

219. *Adams v. Murakami*, 813 P.2d 1348 (Calif. 1991).

220. *Estes Health Care Centers, Inc. v. Bannerman*, 411 So.2d 109, 110 (Ala. 1982).

221. *Fielder v. Bosshard*, 590 F.2d 105, 108–11 (5th Cir. 1979).

222. 570 So.2d 1209 (Ala. 1990).

223. No. 83-11543-7 (Cir. Ct. (Florida) Pinellas Cty., February 1988).

224. Letter from Elizabeth J. Daniels, Plaintiff's Counsel in *Doe v. Walker*, reprinted JVR No. 32121, 1988 WL 366953 (LRP Jury), to Michael Rustad, April 26, 1994.

225. Barbara Johnson, "Nurse Won't Testify in Suit over Alleged Hospital Rape," *St. Petersburg Times* (February 3, 1988): 3B.

226. Id. at 1.

227. Id. at 1–2.

228. Questionnaire of Elizabeth J. Daniels, Plaintiff's Counsel in *Doe v. Walker*, 1988 WL 366953 (Fla. Cir. Ct., Pinellas, Ct., Fla. February 1988).

229. Dave Kidwell, "Hospital Says Victim Didn't Cry during Deposition," *Tampa Tribune-Times* (February 7, 1988): 1.

230. Barbara Johnson, "Woman Says She Didn't Tell Lawyers about Previous Rape," *St. Petersburg Times* (February 7, 1988): 3B.

231. Id.

232. Id.

233. Dave Kidwell, "Rape Victim's Credibility Questioned by Defense," *Tampa Tribune-Times* (February 7, 1988): 1, 6.

234. Id.

235. *McNamara v. Honeyman*, 546 N.E.2d 139 (Mass. 1989).

236. Id.

237. Questionnaire of Harry Miles, Plaintiff's Counsel in *McNamara v. Honeyman*, 546 N.E.2d 139 (Mass. 1989). As with many cases in our study, no punitive damages were ever collected. In *McNamara*, the trial court amended the judgment by striking the punitive damages since the amount exceeded the Commonwealth's cap of $100,000 on recoveries against the state. Miles, Id.

238. Telephone interview with Elden Rosenthal, Plaintiff's Counsel in *Harmon v. Glisan*, conducted April 1994.

239. "Unqualified Doctors Performing Cosmetic Surgery: Policies and Enforcement Activities of the Federal Trade Commission, Part II," Hearing Before the Subcommittee on Regulation, Business Opportunities, and Energy of the Committee on Small Business, 101st Congress, 1st Session (1989) (reproducing advertisements with titles such as "Reshape Your Future," "Be a Knockout," "Free What Ifs," "Dreams," "Facts and Figures," and "If You'd Like to Know How Cosmetic Surgery Changed My Life, Call Me").

240. Id. at 1.

241. Id. at 2–3.

242. When practicing as individuals, physicians have substantial freedom to misbehave without punishment because they have the social and financial resources to conceal their "backstage behavior" with effective impression management. Erving Goffman, *The Presentation of Self in Everyday Life* (New York: Anchor, 1959).

243. No. 34,503 (Tex. Cty. Ct., Harrison Cty., May 4, 1984).

244. See also *Nethery v. Unterthiner*, No. 40095 (Riverside Cty. (Calif.) Super. Ct., May 21, 1985) (assessing punitive damages against cosmetic surgeon for incompetent cosmetic surgery and for molesting plaintiff as she was coming out of anesthesia); *Vitali v. Bartell*, No. 353 206 (Orange Cty. (Calif.) Super. Ct., March 2, 1984) (assessing punitive damages for ghost surgery).

245. *Nethery v. Unterthiner*, No 40095 (Indio Cty. Ct. (Calif.) May 21, 1985).

246. *Ravens v. Maschek*, No. 89-36245 (Dade Cty. Cir. Ct. (Fla.) January 1990).

247. *Mauga v. Rundles*, No. 718261 (S.F. (Calif.) Super. Ct., May 13, 1983).

248. Lewis L. Laska, *Malpractice Experts: Finding and Using the Best!* (Memphis: Laska Publications, 1994), 216.

249. James Harvey Young, *The Medical Messiahs: A Social History of Health Quackery in Twentieth-Century America* (Princeton, N.J.: Princeton University Press, 1967), 25.

250. American Medical Association, *Nostrums and Quackery: Articles on the Nostrum, Evil and Quackery Reprinted with Additions and Modifications from the Journal of the American Medical Association* (Chicago: Press of American Medical Association, 1911), 211–12.

251. No. 82574/74 (N.Y. Super. Ct., July 24, 1986).

252. Id.

253. Id.

254. 722 F.2d 203 (5th Cir. 1984).

255. Id. at 204.

256. Id.

257. Id. at 205.

258. Id. at 2.

259. Id.

260. Id. at 3.

261. *Carlton v. Shelton*, 722 F.2d 203, 206 (5th Cir. 1984).

262. *Reneau v. Ferreri*, No. 88-056 (Del Norte Cty. (Calif.) September 1991).

263. Id.

264. The phrase comes from the title of Dr. Peter Rutter's book, *Sex in the Forbidden Zone: When Men in Power—Therapists, Doctors, Clergy, Teachers and Others—Betray Women's Trust* (New York: Ballantine, Fawcett Crest Books, 1986).

265. See, e.g., *Roy v. Hartogs*, 381 N.Y.S.2d 587 (App. Term 1976).

266. *L.L. v. Medical Protective Co.*, 362 N.W.2d 174, 177 (Wis. Ct. App. 1984).

267. See "Woman Wins Damages from Psychiatrists," *United Press International* (February 11, 1989), available in LEXIS, News Library, Wires File.

268. *Combs v. Silverman*, No. LE 596 (Va. Cir. Ct. Richmond Cty. February 5, 1982).

269. *Greenberg v. McCabe*, 453 F. Supp. 765 (E.D. Penn. 1977).

270. *Chanley v. Pratska*, No. 33-31-88 (Orange Cty. (Calif.) July 23, 1982).

271. In *American Home Insurance Co. v. Stone*, 61 F.3d 1321 (7th Cir. 1995), the U.S. Court of Appeals upheld an insurer's $25,000 cap on liability for sexual misconduct in a professional liability policy.

272. *Rahn v. Lowinger*, No. 940955 (Orange Cty. (Calif.) July 1, 1994), published in *Verdictum Juris Press* 11 (1994): 1.

273. No. 74116 (Kootenai County Dist. Ct. Coeur d'Alene, Idaho, April 19, 1990).

274. *Doe v. Doe*, No. 94-203 (Dade County, Fla., July 1995), reported in *Medical Litigation Alert* (March 1996): 1.

275. 577 A.2d 1081 (Conn. App. Ct. 1990).

276. This statistic is drawn from our database of punitive damages in medical malpractice litigation, 1963–93. See Rustad and Koenig, "Reconceptualizing Punitive Damages in Medical Malpractice," 975.

277. Outlook, *U.S. News and World Report* (October 17, 1994): 15.

278. Given the unregulated nature of much of cosmetic surgery, it is not surprising that this specialty produced a disproportionate number of extreme deviations from accepted practice verdicts. See, generally, "Cosmetic Surgery Procedures: Standards, Quality and Certification of Non-Hospital Operating Rooms—Part III," Hearing Before the Subcommittee on Regulation, Business Opportunities, and Energy of the Committee On Small Business, House of Representatives, First Congress, First Session, Serial No. 101-14 (documenting that cosmetic surgery is often performed in unregulated, unsafe non-hospital settings). See, e.g., *Stone v. Foster*, 106 Cal. App. 3d 334; 164 Cal. Rptr. 901 (Ca. Ct. App. 1980) (awarding punitive damages to female scarred from botched "tummy tuck"); *Mauga v. Rundles*, No. 718261 (San Francisco Superior Court (Calif.)., May 13, 1983) (awarding punitive damages for death of female patient from staph infection after tummy tuck operation). In *Baker v. Sadick*, 208 Cal. Rptr. 676 (Cal. Ct. App. 1984), the plaintiff suffered serious post-surgery infections after breast reduction. The grossly ineffectual post-operative treatment required extensive corrective plastic surgery. Id. at 621; 208 Cal. Rptr. at 678. The arbitrator awarded punitive damages based upon the fraudulent inducement to surgery, falsification of medical records, and uninformed post-operative treatment of an infection. Id. at 625; 208 Cal. Rptr. at 680.

279. Keeton et al., *Prosser and Keeton on the Law of Torts*, 185.

280. For example in *Sapp v. Gottschalk*, ATLA Newsletter 16 (1974): 1, a physician was charged with punitive liability for carelessly operating on the wrong patient.

281. Reproductive injuries accounted for many cases of extreme deviation from accepted medical standards. See, e.g., *Adams v. Golden*, No. CV-87-T-026-N, (M.D. Ala. Alabama, December 16, 1987) (awarding punitive damages in wrongful death action brought against the treating physician, nurse, and hospital, alleging failure to recognize and treat obvious signs of fetal distress). See also *Hernandez v. Smith*, 552 F.2d 142 (5th Cir. 1977) (awarding punitive damages based upon the grossly inadequate facilities of an obstetrical clinic leading to death of baby).

282. A number of cases where punitive damages were based upon extreme deviation from accepted medical practice were unrelated to the gender of the plaintiff. See, e.g., *Scribner v. Hillcrest Medical Center*, JVR No. 0063121, 1990 WL 461701 (LRP Jury) (Nexis File) (awarding punitive damages to plaintiff injured by orderly who mistook her for another patient); *Greene v. Averi*, No. CV-87-1534-PH (Mont-

gomery Cty., Ala., July 1988) (assessing punitive damages for severe foot damage from botched operations); *Florence T. Huelsmann and David R. Huelsmann v. Wallace P. Berkowitz*, 210 Ill. App. 3d 806, 568 N.E. 2d 1373 (1991) (awarding punitive damages for failure to arrest the bleeding during tonsillectomy); *Schaefer v. Miller*, 322 Md. 297, 587 A.2d 491 (1991) (awarding punitive damages against defendant ophthalmologist who performed unnecessary surgery without informed consent and rendered negligent pre-operative and post-operative care); *Larrumbide v. Doctors Hospital*, No. 81-5216-J, (Tex. (Dallas County) 19 First Judicial District Court, November 28, 1984) (assessing punitive damages for grossly inadequate dental surgery). Some of the "gender-neutral" cases involved relational injuries that affected mothers through their children. See, e.g., *Portlock v. Duncanville Diagnostic Center, Inc.*, 1993 WL 5572444 (Tex. Dist. Ct. Oct. 1993) (awarding punitive damages after four-year-old girl dies from overdose given by doctor). See also "Clinic Suit Jury Awards Woman $34.76 Million; Child Died as Result of Drug Overdose at Facility," *Dallas Morning News* (October 12, 1993): 1A.

283. No. 35306, (Verdictum Juris No. 84-46AB, Orange Cty. (Calif.), March 2, 1984).

284. No. 107480, (Johnson Cty. Dist. Ct., Kansas, 1985).

285. See, generally, Mary Adelaide Mendelson, *Tender Loving Greed: How the Incredibly Lucrative Nursing Home Industry Is Exploiting America's Old People and Defrauding Us All* (New York: Alfred A. Knopf, 1974).

286. No. 22306/75 (N.Y. Sup. Ct. 1982).

287. Report to the American Bar Association, *Towards a Jurisprudence of Injury*, 5–189.

288. Linda V. Tiano, "The Legal Implications of HMO Cost Containment Measures," *Seton Hall Journal of Legislation* 14 (1990): 79, 80.

289. Edmund Faltermayer, "The Right to Fire HMO Doctors," *Fortune* (July 11, 1994): 12 (quoting AMA President Dr. Lonnie Bristow).

290. Clarence Morris, "Punitive Damages in Tort Cases," *Harvard Law Review* 44 (1931): 1173, 1184–88.

291. "Group Says Video Proves Aetna Discriminates," *BestWire: A. M. Best Company* (October 14, 1998). The Consumers for Quality released a copy of the video depicting "Aetna lawyers telling disability claims managers to consider a patient's right to sue when determining whether to pay a policyholder's claims."

292. "Physician Gag Orders," *Consumer Watchdog* (visited November 28, 1998) <http://www.consumerwatch.org/public_hts/smokegun/gagorder.htm>.

293. Id. (name of HMO withheld).

294. Id.

295. Mark Murray, "Issues of the Day: Where Bush Stands," *National Journal* (August 7, 1999): 2279.

296. See "Health Administration Responsibility Project: Tort Theories of HMO Liability" (visited January 1, 1999) <http://harp.org/tort.htm>.

297. "Repair Team Files National Class Action Lawsuits Against Five Giant HMO Operators," *PR Newswire* (November 23, 1999).

298. Milo Geyelin, "Courts Pierce HMOs' Shield against Lawsuits," *Wall Street Journal* (April 30, 1999): B1.

299. Id.

NOTES TO CHAPTER 5

1. "ACEC Says Liability Reform Is a Small Business Issue," *United States Newswire* (August 27, 1996) (quoting Stan Kawaguchi, President of American Consulting Engineers Council).

2. Laura Duncan, "New Tort-Reform Coalition Takes Aim at Lawyers, Legislators, Legislation," *Chicago Daily Law Bulletin* (December 1, 1993): 1 (quoting John Davis, State Director of National Federation of Independent Business).

3. Editorial, "Taking on the Tort Tax; Tort Liabilities Raise Costs; View from the Top," *Chief Executive* (November 1994): 68.

4. Id.

5. David Jackson, "Senate to Vote on Limiting Products Liability Awards: Supporters of Cap Doubt They Could Override Veto," *Dallas Morning News* (March 21, 1996): 1D.

6. Much of the business community depicts punitive damages as a monster. Clark Richardson of the Business Council of Alabama was referring to punitive damages when he stated: "We have created a monster in this state." *ABC Nightline*, "Strange Justice: The Law in Alabama" (October 24, 1995). The enlistment of large corporate defense companies as part of the tort reform coalition is reported Rocco Cammarere, "Environmentalists Say Tort Reformers Hide Their Intention," *New Jersey Lawyer* (April 25, 1994): 44 (naming law firms as part of tort reform coalition).

7. See, e.g., APCO Associates, "American Tort Reform Association" (visited February 20, 1999) <http://www.prcentral.com/c96tort.htm>.

8. American Tort Reform Association, *The Reformer* (Winter 1998–99) (quoting Association for California Tort Reform).

9. Id.

10. American Tort Reform Association, ATRA Press Release, "ATRA Presents 'No Foolin' Day'" (Washington, D.C.: American Tort Reform Association, April 2, 1998).

11. Marc Galanter, "An Oil Strike in Hell: Contemporary Legends about the Civil Justice System," *Arizona Law Review* 40 (1998): 717, 726.

12. Michigan Lawsuit Abuse Watch, "Winner of M-Law's Second Annual Wacky Warning Label Contest Announced," December 21, 1998 (visited December 31, 1998) <http://www.mlaw.org/whacky.htm>.

13. Id.

14. 787 APCO Associates, American Tort Reform Association (visited February 20, 1999) <http://www.prcentral.com/c96tort.htm>.

15. Neil A. Lewis, "Senate Takes Up Change in Civil Suits," *New York Times* (April 3, 1995): 6B (commenting on March 6, 1995, editorial in *USA Today*).

16. The tricycle case resulted in a $1.9 million settlement. See *Berju v. Hanover House*, No. 6986/89 (N.Y. County Sup. Ct., June 4, 1990).

17. *McCord v. Sears, Roebuck and Co.*, No. CV-90-35 (Ala. Lowndes County Cir. Ct., February 27, 1992).

18. Id.; see also, *Sliman v. Aluminum Company of America*, 731 P.2d 1287 (Idaho 1987) (awarding punitive damages against bottler in a similar case).

19. American Tort Reform Association, "ATRA Tort Stories," ATRA website (visited December 30, 1998) <http://www.atra.org/ah.htm>.

20. See Robert Keeton et al., *Prosser and Keeton on Torts*, 5th ed. (St. Paul, Minn.: West Publishing Co., 1984), 25 (noting that deterrence through imposing financial liability is a key function of tort law).

21. *Moore v. Jewel Tea Co.*, 253 N.E.2d 636 (1969), aff. 263 N.E.2d (Ill. 1970).

22. American Law Institute, *Reporters' Study: Enterprise Responsibility for Personal Injury* (Philadelphia: American Law Institute, 1991): 1:245.

23. Id. at 342.

24. Id. at 245.

25. Id. at 282.

26. Id.

27. Id. at 243.

28. The CPSC has issued only a handful of safety standards because its final rules are challenged by industry. Industry challenges proposed safety standards at every stage. Approved rules are now being challenged on the grounds that Congress did not delegate legislative authority to promulgate standards in a given area. Industry, for example, is challenging the Environmental Protection Agency's rules on standards for particulate matter as an unconstitutional delegation of legislative authority.

29. Richard Landes and Richard Posner, *The Economic Structure of Tort Law* (Cambridge, Mass.: Harvard University Press, 1987).

30. Philip K. Dick, "Colony," in *The Best of Philip K. Dick* (New York: Coronet, 1977), 127–28.

31. Id. at 134.

32. Id. at 135.

33. No. TCA 83-7037 (U.S. Dist. Ct., N.D. Fla., April 4, 1984).

34. Telephone Interview with E. C. Deeno Kitcher, Plaintiff's Counsel in *Alexander v. Ford Motor*, id.

35. *Rookes v. Barnard*, 1 Eng. Rep. 367 (H.L. 1964).

36. 217 N.Y. 382, 111 N.E. 1050 (1916).

37. Id. at 1053.

38. 150 P.2d 436 (Cal. 1944).

39. Id.

40. See, e.g., *Roginsky v. Richardson-Merrell, Inc.*, 378 F.2d 832 (2d Cir. 1967) (reversing punitive damages); *Toole v. Richardson-Merrell, Inc.*, 60 Cal. Rptr. 398, 403–09 (Ct. App. 1967) (upholding punitive damages); *Ostopowitz v. Richardson-Merrell, Inc.*, No. 587 9/63 (N.Y. Sup. Ct. November 7, 1966) (awarding punitive damages).

41. The MER-29 vignette is drawn from *Toole v. Richardson-Merrell, Inc.*, 60 Cal. Rptr. 398 (Ct. App. 1967).

42. Id. at 404.

43. Id.

44. Id.

45. Id.

46. Id.

47. Id.

48. Id.

49. Id. at 405–6.

50. Id.

50. Id.

52. Id.

53. Id. at 407.

54. Id.

55. Paul Rheingold, "The MER-29 Story: An Issuance of Successful Mass Disaster," *California Law Review* 56 (1968): 116.

56. Id.

57. Id.

58. Id.

59. *Roginsky v. Richardson-Merrell, Inc.*, 378 F.2d 832 (2d Cir. 1967) (reversing punitive damages award).

60. The same evidence led the California court to affirm a $500,000 punitive damages award in *Toole v. Richardson-Merrell, Inc.*, 251 Cal. App.2d 689, 60 Cal. Rptr. 398 (1967).

61. A. T. Kearney Associates ranked the respondents in terms of four levels of safety sophistication: the first stage represented minimal reactive preparedness, with no formal, ongoing safety program or coordinator; the second stage was characterized by a formal, but unsophisticated, plan operating on a sporadic basis with a part-time coordinator; the third stage included a full-time coordinator and safety committee meeting on a regularly scheduled basis, safety audits, and a proactive media program for communicating with consumers; in addition to the advances of third-stage preparedness, the fourth, most sophisticated, level entailed a high degree of management commitment to safety, a safety committee with far-reaching authority and well-defined duties, and a fully integrated pro-

gram emphasizing proactive quality control and systematic corrective action plans.

The disturbing results of the survey were that 272, or 51 percent, of the companies were at the first stage of development; 233, or 44 percent, fell into the second stage; 24, or 5 percent, qualified for third-stage ranking, and only one company had a safety program comprehensive enough to gain fourth-stage status. CCH, *Managing for Product Liability Avoidance*, 2d ed. (New York: CCH, Inc., 1996), §48.

62. Michael J. Saks, "Do We Really Know Anything about the Behavior of the Tort Litigation System: And Why Not?" *University of Pennsylvania Law Review* 140 (1992): 1147, 1254.

63. In contrast to the studies produced for litigation, the research reported in this section has all been peer reviewed and published in social science journals or law reviews. See Michael L. Rustad "Unraveling Punitive Damages: Current Data and Further Inquiry," *Wisconsin Law Review* (1998): 15, for a comprehensive analysis of the nine empirical studies of punitive damages. The leading empirical studies are: Mark Peterson et al., *Punitive Damages: Empirical Findings* (Santa Monica, Calif.: Rand Institute for Civil Justice, 1987) (R-3311-Icj) (Rand I); Stephen Daniels and Joanne Martin, "Myth and Reality in Punitive Damages," *Minnesota Law Review* 75 (1990): 1 (ABF I); U.S. General Accounting Office, Report to the Chairman, Subcommittee on Commerce, Consumer Protection, and Competitiveness, Committee On Energy and Commerce, House of Representatives, *Product Liability: Verdicts and Case Resolution in Five States*, GAO/HRD 89-99 (Washington, D.C.: U.S. Government Accounting Office, 1989): 2–3 (GAO) (finding twenty-three punitive awards in products cases in Arizona, Massachusetts, Missouri, North Dakota, and South Carolina between 1982 and 1985); Landes and Posner, *The Economic Structure of Tort Law*; William M. Landes and Richard A. Posner, "New Light on Punitive Damages," *Regulation* (September–October 1986): 33 (Landes and Posner); Michael Rustad, "In Defense of Punitive Damages in Products Liability: Testing Tort Anecdotes with Empirical Data," *Iowa Law Review* 78 (1992): 1 (reporting findings from nationwide study of punitive damages in products liability) (Rustad and Koenig I); Michael Rustad and Thomas Koenig, "Reconceptualizing Punitive Damages in Medical Malpractice: Targeting Amoral Corporations, Not 'Moral Monsters,'" *Rutgers Law Review* 47 (1995): 495 (reporting results of a nationwide study of punitive damages in medical malpractice) (Rustad and Koenig II); Carol DeFrances et al., U.S. Dept. of Justice, *Civil Jury Cases and Verdicts in Large Counties* (Washington, D.C.: Department of Justice, 1995); Theodore Eisenberg et al., "The Predictability of Punitive Damages," 26 *Journal of Legal Studies* 623 (1997) (Department of Justice Study); Deborah Hensler and Erik Moller, *Trends in Punitive Damages: Preliminary Data from Cook County, Illinois and San Francisco, California* (Santa Monica, Calif.: Rand Institute for Civil Justice, 1995) (DRU-1014-ICJ) (presenting

preliminary updated findings on punitive damages awards, 1960–94); Erik Moller, Institute for Civil Justice (RAND), *Trends in Civil Jury Verdicts since 1985* (Santa Monica, Calif.: Rand Institute for Civil Justice, 1996); Erik Moller, Institute for Civil Justice (Rand), *Trends in Punitive Damages: Preliminary Data from California* (Santa Monica, Calif.: Rand Institute for Civil Justice, 1995) (DRU-1059-ICJ) (presenting patterns of punitive damages in California for 1960–94) (cited hereafter as Rand II); Stephen Daniels and Joanne Martin, *Civil Juries and the Politics of Reform* (Evanston, Ill.: Northwestern University Press, 1995) (ABF II).

64. Daniels and Martin, *Civil Juries and the Politics of Reform.*
65. Id. at 220–21.
66. DeFrances et al., *Civil Jury Cases and Verdicts in Large Counties.*
67. Id. at 1.
68. Id.
69. Id.
70. Id. at 6.
71. See Rand II, 11, table 2.4.
72. See id. at 11–13.
73. See id. at 11, table 2.4.
74. See id.
75. See id. at ix.
76. See id.
77. See Moller, *Trends in Civil Jury Verdicts*, 34.
78. Id.
79. Daniels and Martin, *Civil Juries and the Politics of Reform*, 38–39.
80. Punitive damages in securities arbitration have been on the rise. An industry task force recommended capping punitive damages awards in the arbitration of securities disputes, concluding that "often the mere threat of punitive damages encourages brokerage firms to negotiate settlements with investors." James J. Eccleston, "Task Force Urges Rules Overhaul for Securities Arbitration Cases," *Chicago Daily Law Bulletin* (April 22, 1996): 6.
81. See, e.g., "Top 50 Awards of 1994," *Inside Litigation* (March 1995): 8.
82. See *Schoen v. Schoen*, No. CV 88-20139 (Maricopa County Sup. Ct., Ariz. October 7, 1994) (LEXIS, Verdict Library, ALLVER File).
83. See *Remington Rand Corp. v. Amsterdam-Rotterdam Bank*, No. 87 Civ. 8288 (S.D.N.Y. April 13, 1994) (LEXIS, Verdict Library, ALLVER File).
84. See *Dominguez Energy L.P. v. Shell Oil Co.*, Nos. C736 891, BC030 746 (L.A. County Sup. Ct., Cal. January 31, 1994) (LEXIS, Verdict Library, ALLVER File).
85. See *Alpex Computer Corp. v. Nintendo Co.*, No. 86 Civ. 1749 (S.D.N.Y. August 1, 1994) (LEXIS, Verdict Library, ALLVER File); *Electronics Co. v. Microsoft Corp.*, No. CV 93-413-ER (C.D. Cal. February 23, 1994) (LEXIS, Verdict Library,

ALLVER File) (awarding $120 million in punitive damages arising out of patent infringement).

86. See, e.g., *Babson Bros. Co. v. Sigafoose*, 596 So. 2d 56 (Ala. 1989) (LEXIS, Verdict Library, ALLVER File) (upholding $10 million punitive damages award in fraud case*)*; *In re American Continental Corp., Lincoln Sav. and Loan Sec. Litig.*, MDL Docket No. 834 (D. Ariz. 1992) (LEXIS, Verdict Library, ALLVER File) (reducing jury award from $3.3 billion to $1.75 billion in case arising out of fraud in connection with Lincoln Savings and Loan Association); *Estate of Technical Equities Corp. v. Harry Stern*, No. SM326672 (Sup. Ct., Santa Clara County, Cal. October 20, 1992) (LEXIS, Verdict Library ALLVER File) (awarding $122 million against chief executive officer of company that engaged in Ponzi scheme defrauding investors of $150 million; settlements from KMG Main Hurdman, $9 million); *Amoco Chem. Co. v. Certain Underwriters of Lloyd's of London*, No. BC030 755 (Civil West L.A., Cal. December 7, 1993) (LEXIS, Verdict Library, ALLVER File) (awarding $386,433,000 punitive and $39,243,300 compensatory damages for failure to defend products liability suit); *Riddle v. Southmark Corp.*, No. 518768 (San Diego County Ct., Cal. September 6, 1988) (LEXIS, Verdict Library, ALLVER File) (Remitting $85 million punitive damages award to $22.7 million in fraud case); *John Does v. Technical Equities*, No. 600306 (Santa Clara, Cal. June 29, 1988) (LEXIS, Verdict Library, ALLVER File) (awarding $147 million in case involving Technical Equities); *Garth G. Conlan and Lighting Farms v. Wells Fargo Bank*, N.A., No. 82852, (Monterrey County, Cal. June 10, 1987) (LEXIS, Verdict Library, ALLVER File) (awarding $50 million punitive damages in lender liability action); *Hedrick v. Sentry Ins. Co.*, No. 96-128100-90 (Dist. Ct. Tarrant Co., Tex. December 10, 1993) (LEXIS, Verdict Library, ALLVER File) (awarding $2,170,000 in actual damages and $100 million in punitive damages in bad-faith insurance case; case subsequently settled for a confidential sum); *Janacek v. Triton Energy Corp.*, No. 90-07220-M (Dist. Ct. Dallas County, Tex. May 21, 1992) (LEXIS, Verdict Library, ALLVER File) (awarding $80 million in punitive damages for wrongful termination: Ticor Title Insurance Co., $7.5 million; Security Pacific National Bank, $4.5 million; Bear Stearns and Co., $8 million; miscellaneous other defendants, $3 million).

87. Rick Bragg and Sarah Kershaw, "Juror Says a 'Sense of Mission' Led to Huge Tobacco Damages," *New York Times* (July 16, 2000): 1.

88. See *In re the Exxon Valdez*, No. A89-095-CV (D. Alaska September 16, 1994) (LEXIS, Verdict Library, ALLVER File).

89. *Anderson v. General Motors*, No. BC 116-926 (Cal. Super. Ct., July 9, 1999) (jury award of $107 million compensatory damages and $4.8 billion dollars punitive damages in case where plaintiff was severely burned by exploding gas tank). The trial judge reduced the punitive damages portion of the award to $1.2 billion. Bob Van Voris, "$145 Billion to Send a Message," *National Law Journal* (July 31, 2000): 1.

90. 481 U.S. 1, 4 (1987).

91. Rustad, "In Defense of Punitive Damages in Products Liability," 1.

92. See DeFrances et al., *Civil Jury Cases and Verdicts in Large Counties*, 14, table 3.

93. See Edward A. Dauer, "Future of the Legal Profession Lies in Utilizing Preventive Law," *Preventive Law Reporter* (March 1990): 20.

94. Oliver Wendell Holmes, Jr., "The Path of the Law," in *Collected Legal Papers* (1921; reprint, Holmes Beach, Fla.: Gaunt, 1998), 167, 187.

95. Thomas F. Lambert, Jr., "Suing for Safety," *Trial* (November 1983): 48.

96. Violation of a safety standard is frequently considered to create a presumption of negligence.

97. No. 83-38-COL (M.D. Ga. November 21, 1983).

98. Opening Statement of Neal Pope, Plaintiff's Counsel in *Borom v. Eli Lilly*, No. 83-38-Col. (M.D. Ga. November 21, 1983).

99. *Bhagvandoss v. Beirsdorf, Inc.*, 723 S.W.2d 392 (Mo. 1987) (reversing punitive damages on the grounds that the plaintiff did not prove defendant's state of mind).

100. 551 P.2d 234 (Nev. 1976).

101. Id.

102. Id.

103. *Castro v. Arkansas-Louisiana Gas Co.*, 562 F.2d 622 (10th Cir. 1977).

104. Telephone Interview with Robert Buck, Plaintiff's Counsel in *Castro v. Arkansas-Louisiana Gas Co.*, 562 F.2d 622 (10th Cir. 1977).

105. Id.

106. *Blossman Gas Co. v. Williams*, 375 S.E.2d 117, 119 (Ga. Ct. App. 1988).

107. No. 81-126332 (Ill. Cir. Ct. May 8, 1987).

108. 424 N.E.2d 568 (Ohio 1981).

109. Id. at 572.

110. Id. at 573.

111. Id. at 580.

112. Id.

113. Pretrial Order in *Achord v. Momar, Inc.*, No. 87-D-824-N (M.D. Ala. 1988) (provided authors by Plaintiff's Counsel, Gresham Sykes).

114. *Gillham v. Admiral Corp.*, 523 F.2d 102 (6th Cir. 1975).

115. Id. at 105.

116. Id. at 107.

117. This is a case of a company violating several commandments of public safety. Admiral also violated the Ninth Commandment of failing to warn consumers of a known danger as well as covering up the problem.

118. Interview with Victor Bergman, Plaintiff's Counsel in *Johnson v. Colt Indus. Operating Corp.*, 797 F.2d 1530 (10th Cir. 1986).

119. 464 A.2d 887 (Del. 1983).

120. Questionnaire of Alan Schwartz, Plaintiff's Counsel in *Cloroben Chemical Corp. v. Comegys*, 464 A.2d 887 (Del. 1983).

121. Id.

122. See, e.g., *Moore v. Jewel Tea Co.*, 253 N.E.2d 636, 648–49 (Ill. App. Ct. 1969).

123. This is a paraphrase of Professor Thomas F. Lambert, Jr.'s dictum on the preventive law underlying the law of torts.

124. Anne Saker, "Child Hurt in Drain Accident Talks to Court," *(Raleigh, N.C.) News and Observer* (December 14, 1996): B1.

125. Anne Saker, "Company Papers Reveal 13 Accidents Like Cary Girl's," *(Raleigh, N.C.) News and Observer* (December 11, 1996): B3. See also Brooks Egerton, "Experts Warn of Dangers with Pool, Hot Tub Drains," *Dallas Morning News* (January 27, 1997): 1.

126. Id.

127. Id.

128. Id.

129. Questionnaire of Andrea Curcio, one of the Plaintiff's Counsel in *Lakey v. Sta-Rite*.

130. "Settlements Reached before Trial, Lakey v. Sta-Rite Industries," *National Law Journal* (February 23, 1998): C14.

131. Questionnaire of Andrea Curcio, one of the Plaintiff's Counsel in *Lakey v. Sta-Rite*.

132. Anne Saker, "Girl Adapts to Life since Drain Accident, Verdict," *News and Observer (Raleigh)* (May 27, 1997): B3.

133. Questionnaire of Andrea Curcio, one of the Plaintiff's Counsel in *Lakey v. Sta-Rite*.

134. No. A-80, CA-214 (W.D. Tex., December 1981).

135. 786 F.2d 859 (8th Cir. 1986).

136. Questionnaire of Plaintiff's Counsel in *Mulligan v. Lederle Lab.*, 786 F.2d 859 (8th Cir. 1986).

137. 309 S.E.2d 295 (S.C. Ct. App. 1983).

138. Id. at 298–99.

139. Plaintiff's Counsel Questionnaire sent to Michael Rustad (name and case to be kept confidential).

140. 276 Ark. 486, 638 S.W.2d 660 (1982).

141. Id. at 661.

142. This account is based in part upon a telephone interview with Bernard Whetstone, Plaintiff's Counsel in *Airco v. Simmon First National Bank*, 638 S.W.2d 660 (Sup. Ct. Ark. 1982).

143. Id. at 661.

144. No. D870562-C (Tex. Dist. Ct. January 12, 1990).

145. See *Acosta v. Honda Motor Co.*, 717 F.2d 828, 837 (3rd Cir. 1983).

146. National Safety Council, *Accident Facts* (Itasca, Ill.: National Safety Council, 1998), 78.

147. 714 S.W.2d 329 (Texas Ct. of Appeals 1985).

148. This account is based upon an interview and pleadings filed by David Perry, Plaintiff's Counsel in *Durrill v. Ford Motor Co.*, 714 S.W.2d 2d 329 (Tex. App. 1986).

149. *Nowak v. Ford Motor Co.*, 638 S.W.2d 583 (Tex. Ct. App. 1982).

150. Id. at 593.

151. Id. at 594.

152. Id. See also *Ford Motor Co. v. Bartholomew*, 297 S.E.2d 675, 680 (Va. 1982) (upholding compensatory damages based upon allegation that the Ford transmission had a park-to-reverse defect).

153. No. 23033 (Dist. Ct. Minn., January 11, 1982).

154. *Durallee Estates v. Cities Services Oil Co.*, 569 F.2d 716, 723 (2d Cir. 1977).

155. See, e.g., *Schwartz v. Sears, Roebuck and Co.*, 669 F.2d 1091 (5th Cir. 1982).

156. 726 F.2d 657 (10th Cir. 1984).

157. Id. at 658–59.

158. Questionnaire of John Maum, Plaintiff's Counsel in *Saupitty v. Yazoo Manufacturer Co.*, 726 F.2d 657 (10th Cir. 1984).

159. See also *Keller v. Yazoo Manufacturing, Inc.*, No. 494-932, (Milwaukee Cty. Cir. Ct. (Wis.) August 3, 1981) (awarding punitive damages to a school custodian suffering an amputation injury when the tractor bucked him off the machine after an accidental shift).

160. No. 80-10858 (D. Me. April 1984).

161. *Rosendin v. Avco-Lycoming*, ATLA News 15 (1973): 103.

162. Id.

163. No. C-2853-85 (Tex. Dist. Ct. February 17, 1988).

164. A growing number of states—including Michigan, Missouri, New Jersey, Ohio, and Oregon—are enacting state-of-the-art defenses as either a complete or partial affirmative defense to products liability. American Tort Reform Association, *Product Liability Reform* (June 2000). Iowa established a complete defense in products liability actions where the defendant manufacturer complied with state-of-the art. Id. Missouri, too, recognizes state-of-the-art as a complete affirmative defense. Id. New Jersey's reform statute establishes a rebuttable presumption that a government (FDA) warning is adequate. Id. New Jersey also immunizes manufacturers from punitive damages if their "drugs, devices, food and food additives" received FDA approval and there was no misrepresentation or withholding of material information. Id.

165. *Restatement (Second) of Torts*, §295a cmt. c (1965).

166. 464 U.S. 238 (1984).

167. *Silkwood v. Kerr-McGee*, 485 F. Supp. 566, 576 (W.D. Okla. 1979).

168. Id. at 578.

169. Id.

170. Plaintiff's Exhibit No. 28.

171. Id. at 1055–58.

172. *Silkwood v. Kerr-McGee*, 585 F. Supp. 566, 570 n.1 (W.D. Okla. 1979).

173. Transcript at 7563-65, II J.A. 384; III J.A. 1494; II J.A. 377–79.

174. App. at 75a–75b.

175. 465 U.S. 1074 (1984).

176. *Silkwood v. Kerr-McGee Corp.*, 769 F.2d 1451 (10th Cir. 1985).

177. The case also illustrates the courage that a private attorney general requires to prosecute a corporate giant. Kerr-McGee attacked Karen Silkwood's character, including her "sexual involvements, use of drugs, and purported suicide attempts," in defending the plutonium contamination case brought by her estate. *Silkwood v. Kerr-McGee*, 485 F. Supp. 566 (W.D. Okla. 1979).

178. 821 F.2d 1438, 1445 (10th Cir. 1987).

179. Id. at 1447.

180. *O'Gilvie v. International Playtex, Inc.*, 821 F.2d 1438, 1446 n. 6 (10th Cir. 1987).

181. Id. at 1040–41, 1447–50.

182. 655 F.2d 650, 652 (5th Cir. Unit B, September 1981).

183. Id. at 653.

184. Id. at 654.

185. Id. at 657.

186. Id. at 656.

187. 528 A.2d 590 (Pa. 1987) (Larsen, J., concurring).

188. Id. at 612.

189. 297 N.W.2d 727 (Minn.), *cert. denied*, 449 U.S. 921 (1980).

190. Id. at 734.

191. Id.

192. *National Association of Manufacturers v. Occupational Safety and Health Administration*, 976 F.2d 749 (D. D.C. Cir. 1992).

193. See Marianne M. Jennings, "Perils of Business Practice: Here Are 10 Preventive Strategies to Resolve Disputes, Avoid Litigation," *Preventive Law Reporter* (September 1991): 8.

194. Telephone interview with Larry Rogers, Plaintiff's Counsel in *Duddleston v. Syntex Labs, Inc.*, No. 80-L-57726 (Ill. Cir. Ct. February 28, 1985).

195. *Duddleston v. Syntex Labs, Inc.*, No. 80-L-57726 (Ill. Cir. Ct. February 28, 1985).

196. Id.

197. Interview with John Hayes, Plaintiff's Counsel in *Duddleston and Sheridan v. Syntex Labs, Inc.*, No. 80-L-57726 (Cir. Ct. Ill. February 28, 1985).

198. 526 N.E.2d 428 (Ill. App. Ct. 1988).

199. Id. at 446–47.

200. Id. at 440.

201. No. 82-9 (E.D. Ky. December 19, 1985).

202. Id.

203. Letter from Peter Perlman, Plaintiff's Counsel in *Shackleford v. Joy Manufacturing Co.*, No. 82-9 (E.D. Ky. December 19, 1985).

204. 674 S.W.2d 413 (Tex. Ct. App. 1984).

205. Id. at 417.

206. *Bassin v. National Presto Industries, Inc.*, No. 6773/72 (N.Y. County Sup. Ct. 1975).

207. Telephone interview with August De Fillipo, Plaintiff's Counsel in *Bassin v. National Presto Indus., Inc.*, No. 6773/72 (N.Y. County Superior Court 1975).

208. *Jones v. Lederle Laboratories*, 695 F. Supp. 700 (E.D. N.Y. 1998).

209. *Gearhart v. Uniden Corp.*, 781 F.2d 147 (8th Cir. 1986) (reversing punitive damages).

210. The Sixth Circuit reversed the punitive damages verdict, finding that the warning label evidenced at least some concern on the part of the manufacturer, even though it was inadequate to communicate the danger of the radius of the risk. *Johnson v. Husky Industries, Inc.*, 536 F.2d 645 (6th Cir. 1976) (reversing punitive damages).

211. No. 88-CIV-232 (Jefferson County (Ohio) Court of Common Pleas, 1989).

212. John D. Ingram, "Insurance Coverage Problems in Latent Disease and Injury Cases," *Environmental Law Review* 12 (1982): 317, 333.

213. *Jenkins v. Raymark Indus., Inc.*, 782 F.2d 468, 470 (5th Cir. 1986) (citing Richard A. Seltzer, "Punitive Damages in Mass Tort Litigation: Addressing the Problems of Fairness, Efficiency and Control," *Fordham Law Review* 52 (1983): 37, 37 n. 1.

214. *Borel v. Fibreboard*, 493 F.2d 1076 (5th Cir. 1973).

215. Id.

216. 641 F. Supp. 1429 (D. Kan. 1986), rev'd, 861 F.2d 1453 (10th Cir. 1988).

217. Questionnaire of Paul H. Hulsey, Plaintiff's Counsel in *Menne v. Celotex Corp.*, 641 F. Supp. 1429 (D. Kan. 1986), rev'd 861 F.2d 1453 (10th Cir. 1988).

218. Id.

219. 479 F.2d 1089, 1096-97 (5th Cir. 1973).

220. 948 F.2d 1546, 1561 (10th Cir. 1991) (applying Kansas law and remitting punitive damages award from $25 million to $12.5 million).

221. No. 44359 (Harris Cty., Tex., December 13, 1989).

222. *Rinker v. Ford Motor Co.*, 567 S.W.2d 655 (Mo. Ct. Of App. 1978).

223. Id. at 658.

224. No. 330,209 (Travis Cty. (Tx.) 167th Jud. Dist. Ct., June 15, 1984).

225. Questionnaire of Tom Harkness, Plaintiff's Counsel in *Davis v. Veslan Enters.*, No. 330,209 (Travis Cty. (Tx.) 167th Jud. Dist. Ct., June 15, 1984).

226. Id.

227. *Petrus Chrysler-Plymouth v. Davis*, 671 S.W.2d 749 (Ark. 1984).

228. Questionnaire of Charles Karr, Plaintiff's Counsel in *Petrus Chrysler, Inc. v. Davis*, 671 S.W.2d 749 (Ark. 1984).

229. Id.

230. 592 So.2d 1054, 1061 (Ala. 1992).

231. Id. at 1061.

232. 602 P.2d 1326 (Kan. 1979).

233. 466 N.E.2d 1191 (Ill. App. Ct. 1984).

234. Id.

235. Davis S. Poole and Marc D. Machlin, "Environmental Compliance Audits: Preventive Medicine for Compliance Litigation?" *Preventive Law Reporter* (Winter 1993): 5.

236. Id.

237. Id.

238. Telephone interview with David Perry, Plaintiff's Counsel in *Ford Motor Co. v. Durrill*, 714 S.W.2d 329 (Tex. Ct. App. 1986).

NOTES TO CHAPTER 6

1. Michael Rustad and Thomas Koenig, "The Historical Continuity of Punitive Damage Awards: Reforming the Tort Reformers," *American University Law Review* 42 (1993): 1269, 1330.

2. Marshall S. Shapo, A.B.A. Special Committee on the Tort Liability System, *Towards a Jurisprudence of Injury* (Chicago: American Bar Association, 1984), 3 (tracing concept of tort law as grievance mechanism to the work of Roscoe Pound, who showed that "ancient tort-like rules served as grievance mechanisms" for the protection of the group).

3. Thomas F. Lambert, Jr., "Tort Law—Seeing the '70's: Anticipations in Automobiles Law in the '70's," *American Trial Lawyers Journal* 34 (1972): 60.

4. By interstitial legislation, Professor Kalven meant harmful acts not typically prosecuted on the criminal side of the law, but punished by tort sanctions. See Harry Kalven, "Tort Watch," 1 *American Trial Lawyer Journal* 59 (1972) (coining the term "interstitial legislation").

5. Chris Sieroty, "HMOs Facing Suits, Attorney Claims 'Pattern of Pain' Exists," *Daily News of Los Angeles* (November 24, 1999): B1.

6. "Class Action Filed against Aetna Alleges RICO, ERISA Violations," *Mealey's Litigation Report: Managed Care Liability* (October 13, 1999).

7. "Delays in Payments to Doctors Prompt Class Action Against HMO," *New Jersey Law Journal* 158 (October 4, 1999): 1.

8. Kathy L. Ceminara, "The Class Action Suit as a Method of Patient Empowerment in the Managed Care Setting," *American Journal of Law and Medicine* 24 (1998): 7.

9. Mark Curriden, "Lawyers Inundated with Calls to Sue Hospital," *Atlanta Constitution* (August 26, 1991): C2 (quoting Professor Richard Epstein of the University of Chicago).

10. Greg Groeller, "Nursing-Home Lawsuits Face Limits in Plan by Governor Bush," *Sun Sentinel* (January 10, 2001): 1.

11. Stephen Clare, "Pro Bono," *American Lawyer* (September 1996): 111.

12. David B. Wilkins, "Race, Ethics, and the First Amendment: Should a Black Lawyer Represent the Ku Klux Klan?" *George Washington University Law Review* 63 (1995): 1030, 1051 n. 107 (discussing lawsuit).

13. John Cloud, "Is Hate on the Rise? Racist Groups May Not Be Growing, But They're Finding Deadlier Recruits," *Time* (July 19, 1999): 33.

14. Bill Morlin, "Judge Refuses Butler Request for New Trial; Jury's $6.3 Million Judgment against Aryan Nations Stands," *(Spokane, Wash.) Spokesman-Review* (October 27, 2000): B1.

15. Id.

16. Bill Morlin, "Butler Withdraws His Appeal; Action Kept Sheriff from Beginning to Seize Property," *(Spokane, Wash.) Spokesman-Review* (October 5, 2000): 5.

17. See *Hilao v. Estate of Marcos*, 103 F.3d 767, 787 (9th Cir. 1996) (upholding punitive damages against the estate of Marcos).

18. See *Abebej-Jira v. Negewo*, 72 F.3d 844, 845 (11th Cir. 1996) (upholding $300,000 punitive damages award for each plaintiff).

19. See B. Drummond Ayres, Jr., "Jury Decides Simpson Must Pay $25 Million in Puniti Award," *New York Times* (February 11, 1997): A1, 12.

20. Gary T. Schwartz, "Tobacco Liability and Viscusi," 29 *Cumberland Law Review* (1999): 555.

21. Rick Bragg and Sarah Kershaw, "Juror Says a 'Sense of Mission' Led to Huge Tobacco Damages," *New York Times* (July 16, 2000): 1.

22. Shannon P. Duffy, "Fen-Phen Cases Settle for $3.75 Billion: Federal Judge's 163-page Opinion Says Settlement Passes Muster," *Pennsylvania Law Weekly* (September 4, 2000): 10 (reporting court's acceptance of settlement in *In re Diet Drugs*, PICS Case No. 1739 (E.D. Pa. August, 28, 2000)).

23. Deborah Hensler et al., *Class Action Dilemma: Pursuing Public Goals for Private Gain* (Santa Monica, Calif.: Rand Institute for Civil Justice, 1999) (noting the recent expansion of the use of class actions in mass torts field).

24. Fed. R. Civ. P. 23(a)(1)(b)(3) (explaining how actions may be brought by one or more representative plaintiffs on behalf of a larger class of persons).

25. See, generally, Bruce Hay and David Rosenberg, "'Sweetheart' and 'Blackmail': Settlements in Class Actions: Reality and Remedy," *Notre Dame Law Review*

75 (2000): 1377; John Coffee, "Class Wars: The Dilemma of the Mass Tort Class Action," *Columbia Law Review* 95 (1995): 1343.

26. *Amchem Prods., Inc. v. Windsor*, 117 S. Ct. 2231, 2246 (1997) (quoting Suffolk University Law Professor Benjamin Kaplan).

27. Richard H. Middleton, Jr., "Save Class Actions; Drop the Coupon Scams" (visited December 6, 1999) <http://www.atlanet.org/homepage/classact.ht>.

28. "Nissan Van Owners Lose Out," *Congressional Record* 140 (March 11, 1994) (statement of Rep. Helen Delich Bentley [R-Mich.]).

29. Ruth Gastel, "The Liability System," *Illinois Insurance Issues Update* (October 1999): 1.

30. *Floyd v. Thompson*, 227 F.3d 1029, 1030 (7th Circuit 2000) (discussing $5.9 billion to be paid to Wisconsin under the Master Settlement Agreement).

31. Gastel, "The Liability System," 1.

32. See, e.g., *Camden County Board v. Beretta U.S.A.*, 123 F. Supp. 2N 245 (N.J. 2000).

33. Gastel, "The Liability System," 1.

34. John Helyar, "They're Ba-a-ack!" *Fortune* (June 26, 2000): 222.

35. Id.

36. Harvey Berkman, "Tort Reform Measure, Facing Stiff Opposition, Unlikely to Become Law," *National Law Journal* (October 4, 1999): A5.

37. See H.R. 1875, "The Interstate Class Action Jurisdiction Act" (1999) (passed by House of Representatives). See also Gastel, "The Liability System" (noting that S. 53 is moving through the legislative process in the Senate).

38. Ruth Gastel, "The Liability System," *Illinois Insurance Issues Update* (June 2000).

39. Amy Collins, "Tobacco Stocks Trampled after Rulings," *Reuters* (March 31, 1999).

40. "Sealed Court Records Kept Tire Problems Hidden," *USA Today* (September 19, 2000): 16A.

41. Id.

42. Id.

43. This account of the water slides is found at Public Citizen's website (visited December 17, 1998), <http://www.citizen/org/orgs/public_citizen/congress/civjus/product/hazards_of_secrecy.tm>.

44. *Spivey v. Kubota Tractor Corp.*, No. CV-92-101 (Greene Cty., Ala., February 1993).

45. *Nunnallee v. Sheller-Globe Corp.*, No. 88-CI-099 (Carroll County Ct., Ky., 1988).

46. *Campus Sweater & Sportswear Co. v. M. B. Kahn Constr. Co.*, 515 F. Supp. 64, 107 (D.S.C. 1979), aff.d by 644 F.2d 877 (4th Cir. 1981).

47. See *Stevens v. Humana, Inc.*, No. 88CV1651 Div. 4 (Colo. Dist. Ct. Arapahoe County, March 21, 1990); see also Michael Rustad, "Nationalizing Tort Law:

The Republican Attack on Women, Blue Collar Workers, and Consumers," *Rutgers Law Review* 48 (1996): 673, 751 (reporting numerous examples of brain-damage cases in which awards were reduced arbitrarily by tort reform caps).

48. During the late nineteenth century, corporations successfully argued that they were protected by the Fourteenth Amendment. "In the *Minnesota Rate Case* of 1889, the U.S. Supreme Court agreed that the action of a state legislature to reduce rail rates constituted a deprivation of property without due process. That broke the dam. During the next three decades, the Fourteenth Amendment was used nearly 800 times to protect corporations against hamstringing legislation." Robert G. Athearn, *Age of Steel*, vol. 10 of *The American Heritage's Illustrated History of the United States* (New York: Dell, 1963), 27. The corporate lawyers convinced the Court to treat an entity as the functional equivalent of a person. It was one of the Reconstruction Era amendments, and most people assumed that the "person" referred to was the American Negro. Id.

49. 499 U.S. 1 (1991).

50. Id. at 55.

51. Id. at 23–24.

52. 509 U.S. 443, 460 (1993).

53. 517 U.S. 559 (1995).

54. William L. Prosser, *Handbook of the Law of Torts*, 5th ed. (St. Paul, Minn.: West Publishing Co., 1971), 23.

55. See Margaret J. Radin, "Compensation and Commensurability," *Duke Law Journal* 43 (1993): 56 (highlighting the common complaint that tort damages are uncertain).

56. Justice Felix Frankfurter stated in *McNabb v. United States*, 318 U.S. 332, 347 (1943) that "[t]he history of liberty has largely been the history of observance of procedural safeguards."

57. The use of wealth in assessing punitive damages has been a key factor in several recent U.S. Supreme Court cases reviewing the constitutionality of punitive damages awards. In *Haslip v. Pacific Mutual Insurance Co.*, 499 U.S. 1, 23–24 (1991), the Court affirmed a punitive damages award with a ratio of greater than four times actual damages but observed that the high ratio was close to the line of constitutional impropriety. In *TXO Production Corp. v. Alliance Resource Corp.*, 509 U.S. 443, 460 (1996), the Court acknowledged that one of the key factors in determining whether a given punitive damages award violated due process was whether there was an unreasonable relationship between punitive damages and compensatory damages. In *BMW of N. Am. v. Gore*, 517 U.S. 559 (1995), the Court struck down a punitive damages award with a 500-to-1 ratio. Many courts have found punitive damages to be exceed the constitutional maximum after *BMW v. N. Am. v. Gore*. See, e.g., *Watkins v. Lundell*, 169 F.3d 540 (8th Cir. 1999) (holding that a district court abused its discretion in not reducing a punitive damages award because the award was exaggerated as compared to the harm in-

flicted, the defendant's wealth, and the reprehensibility of his conduct); *Johansen v. Combustion Eng'g, Inc.*, 170 F.3d 1320 (11th Cir. 1999) (upholding reduction of punitive damages award in favor of plaintiff to the constitutional maximum and ruling that it did not invade the province of the jury). The Supreme Court has recently granted a *writ of certiorari* limited to the question: "What is the standard of review of a trial court's ruling on a challenge to the constitutionality of a punitive damages award?" *Cooper Industries v. Leatherman Tool Group, Inc.*, 2000 U.S. LEXIS 6599 (U.S. Supreme Court, Oct. 10, 2000) (granting petition for a *writ of certiorari* to the U.S. Court of Appeals in No. 99-2035). In that case, Leatherman Tool Group was assessed a punitive damages award ninety times compensatory damages in a trade dress infringement lawsuit. The defendant argues that the *de novo* standard of review should apply rather than the abuse of discretion standard. The abuse of discretion standard makes it more difficult to overturn punitive damages, whereas the *de novo* standard gives no deference to the trial court's decision to uphold punitive damages.

58. James Ghiardi and John Kirchner, *Punitive Damages: Law and Practice*, §5.36 at 47-57 (Boston: Callahan, 1985), §5.36 at 47–57 (1994 update).

59. 158 N.Y. 73, 52 N.E. at 679 (1899).

60. Id. at 690.

61. U.S. Sentencing Commission, *Sentencing Guidelines Manual* (Washington D.C.: U.S. Sentencing Commission, 1993).

62. *McNamara v. King*, Ill. (2 Gil.) 432 (Ill. App. 1845) (upholding punitive damages).

63. A few states have enacted tort reforms that prohibit the introduction of the defendant's wealth in setting the level of punitive damages.

64. For example, Clarence Darrow stated, "I speak for the poor, for the weary, for that long line of men who, in darkness and despair, have borne the labors of the human race." *Central of G. R. Co. v. Cole*, 191 Ga. App. 53, 381 S.E.2d 60 (1889). The plaintiff's counsel in another railroad case argued that the millionaire defendant was oppressing the people and should be punished. *Louisville and N. R. Co. v. Crow*, 107 S.W. 807 (Ky. 1907). Similarly, a trial lawyer told a jury that he made his living "'practicing law for the naked and sick and blind in the rain and the cold,'" quoting at length from Masefield's "Consecration." *Maryland Casualty Co. v. Abbott*, 148 S.W.2.d 465 (1941, Tex. Civ. App.) (holding reference to the wealth of the defendant was an improper appeal to jury's emotions).

65. As the New Hampshire Supreme Court ruled in 1870: "When exemplary or punitive damages are to be allowed, the condition and circumstances of the defendant are material, as what would be sufficient damages by way of example and to punish a day laborer would be nothing by way of punishment or example to a wealthy corporation." *Belknap v. Boston and Maine R.R. Co.*, 49 N.H. 358, 374 (1870). The Court stated in *Washington Gas Light and Company v. Lansden*, 172 U.S. 534 (1899) that a punitive damages "verdict [could be] enhanced by the evidence

of the wealth of one defendant, while a poorer co-defendant might be assessed a smaller punitive penalty." Id. at 552.

66. See, e.g., *Louisville and N.R. Co. v. Smith*, 27 Ky. 257, 84 S.W. 755 (1905) (describing railroad as a soulless corporation that made millions of dollars every day); *Missouri P. R. Co. v. Foreman*, 194 Ark 490, 107 S.W.2d 546 (1937) (reversing award where the trial attorney argued that recovery would not result in "a meal missed" by the owners of the defendant railroad); *Southern R. Co. v. Bulleit*, 40 Ind. App. 4547, 82 N.E. 474 (1907) (reversing $2,000 award because of improper statement that "defendant would make that much money in the time they were signing the verdict"). *Louisville and N.R. Co. v. Hull*, 113 Ky. 561, 68 S.W. 433 (1902) (reversing award because of improper comparison of the railroad's wealth to "Solomon's Temple"). Improper references to an individual defendant's wealth were also the basis for appeals. *Crabbe v. Rhoades*, 101 Cal. App. 503, 282 P. 10 (1929) (referring to defendant as "presumably wealthy"); *Handley v. Lombardi*, 122 Cal. App. 22, 9 P.2d 867 (1932) (characterizing the defendant as "this rich dairyman"); *Distin v. Bradley*, 83 Conn. 466, 76 A. 911 (1910) (referring to the defendant as a member of the top "Four Hundred" of fashionable society and noting that he would "stretch the truth like any other millionaire"); *Parsley v. Horn*, 210 Ky. 792, 276 S.W. 800 (1925) (appealing to the jury to "learn rich men" not to employ "our boys" in dangerous places).

67. *Honda Motor Co. v. Oberg*, 512 U.S. 414 (1996) (holding that a corporate defendant's due process rights were violated under Oregon law when there was no procedure for the post-verdict review of the size of punitive damage awards).

68. Id.

69. Gary T. Schwartz, "Deterrence and Punishment in the Common Law of Punitive Damages: A Comment," *Southern California Law Review* 56 (1982): 133, 140.

70. Professors Berle and Means described the growing societal power of America's largest corporations in their classic study of management control:

> One in which production is carried on under the ultimate control of a handful of individuals is replacing a society in which production is governed by blind economic forces. The economic power in the hands of the few persons who control a giant corporation is a tremendous force which can harm or benefit a multitude of individuals, affect whole districts, skirt the currents of trade, bring ruin to one community and prosperity to another. The organizations, which they control, have passed far beyond the realm of private enterprise—they have become more nearly social institutions.

Adolf A. Berle and Gardiner C. Means, *The Modern Corporation and Private Property* (1932; reprint, New Brunswick, N.J.: Transactions Books, 1991), 46.

71. *Louis K. Liggett Co. et al. v. Lee, Comptroller, et al.*, 288 U.S. 517, 565–566 (1933) (J. Brandeis).

72. *Goddard v. Grand Trunk Ry.*, 57 Me. 202, 222–24 (1869).

73. The Court in *TXO Production Corp. v. Alliance Resources Corp.*, 509 U.S. 443 (1993), set forth a number of factors that the jury may legitimately consider in determining whether a given punitive award is "reasonable." Id. at 457, 460–62. These factors include the wealth of the defendant; "potential harm" of the defendant's course of conduct; the degree of bad faith displayed by the defendant; and whether the conduct was part of a "larger pattern of fraud, trickery and deceit." Id. at 459–62 (citing *Pacific Mut. Life Ins. Co. v. Haslip*, 499 U.S. 1 (1991)).

74. Risks in manufacturing are optimally borne by the party in the best position to eliminate excessive preventable danger. Because manufacturers have far more knowledge about potential product dangers, they are in the position to "internalize" the costs of undertaking remedial measures. A company that knowingly permits consumers to face injury unnecessarily in order to save money is said to be "externalizing the risk" by shifting the costs outside of the company. See, generally, Guido Calabresi, "Some Thoughts on Risk Distribution and the Law of Torts," *Yale Law Journal* 70 (1961): 499, 499–534. (offering general analysis of corporate risk distribution).

75. *Goddard v. Grand Trunk Ry.*, 57 Me. 202, 224 (1869).

76. One opportunity for the U.S. Supreme Court to take wealth in creating a new suspect class was the case of *San Antonio School District v. Rodriquez*, 411 U.S. 1 (1973). The Court in *Rodriquez* held that wealth was not a suspect class in a case where a class action lawsuit was filed against school board authorities challenging disparities in per pupil expenditure. The Court rejected an opportunity to open the door to equal protection challenges based upon wealth-based discrimination. The Court has, however, been receptive to corporate defendants who argue against the use of wealth in assessing punitive damages. The capping of punitive damages is in effect a challenge upon wealth-based punishment.

77. Henry Hansmann and Reinier Kraakman, "Toward Unlimited Shareholder Liability for Corporate Torts," *Yale Law Journal* 100 (1991): 1879.

78. Thomas Lambert warned against "peer[ing] ahead into the mists of the 21st century . . . [because] not only is the future misty, but the present itself is also plenty murky." Thomas F. Lambert, Jr., "Law in the Future: Tort Law: 2003," *Trial* (July 1983): 93, 93.

79. Steve Lohr, "Study Ranks Software as Number 3 Industry," *New York Times* (June 3, 1997): D2 (citing study by Nathan Associates funded by the Business Software Alliance).

80. Letter from Mark E. Nebergill, vice president, Software Publishers Association to Carlyle C. Ring, Jr., chair of the Drafting Committee on Uniform Commercial Code; *Article 2B-Licenses* (November 15, 1996).

81. Neil Munro, "Cybercrime Treaty on Trial," *National Law Journal* (March 10, 2001): 1.

82. Letter from Mark E. Nebergill to Carlyle C. Ring, Jr.

83. *State of Washington v. Heckel*, No. 98-2-25480-7SEA (Wash. Super. Ct., King Cty., March 10, 2000).

84. *Ferguson v. Friendfinder, Inc.*, No. 307309 (Cal. Super. Ct. S.F. Cty. June 2, 2000).

85. Id (quoting computer forensics lab manager).

86. *Ex Parte Indiana Transport Co.*, 244 U.S. 456, 456 (1917) (J. Holmes dissenting).

87. *American Civil Liberties Union v. Reno*, 929 F. Supp. 825, 830–31 (E.D. Pa. 1996).

88. "Legislatures have now begun to deal with . . . stalking crimes which often result in serious bodily injury or death." Marshall S. Shapo, *Tort and Injury Law*, 2d ed. (New York: Matthew Bender, 2000), 22. Illinois defines stalking as at least two separate incidents in which a person is followed or placed under surveillance. Id (citing Il. St. ch. 720 §5/12-7.3).

89. The National Institute of Justice found 1.4 million American stalking victims every year. The Antistalking Web Site, "Stalkers and Stalking" (visited November 19, 2000), <http://www.antistalking.com/aboutstalkers.htm> (discussing National Institute of Justice study estimating that 8 percent of American women and 2 percent of American men would be victimized by stalking in their lifetime).

90. Id.

91. Id.

92. *Butler v. Continental Express, Inc.*, No. 96-1204091, *The Blue Sheet of Southeast Texas* (Montgomery County District Court, Texas, June 8, 1998).

93. 2000 WL 96789 (N.D. Ill., June 29, 2000).

94. *Acquinto v. Electriciti, Inc.*, *Media Law Reporter* (BNA) 26 (Cal. Super. Ct. 1997): 1032.

95. Department of Justice, *Report on Cyberstalking: A New Challenge for Law Enforcement and Industry* (Washington, D.C.: Department of Justice, August 1999): 5.

96. Id.

97. Katie Dean, "The Epidemic of Cyberstalking," *Wired News* (May 1, 2000): 1.

98. "E-Mail Stalker Sentencing Likely Will Influence Future Cases" (visited August 30, 2000), http://detnews.com/news.com/menu/storeis/4109.htm>.

99. See Stalking Prevention and Victim Protection Act of 1999 (introduced by U.S. Rep. Sue Kelly) (visited September 27, 2000), <http://www.house.gov/suekelly/pr-02999.htm>.

100. Deborah Radcliff, "A Case of Cyberstalking: Law Enforcement Agencies Appear Powerless to Stop Electronic Harassment," *Network World* (May 29, 2000): 56 (quoting head of New York City Police Department's computer crime unit).

101. Michael Dresser, "New Md. Law Will Ban Harassment by E-Mail," *Sunspot (Maryland) News* (visited June 18, 1999) <http://members.tripod.com/~cyberstalked/sunstory.html>.

102. *Hitchcock v. Woodside Literary Agency*, 15 F. Supp.2d 246 (E.D. N.Y. 1998).

103. Id.

104. See Dresser, "New Md. Law Will Ban Harassment by E-Mail."

105. Id.

106. Id.

107. Id.

108. Lawrence Lessig, *Code and Other Laws of Cyberspace* (Cambridge, Mass.: Harvard University Press, 1999).

109. 47 U.S.C. §230(c)(1)(2000).

110. *Zeran v. America Online, Inc.*, 129 F.3d 327 (4th Cir. 1997).

111. Cf. *Cubby, Inc. v. CompuServe, Inc.*, 776 F. Supp. 135 (S.D. N.Y. 1991) (Finding ISP to be a distributor, not a publisher); and *Stratton Oakmont, Inc. v. Prodigy Servs. Co.*, 1995 WL 323710 (N.Y. Sup. C&, May 24, 1995) (holding ISP to standard of a publisher).

112. Congress enacted another immunity when it passed the Digital Millennium Copyright Act (DMCA). The DMCA immunizes ISPs from copyright infringement claims where the content is produced by third parties. The statute's safe harbor provision, like the Good Samaritan rule of the Communications Decency Act, overruled earlier case law holding service providers liable copyright infringement. See Digital Millennium Copyright Act, 17 U.S.C. §512(c)(2)(2000).

113. Id.

114. 129 F.3d at 331.

115. Id.

116. 992 F. Supp. 44 (D.D.C. 1998).

117. *Blumenthal v. Drudge*, 992 F. Supp. 44 (D.D.C. 1998).

118. 718 So.2d 385 (Ct. of App., 4th Dist. 1998).

119. Id.

120. *Acquinto v. Electriciti, Inc.*

121. Grant P. Fondo and Robert Shore, "Public Property in Cyberspace," *Cyberspace Lawyer* 5 (June 2000): 2 (citing *Compaq Computer Corp. v. John Does* 1-4, No. CV785143 (Santa Clara Cty. Super., October 8, 1999)).

122. "Slander Suit Served against Yahoo! Users," *Reuters*, special to *CNET News.Com*, March 9, 1999 (visited June 18, 1999) <http://www.cnet.com>.

123. Margaret Cronin Fisk, "Anonymous Posting, Termed 'Despicable,' Nets $675,000 Award," *National Law Journal* (December 25, 2000): A19.

124. John N. Walker, "Can You Stop That Anonymous Spammer?" *Cyberspace Lawyer* 4 (May 1999): 6.

125. *Stoner v. E-Bay, Inc.*, No. 3056666 (Sup. Ct. Calif., November 7, 2000).

126. Jeffrey Ghannam, "Libel Online: Suit Raises Issue of Protection for Anonymous Web Comments," *ABA Journal* (March 2001): 28.

127. 2000 WL 816779 (N.D. Ill., June 2000) (dismissing claims on grounds of CDA immunity for website host).

128. Kevin Poulsen, "Federal Rejection," *Cybercrime News, ZDTV* (August 8, 1999) (visited August 16, 1999), <http://www.zdnet.com/zdtv/cbercrime/news/story/0,3700,2310198,00,html>.

129. John D. Benn, "Beyond the Quill: Big Brother Really Is Watching: Following Computers' Trails," *American Bar Journal* (June 1999): 15.

130. Amitai Etzioni, *The Limits of Privacy* (New York: Basic Books, 1998).

131. Nora Lockwood Tooher, "Couple Sues CVS for Breach of Privacy," *Providence Journal* (September 16, 2000): 1.

132. Michael Geist, "Accidental E-Mail Reveals 12,000 Patients' Health Info," *BNA's Internet Law News* (January 4, 2001): 1.

133. Cookie Central, *The Unofficial Cookie FAQ* (visited April 27, 1999), <http://www.cookiecentral.com>.

134. "Spam" is unsolicited e-mail sent to mailing lists on the Internet.

135. *O'Connor v. Ortega*, 480 U.S. 709 (1987).

136. Id. (citing the American Management Association study of large American companies).

137. *Smyth v. Pillsbury Co.*, 914 F. Supp. 97 (E.D. Pa. 1996).

138. *Bourke v. Nissan Motor Co.*, No. YC003979 (Cal. Sup. Ct., Los Angeles Cty., 1991) (upholding right of company's systems administrator to read employees' e-mail and to terminate employees based on the contents of e-mails that criticized supervisor); *Shoars v. Epson Am., Inc.*, No. YC003979 (Cal. Sup. Ct., Los Angeles Cty., 1989).

139. *Restuccia v. Burk Technology*, Civil Action No. 95-2125 (Mass. Super. Ct., Middlesex Cty., December 31, 1996).

140. Peter Kelman, "How to Control Employee Gossip in Web Chat Rooms," *Massachusetts High Technology* (October 25–31, 1999): 27 (noting that a company's proprietary information may be jeopardized by employees' posting statements in Web chat rooms).

141. *McClaren v. Microsoft*, No. 05-97-00824-CV (Ct. App., 5th Dist. Tex., May 28, 1999).

142. Maria Trombly, "*Dow to Fire up to 40 More Employees for E-Mail Abuse,*" *Computer World* (August 28, 2000): 28.

143. Id.

144. See, e.g., "Federal Agency Files Harassment Suit Against Texas-Based Company," *Houston Chronicle* (September 25, 1999): 1 (reporting EEOC investigation of a computer company for failing to prevent sexual harassment at a Texas store after notice from prior incidents of sexually oriented remarks).

145. "Nosy Bosses Face Limits on E-Mail Spying—Workers Gain New Freedoms," *P.C. World* (September 2000): 1.

146. Id.

147. Stan Burger, "The Spotlight-Junk E-Mail," October 3, 1997 (visited June 18, 1999), <http://www.newmmedianews.com/100397/ts_junk.html>.

148. James W. Butler, "The Death of Spam: A Bill to Ban It Could Backfire," *Internet News: Legal and Business Aspects* (September 1998): 3.

149. A trespass to chattels is an intermeddling with personal property.

150. Id.

151. Stan Burger, "The Spotlight-Junk E-Mail," Id.

152. Id.

153. Michael Geist, "Two Spammers Get Jail Time," *BNA's Internet Law News* (January 3, 2001): 1.

154. *Rosenblatt v. Zimmerman*, 766 A.2d 749 (N.J. 2001) (discussing distinction between tort actions for spoliation and fraudulent concealment).

155. *In re Prudential Insurance Co. of American Sales Practices Litigation*, 169 F.R.D. 598 (D.N.J. 1997).

156. "Computer Virus FAQ for New Users" (visited July 19, 1999). <http://www.faqs.org/faqs/computer/virus/new-users>.

157. Computer viruses include a wide variety of malicious computer code with common examples being trojan horses, logic bombs, mutation machines, and stealth viruses.

158. Wendy R. Leibowitz, "In New U.C.C. Software Contracts: Is the Customer Always Wrong?" *National Law Journal* (February 23, 1998): B8.

159. "Melissa Author Admits Guilt," *Information Security* (January, 2000): 11.

160. Id. (quoting Peter Tippett, chief technologist at a major information security company).

161. "Love Bug Suspect Can Still Face Civil Suits: Philippine Prosecutor," *Agence France Presse* (August 23, 2000).

162. Leibowitz, "In New U.C.C. Software Contracts."

163. U.C.C. §2B-406 (Tentative Draft, April 15, 1998).

164. Jennifer Couzin, "Suing eBay: Going, Going, Going?" *The Industry Standard* (November 13, 2000): 1 (noting that it is unclear whether online auction houses are immunized by the CDA).

165. *Federal Trade Commission v. Hare* (S.D. Fla., April 1998), reported in Perkins Coie Law Firm, *Internet Law Digest* (July 1999).

166. Id.

167. David L. Wilson, "Your Passport Please: Helping to Ferret Out Fakes and Frauds on the Web," *Buffalo News* (January 13, 1998): 7D.

168. *Andrews v. Trans Union Corp.*, 7 F. Supp.2d 1056 (C.D. Cal. 1998).

169. Id. at 1062.

170. Ian Black, "Internet Giving Race-Hate Groups New Lease of Life, EU Watchdog Says," *The Guardian* (London) (November 24, 2000): 17.

171. "German Far-Right, Hate Websites More Than Double," *Agence France Presse* (January 14, 2001): 1.

172. Black, "Internet Giving Race-Hate Groups New Lease of Life."

173. Cloud, "Is Hate on the Rise?" 33.

174. Tony Perry and Kim Murphy, "White Supremacist, Three Followers Charged with Harassing Four Officials," *Los Angeles Times* (November 11, 2000): A1: 20.

175. Id.

176. Id.

177. "Pardon My Yahoo! Not Finished," *BNA's Internet Law News* (January 4, 2001): 2.

178. Roscoe Pound, *Social Control through Law* (1942; reprint, Hamden, Conn.: Archon, 1968).

179. *Rookes v. Bernard* (H.L. 1964) 1 All Eng. Rep. 367.

180. William M. Landes and Richard R. Posner, *The Economic Structure of Tort Law* (Cambridge, Mass.: Harvard University Press, 1987), 160–61.

181. Richard A. Posner, *Law and Legal Theory in the UK and USA* (Oxford: Clarendon Press, 1996), 54.

Index and Table of Cases

About the Authors

Thomas Koenig is a professor of sociology and a founding faculty member of the Law, Policy and Society doctoral program at Northeastern University. His empirical research in tort law, which has been cited by federal courts including the U.S. Supreme Court, has earned him national recognition.

Michael Rustad is the Thomas F. Lambert Jr. Professor of Law and Director of the High Technology Law Program at Suffolk University Law School in Boston. Professor Rustad is the author of numerous articles and books, including *The E-Business Legal Handbook* (with Cyrus Daftary), *Women in Khaki: The American Enlisted Woman*, and *Demystifying Punitive Damages in Product Liability*, and the coauthor of *Social Problems: The Contemporary Debates*.